SKETCH

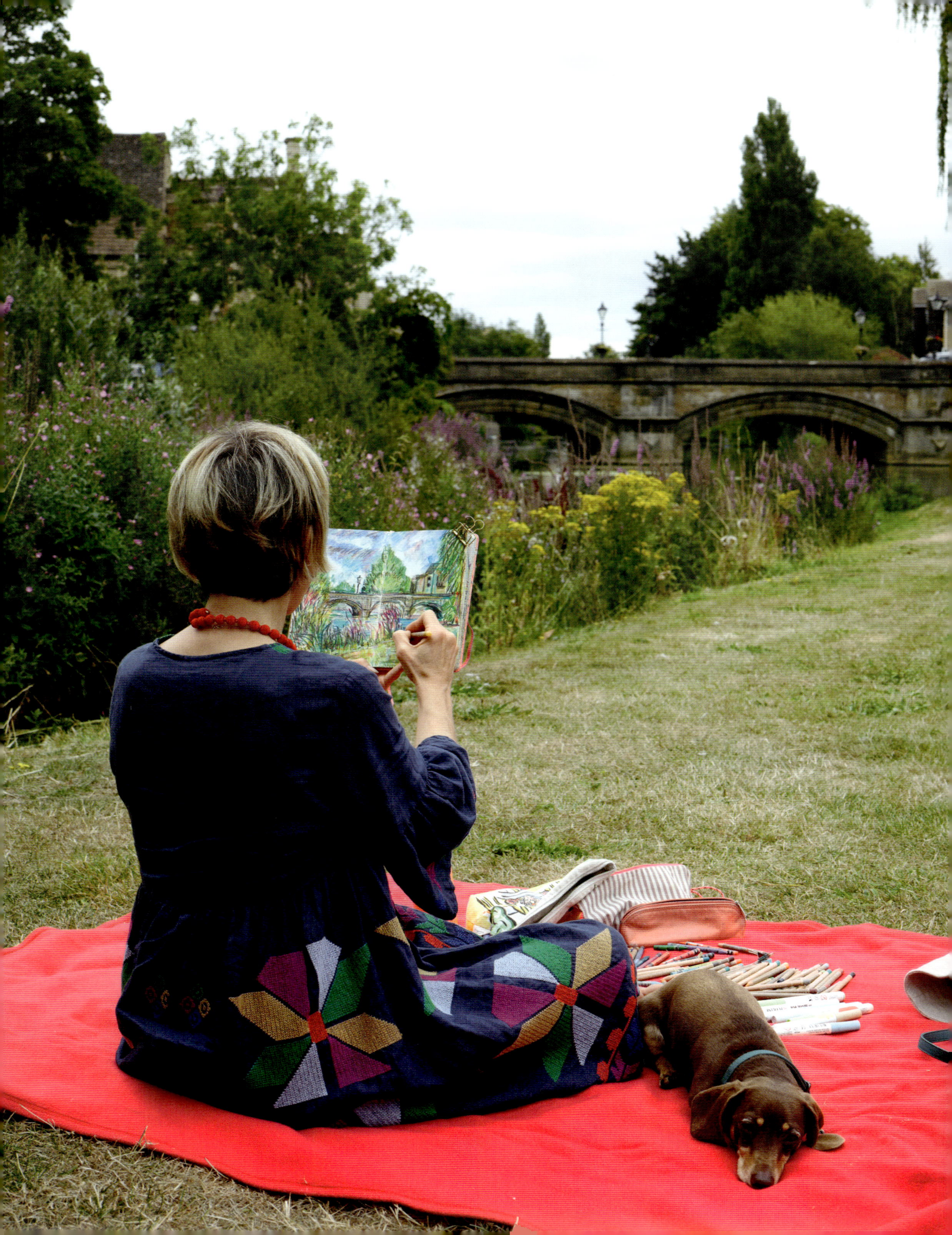

SKETCH

A Project Guide to Drawing
with Confidence

Sam Marshall

HERBERT PRESS

LONDON · OXFORD · NEW YORK · NEW DELHI · SYDNEY

HERBERT PRESS
Bloomsbury Publishing Plc
50 Bedford Square, London, WC1B 3DP, UK
Bloomsbury Publishing Ireland Limited
29 Earlsfort Terrace, Dublin 2, D02 AY28, Ireland

BLOOMSBURY, HERBERT PRESS and the Herbert Press
logo are trademarks of Bloomsbury Publishing Plc

First published in Great Britain in 2026

A catalogue record for this book is available from the British Library
Library of Congress Cataloguing-in-Publication data has been applied for

ISBN: 978-1-7899-4310-8; eBook: 978-1-7899-4311-5

2 4 6 8 10 9 7 5 3

Typeset and designed by Tina Hobson
Printed and bound in China by Toppan Leefung Printing Ltd

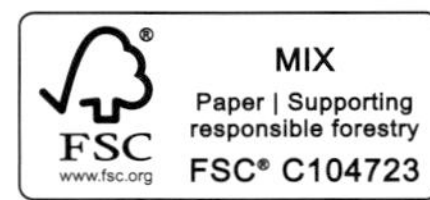

To find out more about our authors and books visit www.bloomsbury.com and sign up for our newsletters
For product safety related questions contact productsafety@bloomsbury.com

Contents

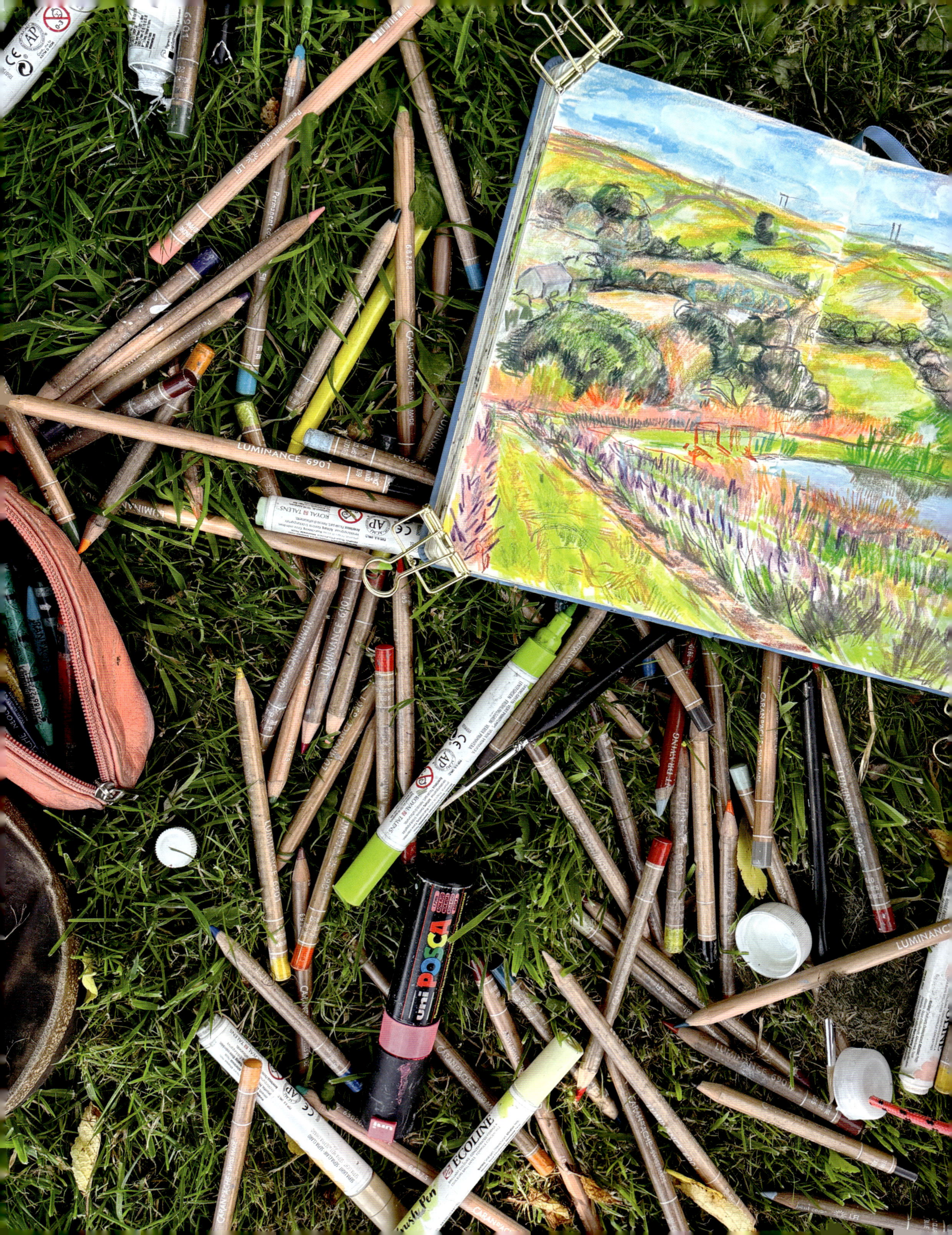

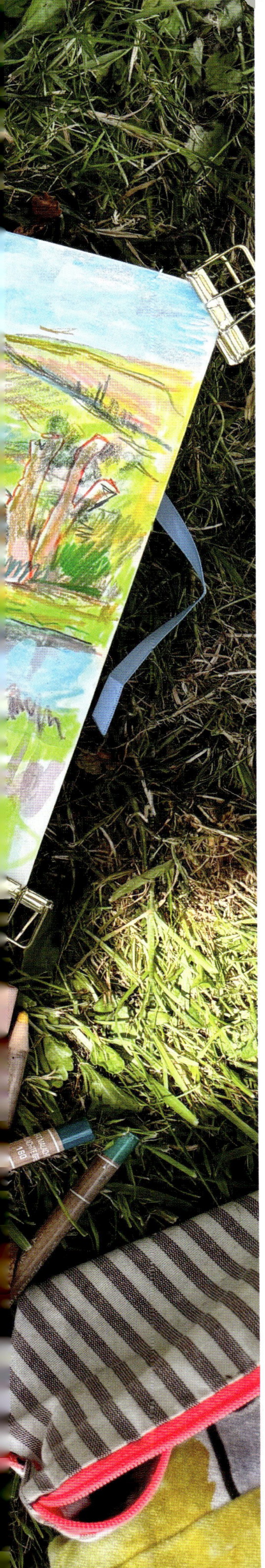

Introduction

'To make art is to sing with the human voice. To do this you must first learn that the only voice you need is the voice you already have'

Art & Fear, David Bayles and Ted Orland

Have you ever picked up a 'how to draw' book and felt inadequate and out of your depth? Did you get the impression that to draw well you needed to draw like the author of the book? If you've ever felt disillusioned by an art book, you've come to the right place. This is not a 'how to draw' book; there are plenty of those already. I'm not going to show you how to draw accurately or teach you to draw like me. I want to give you the confidence to draw like you; to help, guide and support you to draw in a sketchbook, however that might look. I hope that you find *Sketch* to be an inspiring and helpful guide to encourage you to start and maintain a regular drawing practice.

Over my many years of teaching art, the most common phrase I've heard is 'I can't draw'. Many of us feel we can't draw, even though as children we loved drawing and did it unselfconsciously. For many reasons, we develop the belief that the basic, innate quality of making marks on a surface is beyond us. I believe that we can all draw and it's a myth that a special talent is needed. The most common barrier to people having a go at drawing and keeping at it is a conviction that the purpose of drawing is to make the artwork as realistic as possible, to make it look like what we are drawing – for example, if we can't make an orange look like an orange, we might as well give up. This book will change the way you think and feel about drawing.

Throughout my years as a teacher, I have seen many students give up drawing in their early teens. I've witnessed the joy that drawing gives to children under eleven – we give crayons, pencils and paper to young kids and they can draw for hours. Around the age of twelve, when children become more aware of their peers and the world around them, they quickly become self-conscious and critical of their work. This is often accompanied by teachers celebrating students whose drawings are 'realistic', and grading them accordingly. Sadly, art in school is so limited that it becomes prescriptive; artwork needs to be quickly graded and in the system, leaving no time for experimentation and exploration. So many times, in my drawing workshops, older students have been brought to tears because a teacher sixty years ago told them they couldn't draw. This stunted their creativity and held them back; in worst-case scenarios, it changed the course of their lives.

I believe we are all inherently creative. We may create marvellous meals, plant beautiful gardens, knit colourful clothing or throw lovely ceramic pots. Drawing can be a practice that connects us to our true creative selves again. It takes us out of our linear, rational minds into our feeling, intuitive minds. The simple process of making marks on paper can benefit everyone.

People often say to me that they don't know what to draw, and I suggest that they draw anything. It doesn't matter what you draw; as soon as you start to draw, you will spot something you hadn't noticed before. Drawing helps you see. By drawing something – whether it be an object, a person, a landscape or a painting – we see it in an entirely different way. Take a simple apple to look at and draw. First, you notice its shape: a roundish form that tapers in slightly at the bottom. Next, you look at its shiny, slightly waxy surface, its curved, light-brown stem ... I could go on. The more you draw, the more you look, and the more your world opens up. I remember leading an 'Introduction to Drawing' workshop here in my studio and getting the students to draw a pear – all of them said at the end that they would never look at a pear in the same way again!

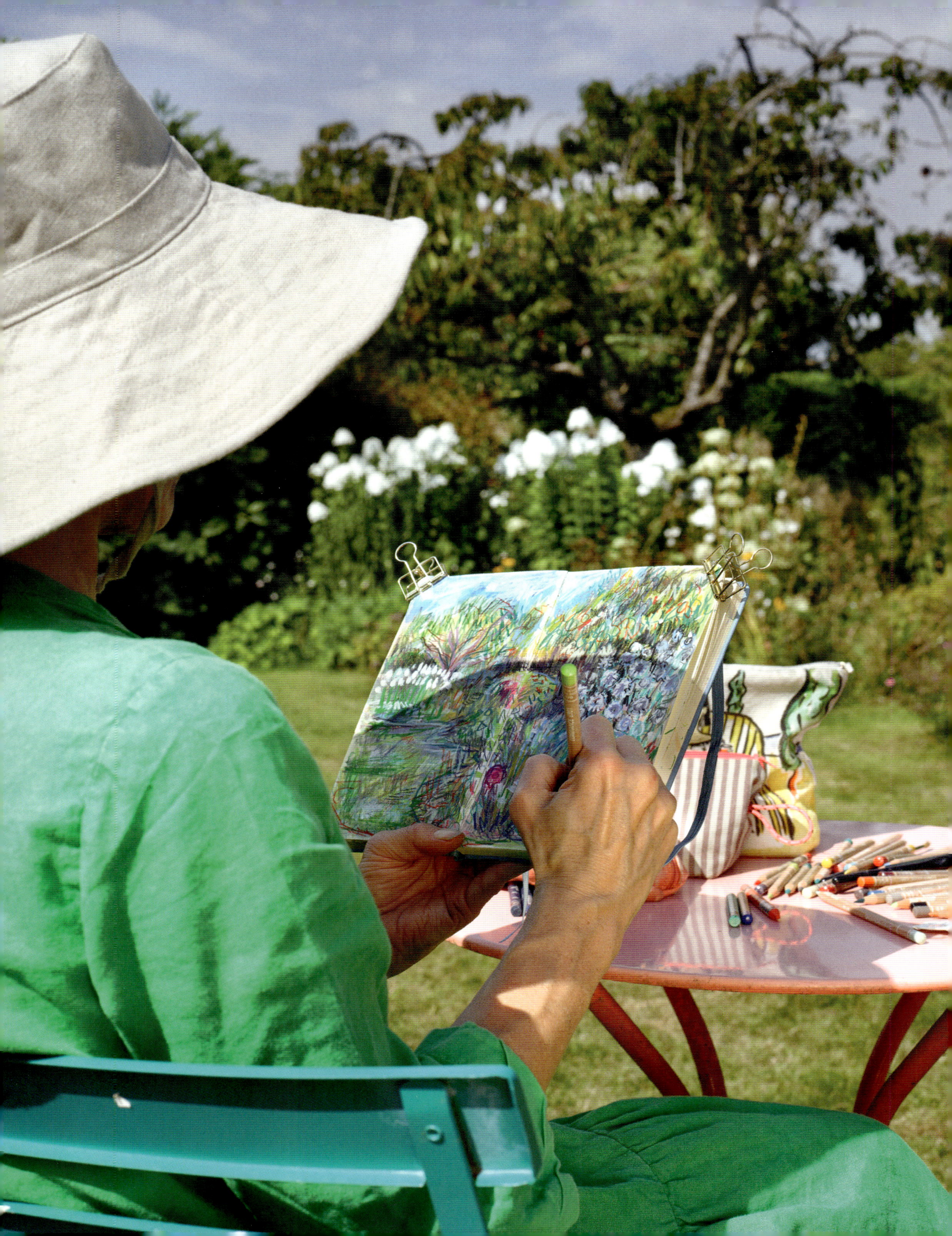

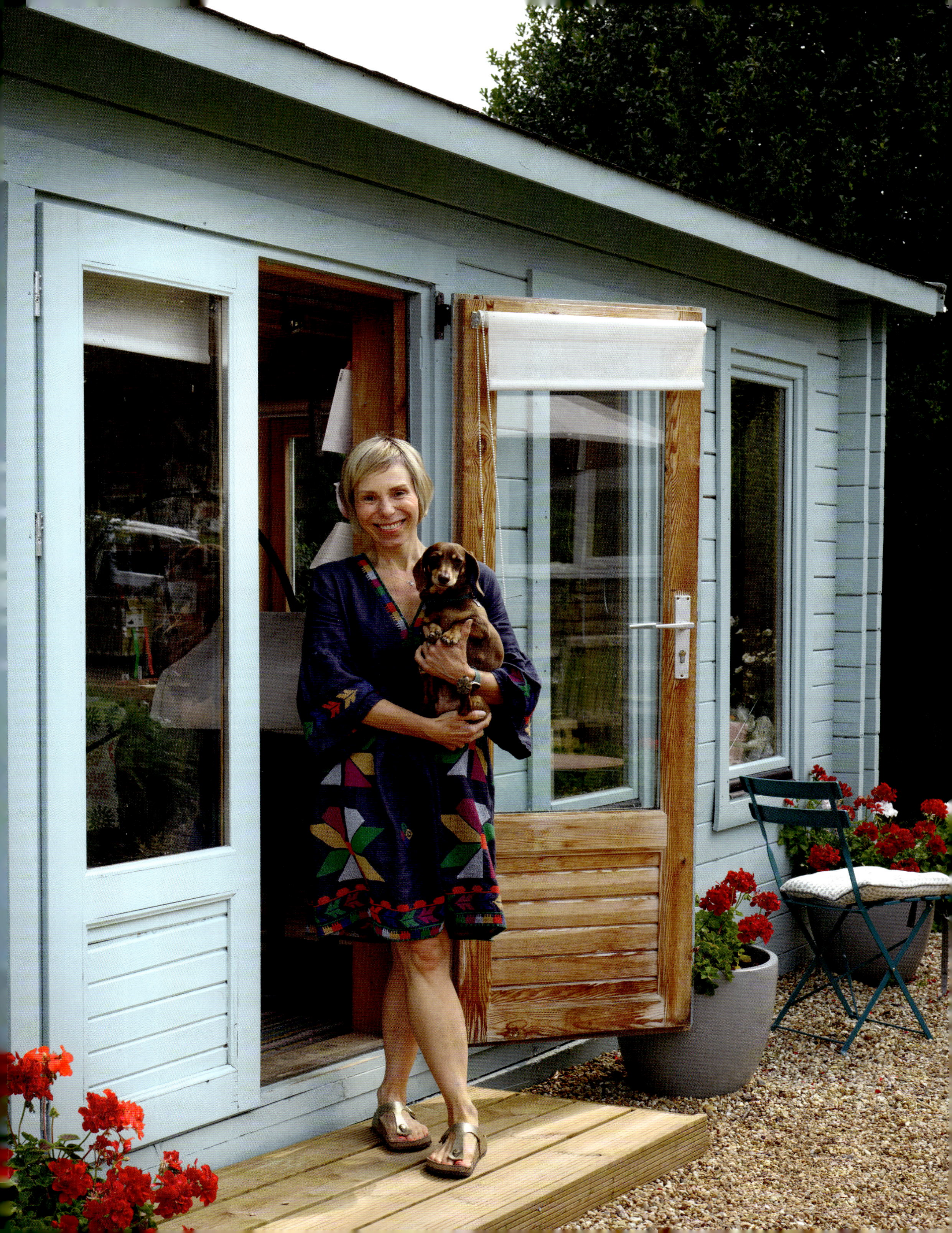

A little about me

As an only child growing up in the flat fens of Lincolnshire, drawing was my entertainment. It was my way of exploring the world around me and a means to escape into my own inner world. Forty years on, not much has changed; drawing is still at the heart of my practice. I draw to calm my busy mind, to slow down and to connect with my surroundings. I guess you could say that drawing is my meditation. When I'm drawing, I'm totally present. I forget myself. I look, and I make marks on paper.

I drew through my childhood and into secondary school. Art was my favourite subject, and I wanted to pursue it. I left Lincolnshire as soon as I could and headed to London to do a Fine Art BA at the Slade School of Fine Art. It was in the early nineties and conceptual work was everywhere; I eventually ended up making short films about my dad and his cabbages (he was a cabbage farmer). During my time at the Slade, I hardly picked up a pencil. I got out of the sketching habit and I left feeling disillusioned.

It was in my early thirties when I studied for my MA diploma in drawing at the Royal Drawing School that I rediscovered my passion. We were encouraged to draw consistently; to draw what we were seeing. I filled up sketchbook after sketchbook. I felt happier than I had done in years, and I knew I'd found my way again.

'I draw to calm my busy mind, to slow down and to connect with my surroundings. I guess you could say that drawing is my meditation'

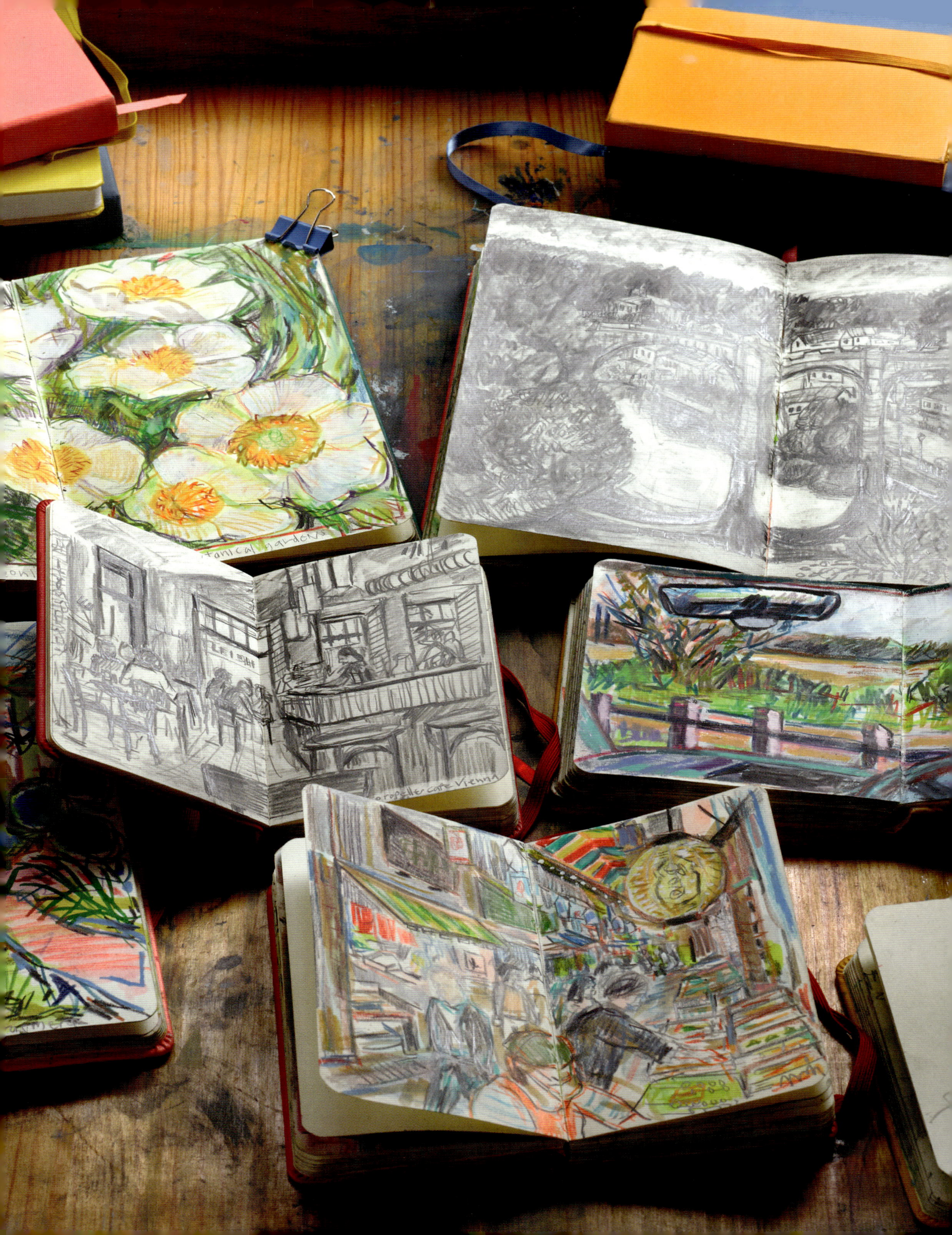
botanical gardens
propeller cafe Vienna

About this book

I wanted to do something different with my drawing book, to look at drawing in a way we weren't taught at school. I've come across a huge variety of ways to approach different types of drawing, so I thought it would be helpful to see various methods of drawing showcased in one book. From this germ of an idea grew the evolution of the Sketch Squad. I carefully selected eleven of my students – some of whom had done my online workshops, while others I had worked with as a creative coach – and asked them if they would like to take part in the book. I chose them specifically because I knew they were interested in drawing and they had struggled in the past with motivation, doubts and insecurities. Most importantly, I believed they could commit to a year of drawing and were willing to give it a go. I also invited my seventy-nine-year-old mum, who was eager to get involved, as I knew she would be a great addition.

All the drawing exercises in this book have been done by me and the members of the Sketch Squad, so you will see all of our interpretations. I want the book to feel like we are in a drawing class, drawing together and sharing the work we have done. The exercises are designed to be done in a sketchbook as they are such a versatile and portable way of keeping your work in one place. I will go into greater detail regarding the benefits of keeping a sketchbook in Chapter 1.

This book is suitable for beginners and for those of you with more experience who want to establish a regular drawing practice. I have designed the book to build up in complexity, and to get the maximum benefit from the book I would advise following along sequentially. In my practical chapters, I include drawing exercises to complete in your sketchbooks, along with material suggestions. I then show you my own drawings, along with a selection of drawings from the Sketch Squad, chosen to highlight certain points based on their reflections on their drawings. I haven't chosen them as I think they are 'good' drawings – this book isn't about 'good' or 'bad', it's about celebrating drawing in whatever form it takes.

We'll start with a warm-up chapter, with exercises to encourage you to be experimental in your mark making, before we progress to drawing in the comfort of your own home. Next, we move outside to have a go at drawing the exterior of your home and your garden or green space, before moving a little further afield and drawing in your local area.

We then move on to drawing self-portraits and portraits of family and friends. This chapter will encourage you to share your work with others, as well as gaining confidence in how to draw people and faces. After the intensity of this chapter, we'll have a palette cleanser in the form of a daily drawing challenge – the purpose of this is to get you into a regular drawing habit and spend some time each day with your pencil and sketchpad.

Next, we start to draw out and about in public. You'll draw in cafés, art galleries, museums and in your car, so you'll become familiar and more comfortable with taking your kit out and drawing where people can see you. We then pack our sketchbooks in our suitcases and discover the joys of drawing on holiday – how to make sure you carve out some time for yourself and ensure you don't come back with an empty sketchbook.

You'll get the chance to draw from a painting of your choice in a local art gallery or museum, before exploring experimental drawing from music, collage and films. The final chapter culminates in creating your own personal project – one consolidated piece of work in whatever medium(s) you choose, inspired by the drawings in your sketchbook. At this stage, your sketchbooks will be bursting with sketches showing your commitment and dedication to drawing. They will be full of memories, and each drawing will transport you back to the exact day and time you put pencil to paper.

Interspersed throughout the book are chapters on the things we all struggle with: the inner critic, imposter syndrome, comparison and envy, and self-sabotage. By facing these issues head on, and dealing with them as they come up, it will enable you to progress through the book with increased confidence and awareness of what obstacles you may be putting in your own way.

I've written this book for you, as I know you can draw. I want to encourage and inspire you to see, to look carefully and enjoy making marks on paper. The book is designed to help you devise a personal approach to drawing, with exercises you will be able to revisit again and again. I hope that, like me, you find a way to incorporate drawing into your routine so it enriches your life and increases your sense of well-being.

Right, let's get started!

'I've written this book for you, as I know you can draw. I want to encourage and inspire you to see, to look carefully and enjoy making marks on paper'

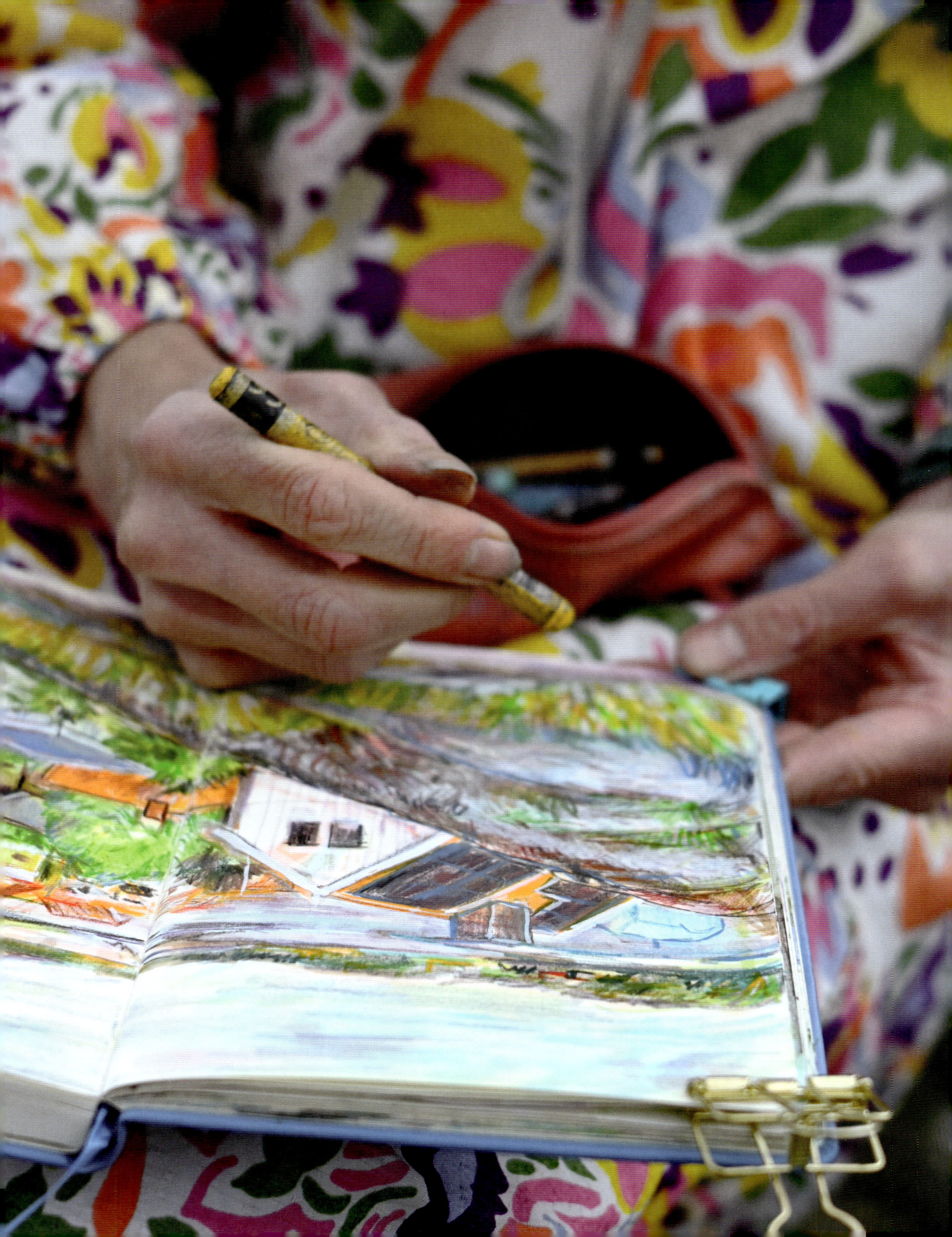

Meet the Sketch Squad

'Drawing is the artist's most direct and spontaneous expression, a species of writing: it reveals, better than does painting, his true personality'

Edgar Degas

You now have an idea of what the book is about, and what you are going to need both mentally and materially to get drawing in your sketchbook, so let's introduce you to the Sketch Squad. Over the course of a year, every two months, I sent the Squad a section of the exercises to complete in the order they appear in this book. Once they had finished each exercise, they uploaded their drawings along with their notes to a shared online platform. This meant that I could see what they had done and they could see each other's drawings. This was a great way for them to get to know one another and to see how differently they were all approaching the same exercises. It's important to note that the Squad didn't see my drawings as I didn't want to influence them in any way.

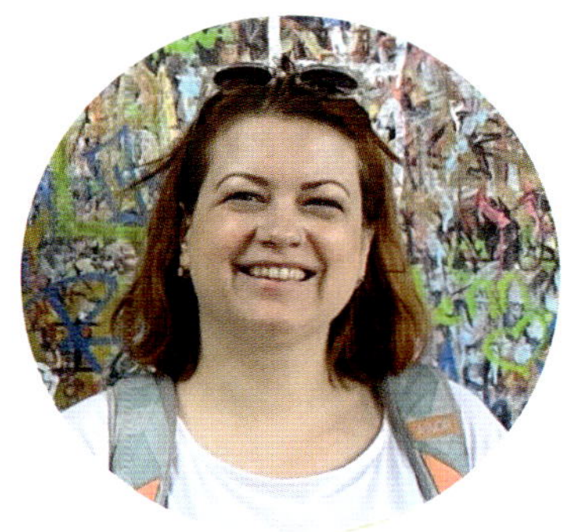

Kathi

'I'm in my late thirties and I live in Austria. I work in a museum here in Vienna, which is my home city. A few years ago, I decided to follow my dreams by returning to painting and printmaking and taking acting classes.

I have taken many of Sam's online workshops. I am very excited, happy and proud to be part of this drawing book.'

@kathi.loves.art

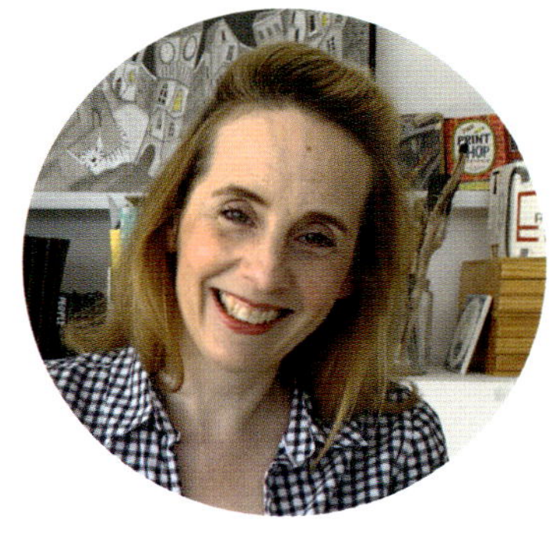

Niki

'I'm in my forties and I live in the remote Scottish Highlands. I used to be a project manager but I'm currently studying for an illustration degree. After years of not drawing at all, I had the opportunity to pursue my original goal! I find sharing my drawings intimidating, but I'm hoping it will challenge me to become a bit more confident.'

@nikij_illustration

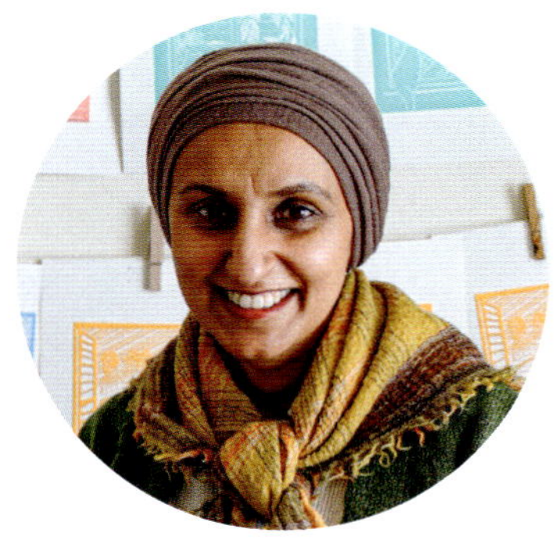

Safa

'I am in my early forties and I live in Bristol, UK. I work in a primary school as a specialist reading teacher. Travel is an important part of my life, and I've recently been drawing on my trips. I'm very excited to be part of the book and a little nervous as I know it will be a challenge for me, but I know I will learn and grow through the experience.'

@safa.aslam

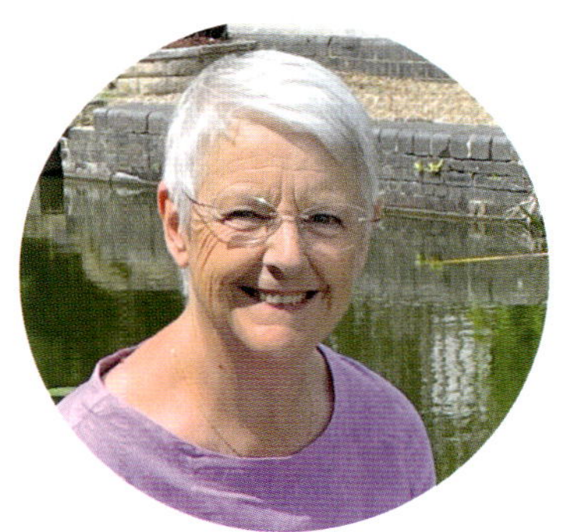

Paula

'I'm in my early seventies and I live in Leicestershire, UK. I used to work as an early years education adviser. I've been intermittently drawing over several years and I was delighted and daunted at the same time to be asked to be part of the book. I feel apprehensive about sharing my work with others but know that this will get easier, as I know we all feel the same.'

@paulawillis593

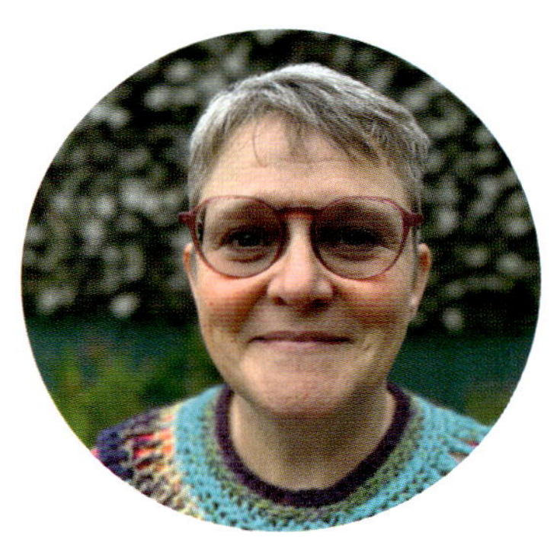

Anne

'I'm in my late fifties and I live in Sheffield, England. I've had a varied career. I've worked in the NHS, established a successful art gallery, taught creative workshops, all while making my own work.

Even though I feel like a novice, I recognise that the process will help me develop my creativity and teach me how to look and observe in ways I haven't before.'

@anne_madbird

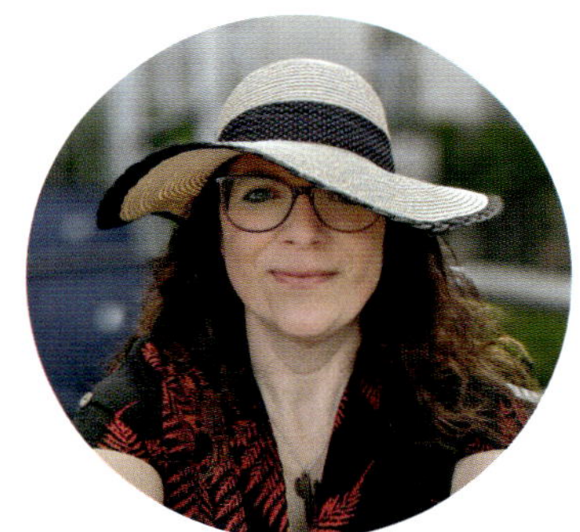

Claire

'I'm in my early forties and I live in north-east Scotland. I'm an archaeologist in a local authority planning department but have a long-held ambition to work in a more creative field. It was after the pandemic that I knew I needed to make a concerted effort to go back to basics and fully embrace my creativity as I know how many benefits – both emotional and physical – it can bring.'

@claire_bck_creates

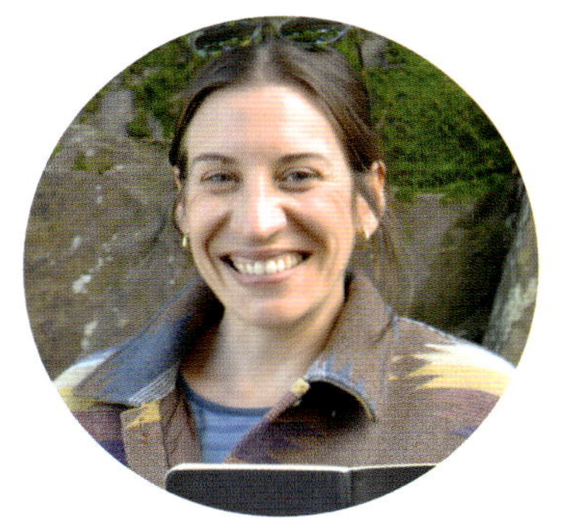

Eva

'I am in my late thirties. I'm from Spain, but I now live in north Wales. I work in tropical forest conservation. I loved drawing when I was a child, but I stopped and started to see myself as a 'science person'. I took up a pencil again a few years ago and art and creativity have since become a priority.

I am really enjoying the process; it is taking me out of my comfort zone.'
@evapintadoart

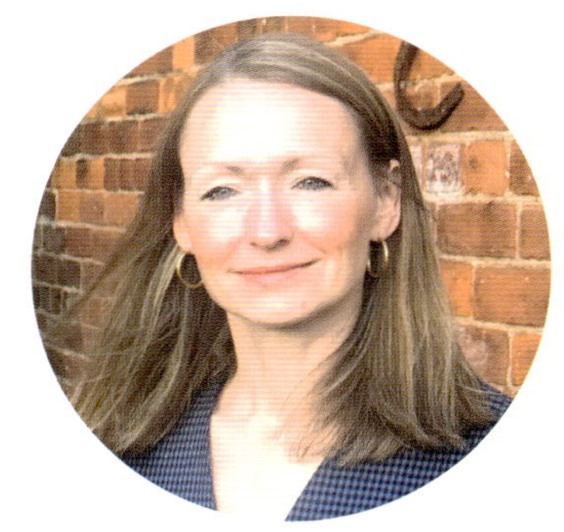

Hannah

'I'm in my forties and live in Lincolnshire, UK. I am self-employed, working with artists on the production and realisation of their artworks in the public realm. Prior to working with Sam, the last time I drew was as a child. I was happy and honoured to be asked to be part of the book and, although anxious, I am excited to give it a go!'
@hannahstandenworks

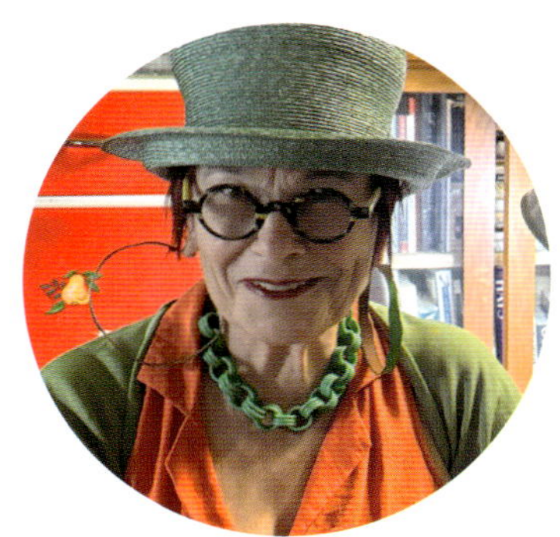

Phyllis

'I'm in my early seventies and I live in Northern California. I'm a milliner, musician, printmaker, paper cutter and a hooked rug maker. Drawing has always been part of my life.

When Sam asked me to be part of the Squad, I was surprised, honoured and excited. However, I was anxious in the beginning, thinking I had to live up to an imaginary ideal.'
@phyllisbeals

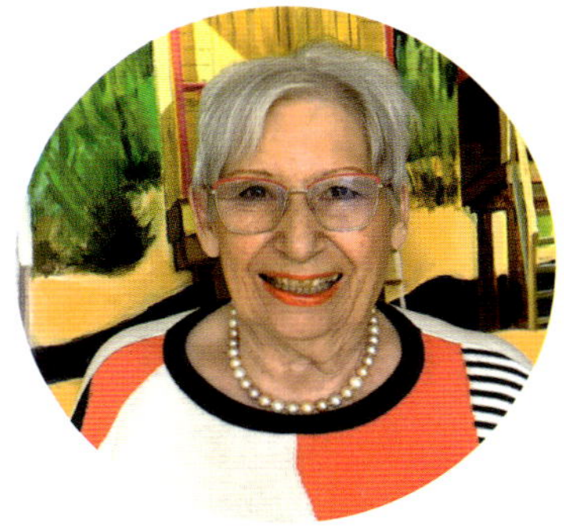

Jane

'I'm in my late seventies and I'm Sam's mum. I worked for many years as a florist, and I found this a good way to express my creativity. Once I retired, I took a weekly watercolour class and discovered that I really enjoyed painting and drawing. I'm totally untrained and do things my own way, so I'm excited to see what happens during this process.'
@janeissamsmum

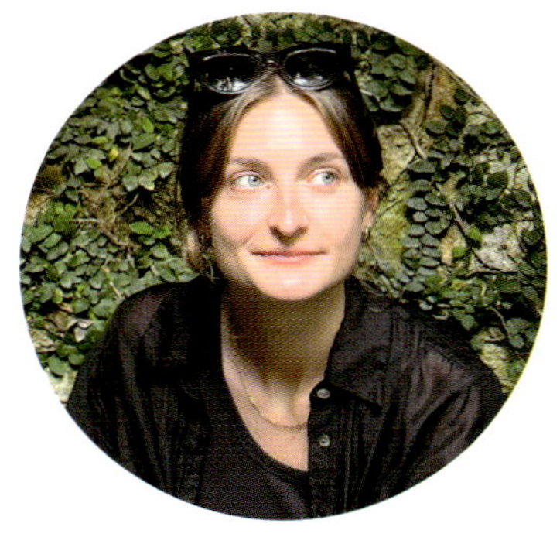

Diane

'I'm in my late twenties and I live in Paris, France. After finishing my BA in textile design, I worked on commissions and collaborations using geometric stencils and screen-printing. However, I realised my drawing skills were lying dormant, so I started working with Sam to build up my practice again. The book gives me reason and motivation to keep going!'
@dianebrsn

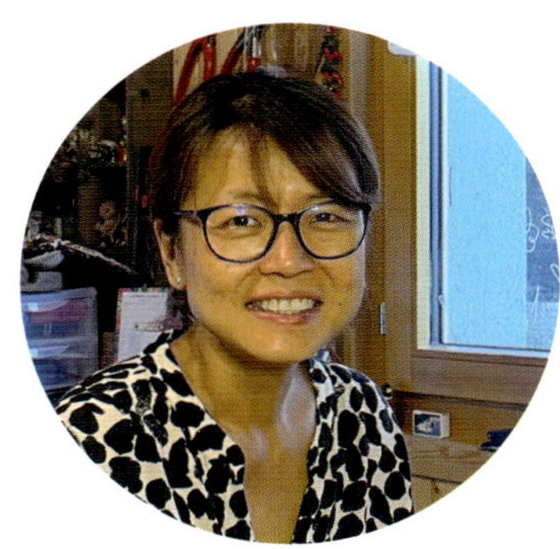

Lucy

'I'm in my early fifties and I live near Bern in Switzerland. I work as an accountant, and I am also an artist, paper cutter and illustrator. I have been drawing since I was a child but I stopped for many years. Now that I have more time, I have returned to it. Last year, I published a children's book that I illustrated and wrote myself. I'm ready for the challenge and to see what happens.'
@lucy.huegli

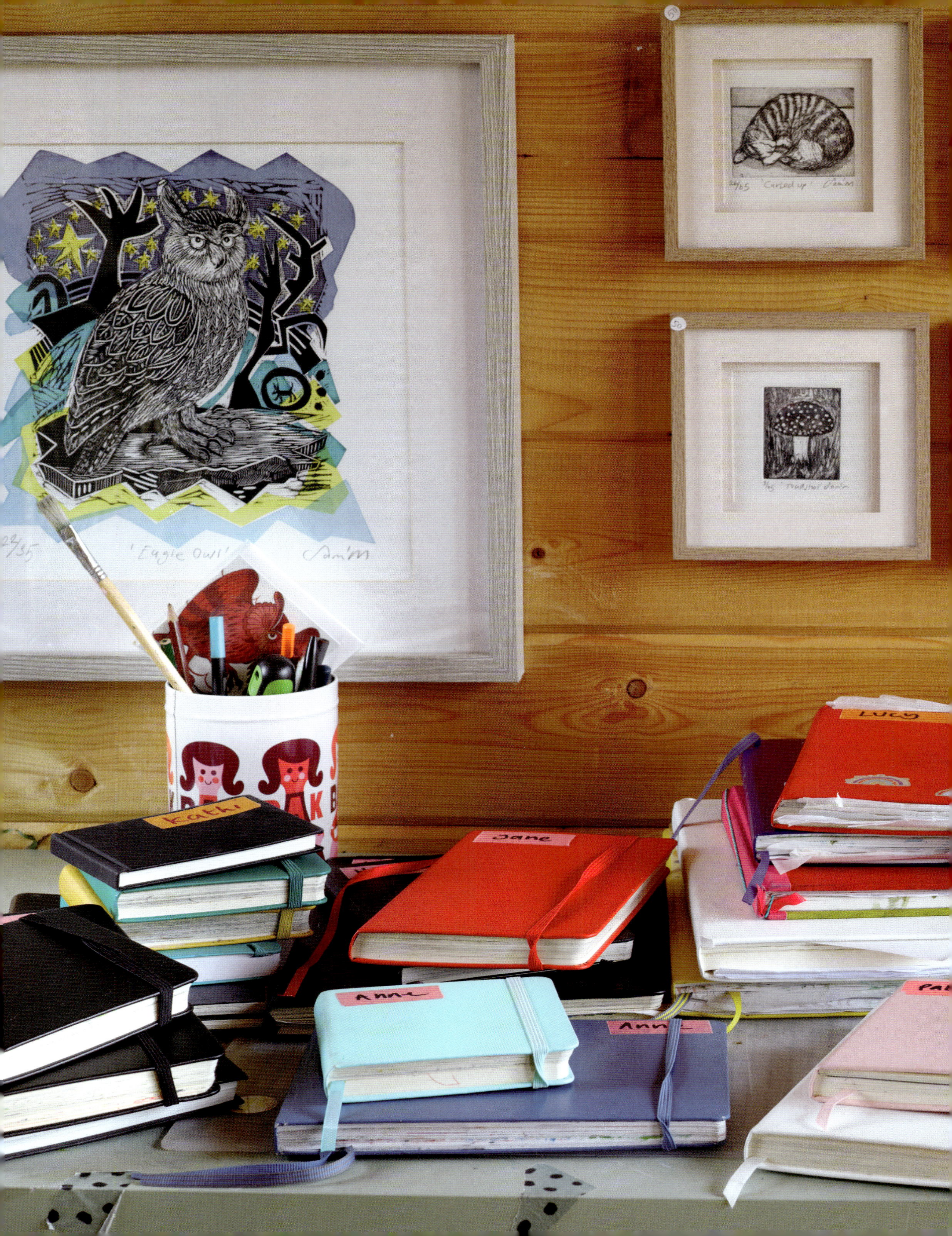
'Eagle Owl'
'Curled up'
'Toadstool'
Kathi
Jane
Anne
Anne
Lucy

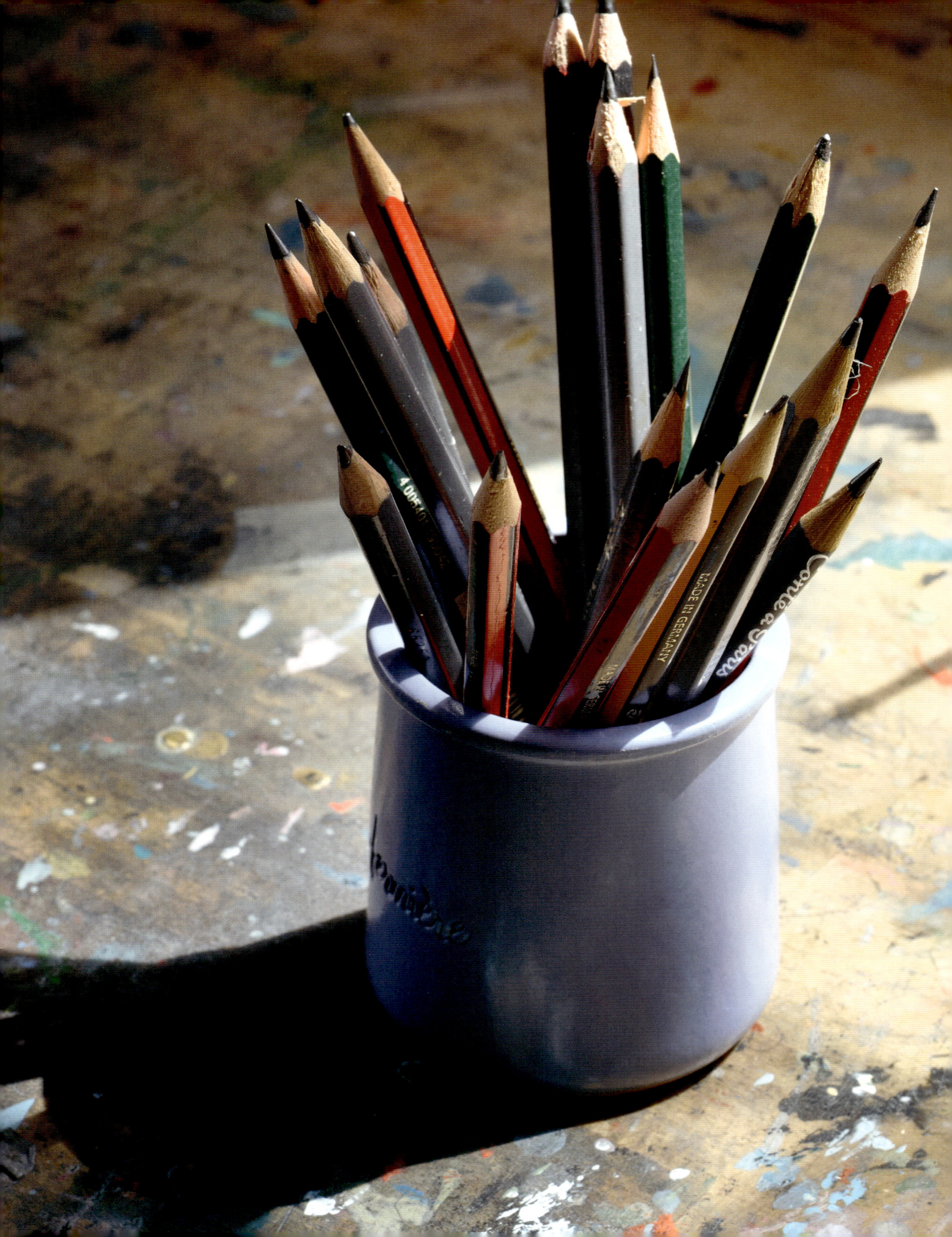

1

Why sketch?

Drawing makes me happy, it's as simple as that. Keeping a sketchbook means I can draw anywhere I choose, and it becomes a record of my life in pictures. These are just two of my reasons why I draw and keep a sketchbook. What are yours?

You might be wondering what the difference is between a drawing and a sketch. Traditionally, a sketch is considered to be a looser, less refined way of drawing, and a drawing is a consolidated sketch. However, for the purposes of this book, I am going to use the terms interchangeably to keep it simple, so a drawing is a sketch and a sketch is a drawing.

'Je suis le cahier'

Pablo Picasso

Reasons to sketch

Here are some reasons to get creative with your sketchpad
and pencil that might resonate with you.

A space to call your own

Your sketchbook can be your own private sanctuary.
It's a place for you to express yourself freely, without
judgement or criticism. It can contain anything you want
it to: shopping lists, drawings that have tea spilt on them,
plans for your kitchen space … whatever you want. It can
be a place to work through ideas.

A gentle way to explore your creativity

A small sketchbook and a pencil are all you need to begin
to explore your creativity. Drawing is the simplest form of
art out there.

A way to help you slow down and be more mindful

Sketching helps me slow down, and it might just do the
same for you. I've got a tremendous amount of energy,
and when I'm visiting somewhere new, I can whizz
around it quickly and cover a lot of ground in a few
hours, thus stimulating my nervous system and making
me feel even more wired. However, when I sit and draw,
I feel my breathing changing and time just stops. I'm
totally absorbed. I feel I emerge out of a drawing in a hazy
state – almost like I've had a massage – a mind massage.
You enter a flow-like state when it's impossible to think or
worry about anything else.

A way to help you see more

When you take the time to draw something – anything – you notice details you might otherwise miss. It helps us see what is there, rather than what we *think* is there. We often have preconceived ideas of what something looks like, and drawing helps us see more clearly.

To lift your spirits and create connections to the world

Drawing helps you strengthen your connection with a place, whether you want to get to know a new location or see somewhere familiar with new eyes. I feel so connected to the places I've drawn; they are special places in my mind, and because I've committed them to memory through drawing, I feel I'm able to visit them anytime. When I'm outside, drawing in my sketchbook, I feel connected to nature. I react with awe and curiosity, and I become part of the landscape.

To help you reconnect with yourself and fulfil your goals

To some it might just be a 'sketch', but I believe it can be so much more. If you've had a rocky road with drawing in the past, if you've felt that you aren't creative, then just proving to yourself that you can draw can be incredibly healing. This may start to have a big impact on the rest of your life – all those things you have been putting off because you were scared or didn't have enough time might just start to get done!

A tool to help you remember

When we draw something, we create a visual record of it in our minds. By looking at anything for a long period of time and committing it to paper, it increases the strength of our memory. When I look through my sketchbooks, I'm transported back to the places I've visited. I look at my drawing of a street in Antibes, and I remember what time of day it was, how warm it was, what I was wearing and how I was feeling. My sketches evoke more memories than any of my photographs do.

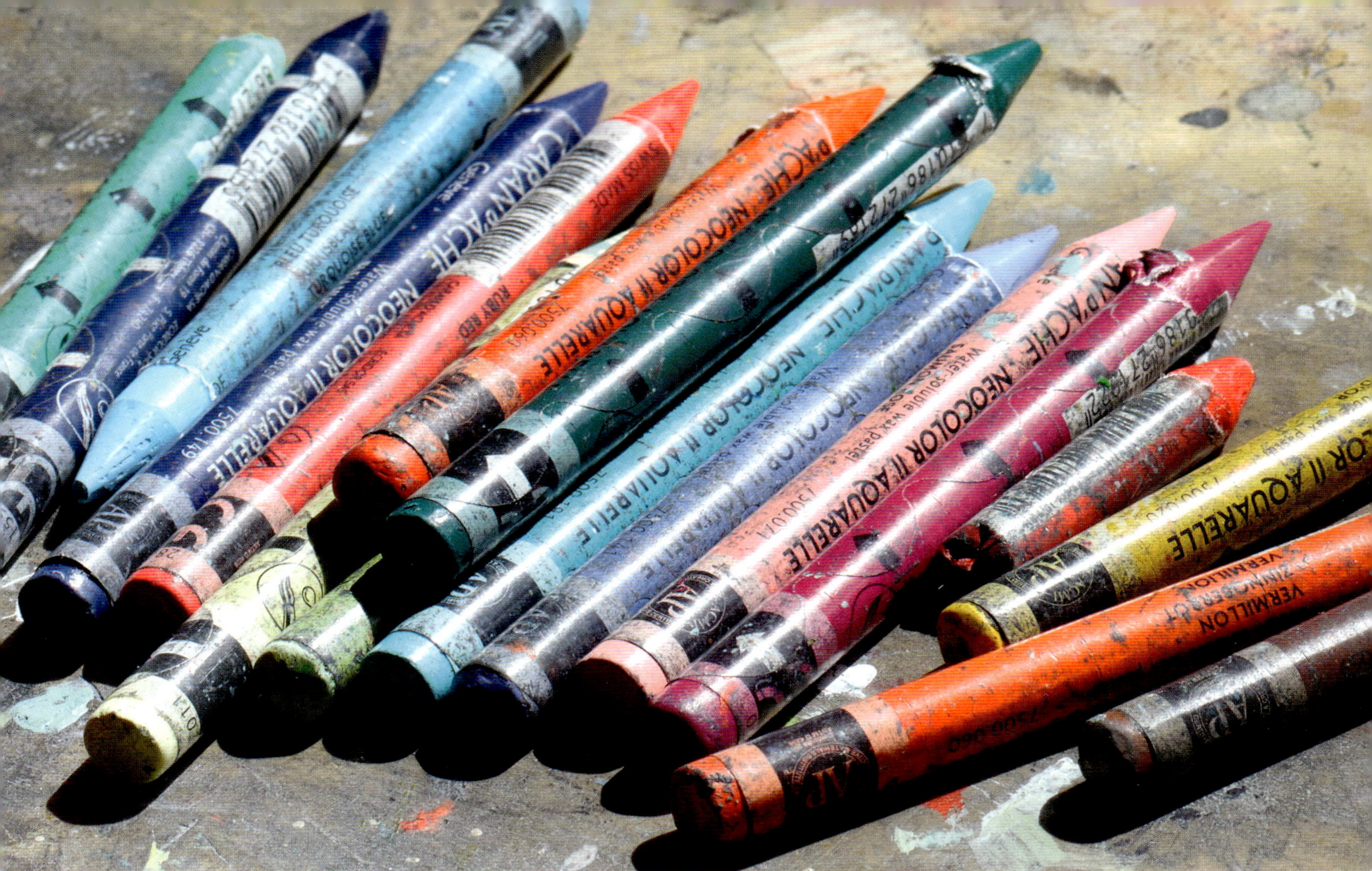

Why have you picked up this book?

Did any of these reasons click with you? If so, which ones? Write down your reasons why at the start of your sketchbook and keep coming back to them whenever drawing gets tough, when you are lacking in motivation and those negative thoughts are swimming around in your head.

I'll be frank, it will get tough. We live with constant chatter in our heads that goes, 'I'm not good enough', 'What's the point?', 'It's too late', 'My drawings look like a child's', 'Who do I think I am?', 'I never went to art school', and so on. It may take a while to unpick these thoughts.

This is a new way of drawing, not the way you learnt at school. You might still be seeking affirmation from your art teacher forty years ago who thought a good drawing was a hyper-realistic drawing. However, if you keep coming back to your why, and reminding yourself of your reasons for picking up this book, then that is one of the most powerful motivational tools you have.

What's preventing you from keeping a sketchbook?

We have discussed why you want to draw, now let's look at why you aren't drawing or what has prevented you in the past. When I ask this question in my workshops, many respond that time is a factor, but what else is stopping you or has stopped you in the past?

Fear

There will be a variety of answers to this question, but I can almost guarantee behind most of these reasons is fear – fear of your drawing not looking as you want it to look, fear of not knowing what to draw, fear of 'messing it up' … I could go on. This whole book is structured around helping you navigate and manage these fears.

One sentence that has helped me enormously throughout my years of drawing, when the fear of the blank page has taken hold, is this: 'There is nothing to be afraid of, it's just a pencil and a piece of paper.' I find this simple sentence so powerful that I often write it at the start of my sketchbooks as a reminder – if you find it helpful too, write it alongside your 'why'.

Finding the time

'We are what we repeatedly do.
Excellence, then, is not an act, but a habit'

Will Durant

The truth is, the more drawing you do, the more it becomes part of
your life, the easier it will get and the more likely you are to do it. One
of the main obstacles that gets in the way of drawing is our perceived
lack of time. We tell ourselves that there are plenty more important
things to do than drawing. My students often tell me that they feel
guilty for drawing, and that it feels self-indulgent. They worry that
drawing is a frivolous pursuit compared to other responsibilities like
work or family obligations. Part of the problem is that activities such
as swimming are celebrated as being good for your mental health,
but society hasn't yet fully understood or embraced the benefits of
drawing for your sense of well-being.

We all have time to draw. Most of us aren't limited by time; in fact,
what we lack is a structure and a plan. So, let's see how you can make
it happen by thinking carefully about when you can fit drawing into
your day. Here are some suggestions:

- In the morning before you have breakfast
- When you reach for your phone, pick up your
  sketchbook instead
- With your morning coffee
- While waiting for the kettle to boil
- While waiting for your food to cook
- While waiting for your train or plane
- After dinner, to relax into the evening and unwind from the day
- When everyone else is watching TV
- On your lunch break
- While in the car, waiting to pick someone up

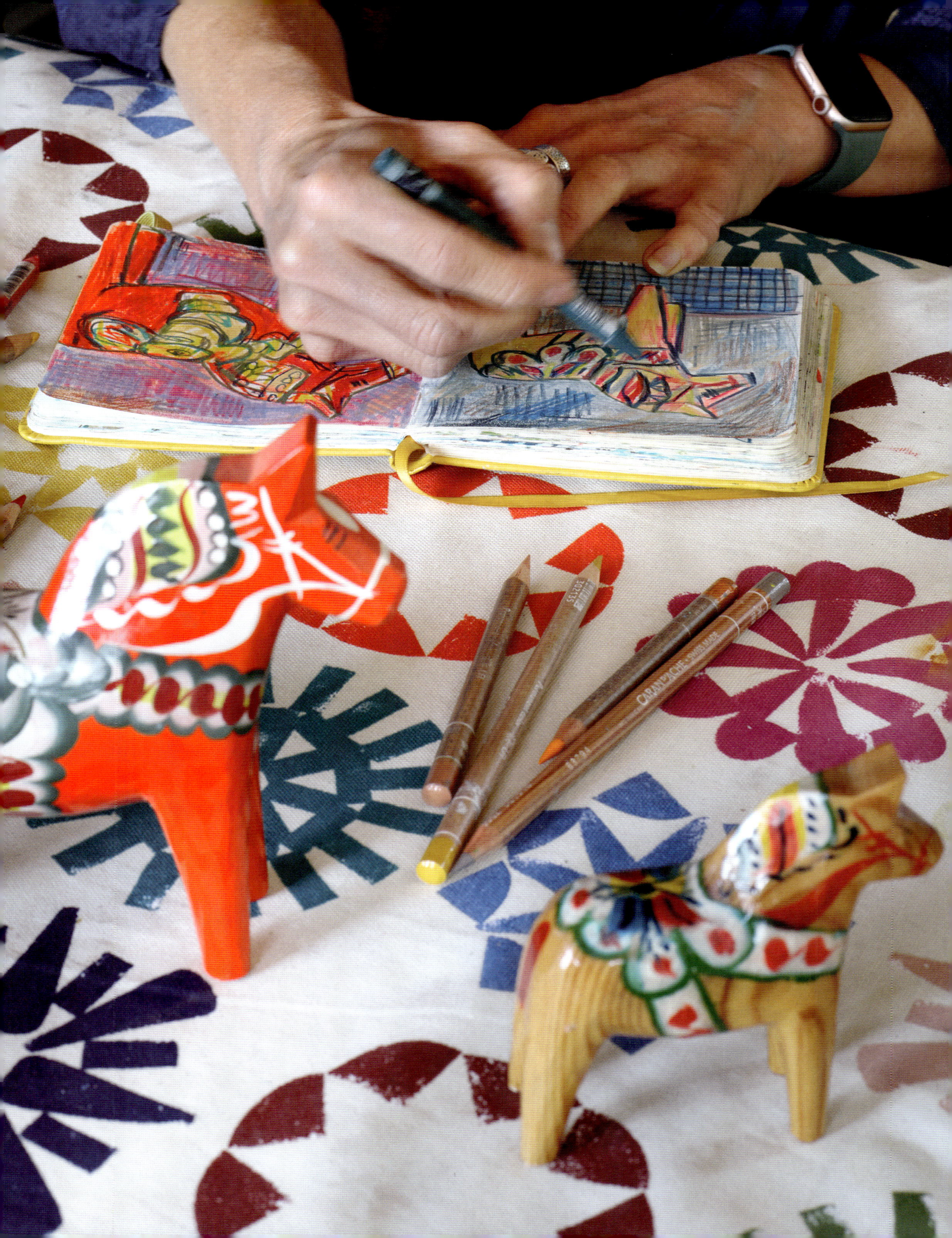

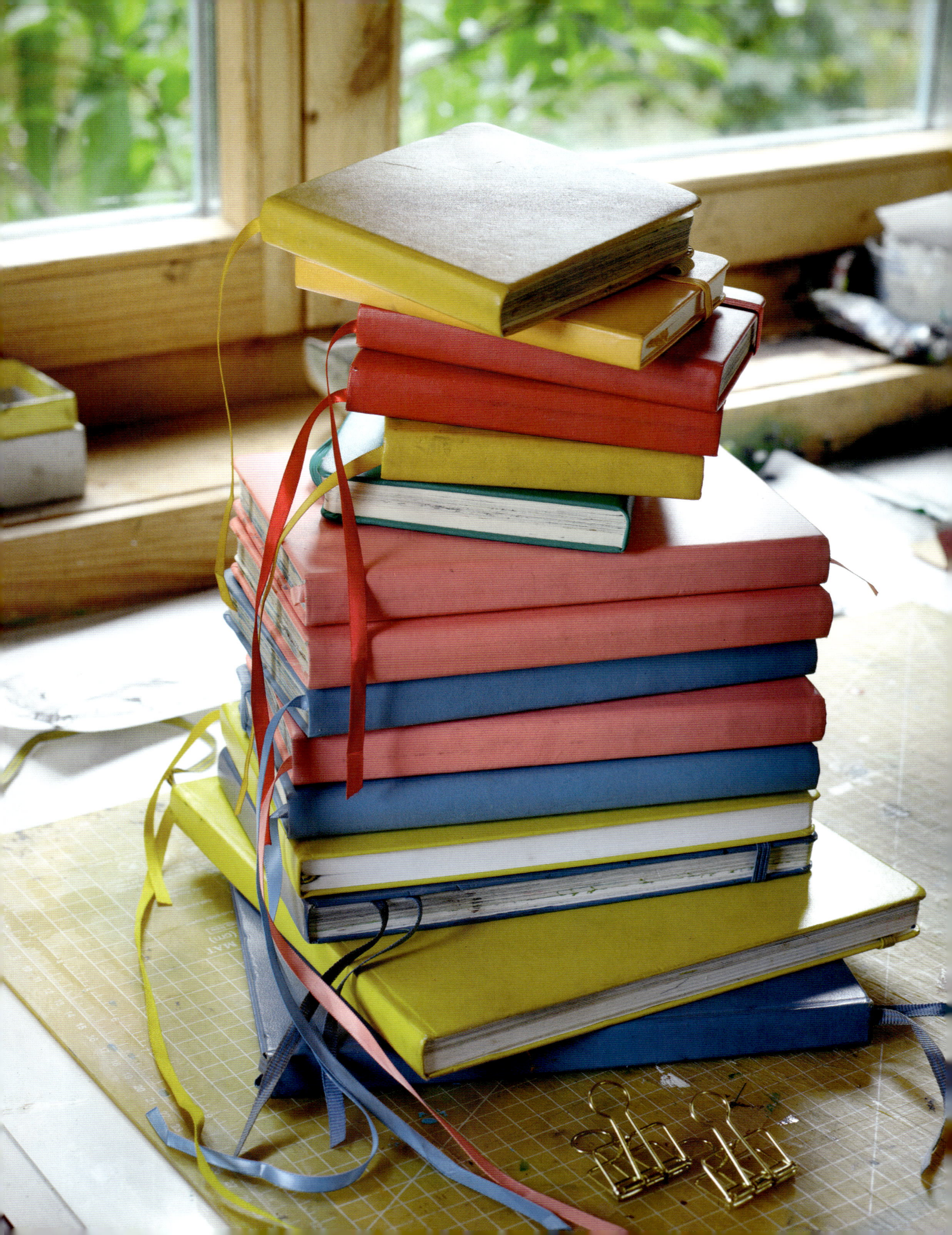

2
Your sketchbook and other materials

Now we have looked at why you want to draw and how you are going to fit your sketchbook drawing into your schedule, let's discuss what materials you might want to use. Don't rush out and buy loads of new supplies, though; use what you have at the start and build your kit up slowly. All materials are a personal preference – these are mine; they might not be yours.

Sketchbook

As an artist, my sketchbook is my most treasured and versatile tool. This is one of the reasons I decided to centre this drawing book around keeping a sketchbook, to help you to discover the joy of having a portable book of creativity to dip in and out of.

As you will be doing most of your drawings in your sketchbook, make sure you find the right sketchbook for you. I'm sure many of you have abandoned a sketchbook because the paper is too thin or too thick or you don't like the feel of the pencil on the page. We are more likely to make drawing a habit if we can make it appealing, and finding a sketchbook is part of this.

My favourite sketchbooks are from Royal Talens. I like the sizes that they come in, the cover colours and the cream paper, which is smooth yet robust. The choice is personal, though, so the best advice I can give you is to go with a book that feels good in your hands and that brings you joy – you might have to try a few before you find your match! You don't need to pay a fortune for a sketchbook. If it's too precious, you might feel inhibited, and this would defeat the purpose.

For the exercises in this book, I would suggest having two sizes – a pocket-size sketchbook and a larger one (no bigger than A4).

Tools and materials

The basic tools and materials you will need for drawing include a range of pencils, erasers and sharpeners. To add colour, you'll need coloured pencils, watercolour brush pens, water-soluble pastels, paints and paintbrushes, plus a pencil case to keep everything together.

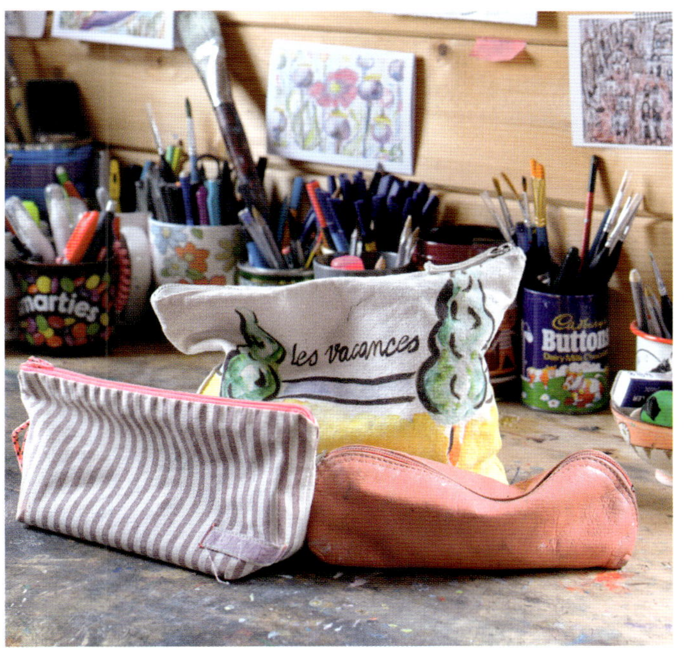

Pencils

Graphite pencils are an essential tool in your kit list. They come in different grading scales, ranging from 10B, the softest, to 10H, the hardest ('H' stands for hard, and 'B' stands for blackness). Hard pencils contain less graphite and are good for sharp, technical drawings. Soft 'B' pencils contain more graphite and produce thicker, darker lines. An HB pencil is hard and black, the middle grade, and the one we most commonly see.

Again, pencils are a personal choice. The hardest graphite weight I use is an HB – I gravitate towards the softer grades as my drawings are more tonal and gestural. Graphite grades can range slightly among different brands; I would recommend trying out different pencils in an art shop. My favourite pencils are Caran d'Ache Grafwood – I've used them for years and they've totally transformed my drawing experience. They are a little more expensive than most, but well worth the cost. I also use a range of Faber-Castell's 'Castell' pencils – in particular 4B, which I find very versatile.

The most important thing is to have a range of pencils; don't just have an HB. You want to be able to create a variety of marks.

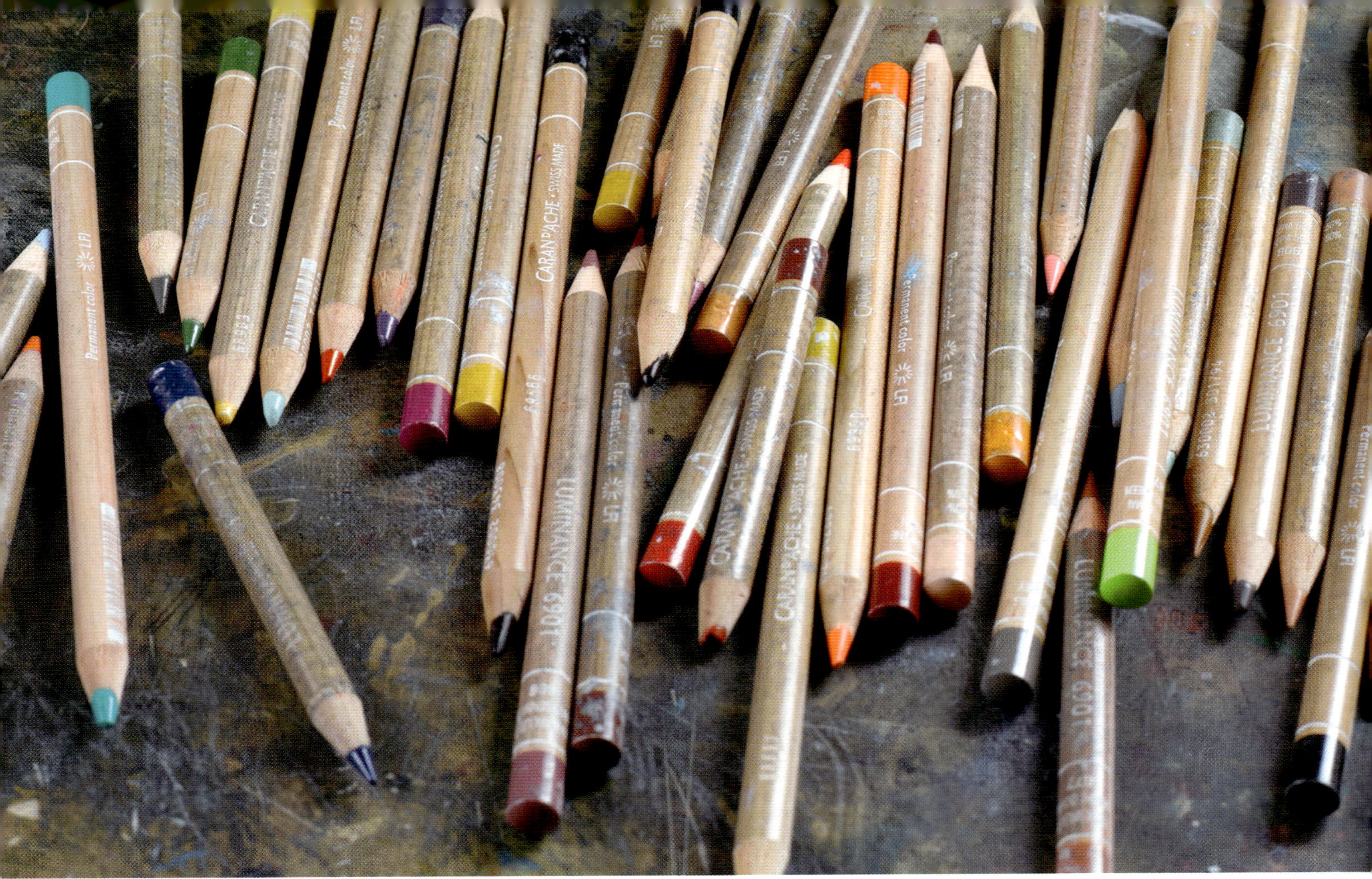

Erasers

I recommend you try out a few erasers and find what suits you. Some people like putty erasers, but I find them difficult to use. My favourite is a Faber-Castell latex-free eraser.

Pencil sharpeners

I always use a travel pencil sharpener that has a container for the shavings. I also have a desk sharpener, which I tend to use before I head off on a drawing trip.

Paints and paintbrushes

You can add a small watercolour or gouache set to your kit if you want to experiment. I always have a tube of white gouache in my pencil case as I use it to paint over areas and build up layers, and I find small inexpensive watercolour brushes work well for this.

Coloured pencils

I used to struggle with using coloured pencils as I found them too hard; then I discovered the Caran d'Ache Luminance pencils and my drawing life changed! They are so soft and buttery, and the colours are rich, bright and opaque. They make drawing in colour an absolute joy. They aren't cheap though, so you might want to build your collection up in stages. Other coloured pencils that come highly recommended by the Sketch Squad are Derwent Chromaflow, Derwent Inktense and Faber-Castell Polychromos.

Pens

I tend not to use pens for drawing, but many of the Sketch Squad do and they recommend Pigma Micron™ or Coptic Multiliners. Most fine-line drawing pens come in different weights or line thicknesses, so try out a few in the art shop to see what suits you.

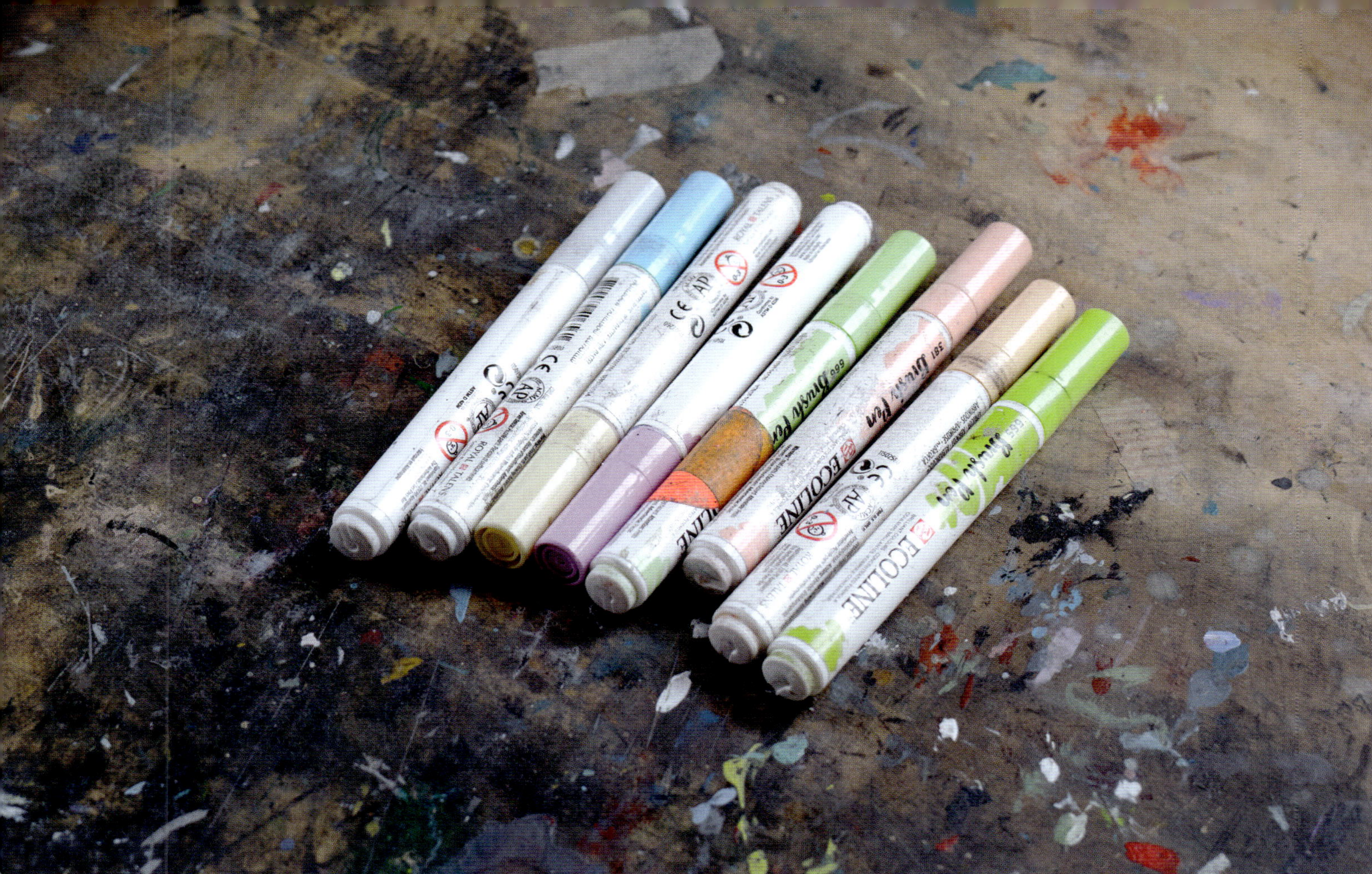

Watercolour brush pens

For adding a background wash on a drawing, I use Ecoline watercolour pastel brush pens. I only use the pastel colours, as the other colours are difficult to work on top of and too intense.

Pencil case

You will want something to hold all your materials together. I keep my pencils and coloured pencils in one pencil case, my marker pens in a second, and my wax crayons in a third. Some people prefer using a pencil roll or wrap. Experiment to see what works best for you.

Other bits and bobs

Something to sit on As you will be drawing outside, I would advise investing in a portable stool. Camping stools are a good option, or my preference is a telescopic expanding stool. This collapses down neatly and easily fits in my backpack.

Clips When you are drawing outside, it's helpful to have little fold-back clips to hold back your sketchbook pages. I find them invaluable.

Charcoal Charcoal is a very flexible drawing material and one you might want in your kit. Be aware, it can get very messy, especially in sketchbooks!

Fixative To prevent your drawings from smudging, you can use fixative. You can buy proper fixative, or hairspray works as a cheaper alternative.

3

Navigating your inner critic

I want to talk to you about something else that will be accompanying you as you work through this book, something that is familiar and unique to every one of us: our 'inner critic'. It's that negative voice in our head that tells us we aren't good enough or talented enough – the voice that often makes us feel small and incompetent. There's no use beating around the bush, this voice will be with you throughout the book, and it'll be much louder at the start.

From a young age, this voice has been nattering away at us, narrating our day and criticising our every move. We develop our inner critic as we internalise the messages we hear as children about what is 'good' and what is 'bad'. Often, our inner critic comes from our parents or primary caregivers; as children we pick up on the negative attitudes that parents not only have towards us but also towards themselves. Our inner voice can also come from interactions with peers, siblings or influential adults. This voice is not our own; we have internalised someone else's judgement.

Be aware of your inner voice

Often, this inner voice becomes so integrated in our thoughts that we see it as us and not just a part of us. For many years, my inner critic was deafening, distracting me from making the work I wanted and making me question my abilities. However, once I realised that the voice wasn't me, just a part of me, I was able to develop strategies to help quieten it. I share these methods with you here to enable you to lessen the power of your inner critic to guide your thinking, feelings, decisions and actions around the art you are making. The more familiar you get with your inner critic, the more capable you will be to notice it and choose to ignore it.

You might want to grab your sketchbook and a pencil to make some notes here.

Tune into your thoughts – what does the voice sound like?

There will always be common themes that your inner critic keeps returning to. It might be that you are too old to start to draw, that you can't be an artist because you have never been to art school or that you have never exhibited any of your work. Think carefully and write the themes you identify down.

Give the voice a name and describe what it looks like

This is a helpful tool that will allow you to get some distance between yourself and your inner critic. Ask yourself, does your inner voice have a gender? What name would it fit? Can you describe it? My inner critic is called Chip; it doesn't have a gender. I gave it that name because that's what it feels like – a constant whittling away at my confidence.

Change the narrative and challenge your inner voice

*'If you hear a voice within you saying,
"You are not a painter" then by all means paint …
and that voice will be silenced'*

Vincent van Gogh

Once you are aware of what your inner critic sounds like, the next step is to talk to yourself with kindness and compassion, like you would to a friend.

Turn up a kinder voice

Think about someone who has been or is supportive and considerate, and think about what they might say to you. You might want to think of me as your cheerleader; if it helps to think about having me on your shoulder as you work, that's great (that also might be your worst nightmare, though!).

Remember, thoughts aren't facts

Let's say your inner voice tells you, 'You are useless'. Just keep asking, 'Is this true? Can I categorically say that this is true?' Most often you can't. Just because you are thinking it doesn't mean you have to believe it. I find it reassuring to remind myself that thoughts aren't facts; they are mental events that pop up in our minds depending on our moods.

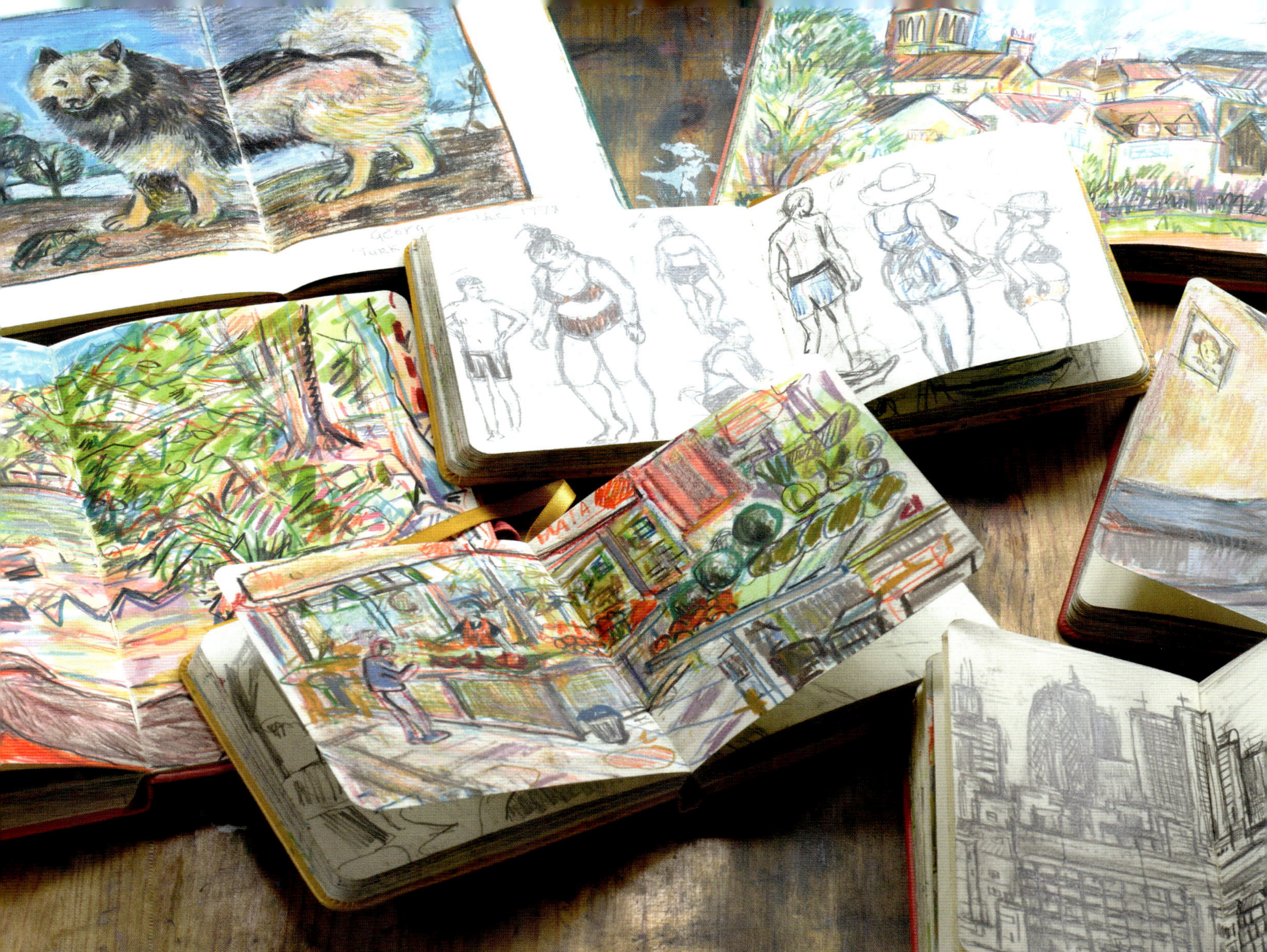

Ask yourself, 'Is this thought helpful?'

This simple question is so powerful. All you need to do is pause and ask yourself, 'Is the thought that I'm untalented and useless helpful to me in any way?' I think you know the answer.

Let your inner voice sit in the corner

The truth is, we are never going to get rid of this inner voice; it's part of us. However, when I'm going through a hard time and my inner critic is loud, I often envisage it entering the room and announcing its presence. I then have a choice: I can sit it down, offer it tea and cake and listen to what it has to say, or just let it sit in the corner, chuntering away to itself. I can choose to ignore it and not to feed it. One of my friends describes it as background music, like you hear in a coffee shop or lift.

When I was in a tutorial at art school, my tutor and I were discussing the inner critic and he said something I will never forget: 'I just get my inner critic drunk, and when he passes out, I get some of my best work done. Then, the next day when he wakes up, he's usually so hungover he can't think straight. I tell him all the great things I've painted so he'd better keep quiet.'

On that note, now we have learnt to identify and ignore our inner critics, I think it's about time we start sketching.

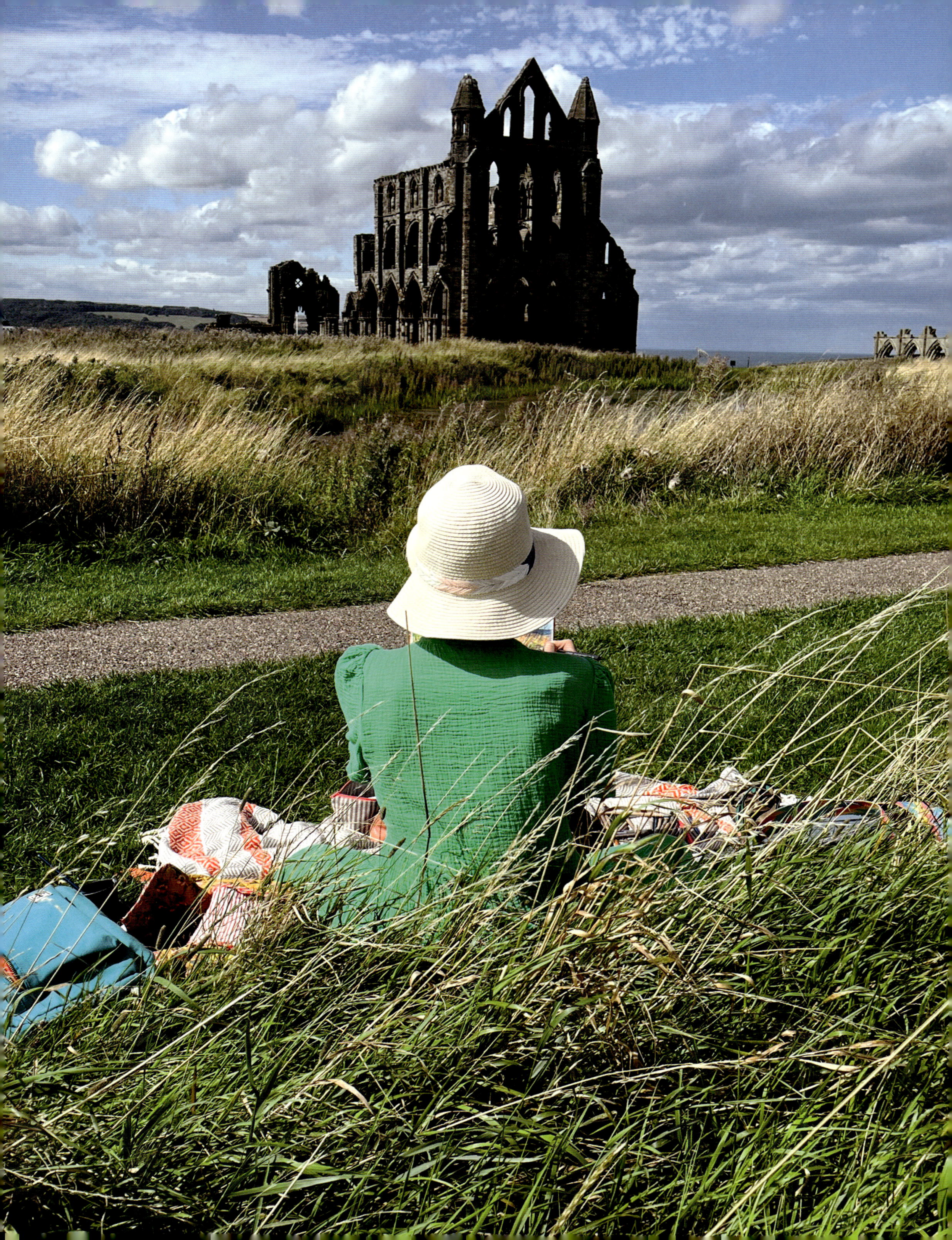

Warm-up exercises

The initial steps in any new creative endeavour are always nerve-racking, no matter how excited you may be. This chapter contains a series of exercises to get you started and ease you into your sketchbook habit. It's a way to break in your sketchbook, loosen up and let go of control. As with all the exercises in the book, these warm-ups are designed to be enjoyable, so take the pressure off and just have some fun.

'It's not what you look at that matters, it's what you see'

Henry David Thoreau

Mark-making exercise

To begin with, we will start with a very simple exercise that will show you how much can be achieved with just a pencil on a page. Keep changing your pencils as you work; don't just use the same one.

What you need
- A range of pencils: HB to 9B
- Your larger sketchbook
- Eraser
- Pencil sharpener

Open your sketchbook so you are working across a double page. Start to make different marks with your pencil. Push and pull it across the surface, applying hard and then soft pressure. Create patterns, scribbles, cross-hatching, circles, lines, dots and dashes. Just create marks – make them messy, fluid and carefree. Close your eyes and see what happens. Fill the whole page, trying to be loose and free, making the lines go from edge to edge.

Look carefully at the marks you have created. Are there any that surprise you? Ones you perhaps haven't used before? Make a note of those that excite you and commit to using similar marks in the future.

Sketch Squad: Mark-making exercise

Here is a selection of the Squad's sketchbooks, showing
how they interpreted this mark-making exercise. Every
one of them said how much they enjoyed this exercise.
You can see how varied their marks are.

Phyllis

Jane

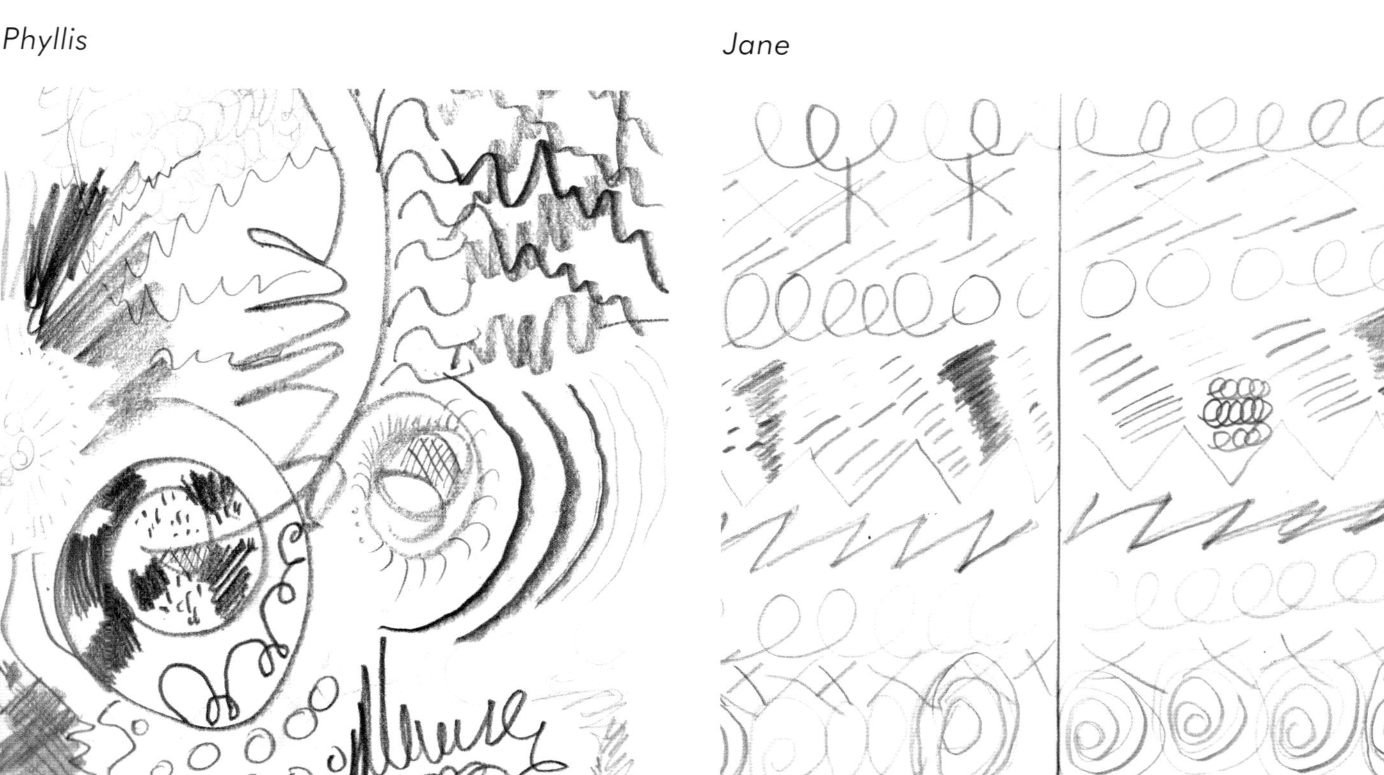

Safa

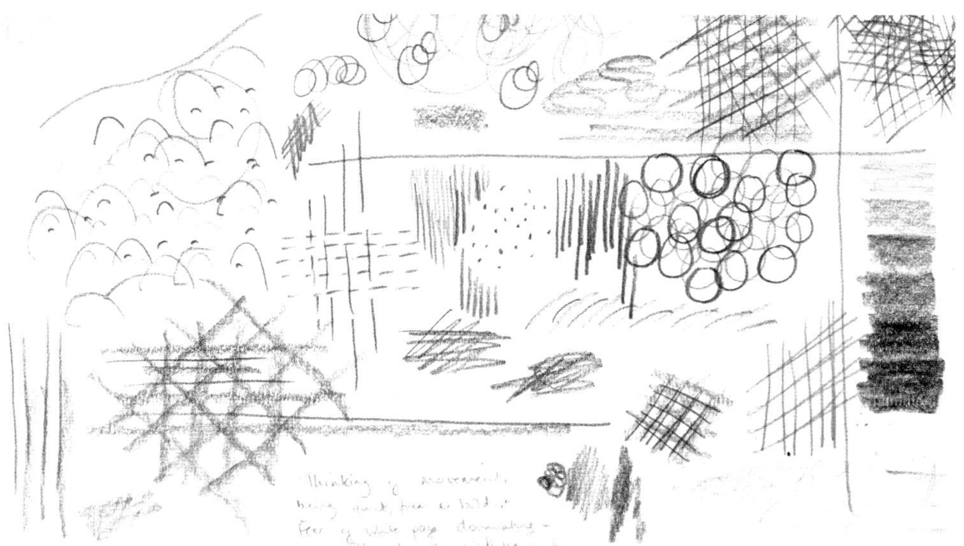

Six warm-up drawing exercises

For these exercises, you are going to draw one object in six different ways.

First, choose an object that fits in your hand. Find something that you see or use every day, something you are familiar with. Don't overthink this; it doesn't really matter what you draw. Remember, we aren't here to create a 'good drawing', we are just having fun and making some marks.

Aim for each drawing to fill at least half the page. The timings (apart from the one-minute quick drawing) are rough guidelines – you don't have to stick to them exactly.

I will include prompts to get you to consider how you feel about your drawings. Include these notes in your sketchbook. It might be helpful to create a list of the exercises on a separate page and record your thoughts and feelings there.

Make a note of each exercise underneath each drawing, just to remind you of the task.

What you need
- A simple object of your choice
- A range of pencils: HB to 9B
- Your larger sketchbook
- Eraser
- Pencil sharpener
- Something to time yourself with

Exercise 1: Quick drawing
(1 minute)

Let all your other thoughts fall away and focus on looking at your object. Draw quickly, trying to capture the whole object in one minute. Use different pressures and marks to describe what you see. Do at least five of these drawings.

How did you find this exercise? Some people really enjoy having a time limit as it prevents them from thinking too much.

Exercise 2: Non-dominant-hand drawing
(5 minutes)

Draw your object with the opposite hand to the one you normally draw with. Just let the lines flow and enjoy not being in control.

How did you find drawing in this way? Maybe you made marks that surprised you, marks that you wouldn't normally make. Take note of this.

Exercise 3: Tone-only drawing (10 minutes)

For this exercise, you are not going to create an outline but just to use tone to describe your object. Put simply, tone refers to how light or dark something is.

Look carefully at your object and ask yourself what the lightest and darkest parts are. It might help you to squint while doing this, as it helps you to see tonal value areas more easily.

Turn your softest pencil on its side and use the lead to create broad marks. Build up the drawing, holding your pencil in this way.

How did you find this? Many people rely on using only lines to create their drawings. There's nothing wrong with this, however it's good practice to use tone in your drawings as it adds another dimension.

Exercise 4: Angry drawing

(10 minutes)

Think back to a time when you were angry. Let that emotion build up in your body and then use your pencil to channel that energy into a drawing of your object.

What does an angry mark look like to you? Remember, there is no right or wrong way to do these drawings – your anger will feel different to my anger – and this is what makes comparing these drawings exciting.

Exercise 5: Sad drawing

(10 minutes)

Now let's do the opposite. I want you to create a sad drawing of your object. What marks can you use to convey sadness? It might help to put some sad music on to help you get in the mood.

How did you find doing these emotional drawings?

Exercise 6: Final drawing

(15 minutes)

To wrap up these exercises, you are going to do a fifteen-minute drawing considering all the exercises you've done so far. Look carefully at your previous warm-up exercises and consider what you might want to bring into this final drawing. Perhaps you liked your use of tone in the tonal drawing or maybe you liked the scribbly lines of your mark-making exercise. It's entirely up to you – just enjoy these final minutes with your object.

After you have finished, you can place the object back where it came from. I guarantee you will never look at it in the same way again!

My warm-up drawings

▶ Exercise 1: Quick drawing

I chose a small Swedish Dala horse as my object. It's an object I'm very familiar with and one I thought I knew quite well but, when I started these one-minute drawings, I was surprised by the complexity of the shape. I assumed it would be an easy form to draw but quickly discovered that this wasn't the case. However, by the end of the exercise, I felt that drawing at such speed had enabled me to get a grasp of the basic shape.

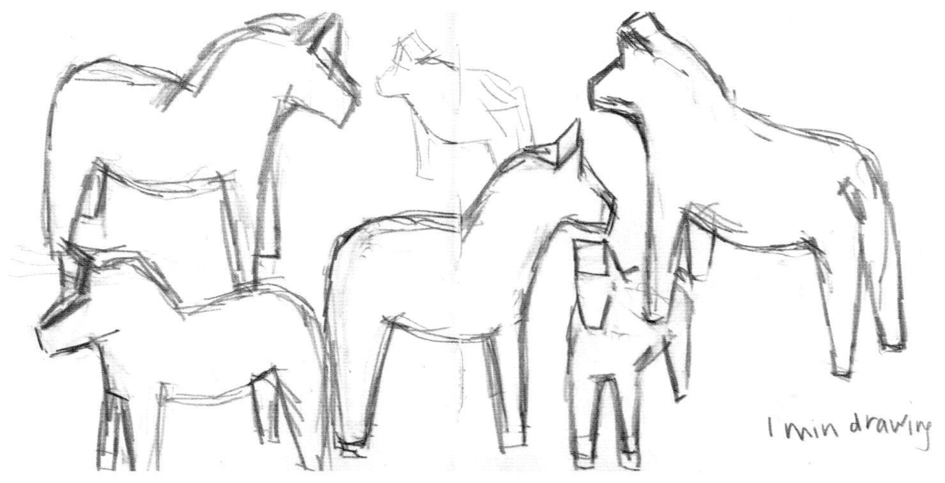

▼ Exercise 3: Tone-only drawing

My drawings are normally very tonal, so this was an exercise that I found straightforward. With tone-only drawings, I tend to squint so that I can see the tonal variations more clearly.

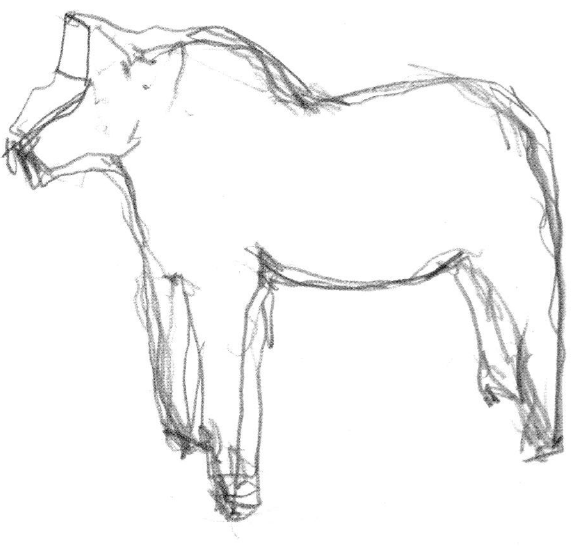

▲ Exercise 2: Non-dominant-hand drawing

I enjoy non-dominant-hand drawings. I find the lack of control really liberating and I make marks that I wouldn't normally, which surprise me. I like the uncertain, hesitant lines that appear in this drawing.

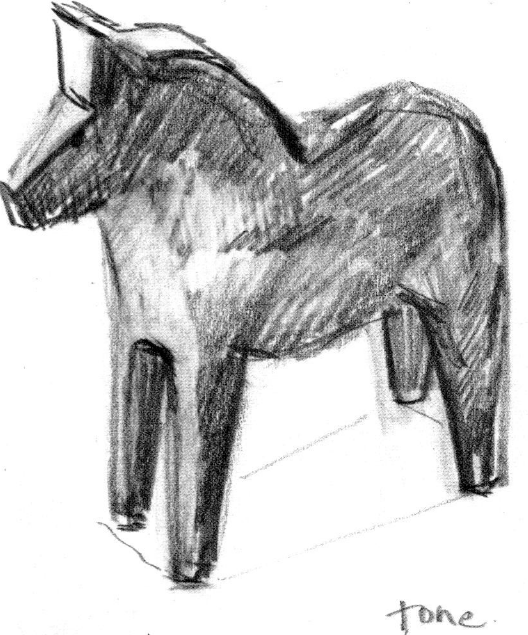

▼ Exercise 4: Angry drawing

I loved this exercise. I often draw when I'm feeling grumpy or angry as I find the very act of making thick, dense, dark pencil marks on paper very cathartic. For me, this is what anger feels like – dark and dense.

▼ Exercise 5: Sad drawing

For my sad drawing, I wanted to use composition – the way in which different elements of an artwork are arranged – as the main element to convey sadness. I placed the horse in the bottom right-hand side of the paper, so it looked a little misplaced and dejected. I also used a lighter HB pencil.

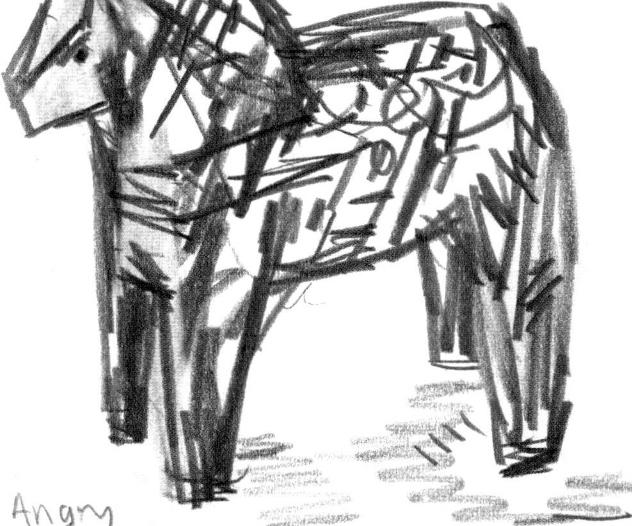

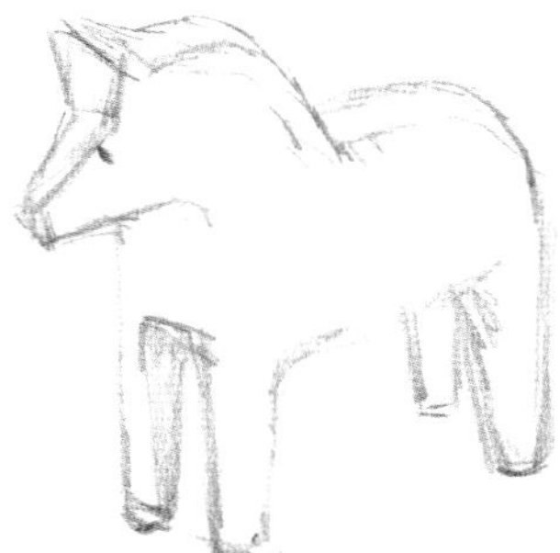

▶ Exercise 6: Final drawing

By the end of the six exercises, I felt very comfortable and confident drawing the horse. The fifteen minutes flew by, and I could have continued for longer.

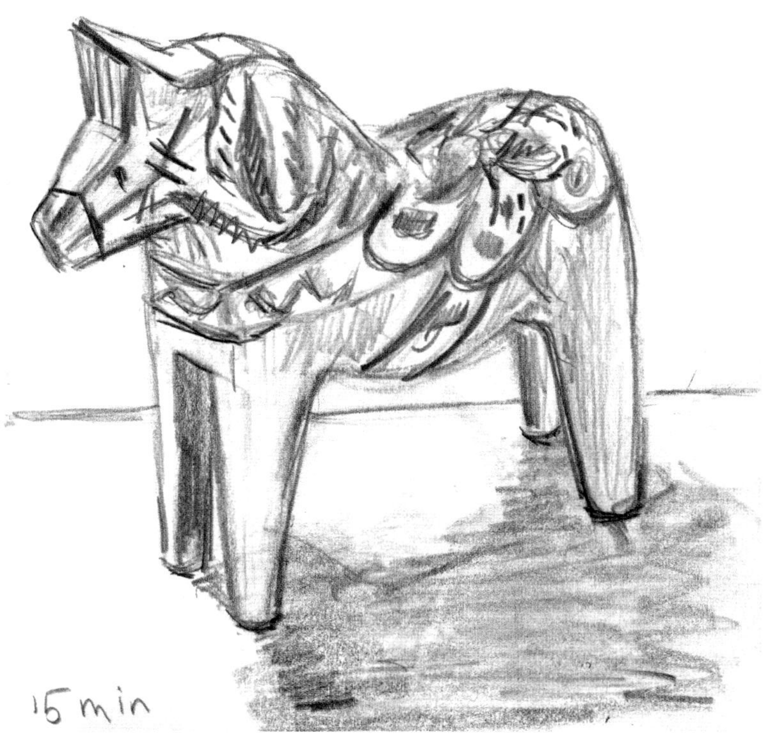

Sketch Squad: Warm-up drawings

Now let's look at a selection of the Sketch Squad's drawings for these six exercises.

Exercise 1: Quick drawing

▶ *Kathi*

Kathi chose to draw her headphones. She admits she isn't good at time management, so she was anxious about doing this sketch. However, after doing five drawings, she felt much looser and ready for the rest of the exercises.

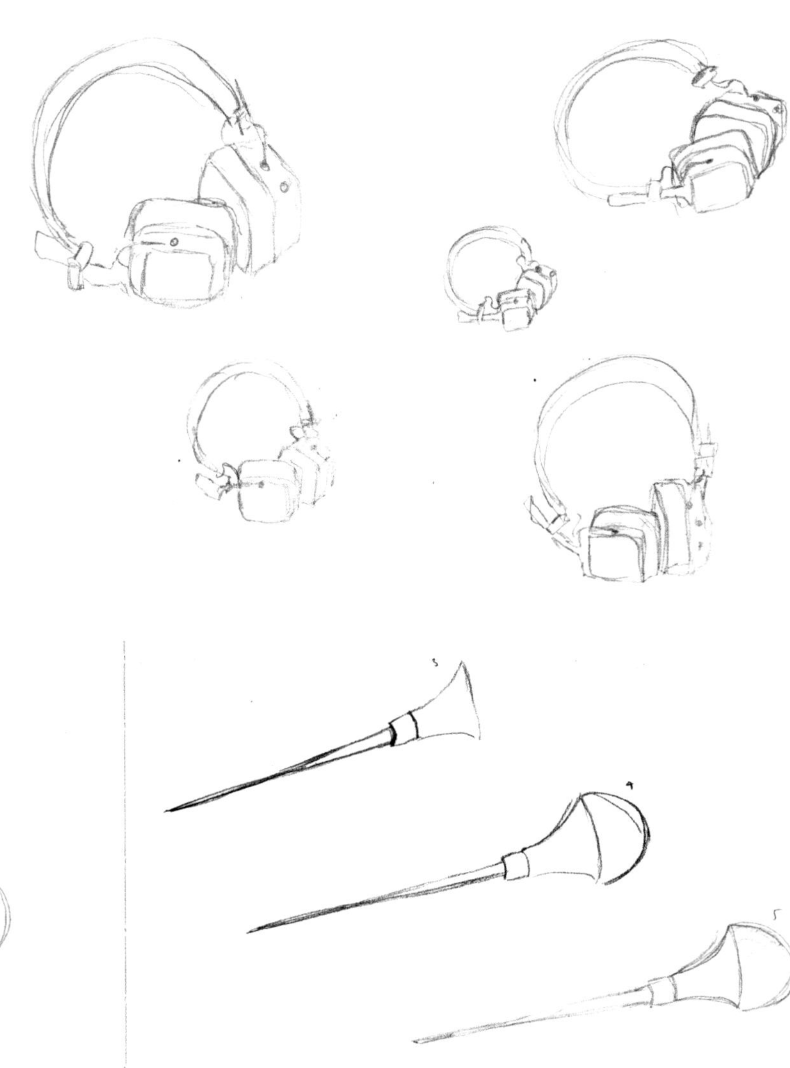

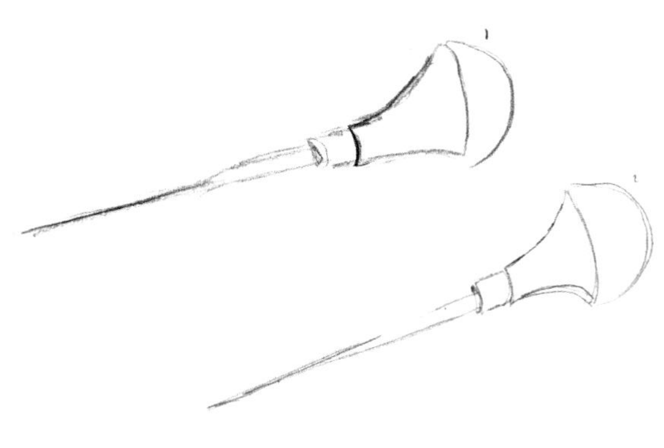

▲ *Safa*

Safa is a printmaker and she chose to use one of her carving tools for the warm-up exercises. On reflection, she wished she had chosen an object with more volume as the tool was thin and spindly to draw. If, at this stage, you are questioning your choice of object, feel free to choose another.

Exercise 2: Non-dominant-hand drawing

▶ *Claire*

Claire chose to draw this soapstone figure, which has sentimental value to her. Although she breezed through the first few drawings, she found this non-dominant-hand one difficult. She notes, 'I'm strongly right-handed, so this was hard. However, by the end, I was quite pleased with the drawing. It feels like it has some vitality to it.'

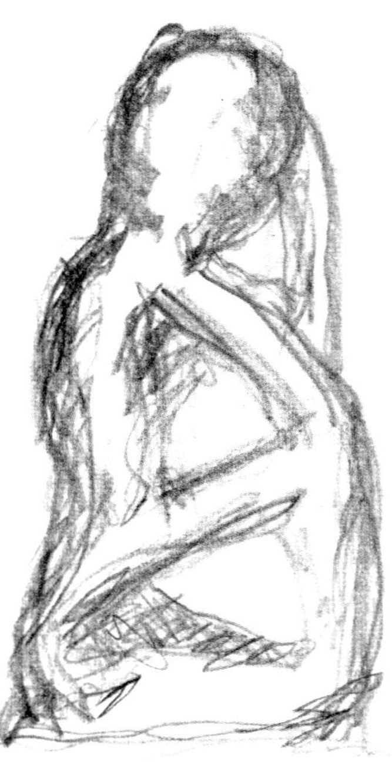

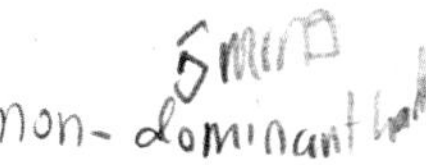

◀ *Lucy*

This was the first time Lucy had done a non-dominant-hand drawing, and she really enjoyed it. Despite having hardly any control over the pencil, she felt liberated from the pressure of creating a 'good' drawing.

Exercise 3: Tone-only drawing

▼ *Hannah*

If you, like Hannah, are someone whose drawings are more line-orientated, the tonal drawing may be tricky. Hannah admits that she did struggle with this drawing. However, she also notes that it really helped her get to grips with understanding the form and curve of the mug.

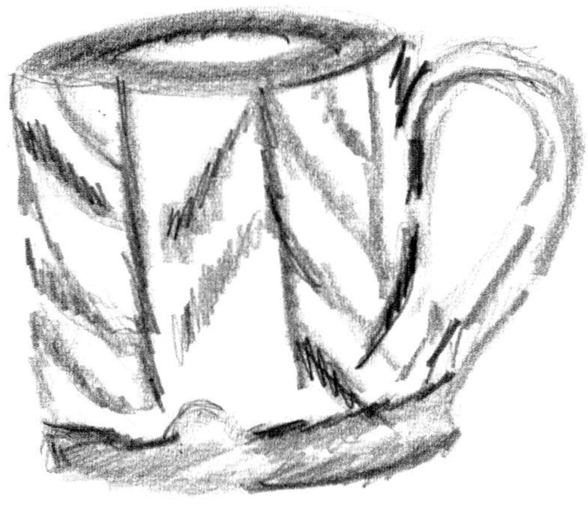

▼ *Paula*

Paula's drawings are always very tonal, so she was excited about this exercise. She used a 6B pencil, turned it on its side to get broader marks and pressed heavily to get the darker tones. She squinted too, as that helped her see the tonal values more clearly.

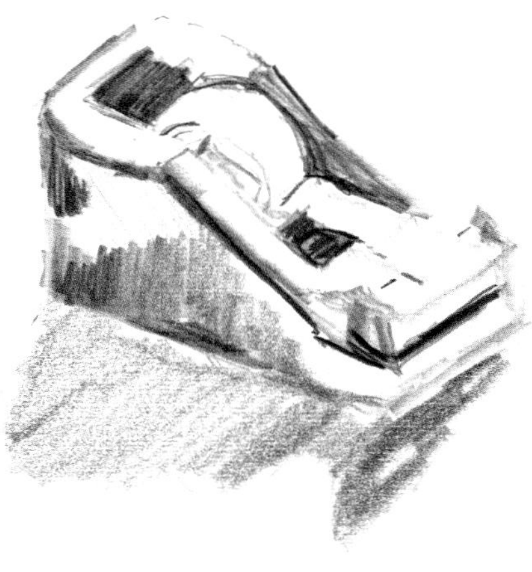

Exercise 4:
Angry drawing

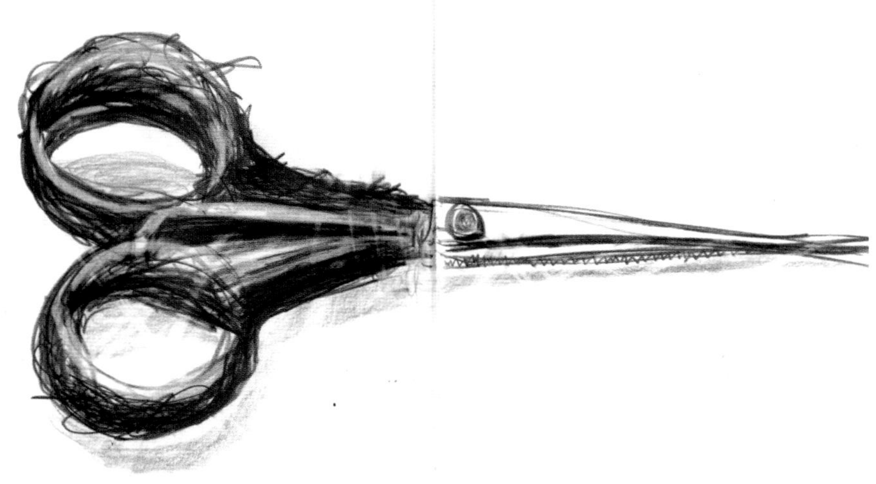

▶ *Niki*

It can be difficult to conjure up emotions as Niki found out: 'I'm not a naturally angry person so I was surprised at how much I enjoyed drawing this one. It felt incredibly freeing to just go for it and make some powerful marks. Perhaps I should draw like this more often!'

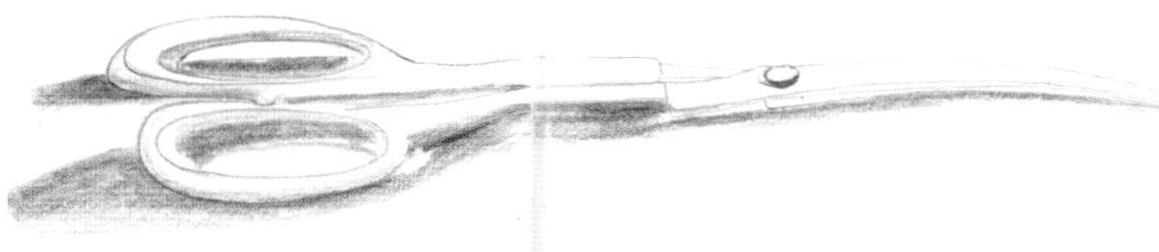

◀ *Anne*

Anne decided to do this exercise when she was feeling angry. She felt so furious that the marks came naturally, and she found it useful as it helped dissipate her anger.

Again, we can see how beneficial drawing can be to help regulate our emotions. When you are having a bad day, drawing can be something that you can turn to. I find that just making marks, scribbling or doodling can help me to solve problems and process emotions.

Exercise 5: Sad drawing

▶ *Diane*

This is Diane's sad electric toothbrush drawing. She intentionally drew the head of the toothbrush with a slight curve 'to give it a slumped feeling, a feeling of lethargy'.

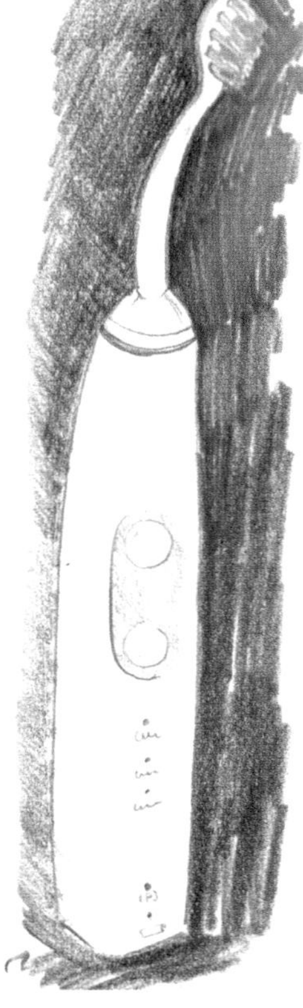

▲ *Niki*

In Niki's sad drawing, we find her scissors looking a little worse for wear. They do, in fact look a little sad. Niki notes: 'I tried to make my marks weary and tired. I used a lighter touch with my pencil and was just stroking the pencil on the page with very little energy.'

▶ *Jane*

Jane admits she had never thought about using her emotions to create a drawing, and she did feel a little lost as to what to do. She reflected on what sadness feels like to her: 'To me, sadness feels like soft, gentle rain, so I decided to cover my mug with marks like rain and use a light, soft touch with my pencil'. She chose to use an HB pencil for this drawing.

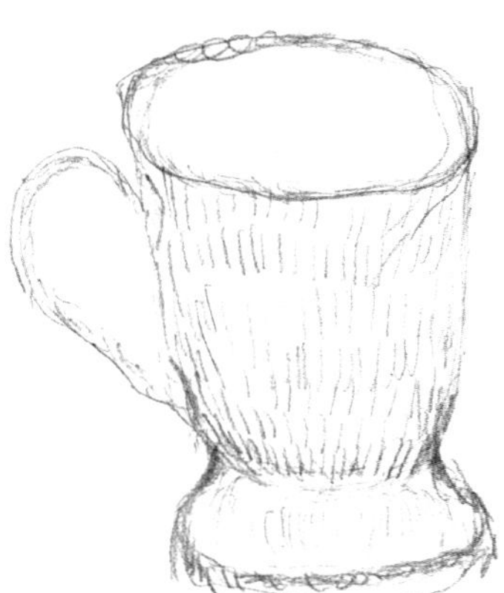

Exercise 6: Final drawing

▼ *Phyllis*

Phyllis observed that during the other exercises, she found herself enjoying making bold lines, cross-hatching and, in her words, 'scribbling'. She was then intentional in ensuring that she incorporated those marks into her fifteen-minute drawing.

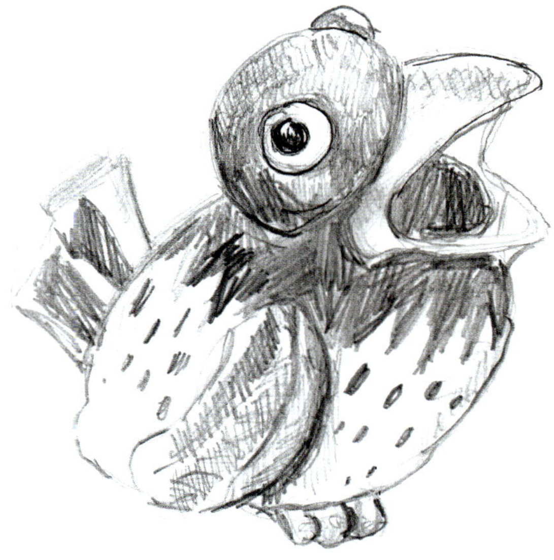

▼ *Eva*

Eva noted that on the final drawing, she spent more time working on the tone and the shape: 'I tried to do a more "serious" drawing here, but I enjoy it more when I am playing a bit more.'

It is interesting to notice that when we are asked to do a final consolidated piece of artwork, the result is sometimes less interesting. When I worked in schools, and students were asked to put together a final work, it was often less engaging than the preparatory work. I think this is because we tend to tidy things up, make them look pretty, put a 'bow' on them. If you find yourself doing this – overworking a piece – it's a good idea to give yourself a time limit.

Final thoughts

I hope you found these warm-up exercises helpful, fun and challenging. Any of these can be used as preparation for the forthcoming exercises in the book. They are such a good way to perfect your hand-eye coordination and to get you in the mood for drawing. I always compare it to a warm-up in an exercise class; you wouldn't go straight into an intense workout without loosening up, and it's the same with drawing.

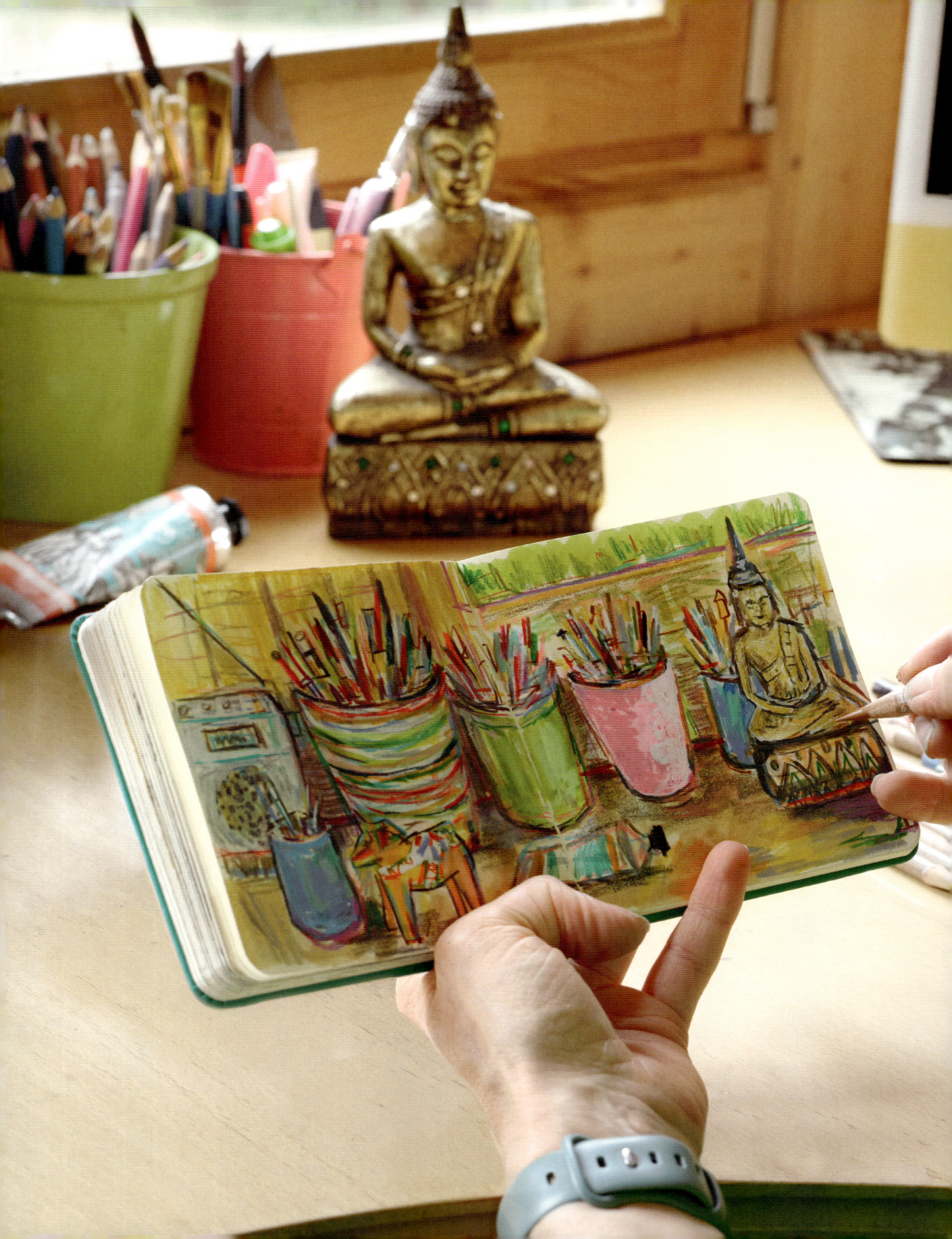

5
In the home

This chapter contains four different exercises that encourage you to look at your home space with fresh eyes. I hope to prove that you don't need to travel far to find something engaging to draw; if you look carefully, anything can become of interest.

*'Blessed are they who see beautiful things
in humble places where other people see nothing'*

Camille Pissarro

Things to consider

Before starting these exercises, ask yourself how you feel at the start and end. Write down your answers in your sketchbook.

Composition

Composition is the way in which different elements of an artwork are combined or arranged. Put simply, it's where you place things on the page. When most people begin a drawing exercise, they just start drawing anywhere on the page. I want you to be mindful of the four corners of your sketchbook – think of the page as a viewfinder. Where you place your drawing will influence how you see and interpret it. For example, a small mug placed in the middle of a page will have a different reading to a large mug that fills both pages of a sketchbook. I love filling the pages in my sketchbook; I like my drawing to burst across the page. That's just me, though – you can use the page as you want.

Materials

In all these exercises it's up to you what materials you use. You might want to do some of them in pencil and others in colour, to use inks or felt-tip pens. It's entirely your choice. If you do choose to use pencils, make sure that you use a wide selection of grades.

Timing

I will give you a rough time limit with all these exercises but feel free to adapt them to your needs. Many students work better when there is a time limit. You might find it helpful to set yourself your own time within which to complete each exercise – and when the time is up, that's it, the drawing is done. This can be useful if you struggle with knowing when to stop.

Exercise 1:

Take a break (roughly 1 hour)

For this exercise, I want you to draw what you would normally have as a drink and snack when you take a break. What might that look like to you? Perhaps it's a strong cup of tea in your favourite mug with a couple of biscuits or maybe it's your evening aperitif with some crisps and nibbles.

Once you have selected your drink and snack, it's time to start drawing. You might want to do some preliminary warm-up exercises to get you going (see pages 42–3).

Look closely at the surface of your drinking vessel. How can you use marks to describe its smoothness? Similarly, study your snack. If it's a biscuit, how can you use your marks to evoke its crumbly texture? Do as many drawings as you like of your drink and snack.

Once you have finished, reward yourself with a fresh cup of tea or coffee (or wine!) and enjoy your snack.

Exercise 2:
What's on your desk? (roughly 1 hour)

Next, you are going to draw a surface in your home. It doesn't have to
be your desk; it could be your kitchen table, dressing table or another
flat surface that stuff sits on.

Exercise 3:

Out of the window (1 hour or more)

Choose a window in your house and draw the view from it. Make
sure that the drawing contains the window frame, so there is a sense
of inside and outside. The window frame will also help you with
your drawing by providing a natural viewfinder from which you can
work. You might want to do this in stages – as the view will most likely
remain the same, you can take your time and build up the drawing
over a few hours.

Exercise 4:

A corner of the room (1 hour or more)

First, reflect on how helpful it was to have the window in the last
exercise to help with the framing of your drawing – it provided you
with a contained space in which to compose your sketch. Select
a corner in your house that you would like to draw, and choose
something on the left and right of the corner that will serve as your
boundaries. You are then to draw everything in between. As with the
previous exercise, you can curate your corner, remove or add things of
interest. And if you can leave the corner undisturbed, you can work on
it over a period of time.

My drawings: In the home

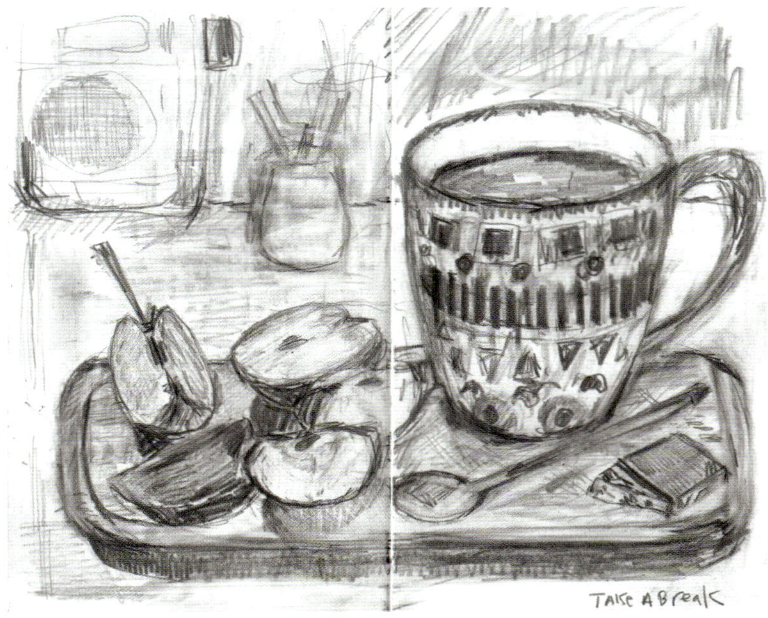

◀ **Exercise 1: Take a break**

A cup of tea, a sliced apple and some chocolate is my go-to drink and snack. I used a heavy 6B pencil, as I wanted my drawing to be bold and strong. The drawing took me just under an hour and it was interesting to observe the colour change in the apple during that time. This is one of the things that I love about drawing from observation – especially drawing organic materials – the scene can change so quickly.

▼ **Exercise 2: What's on your desk?**

The desk in my studio is always crammed full of stuff, so it was the perfect subject for this exercise. It's a place where things gather and accumulate.

I started the drawing with a loose sketch using a light-brown marker pen to get in the main structure. I then built up the drawing using my coloured pencils and used white gouache to lighten areas so I could then draw over them again. To see how I build up my coloured drawings in this way, go to pages 78–9.

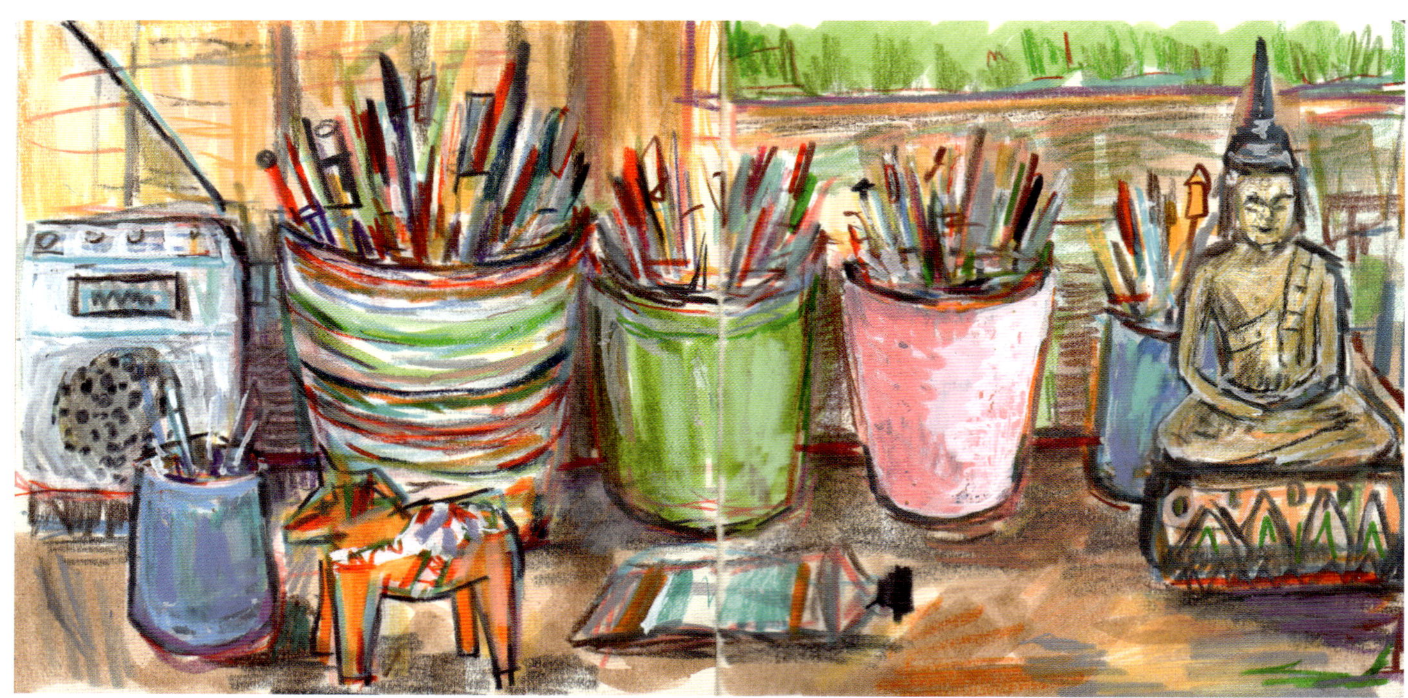

▶ Exercise 3: Out of the window

This is the view from my studio. It's a scene I'm familiar with and I enjoy watching how it changes with the seasons. This drawing was done in March. The trees are still bare, so you can see their structure – you see the trees as they really are. I used a small sketchbook for this and limited myself to one hour.

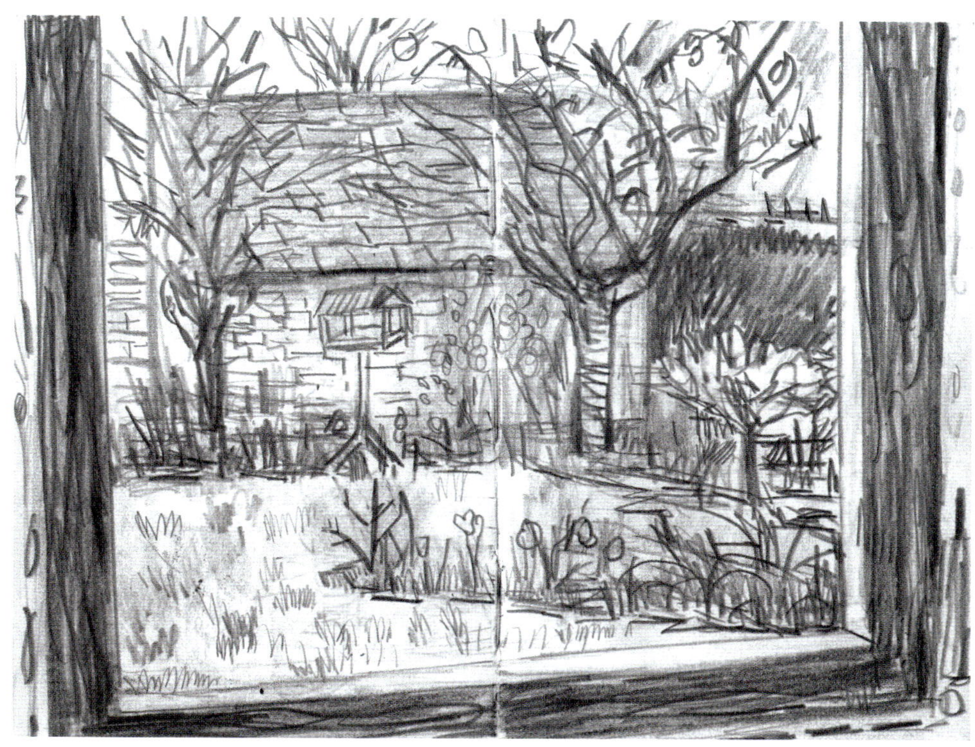

▶ Exercise 4: A corner of the room

I drew a corner of my studio on one of the first sunny days of the year. I love how the sun makes everything warm and inviting. I used my Caran d'Ache Luminance coloured pencils for this drawing, which took me just over one hour.

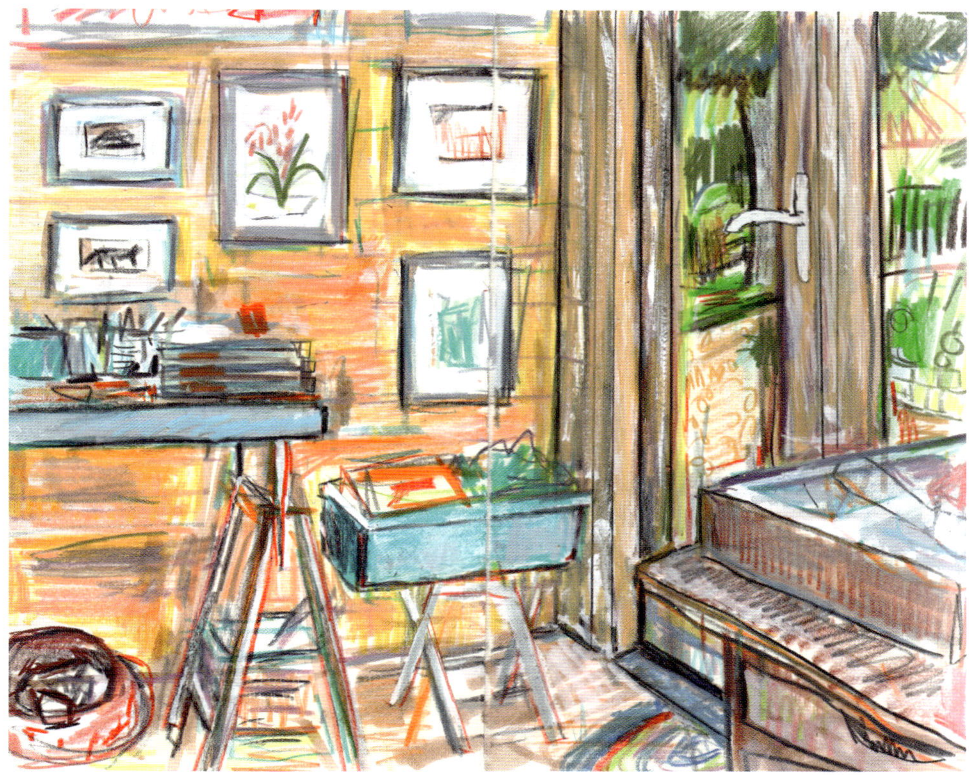

Sketch Squad: In the home

Let's now look at the Sketch Squad's drawings and see how they found each of these exercises.

Exercise 1: Take a break

▼ *Paula*

Paula had to improvise here as she doesn't normally snack and she didn't have any interesting mugs to draw, so she borrowed one from her neighbour.

She chose to use her new coloured pencils as she was eager to try them out. It takes a while to feel comfortable using any new materials, and this was the case for Paula. She noted: 'At first, I felt really hesitant with the pencils, unsure about the colours, as they were more vibrant than my old set, but by the end of the hour I felt I had the measure of them.'

If, like Paula, you don't snack or aren't feeling inspired by your choice of drink and snack, then please do improvise – treat it as if you are setting up a still life. Make sure you are happy with your choice, as you will be spending time drawing it.

▼ *Niki*

Niki decided that, instead of a cup of tea, she would go for a glass of wine with some nuts. She was waiting for her husband to finish an important phone call, and she didn't want to start drinking her wine without him, so she decided to draw it while waiting for him. She drew the outline of it quickly as she didn't know how long he would be, but, as he took a lot longer than she anticipated, this enabled her to add tone and texture.

Drawing while waiting is such a good use of your time, much more rewarding than scrolling purposelessly on your phone (see also the exercise on page 119).

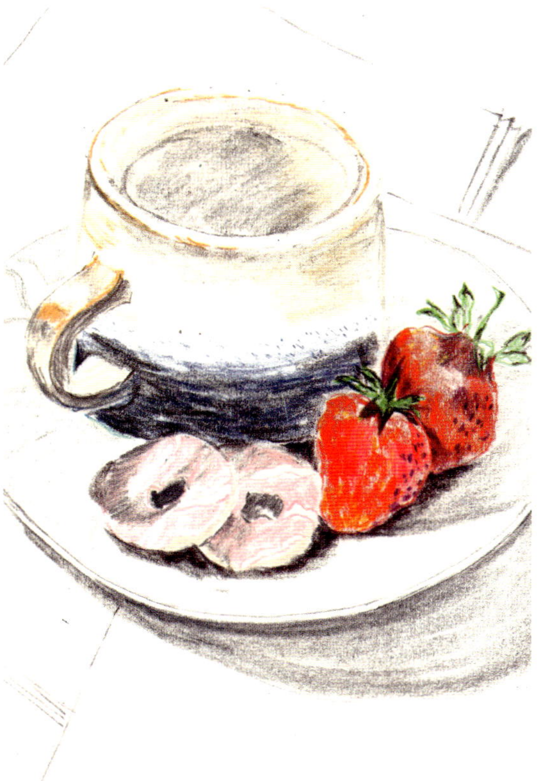

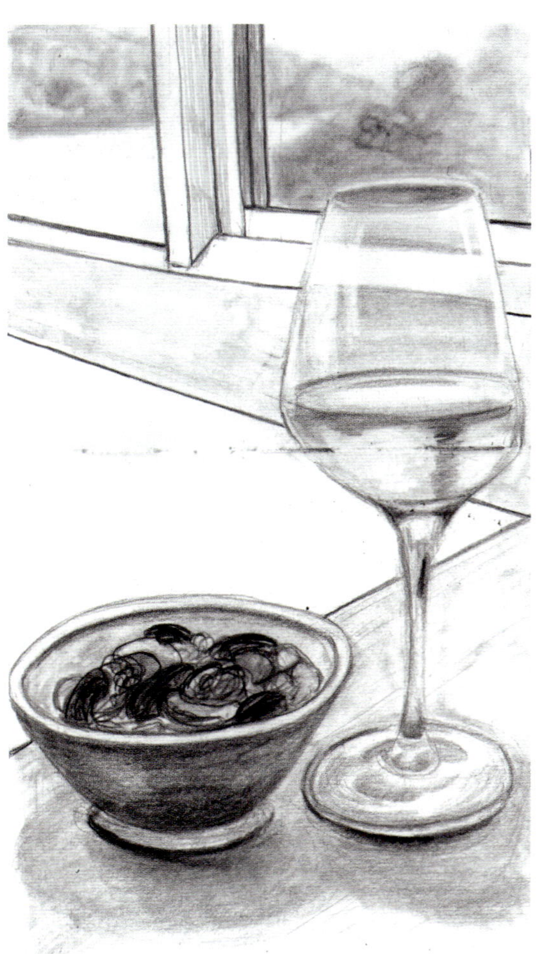

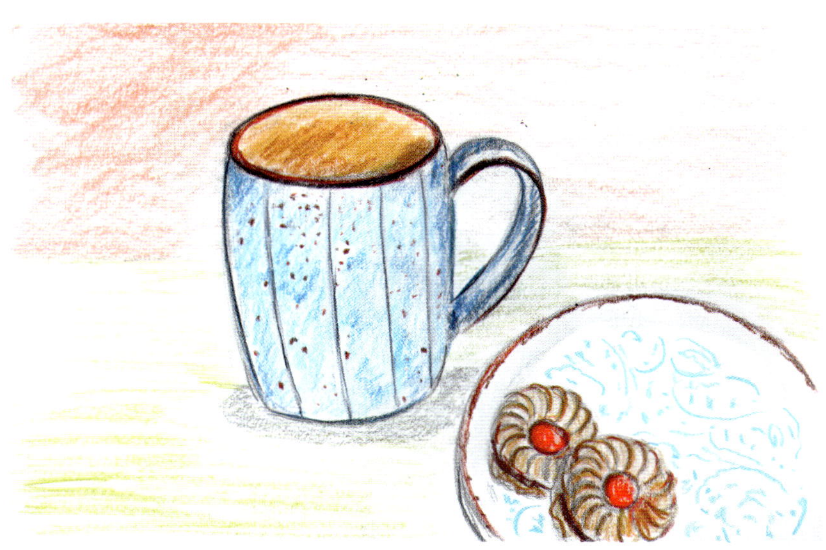

▶ *Safa*

Before Safa started this drawing, she did some of the warm-up exercises from the previous chapter (see pages 42–3). She noted, 'At this point, a blank page still intimidates me, so the warm-up exercises are helpful as they help me loosen up and relax.'

This drawing took her forty minutes. Safa used her Caran d'Ache Luminance coloured pencils, and it's clear in her drawing just how highly pigmented they are.

Exercise 2: What's on your desk?

▶ *Hannah*

Hannah carefully considered the composition of this drawing of her mantelpiece. She wanted to present the items off-centre, from an unusual angle and to add more tone to her drawing than she had previously. It's interesting to note just how thoughtful Hannah was in the lead-up to this drawing. Rather than just getting stuck in, she approached it with real intention and set herself specific goals to achieve.

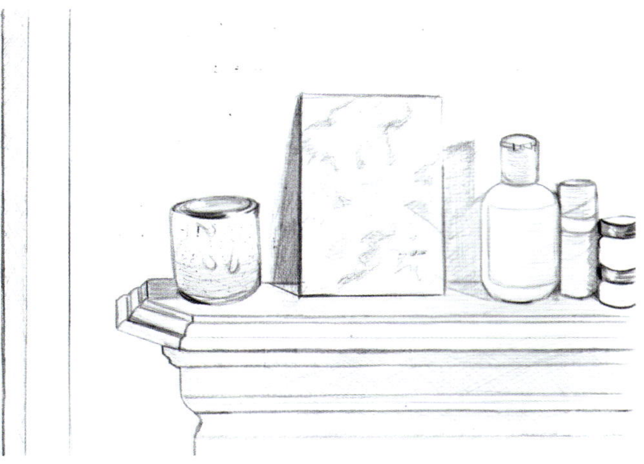

▼ *Anne*

Anne really struggled to get going with this drawing. The task felt enormous as every surface in her home has multiple uses and it's usually chaotic. However, she managed to navigate this by reminding herself that it's the process – not the result – that counts. She also found giving herself a time limit helpful.

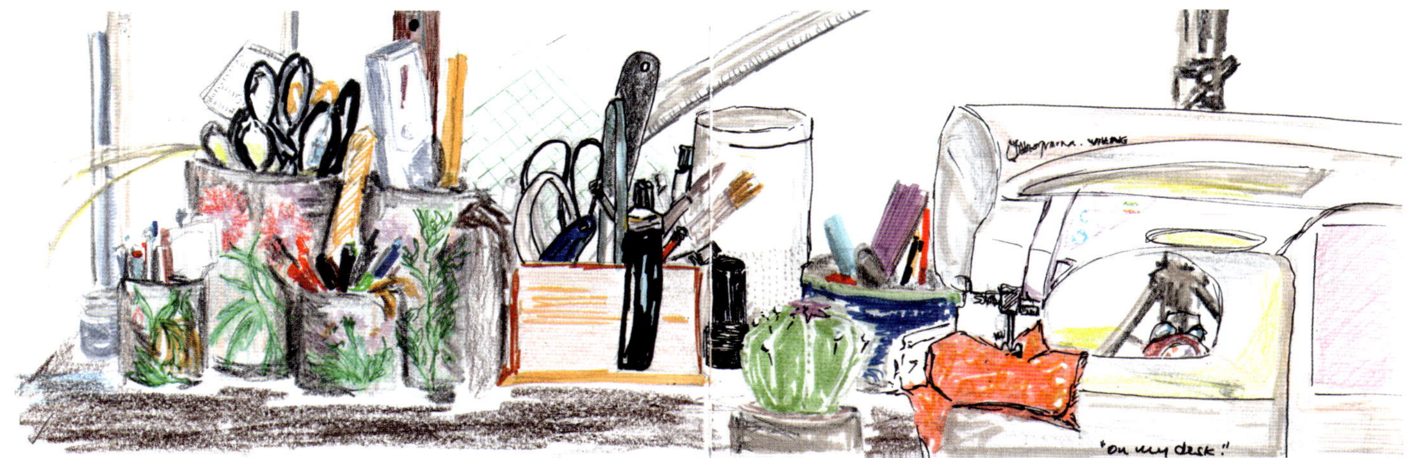

▶ *Phyllis*

Phyllis had no intention of doing this drawing, in fact, she had prepared something very different for this exercise. However, she got back from shopping one morning, placed her shopping bag on the table, and then was struck by how much she liked the composition and the colour of the scene in front of her, so she set about drawing it.

The drawing took her thirty minutes, and she used coloured pens, pencils and fineliners. Phyllis also noted that she probably wouldn't have noticed this before, but as she was in drawing mode, everything in front of her had potential for a drawing. Like I've said before, when we draw, we start to see more.

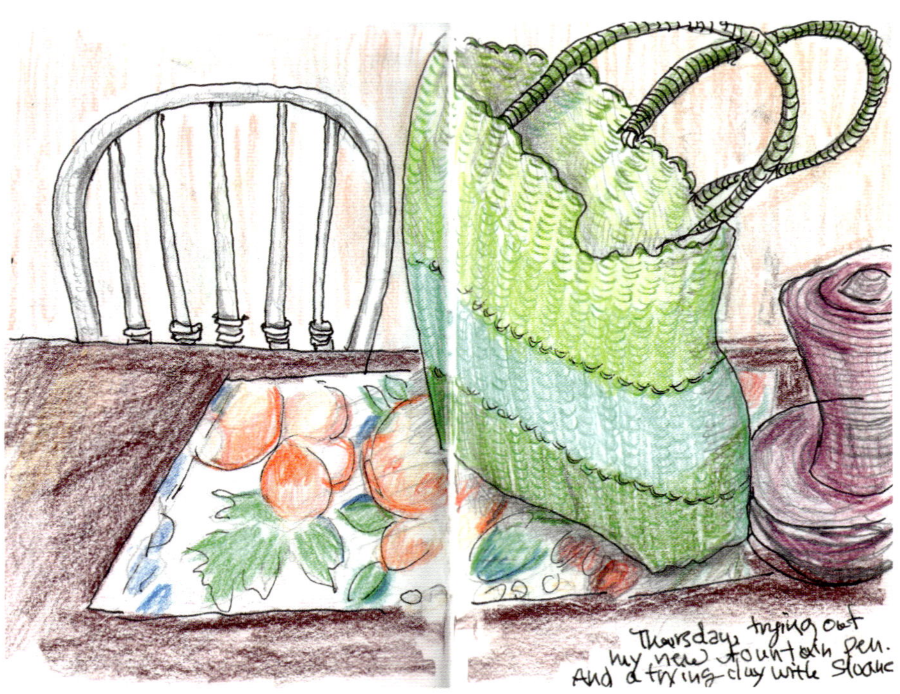

Exercise 3: Out of the window
▶ *Diane*

At the time of this drawing, Diane lived in a flat in London. Every window overlooked another property, highlighting just how cramped living in London can be. At this point, she was feeling claustrophobic in her flat and wanted her drawing to convey this. She was deliberate with her composition and chose to draw the window with the balcony barriers to emphasise that sense of containment.

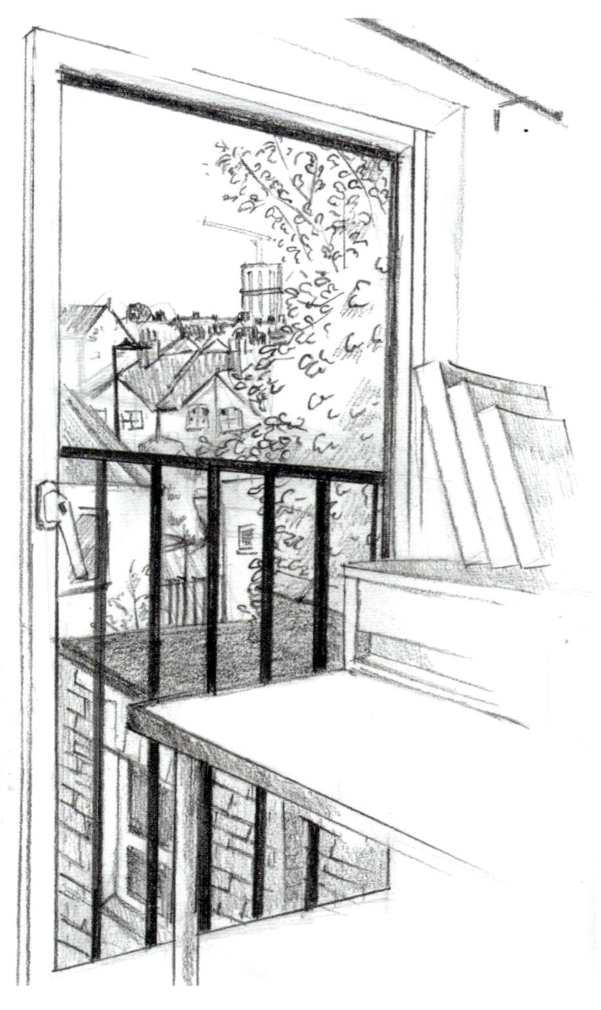

▶ *Jane*

Jane chose to draw a window with lots of plants on the windowsill. She had planned to draw the view out of the window, but she ended up getting carried away with the plants and curtains inside. She purposely changed pencils during this drawing, using softer pencils in contrast with the harder pencils she ordinarily uses.

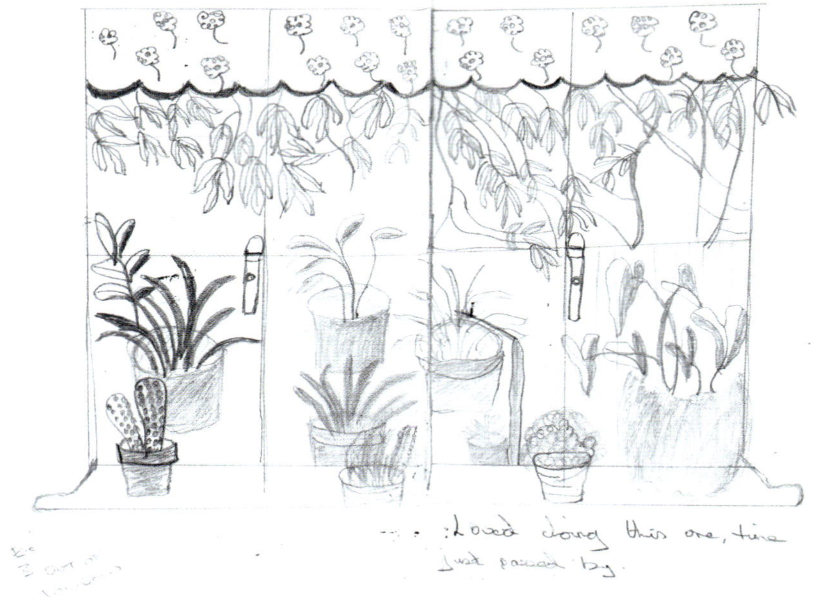

▶ *Eva*

This is a drawing from Eva's bedroom window. It's a view that she had been meaning to draw ever since she moved into the house. She was anxious about the drawing as it was a complex scene; however, once she started drawing and relaxed into it, she really enjoyed it. She took longer on the drawing than intended as she was having such a good time.

I loved reading this feedback from Eva. The fact that she had such an enjoyable experience while drawing is really the point of this book. If you lose track of time when you are drawing, then that is time well spent.

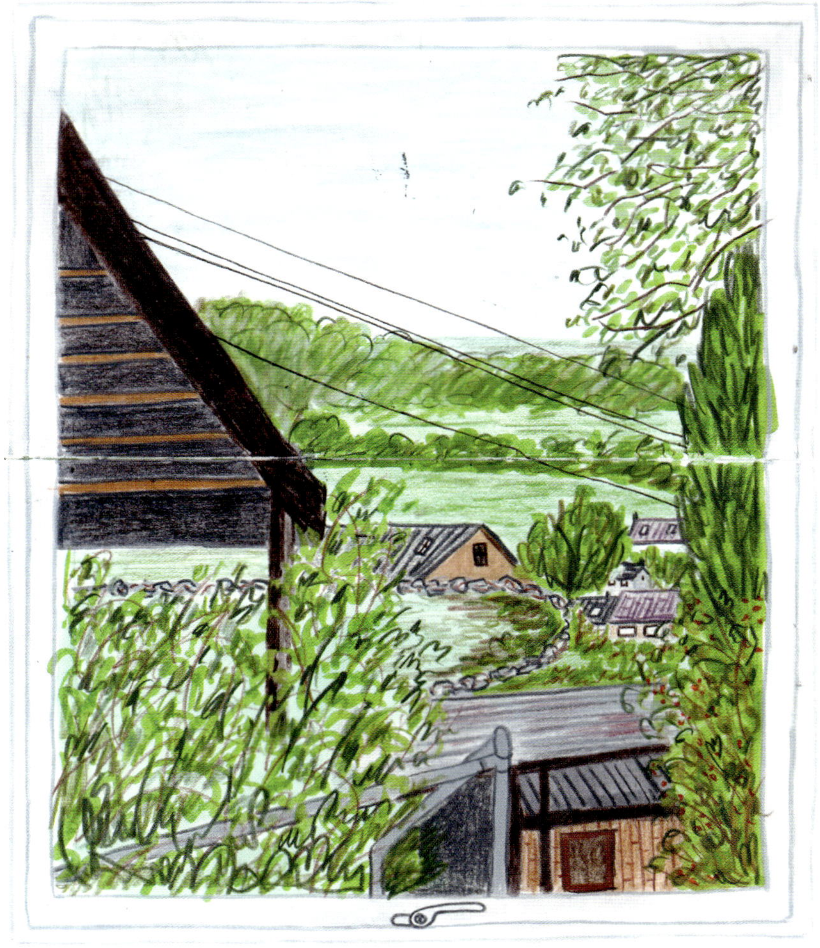

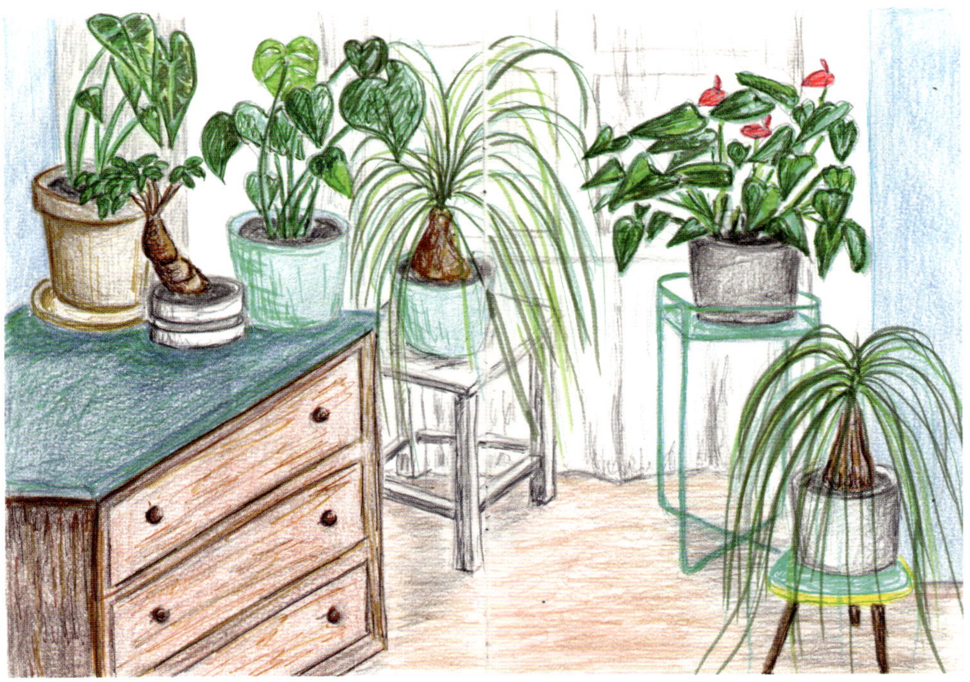

Exercise 4: A corner of the room

▲ *Kathi*

For Kathi, this was the first drawing where she felt more comfortable using her coloured pencils. She chose this corner as it's her favourite part of her apartment in Vienna: 'It feels like it's an indoor garden.'

She built the drawing up slowly by approaching one plant at a time and coming back to the drawing over the course of a week. This is a great strategy to help you feel less overwhelmed by your subject. Just take it step by step – maybe five minutes one day, ten the next, whatever makes you feel comfortable.

▼ *Lucy*

Lucy enjoyed this exercise the most as this is her favourite corner of her home. 'I love the comfy worn-out sofa. I spend a lot of time there reading or watching a movie. It's a very special place for me. I felt really relaxed as I was drawing, and this enabled me just to look and draw what I saw.'

It's interesting to note that many of the Squad members noted that they felt a sense of calm while drawing corners of their homes, especially if they were drawing a favourite space. Rooms can hold so much meaning and evoke such wonderful memories, and drawing them can be a wonderful way to record this.

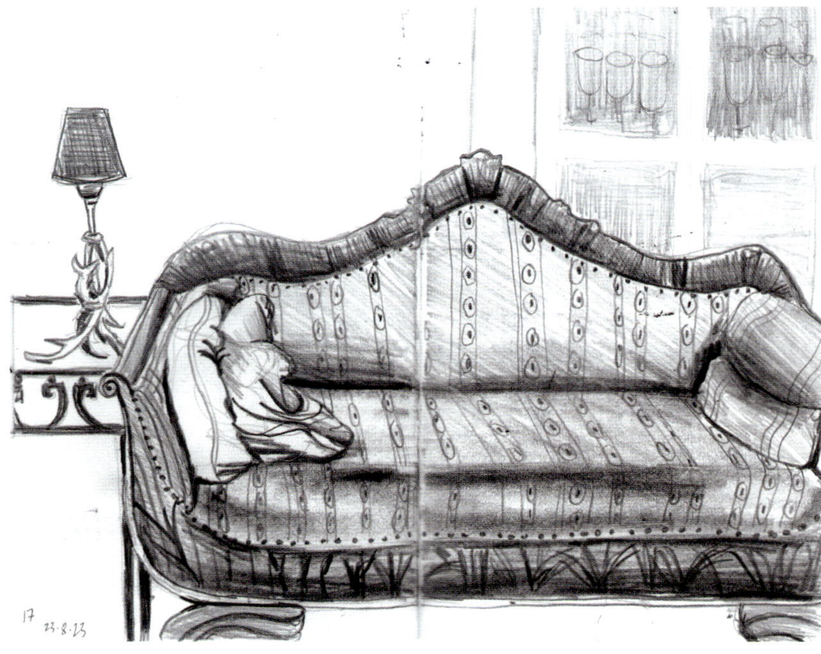

Claire volunteers in a museum and is there so regularly that she thinks of it as her second home. This corner took her interest because of the sharp angles and intriguing composition. She purposely used a ballpoint pen for this exercise as she likes the directness of it: 'Using a pen stops me fussing and forces me to draw quickly. I enjoy the crispness of the line.'

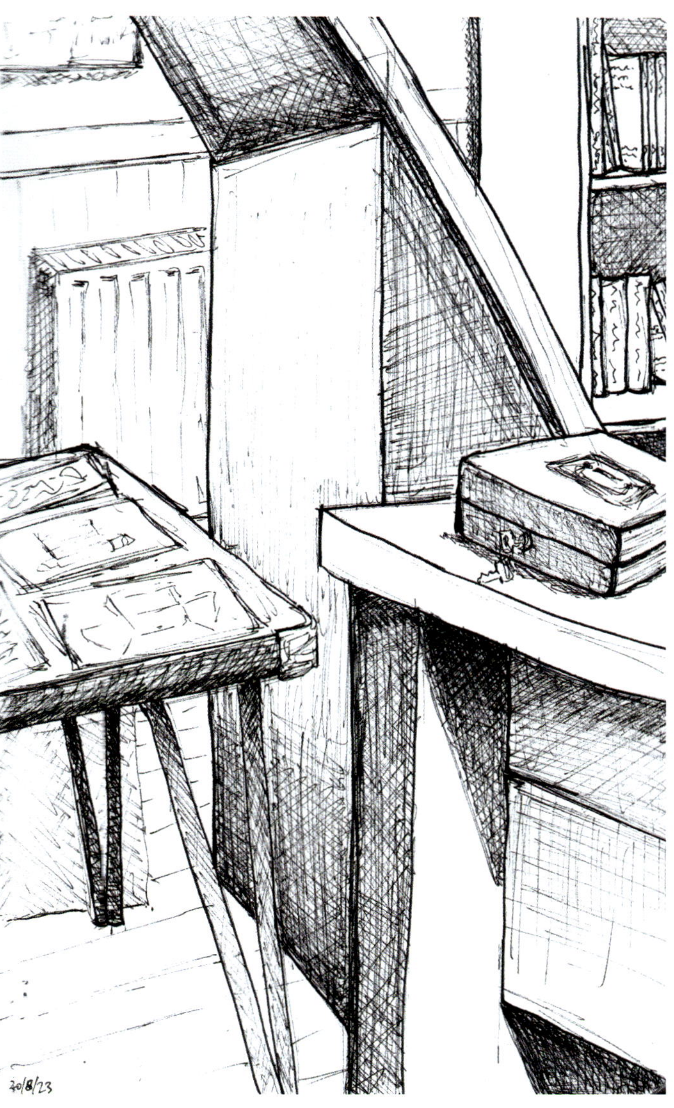

Final thoughts

The general feedback from the Sketch Squad on these exercises was how much they enjoyed them. Some felt a little daunted at the start; however, by the end of the four drawings they felt a sense of accomplishment. Diane had never really looked at her flat that closely before, but even the process of choosing which window or corner to draw enabled her to discover something she hadn't seen before. For Anne, it highlighted to her just how much stuff she has accumulated on windowsills and in corners – a perfect prompt to start to declutter. Despite their apprehension at the start of the chapter, all the Squad said that after finishing the drawings they felt focused and in a better mood –a reminder of just how beneficial drawing can be for our mental health.

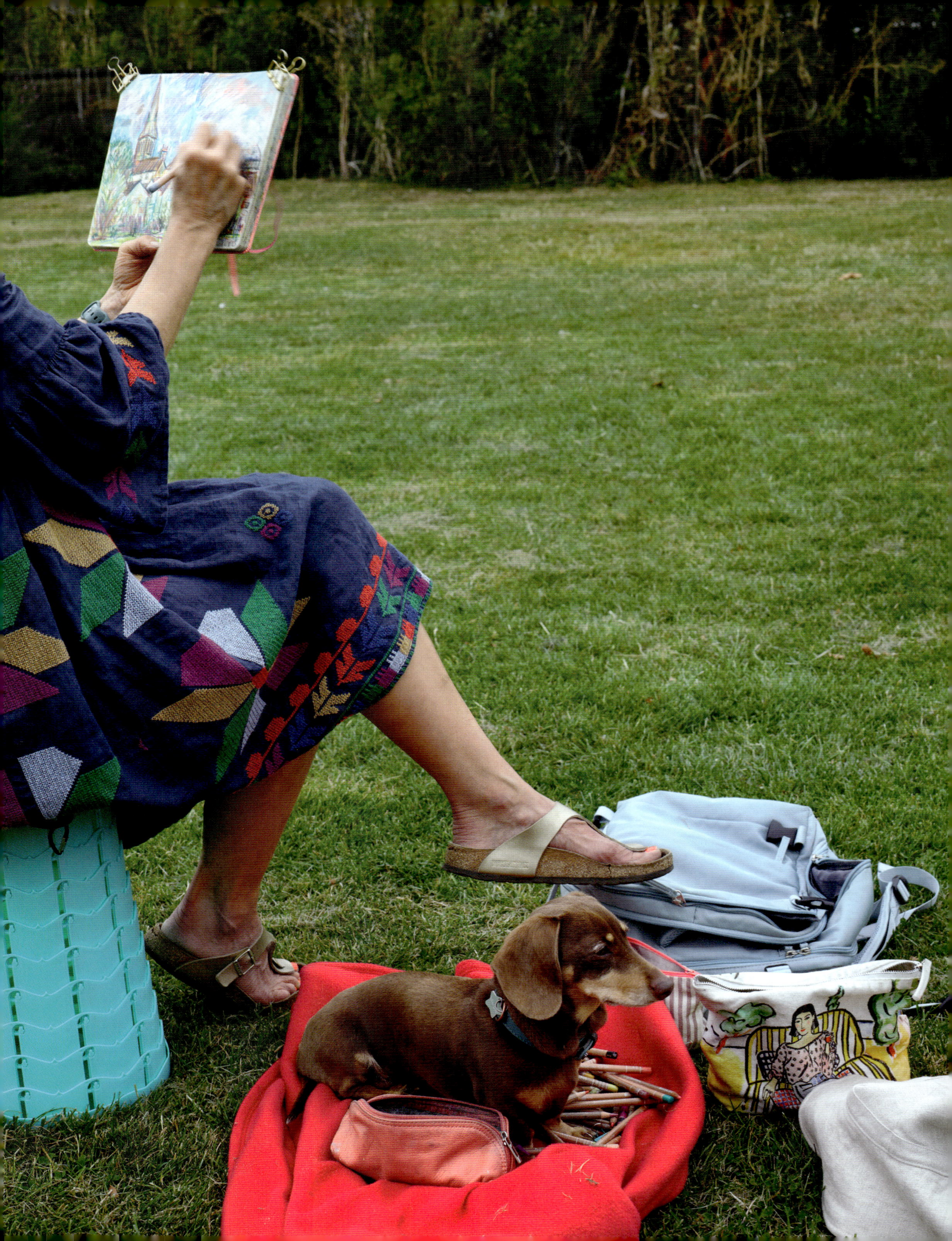

6
Outside the home

Now that you have spent time exploring the inside of your home, it's time to move outside. This chapter is all about building on the confidence you have gained from drawing in the home and challenging you to try drawing outdoors. I know many of you will be clenching your jaws and starting to feel anxious about this task – stepping outside with a sketchbook can be a daunting experience. However, we are going to start slowly and take small steps, so you can get used to getting your kit together, sitting on a stool and drawing outside.

Take a few minutes to reflect on how you are feeling about your drawings so far. I'm hoping you are feeling inspired and eager to continue. I'm also aware that your critical inner voice (see Chapter 3) might still be inhibiting you and I want to reassure you that this is normal. You have lived with this negative chatter for so long, it's not going to quieten down immediately. I can guarantee that the voice will take a back seat – it's just a matter of keeping going, regardless. The more drawing you do, the more immersed in drawing you become.

What to take

Before you start to draw, make sure you have the right kind of kit (see Chapter 2). I have a comfortable rucksack that I take all my drawing materials in. It's always packed and ready to go, which means I have no barrier to getting out there and doing it. As the book progresses, you will be taking your drawing kit outside more, so this chapter is an ideal opportunity to experiment with your portable kit without straying too far from home – you can always nip back if you have forgotten something!

What follows is a list of materials that you could take with you – some are optional, others are essential. When you are first starting out, be selective with the drawing materials you take. I would recommend just using graphite pencils so you don't feel overwhelmed. It's easier to use more materials when you are drawing at home as you can spread out; it's not so easy on location. Just take what you need and build up slowly.

What you need
- A bag to hold all your kit
- Sketchbook – it's up to you whether you choose the small or large sketchbook
- Selection of graphite pencils
- Selection of coloured pencils (optional)
- Marker pens (optional)
- Charcoal (optional) – if used, make sure you fix your drawings (I use hairspray) or put a sheet of paper in between
- Clips to hold sketchbook pages open
- Pencil sharpener
- Eraser
- Headphones
- Water and snacks
- Sun hat/warm clothes, depending on temperature
- Something to sit on (ideally a portable stool) – I use an expandable telescopic stool (see page 33)

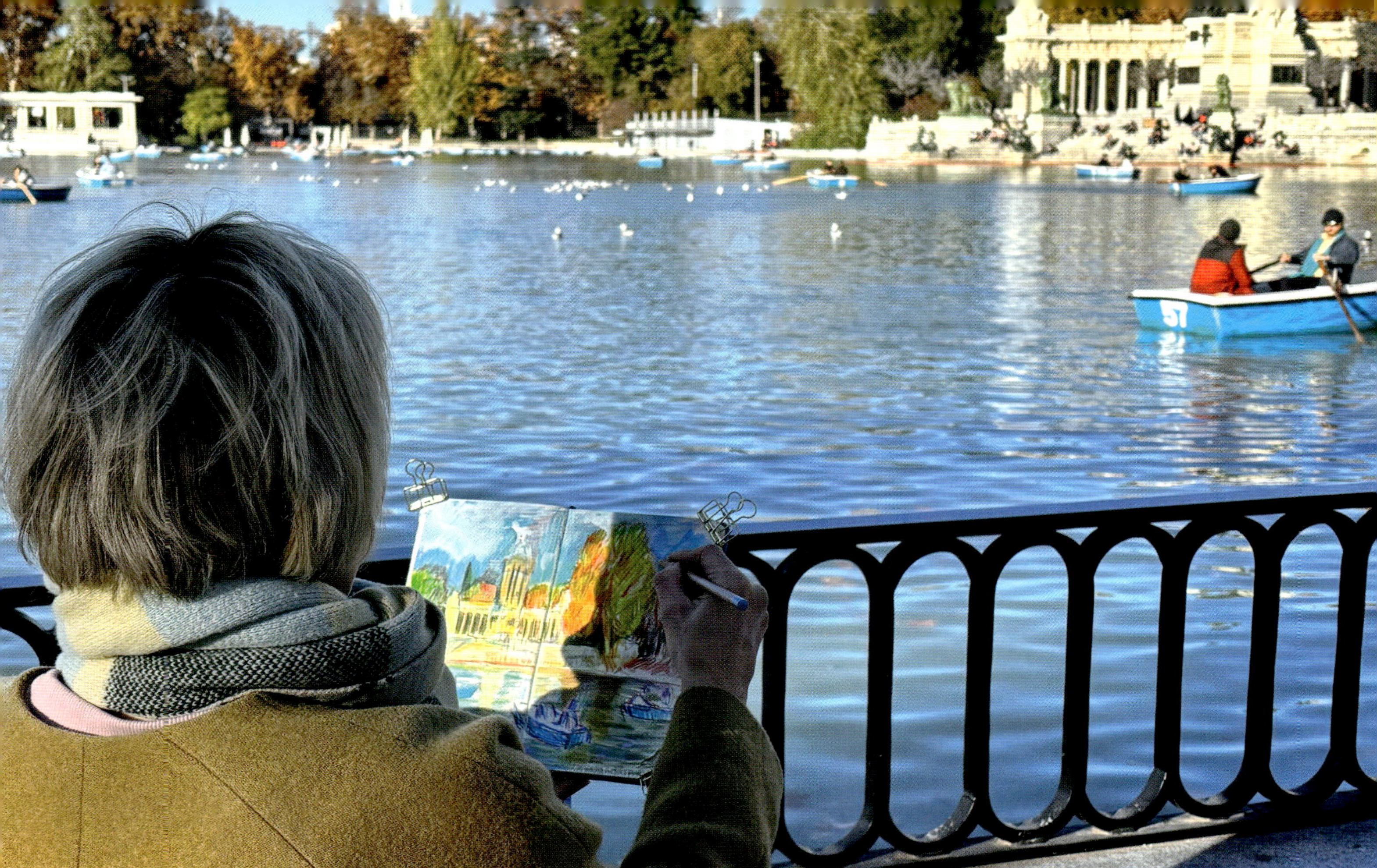

Weather

Before you draw outside, look at the weather as it will affect what and how you draw. You may think that a bright sunny day offers the best drawing conditions but that's not always the case – to be comfortable you'll need to find shade, which limits your options. A grey day can be fabulous as the light is constant and you won't overheat. I like drawing outside in the winter, all wrapped up, with my thermals on and a flask of hot tea.

The weather can also provide a time structure for your drawing. This summer I was drawing on the Norfolk marshes with a clear view of the sky. In the distance, I could see rain clouds looming so I had to quickly finish my sketch, making rapid and urgent marks, which resulted in an interesting drawing.

Timings

When I draw outside, I find there is a natural time limit on my drawings. After about an hour and a half to two hours, I can guarantee that I need the toilet and something more substantial to eat – I need a break.

When you are starting out, I recommend spending no more than an hour on your drawings. Aim to have them in a relatively finished place by the end of that time.

Be flexible

Please don't take these exercises too literally. For example, if it's not possible to draw your home for some reason, choose another building to draw. The main idea behind these exercises is that you aren't too far from home, you feel comfortable and you are away from prying eyes.

Exercise 1:

Draw your home

The first exercise is to draw your home. But before you go out and draw, take a moment to describe your home. What does it look like? How many windows does it have? What kind of windows are they? What sort of roof does it have? If you are anything like me, before I did this exercise, I could only describe my cottage in vague terms. However, after drawing it, I was able to describe it much more accurately.

Before you start drawing, I would encourage you to do some thumbnail sketches of your home and its surroundings. Thumbnail sketches are small, quick sketches that help you get a sense of placement and composition, which can be useful when embarking on these drawings. They are especially helpful in combatting the feeling of being overwhelmed.

It's important to give your home a context: make sure you place it in the space – don't just have a floating house on a white page! After you have completed your thumbnail sketches, decide which one works best and then work on a larger drawing, filling your sketchbook pages.

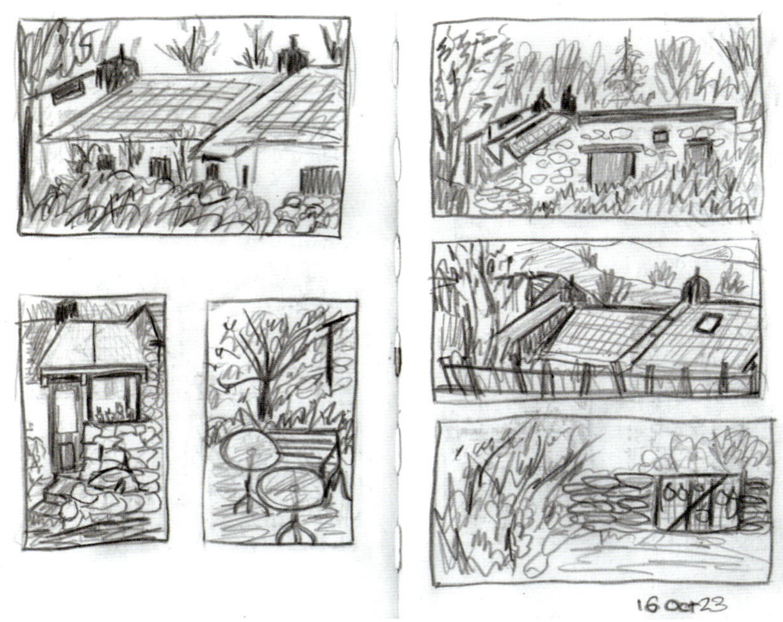

Eva's thumbnail sketches

Exercise 2:

Draw a green space

If you are lucky enough to have a garden, focus on this. If you don't have a garden, you can draw any green space near to your home. The idea here is that you are drawing the space, not just a few pots or flowers. To make it less overwhelming, again it might be helpful to do a few thumbnails – choose something on the left-hand side of your vision and something on your right and draw everything in between.

You may feel this is too much for you at this time; however, just have a go. Take it slowly and build up the drawing step by step. What marks can you use to describe the green foliage you see in front of you? How can you simplify that group of flowers? Keep chipping away at the drawing until you have run out of steam or need the loo, a cup of tea, a bar of chocolate or glass of wine.

Exercise 3:

Draw something close to your home

Think about somewhere roughly ten minutes from your home that you might like to draw. It could be a postbox with a fence behind it or a corner of the street that takes your eye – anything that springs to mind that has got your attention in the past. Once you have chosen your spot, head out to it and draw the scene.

Draw something interesting in your local area

Spend a few minutes thinking about your local area. Think about something that you have always been interested in that you would like to discover more about through drawing. It could be an old, dilapidated building that takes your fancy, or a stream that you often pass but have never taken the time to look at properly. Once you have decided what you want to draw, go on a recce and just spend some time familiarising yourself with it.

Once you have spent some time in the space, now is the time to return and draw it. Again, be selective with what you draw – choose an area to focus on, keep it simple and try to enjoy it.

My drawings: Outside the home

▶ Exercise 1: Draw your home

This is the view from my front gate, looking at my cottage and studio. I wanted to include both my cottage and my studio as they are both technically my 'home' – I spend equal time in both. I have two holly trees in my garden, and it was important for me to feature at least one of them as they are such an important feature in my environment. I planned the composition carefully with the help of thumbnail sketches so that the cottage, studio and holly tree all had equal weight. This drawing took me one hour.

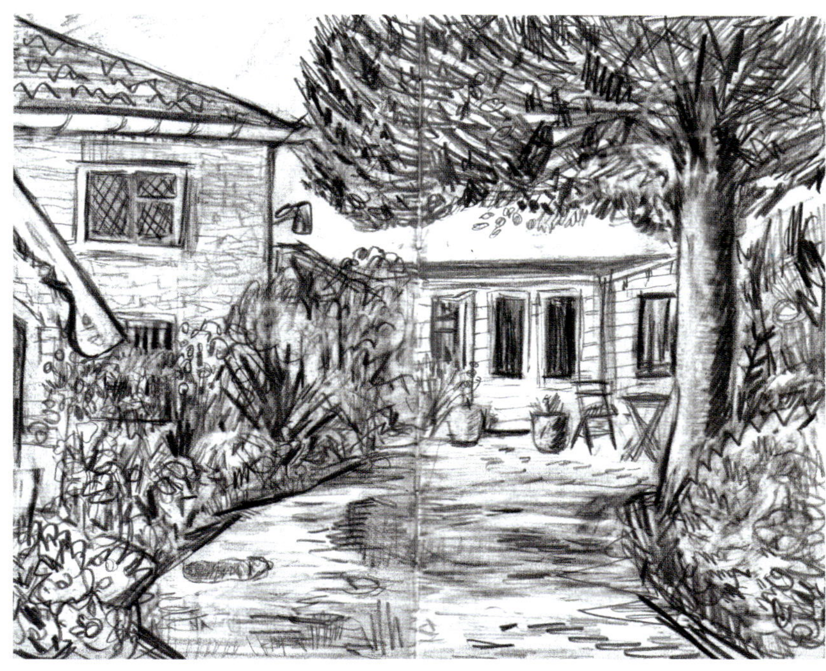

▶ Exercise 2: Draw a green space

This is a drawing of part of my garden and pond. I drew it in early spring when the garden was just beginning to come alive. I wanted to do this drawing in coloured pencils to capture the lovely greens that are so prominent in English gardens in early April. It took me an hour and a half. You can see how I build up this drawing in colour at the end of this chapter (see pages 78–9).

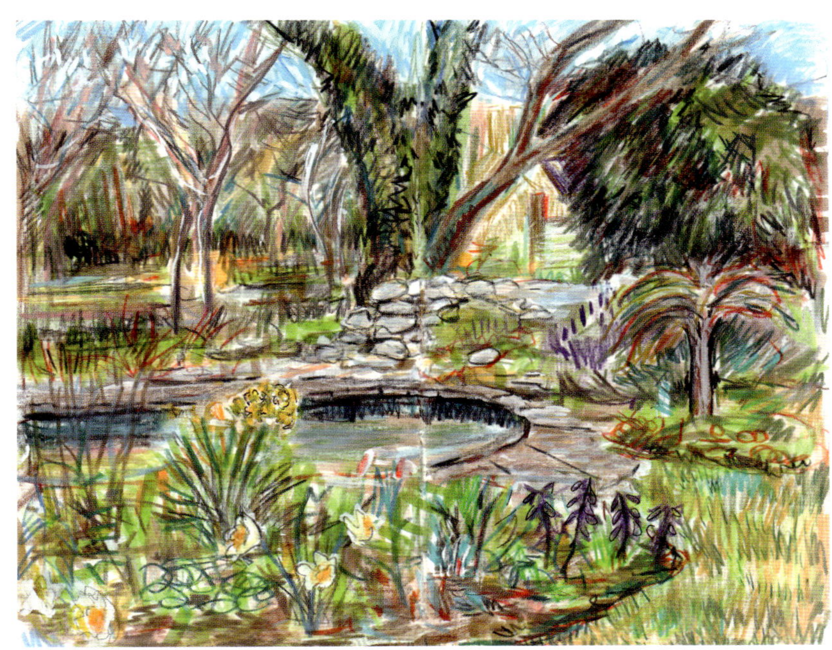

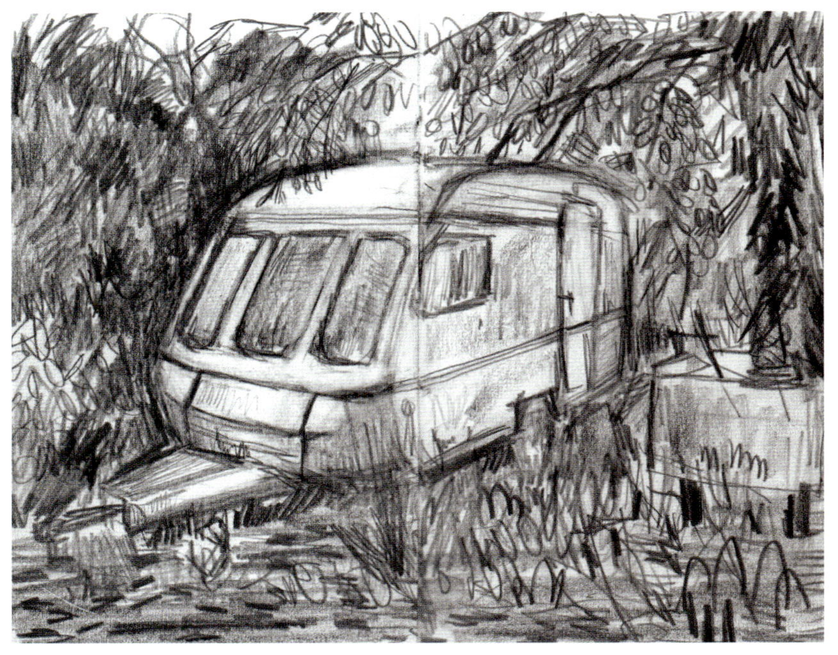

◀ Exercise 3: Draw something close to your home

I run past this old caravan every morning. It's just behind my cottage, before I reach the woods. It was my neighbours' old caravan and now it's just parked in their yard. There's something poetic to me about it, a space that used to provide adventure and fun now sitting sadly, unused. I love drawing caravans too, so this was the obvious choice for me. It took me around one hour.

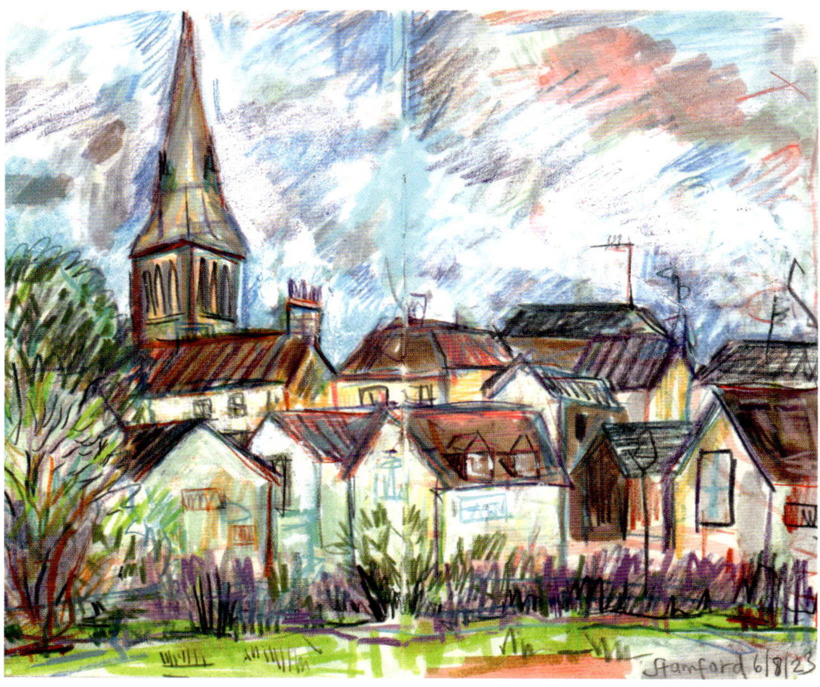

◀ Exercise 4: Draw something interesting in your local area

I live near Stamford in Lincolnshire. It's a small town of many churches – five in total – a picturesque place with wonderful cream stone buildings. There's a meadow in the heart of the town that has a great view of the overlapping buildings and the churches. I've always been meaning to draw in the meadow, and this exercise was the perfect prompt. It made me realise, however, that I don't often think to draw in my local area – I tend to draw while I'm away. This drawing has changed the way I think about where I live; I'm now always looking for interesting places to sit and sketch. It's true what they say – there's beauty on your doorstep.

Sketch Squad: Outside the home

Now we have looked at my sketches, let's see how the Sketch Squad got on.

Exercise 1: Draw your home

▶ *Kathi*

Kathi lives in Vienna; however, she chose to draw her great-grandmother's home in South Austria. Her great-grandmother lived there until her death in 1993, and no one has lived there permanently since.

Kathi wanted the drawing to create a sense of calm and peacefulness to reflect her feelings. She said after completing the drawing, she felt wistful and nostalgic – the process of sitting down to draw made her remember all the happy times she had spent there as a child. She purposely drew slowly and carefully.

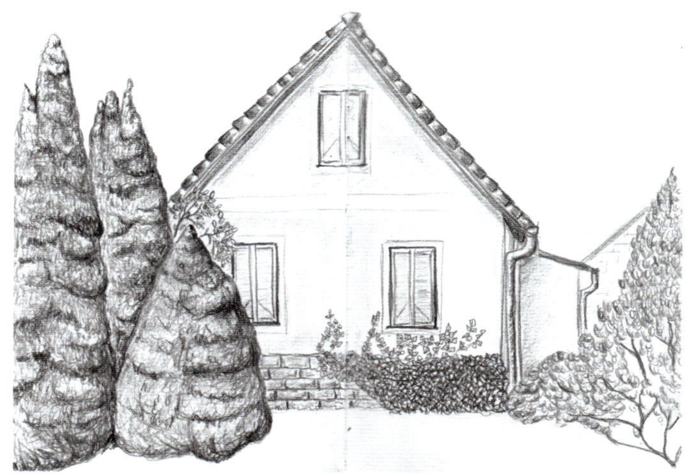

▶ *Safa*

This is Safa's drawing of her home. She sat outside on a stool to do the drawing, and her curious neighbour came out and asked what she was doing. He was encouraging and complimentary about her drawing, which motivated her to keep on going and in turn made her feel less self-conscious. This drawing made Safa think about her dad, who helped her buy her house and who is sadly no longer alive; it brought back lots of memories.

Safa is the only one in her street who has kept the original heart-stained windows– something she hadn't noticed until she did this drawing. Again, it's often only when we take the time to sit and draw something like our home that we see things we never noticed before.

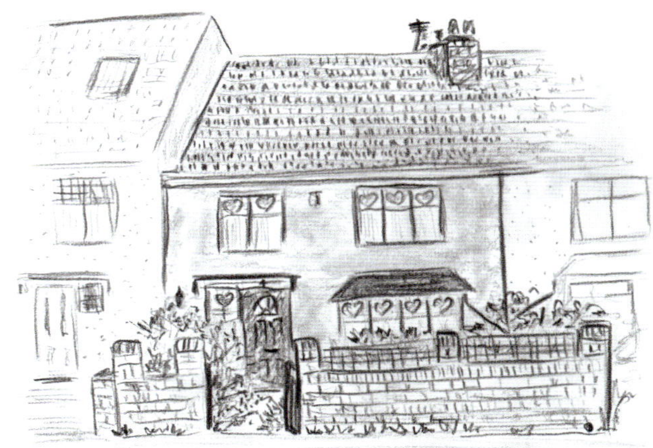

▶ *Eva*

This is Eva's home in Wales. It was the start of autumn when she drew this – cold, bright and sunny. She had just returned from a busy overseas work trip and found the drawing helped her feel grounded and back at home. She used watercolours and coloured pencils for the drawing. Even though she wasn't particularly happy with it in the end, the memories of the drawing experience made it worthwhile.

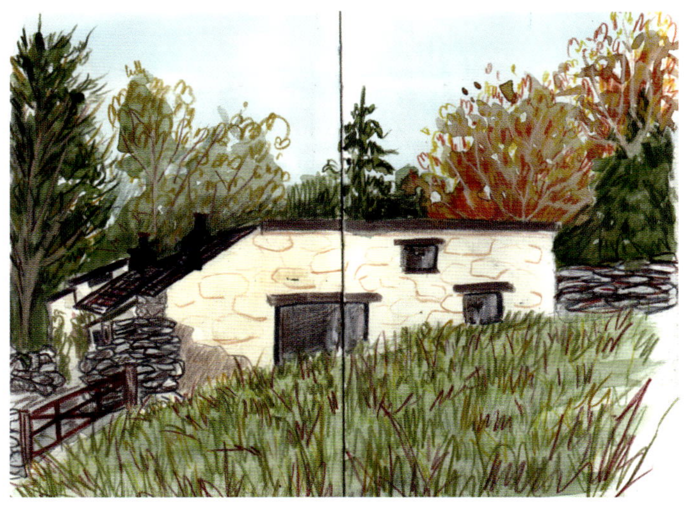

Exercise 2: Draw a green space

▶ *Paula*

This is Paula's backyard. She found the space a bit intimidating at first, but doing a series of thumbnail sketches helped her narrow down and frame the area she wanted to draw. She lightly sketched the areas in first, then used stronger marks as she became more confident with the composition.

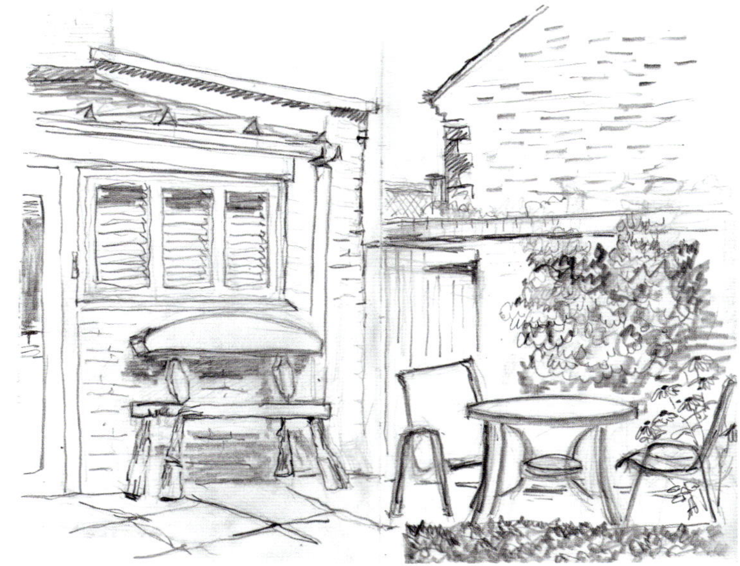

▼ *Niki*

Niki lives in a very remote part of Scotland where the landscape is huge. She admits to finding the sheer scale of it very intimidating: 'Wherever I look, the huge volume of similar data is hard to process, and I lose my place whenever I look down to make a mark on the paper.'

She was determined to complete the drawing and reminded herself: 'It's just a piece of paper, what's the worst that can happen?' After finishing the sketch, Niki was still unhappy with it – she felt it was stiff and overworked. This meant that she quickly got on with another drawing, which enabled her to put this one in the 'rear-view mirror'.

I think Niki's honesty here is refreshing. We aren't always going to be pleased with what we draw, but if we think hard enough there will be something that we have learnt during the process. I always say: any time spent in your sketchbook is time well spent.

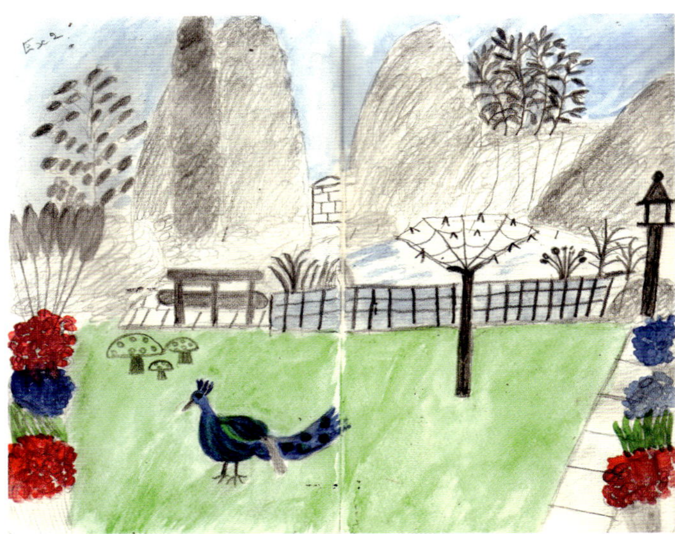

▲ *Jane*

Jane has a resident peacock called 'Percy' who spends a lot of his time in the garden. 'Percy is such an integral part of the garden that I had to include him, and the washing line too as I spend so much time hanging out clothes!'

Jane admits that she had never thought about drawing her own back garden and was surprised by how much she enjoyed it and how many things she hadn't noticed before. She started off with just pencil and then added watercolour at the end.

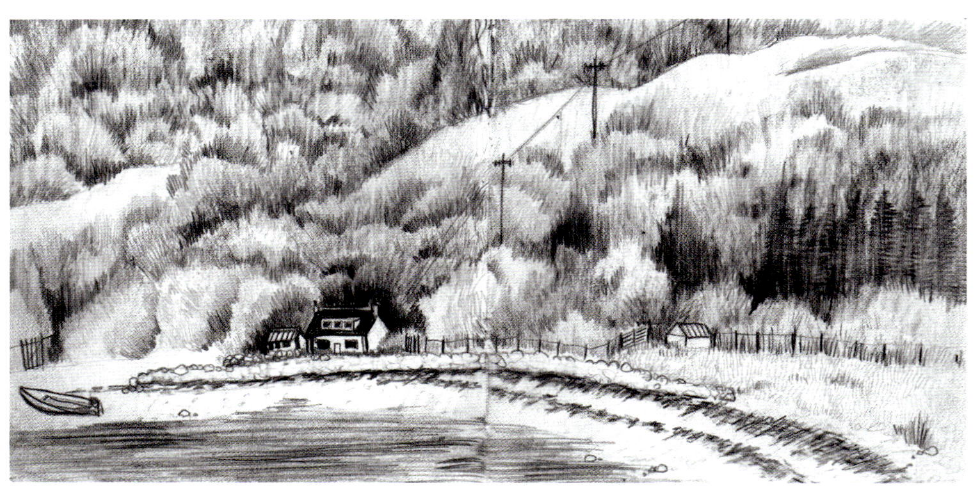

Exercise 3: Draw something close to your home

▶ *Diane*

When Diane lived in London, she used her bike as her main means of transport. She took her sketchpad out with her with the intention of drawing at the local park. As she was cycling down the canal, she realised what an exciting viewpoint she had from her bike, so she stopped and did this twenty-minute pencil sketch. This is a great reminder of how beneficial it is to have our sketchbooks with us whenever we are out and about, as you never know when inspiration might take hold.

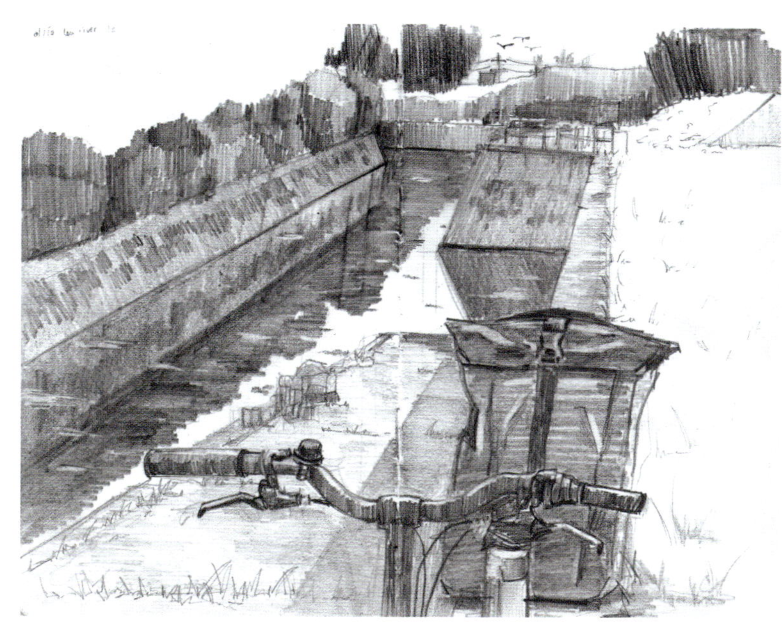

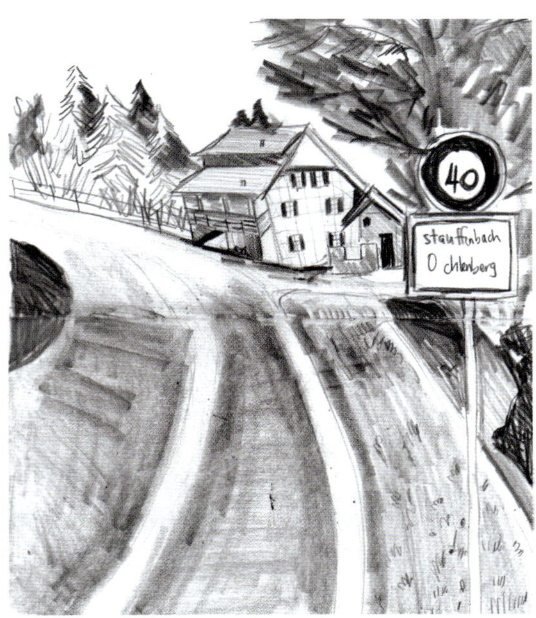

◀ *Phyllis*

Phyllis chose to draw the lending library as it's something she sees every day and an important feature in her neighbourhood. She regularly donates books and, whenever she passes, she looks to see what's in there. 'It's a bit of an addiction as I'm always taking home books, and I'm running out of space.'

She spent just over an hour doing this drawing, and several of her neighbours stopped to see what she was doing. Phyllis is confident with sharing her work, so she enjoyed the interaction. This is something we will discuss at length later in the book (see page 115), but at this stage, if you find yourself feeling awkward if you are approached by an eager passer-by then rest assured that this is perfectly natural. Along with my tips and support, I promise you it will get easier.

▶ *Lucy*

This street in Lucy's local area is one that she always finds intriguing. She had wanted to draw it in the past but never made the time. She admitted she felt nervous about drawing outside – her main concern was people noticing her drawing and her feeling exposed. However, she committed to doing the drawing and found that she really enjoyed pushing herself out of her comfort zone. She also set herself a strict time limit of an hour, which helped her focus and complete the task.

Exercise 4: Draw something interesting in your local area

▼ *Claire*

This is Claire's drawing of a group of fishermen's houses known as 'The Yardie' in an old part of her town. The houses all have their own unique character, and she wanted to highlight this in her sketch. She knew if she used pencil she would get too caught up in the detail, so she chose to use a fineliner and her Ecoline marker pens.

It was a cold day, so she was unable to spend too much time on the drawing, which on reflection she feels is a good thing. 'Having to complete it so quickly made me just get down the basic shapes, and I'm really happy with the result.' This is a perfect example of how weather can force us to make decisions. If Claire had been drawing from a photograph, she most probably would have added more detail and lost the essence of the scene.

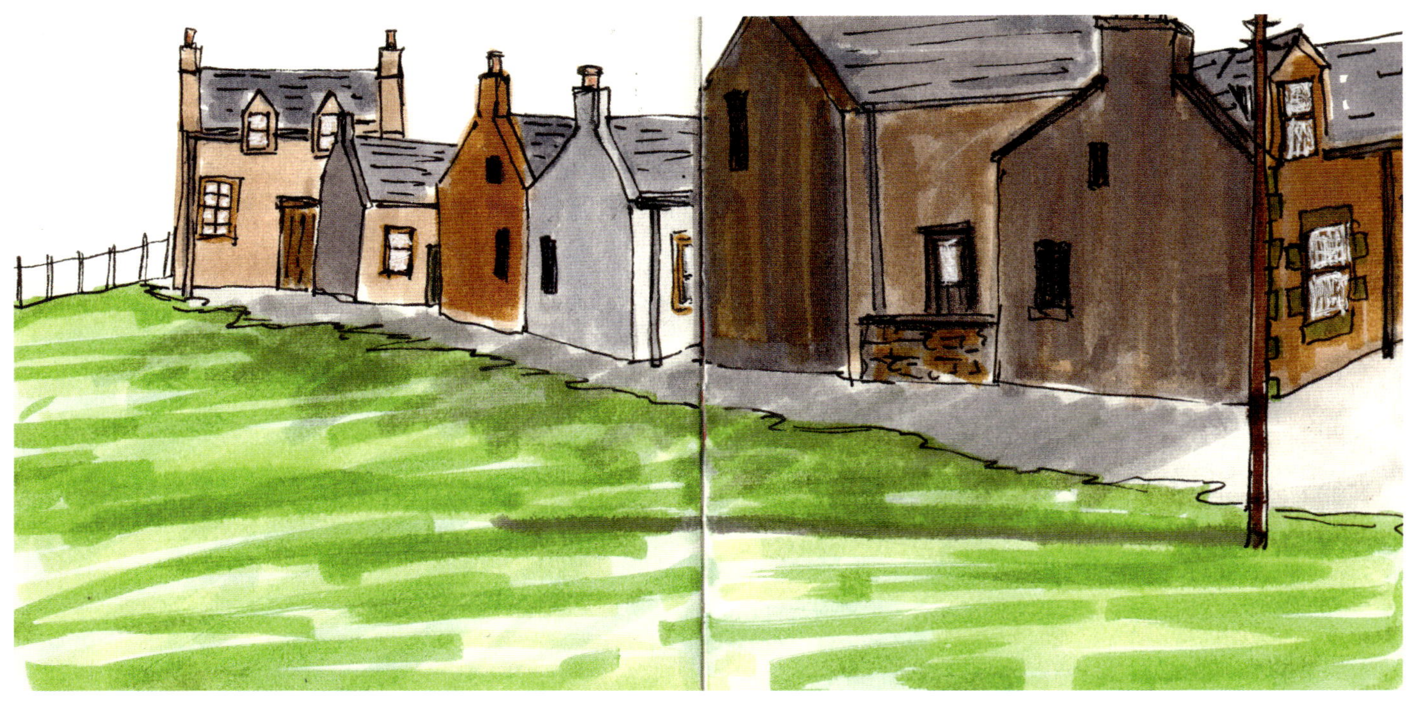

◀ *Anne*

Anne dithered over what to draw for ages. She couldn't choose between an expansive city skyline of Sheffield, her city, or a slice of history that goes unnoticed by the daily commuters. She decided on the latter as she felt more comfortable with the scale of it. It's a tollbar cottage dating from 1830, which provides its own natural boundary.

She noted that before drawing, she felt her usual sense of anxiety about how she would handle the scale, colours and proportion, especially as it also meant that she would be sitting in a corner of a busy local park. However, as is often the case with Anne, she eventually enjoyed this drawing. She did get a few people approach her – friends and acquaintances – and she felt comfortable sharing what she was working on. On reflection, she feels there are things she would do differently with the drawing if she did it again, but overall she was satisfied with the result.

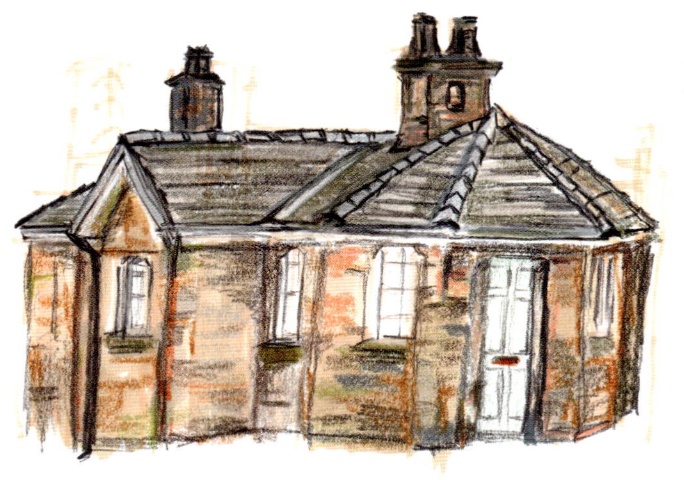

Hannah chose to draw this house directly opposite her home as it's a view she looks at daily and one she is fascinated by. 'It's a family with five children so it's always buzzing with life, and I love the red brick, tiled roof and white window frames.' She wanted to challenge herself to draw lots of patterns and textures in a short time. She described the drawing as 'fast and furious, but lots of fun'.

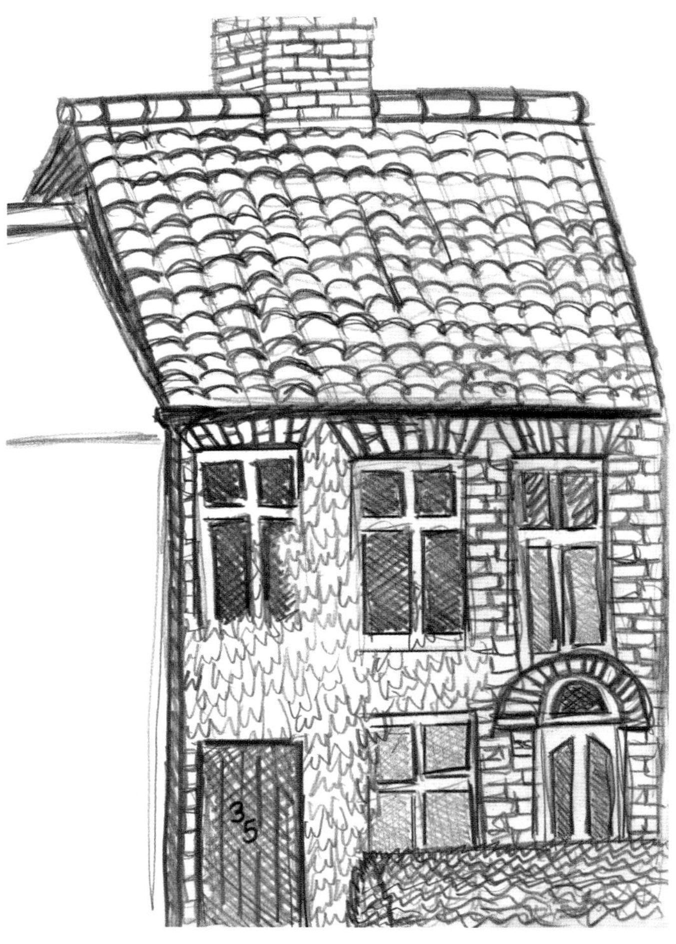

Final thoughts

I hope you have enjoyed this chapter, and that it has enabled you to stretch yourself and your drawing practice. Drawing outside for the first time is never easy; there's your materials to think about, what you are drawing and the weather. However, with determination and enthusiasm, it does get easier – and as we have seen with the Sketch Squad – it can be enjoyable, even if you were full of nerves at the start.

How I create my coloured pencil drawings

To help you understand how I create my coloured pencil drawings, I documented the process of my drawing in stages while I was working on Exercise 2: Draw a green space (see page 71).

This is just to give you an idea of how I draw and use colour; it's not meant as a guide on how you should draw as you know by now that this isn't the purpose of the book. It's purely meant as a way for me to share my process.

I drew this on the first sunny day of spring. The weather was changeable hence the light shifts in the photographs. I used my larger sketchbook for this drawing.

1. Sketch the structure using marker pens

First, I select the scene in my garden that I want to draw, including the large tree as an anchor point in the composition. I then loosely sketch the main elements and establish the basics of the composition using Royal Talens Ecoline marker pens.

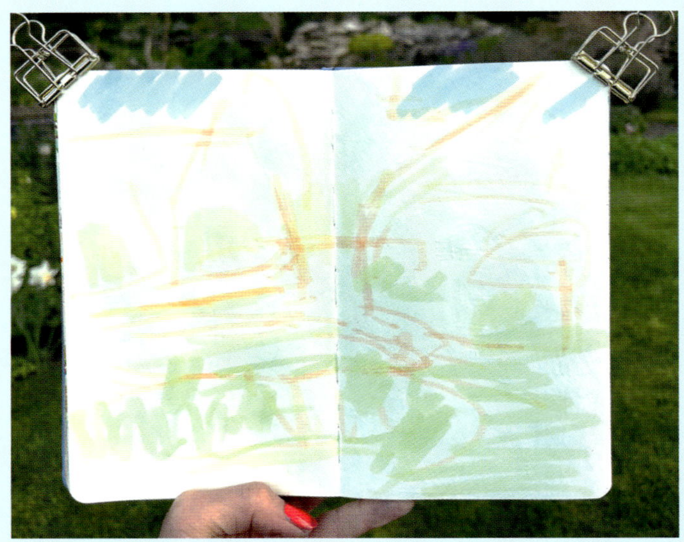

2. Build up the drawing using coloured pencils

Next, I start to build up the drawing using my Caran d'Ache Luminance coloured pencils. I sketch in the details, keeping my marks free flowing and organic.

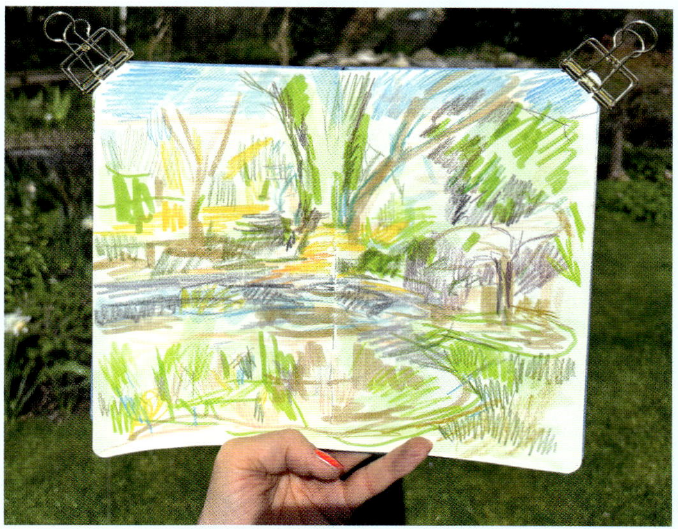

3. Add tonal values using darker colours

Moving quickly across the page, I start to use darker pencils to create the different tones in the drawing. I tend to use whatever dark colour comes to hand. I don't rely on black – I will use dark purple, dark red, dark green, for example.

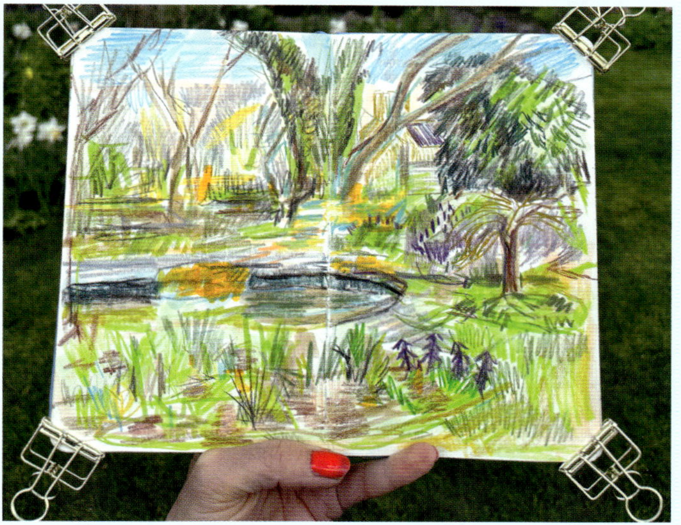

4. Add white gouache

It's difficult to use an eraser to successfully rub out the coloured pencil marks, so I often use white gouache to whiten areas that I want to rework. It's important to ensure that your sketchbook paper is tough enough to withstand water and paint.

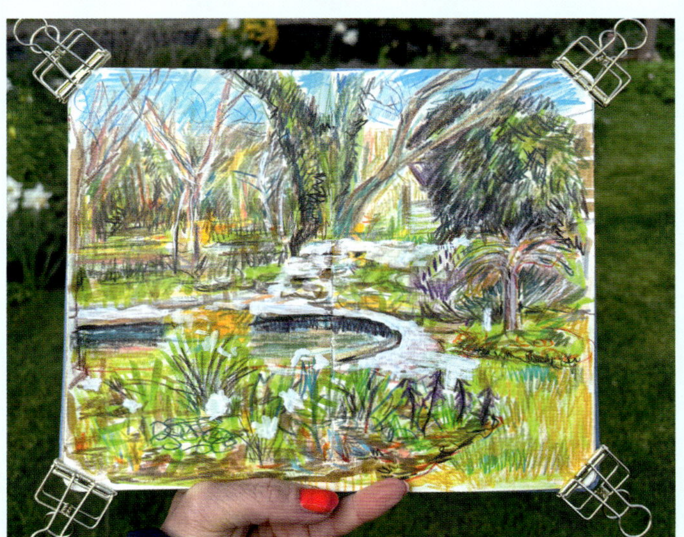

5. Final drawing with addition of wax crayons

Once the white gouache has dried, I then draw over the top of it to create more layers. To finish the drawing, I use Caran d'Ache Neocolor® II crayons in small areas to add pops of colour.

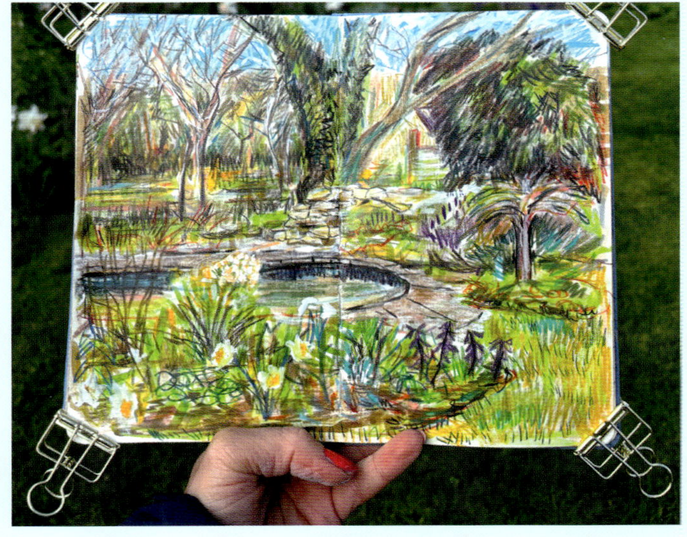

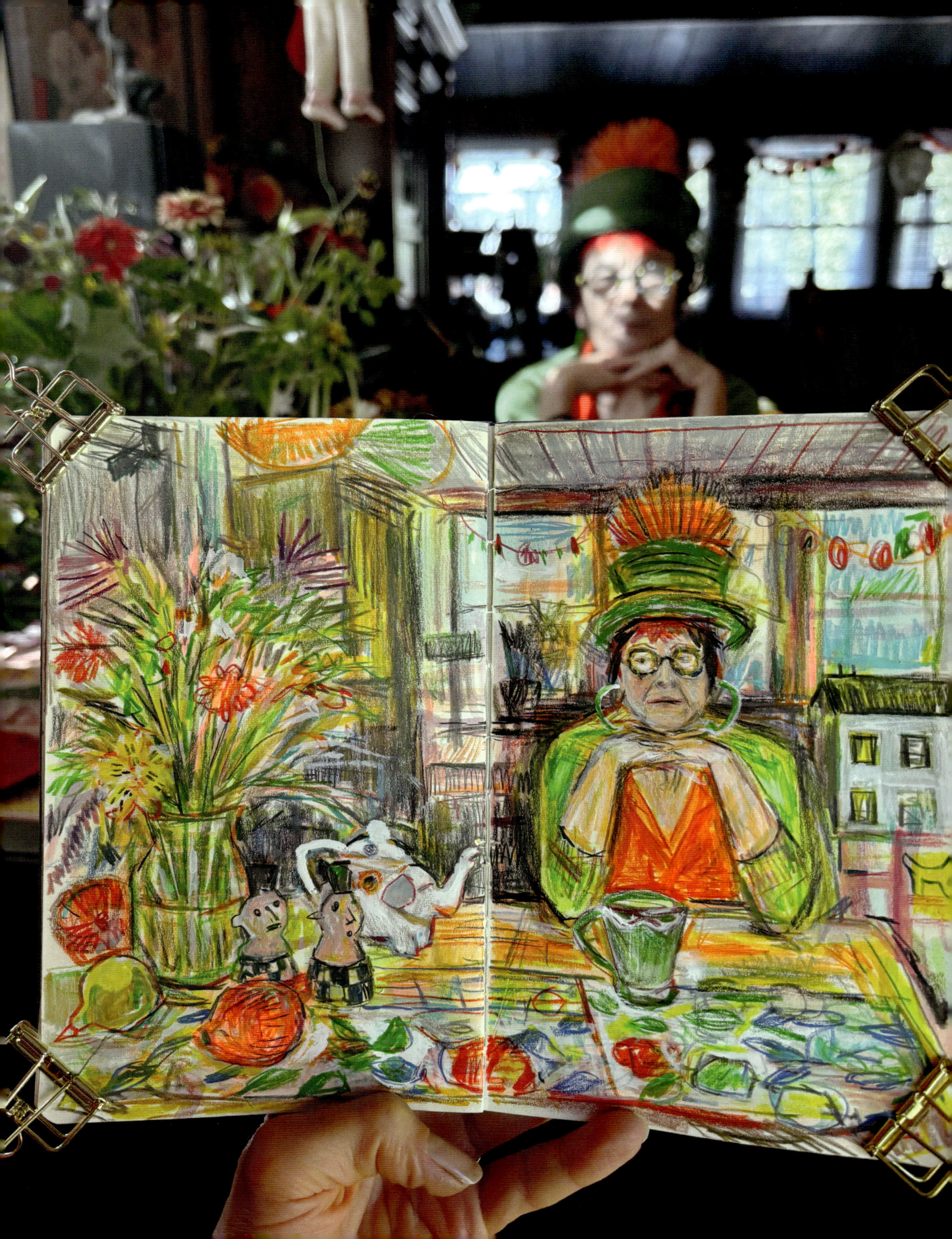

7
Drawing portraits

By now, you have completed a series of drawings both inside and outside of the home that have challenged, enabled and encouraged you to build a regular sketchbook practice. Your sketchbook is filling up. Before we start this series of portrait exercises, take a moment to reflect on the work you have done and congratulate yourself on your commitment to building up your new skills.

If you haven't already done so, show your drawings to someone you trust. This is an important step in building confidence and solidifying the idea of you as a creative person, not only to them but also to yourself. Many of us feel awkward about sharing our work due to a fear of being judged, of being told it's not good enough. But the more you do it, the easier it will become. Hopefully, they will be encouraging and positive, however, if they say something critical, try and let it wash over you. Remember why you are doing this and how it makes you feel. Tune into how much you have enjoyed the drawings so far, and how much you have got from them. This is way more important than if someone thinks you haven't got the perspective of the house quite right.

In this chapter, you will be drawing self-portraits and portraits of others. A portrait is a representation of a person, often focused on the face, head and shoulders but can include the whole body. I can picture some of your faces filling with horror as you read this – if there is one thing that people will insist they can't do, it's drawing faces or the figure. However, most people would like to do this, so together – without any pressure and in the spirit of fun and adventure – we are going to give it a go.

A human being is, of course, a complicated object. You are very familiar with your appearance, having seen it in the mirror for many years. You will know the way your hair falls, the way it won't go in a certain direction. You will think you know how your nose looks, and what your eyes look like. You will have first-hand knowledge of the structure of your face. It's for this reason we're starting here, with you.

Set up

For the first three exercises, choose a place where you won't be disturbed or be disturbing others. You want to avoid being pressurised by anything.

Place your mirror so you can see yourself with ease. The height, the distance and the angle of where you place the mirror will all influence the drawing you create. Experiment with these three factors and see what suits you.

Consider the lighting. Ideally, you want a constant source of light, especially if you want to return to the drawing. You might want to set up a lamp that lights one side of your face, or you might choose a more direct source of light.

Materials

For all these exercises I would suggest you use your larger sketchbook. If you are new to drawing people, keep the materials simple – just stick to pencil and you won't feel even more overwhelmed. You may want to use masking tape in Exercises 4 and 5.

Self-portrait from memory

(30 minutes maximum)

For the first exercise, you are going to draw a self-portrait from memory. Use some of the warm-up exercises (see Chapter 4) to get you started.

We all think we know what we look like, but it is surprising how little we really know when we commit pencil to paper. What tends to happen is that we overemphasise certain areas, so if we think we have a big nose we will draw it bigger than it really is. Or we will draw the eyes higher up the head than they are. Just have a go and I'm sure the result will cause a few giggles.

Exercise 2:

Self-portrait using a mirror (30 minutes maximum)

For this exercise, you will be using your mirror. Treat this drawing as formally as you can; it's about gathering information. Be as honest as possible – observe your face as just a face, not your face – and stay coolly objective. If it helps, imagine you are meeting someone for the first time and that there are no cameras or photos, so you must send them a drawing of yourself in order for them to recognise you. Here are some suggestions to get you started.

Roughly draw in the main shape of your head, making sure you include all of it. You could choose to include the mirror in your drawing – this kind of device can be a great aid for sorting the relative positions of features. For instance, does your left ear come halfway down the edge of the mirror?

Feel your head and face. Think about your skull, which is a firm base for your head, and feel how it swells out from the nape of your neck. Study the way your face is divided into surfaces or planes, sloping in different directions, running gradually or sharply from one another. Thinking about how your face and neck are constructed will help you better understand what you are looking at. If it helps, think of your face like a landscape with all its crevices, peaks and valleys.

Continue to build up your drawing. Don't be afraid to alter it, rub it out and edit it. Use whatever methods you wish to put across your thoughts. If drawing shadows seems like a good way of explaining how the head is solid and how the nose protrudes then use shadows and tones. If you are intrigued by the edges of elements of your face, use a fineliner pen.

Consider how to express the way the skin on the lips is different from the flesh on your cheeks in drawing terms. How can you use marks to convey this? How can you describe the quality of your hair – is it smooth or coarse? Use appropriate lines to help convey this.

You might want to work on this drawing in stages. If you do, make sure you take note of how you are sitting, what the light is like and what angle and position the mirror is in.

Exercise 3:

Self-portrait with character (1 hour minimum)

The first step in this exercise is to ask someone close to you to describe you and your character. Make a note of what they say as you are going to use it in this self-portrait.

Think about the words they have used to describe you and consider how you can create the sense of these characteristics through the elements you have to hand. For example, how are you sitting? How could you position yourself that might convey something about your character? Let's say someone describes you as a little cold, a bit cut off – perhaps you could sit behind something.

Consider what you are wearing. What do your clothes reveal about your personality?

Think about the background. What could you include in the background that might give us insights into your character? Perhaps you are described as tidy and organised – you will then want your background to highlight this.

This is a drawing done from observation, so please don't include anything from memory or imagination. If you want to include an object to reflect your character, ensure it is drawn from life.

Portrait of someone close to you (1 hour minimum)

Now you have spent time drawing yourself, you are going to draw someone else. Ideally, this will be someone close to you, whose features you know well. Ask them nicely to sit for you, offer to take them out for coffee and cake – or whatever you can bribe them with.

Set up your space beforehand with everything prepared. You want to make sure that, when your sitter arrives, you have all your materials to hand. This gives them the sense that you are taking this seriously and you require them to do so too. It's inevitable that this will feel a bit awkward, for you and for them, but if you are calm, organised and clear with your instructions, it should go smoothly.

Make sure you have them sitting opposite you and ensure that you are both sitting comfortably. You may choose to concentrate just on their face, you might want to include their shoulders and arms, or you could draw their whole body in the chair. The choice is yours.

It's important that the sitter remains as still as possible, so make sure you give them regular breaks. Before they take a break, it's important that you note carefully where they are sitting. You might want to use masking tape to mark where their feet are on the floor as this will affect how they position their body on the chair. You could also take a photograph for reference.

Be as objective as you can with your drawing. Try not to flatter the sitter. You are not here to do a pretty drawing – draw what you see, not what you think the sitter wants you to see. They will be keen to see the drawing and their feedback might be helpful; it might not be. If it is the latter, let this wash over you and continue on.

Exercise 5:

Drawing a person or people in context (1 hour minimum)

For the final exercise, I would like you to draw a person or a couple of people together in a relaxed environment. Ideally this will be members of your family or friends – people you know well and feel comfortable with. You could choose to draw someone watching TV, working at the computer or sleeping, or draw a couple of people relaxing on the sofa or eating at a table. The idea here is that you are capturing a person in a moment in time in a specific context, so the background is very important. Try and do a few of these drawings as this will be good practice for the next chapter.

My drawings: Portraits

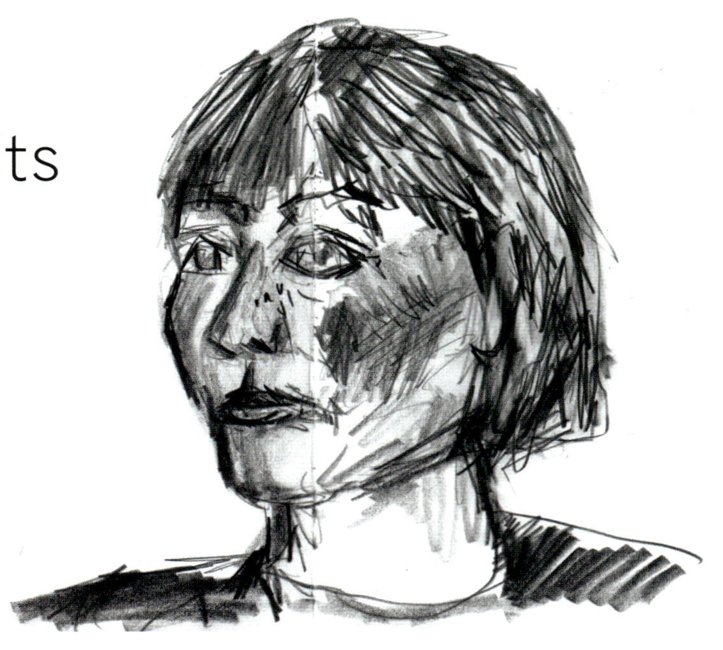

▶ Exercise 1: Self-portrait from memory

As someone who looks in the mirror a lot, I thought
I would have a better memory of what I looked like.
However, I was surprised when I started drawing that
I only had a rather generalised recollection of what
my features look like and that drawing my face from
memory was much more difficult than I anticipated.
This drawing took around fifteen minutes, as I thought
that any longer would mean I was just moving my
pencil around the page without purpose.

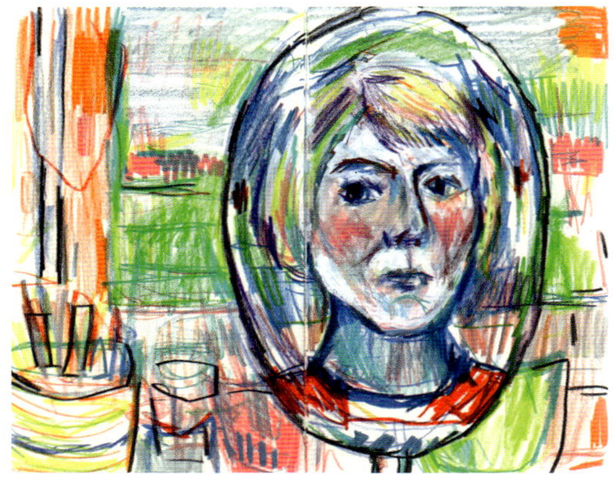

▲ Exercise 2: Self-portrait using a mirror

I chose to include the mirror in my self-
portrait as I thought it would help me frame
my face better. I loosely sketched in the
main areas with marker pen then continued
drawing with coloured pencils. I also used
white gouache to whiten out areas so I could
then go over them again (see pages 78–9).

▼ Exercise 3: Self-portrait with character

When I asked a close friend to describe me, she said I was warm,
energetic, creative, comforting and focused. I chose to draw myself in
my studio, with my artwork surrounding me, sitting at my desk with
Marple, my dog, on my lap.

I kept my mark making quick and loose to convey the feeling of
energy and busyness. I chose a warm colour palette to emphasise
the cosiness of the studio and highlight some of my comforting
character. I'm looking directly at the viewer with quite a serious face,
which I hope conveys my focus and determined spirit.

I really enjoyed this drawing, it was helpful to get feedback
from another person, as often they are more generous with their
descriptions of us than we are about ourselves.

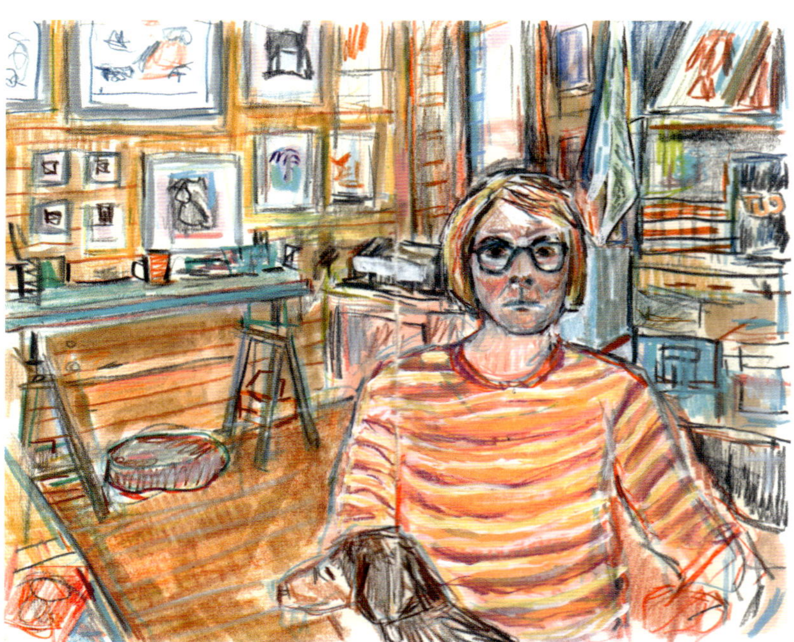

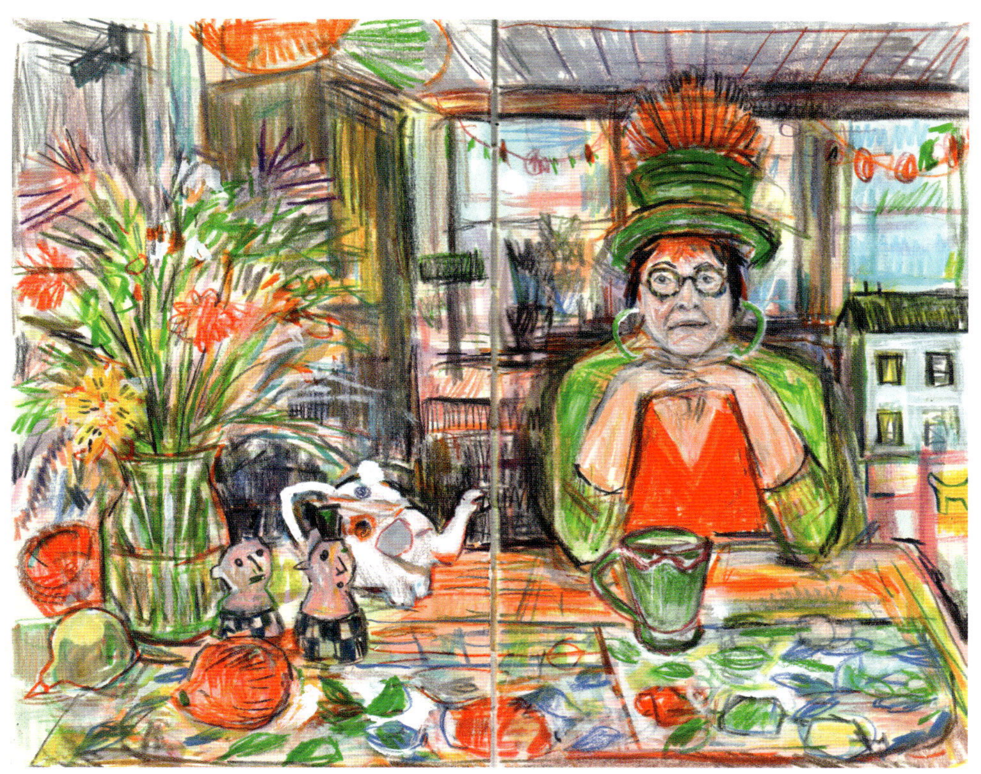

This is a drawing of Phyllis from the Squad. Last year, I visited her at her home in Santa Rosa, California. Her joyful, colourful, eclectic home is such a reflection of her personality that my portrait of her had to include her surroundings. I thought carefully about where I wanted her to sit and what position I wanted her to be in. This drawing took around two hours with breaks.

► Exercise 5: Drawing a person or people in context

This is a drawing of Jane, my mum. We decided to do the last exercise of this chapter together – me drawing her, while she drew me. You can see her drawing of me later in this chapter (see page 94).

It was a couple of weeks before Christmas and we were staying for a few days in a cottage in Derbyshire. Even though we have drawn together in the past, this was the first time we had drawn one another. It was a challenging task, as we both kept looking up and down at different times, but it was fun to do and it's a special memory for both of us.

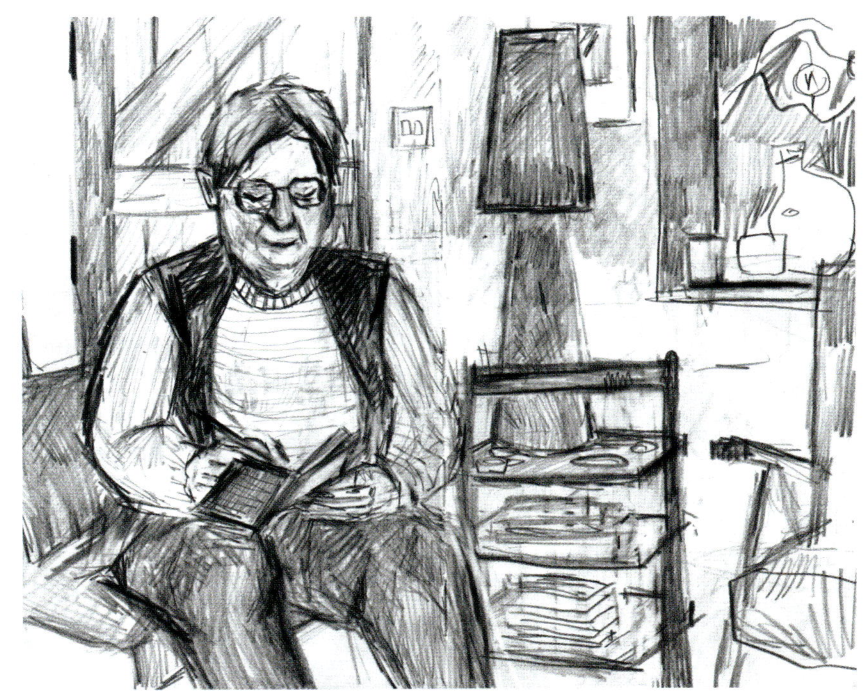

Sketch Squad: Portraits

Now we have looked at my interpretations of the drawing exercises, let's see how the Sketch Squad got on.

Exercise 1: Self-portrait from memory

This isn't an easy exercise to do, and indeed, many of the Sketch Squad found it challenging for a number of reasons. Some found it difficult as they simply aren't used to drawing faces; others found it tough as, in preparation for the exercise, they studied their face in the mirror for longer than normal and found it an uncomfortable experience. It is important to study our faces first, though, as it makes us aware of what to look out for when we draw from our reflection in the mirror.

Treat this exercise light-heartedly. Even though it was a difficult exercise for some of the Squad, they all had a good giggle at the result!

▼ *Eva*

Eva had a lot of resistance to doing this exercise as she believed it would be a 'bad drawing'. The only way she could get herself to do it was to have a ten-minute time limit to prevent her overthinking it. She accepted that she most probably wouldn't like the drawing but told herself that it didn't matter as it was all practice and to just accept it for what it is. An important part of this exercise is to not worry about the outcome. Approach it with curiosity and ask yourself, 'Do I know what I really look like?'

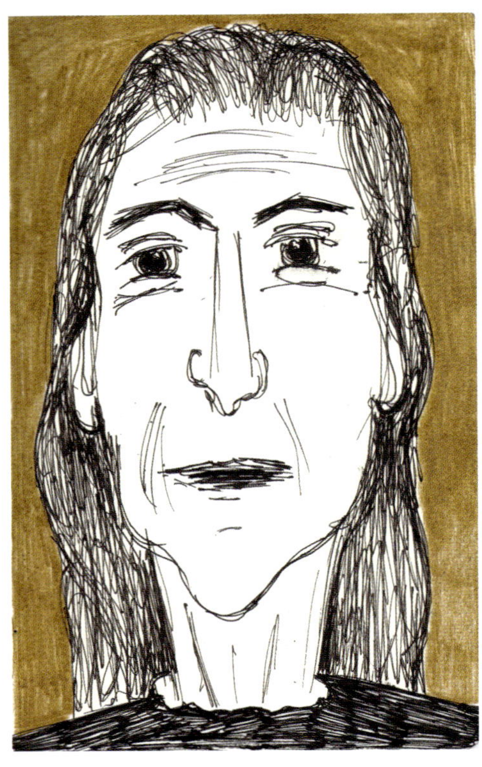

▲ *Niki*

Niki completed this twenty-minute drawing at the end of the day, after a long online meeting. During the meeting, she had been distracted by how tired and old she thought she looked, and she felt that this affected the way she drew herself from memory. Looking back on the drawing, she was surprised by how harsh she had made herself appear.

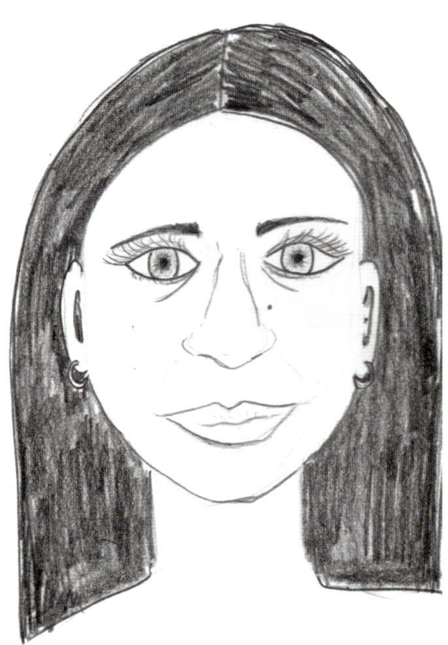

▶ *Jane*

Jane enjoyed this drawing. She has always been someone who enjoys make up and has consequently spent a lot of time looking in the mirror. Even though she wasn't sure about her ability to draw herself, she has a clear visual memory of what she looks like, and she found this helped with her drawing.

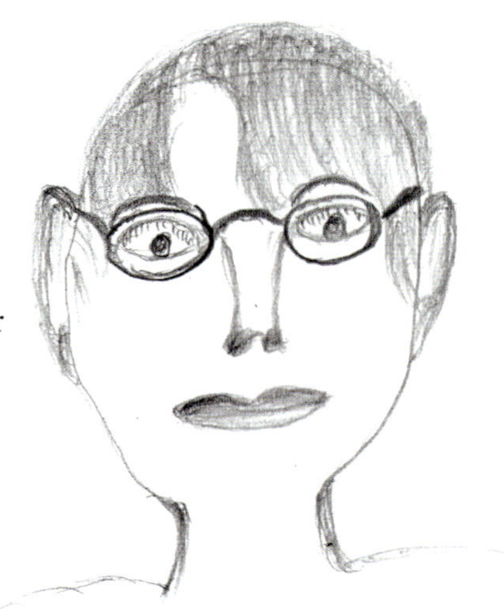

Exercise 2: Self-portrait using a mirror

▼ *Kathi*

Kathi decided that instead of telling herself she was drawing *her* face, she would approach this exercise as if she was drawing *a* face, enabling her to approach it more formally and less emotionally. She started by sketching in the overall shape of her face and then concentrated on her left eye, her right eye, and so on, building up the structure of her face in stages.

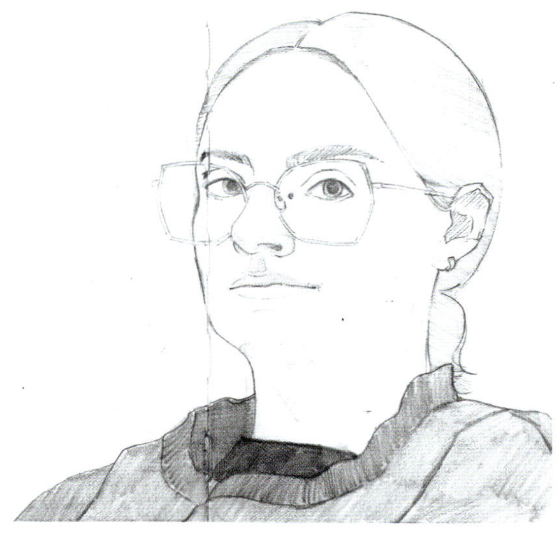

▲ *Diane*

Diane found this exercise much harder than she had anticipated. She found staring at herself in the mirror, for such a long time, an odd experience. She hadn't done a self-portrait for years so admitted to feeling daunted by the task. However, she gave herself a one-hour time limit and this enabled her to just get on with it without too much overthinking and procrastinating.

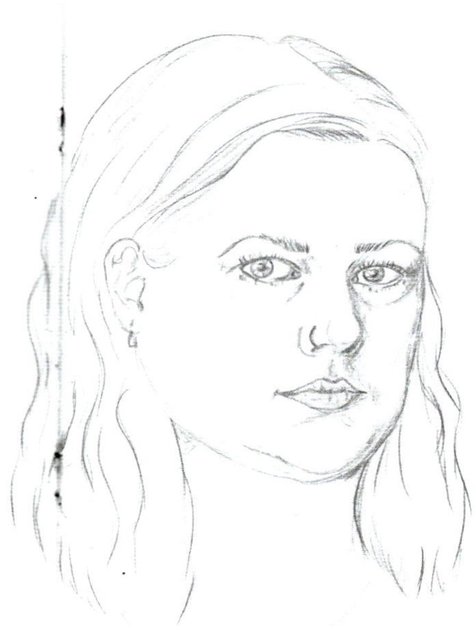

▶ *Eva*

Eva found the self-portrait from memory difficult, so she was dreading this exercise. She stained the page of her sketchbook with ink to take away the challenge of the blank white page and used charcoal as it's a medium she is confident with – she enjoys its flexibility. Despite her initial reservations, she enjoyed this drawing and got completely 'in the zone' while doing it.

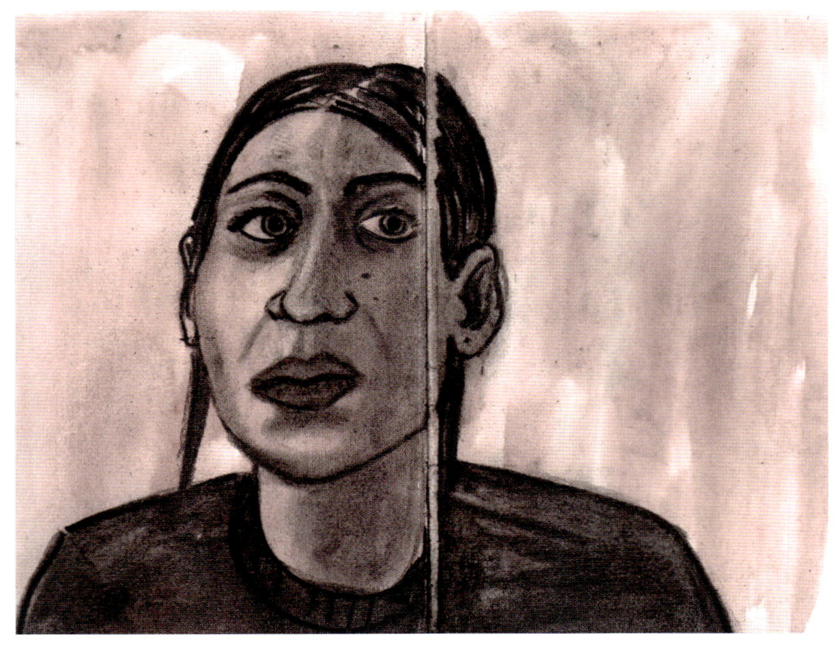

Exercise 3: Self-portrait with character

▼ Anne

Anne spent time researching self-portraits over the last century to understand the various ways people drew themselves. After asking close friends and family to describe her, one of the most frequent comments was how creative she was, so she chose to draw herself sitting at her sewing machine.

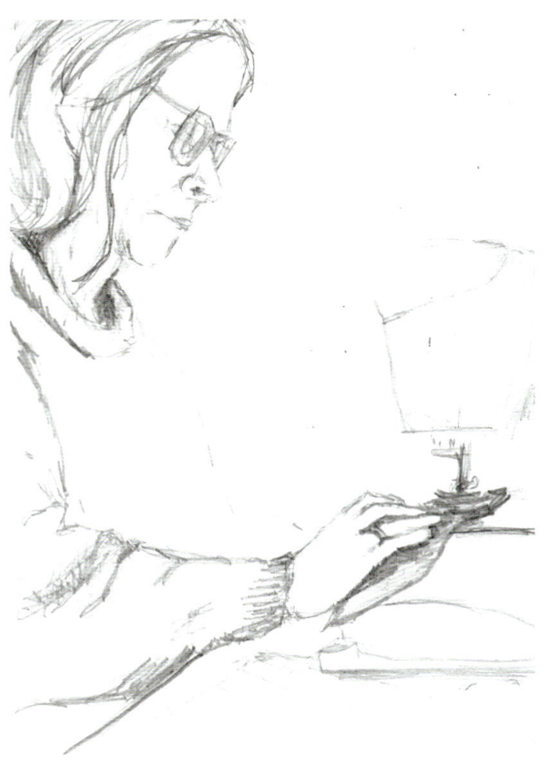

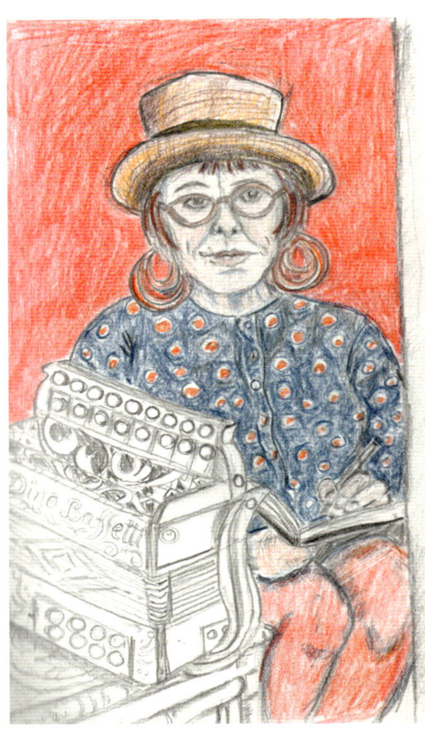

◄ Phyllis

Phyllis's close friend described her as 'joyful, passionate, disciplined, strong, quirky, artistic and very creative'. After hearing this, Phyllis chose her setup carefully. She selected the background colour to give a sense of strength and she chose to include her accordion as it's her favourite musical instrument to play. She also selected her outfit carefully, wanting to wear a hat that she had made, quirky earrings and red tights. All these additions give us a clear sense of Phyllis as a person and her strong sense of style.

► Hannah

Hannah's husband described her as 'luminous, kind, diligent, musical and open'. Hannah chose to concentrate on the word 'luminous'. She covered the whole page with charcoal and then used an eraser to highlight the lighter areas. She enjoyed this way of working as it felt like she was sculpting her face.

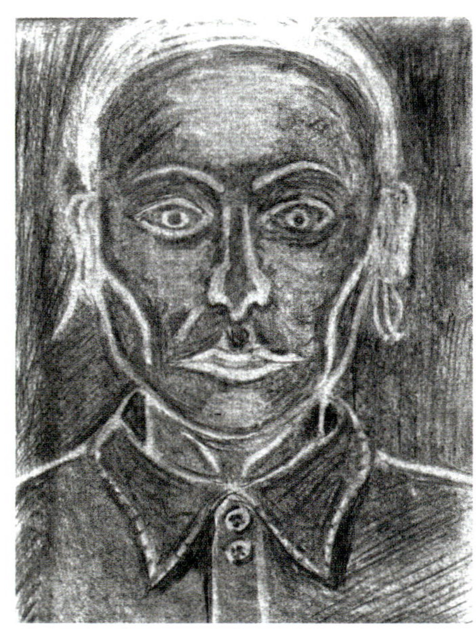

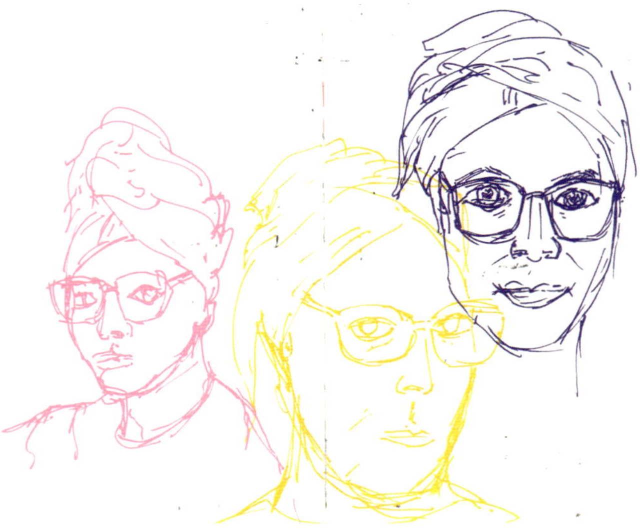

◄ Claire

Claire asked one of her friends to describe her and they said 'wacky, fearless and inquisitive'. Claire decided to use coloured Posca pens to convey this sense of freedom and abandon. The pens create a strong, playful and purposeful line, which describes Claire perfectly.

Exercise 4: Portrait of someone close to you

Spending time drawing someone close to us can be very revealing, as many of the Sketch Squad noted while doing this exercise. It gives us the opportunity to look carefully at those we love and notice things about them that we wouldn't ordinarily see.

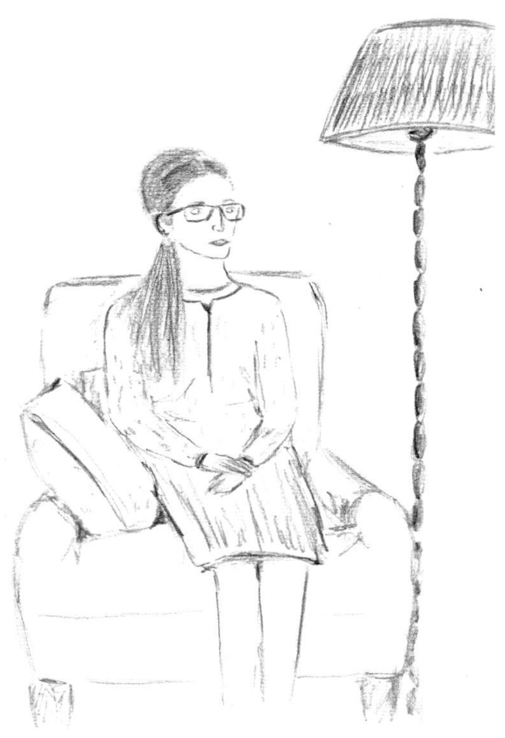

▲ Safa

Safa asked her niece to pose for her for one hour. Her niece was flattered to be asked and eager to please, although she confessed she was a little worried about how she would be seen and portrayed. She also said it was hard to sit still and not chat too much. Safa noted how pleased her niece was with the final drawing and was keen to pose again.

This highlights how important it is to choose your sitter carefully. Make sure you ask someone who is supportive of your work and takes the challenge seriously. You want to make sure both you and the sitter are comfortable.

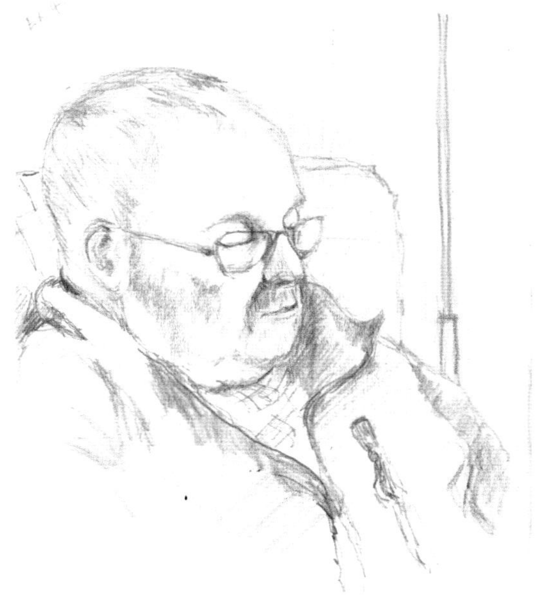

▲ Paula

This is a portrait of one of Paula's friends. He was eager to sit for her, but then promptly fell asleep! This didn't bother Paula, as she felt she could relax more and take her time. She noted that it was a very peaceful, calm and gentle hour – this gentleness comes across in the sensitivity of the drawing.

▼ Anne

This is a drawing of Anne's son, Ben. Ben is supportive of his mum's work and always willing to help, and he proved to be a patient sitter. Anne noted that she found drawing Ben very interesting. She realised that instead of seeing him as her son, she was seeing him as a grown man. She noticed things about him that she hadn't seen before and parts of his face that had changed over the years. After the drawing session, she realised just what a special moment it had been for them.

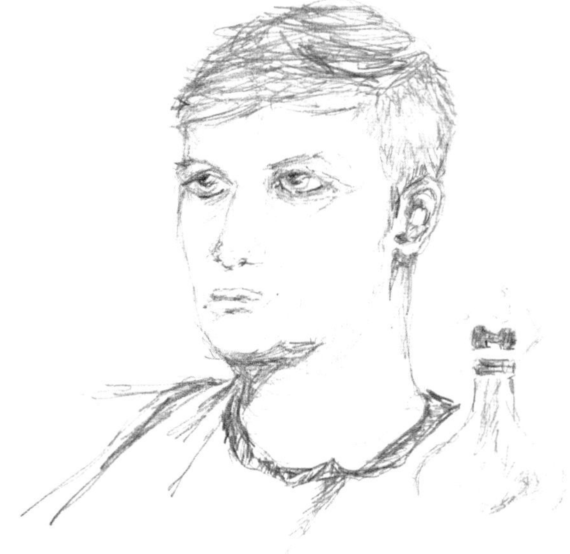

Exercise 5: Drawing a person or people in context

▶ *Jane*

As I mentioned earlier (see page 89), Mum (Jane) and I took the opportunity to draw one another while we were away for a few days before Christmas. This is Mum's drawing of me drawing her. Drawing someone while they are drawing you is a great way to expand your practice and have a good chat at the same time.

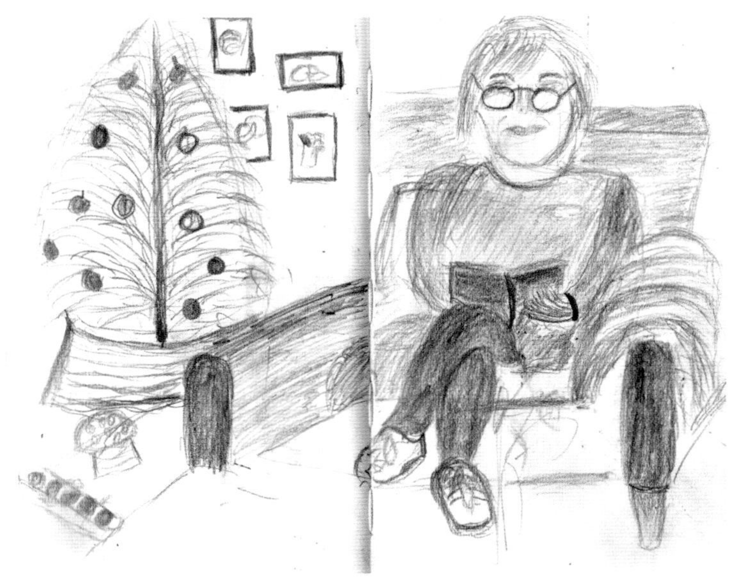

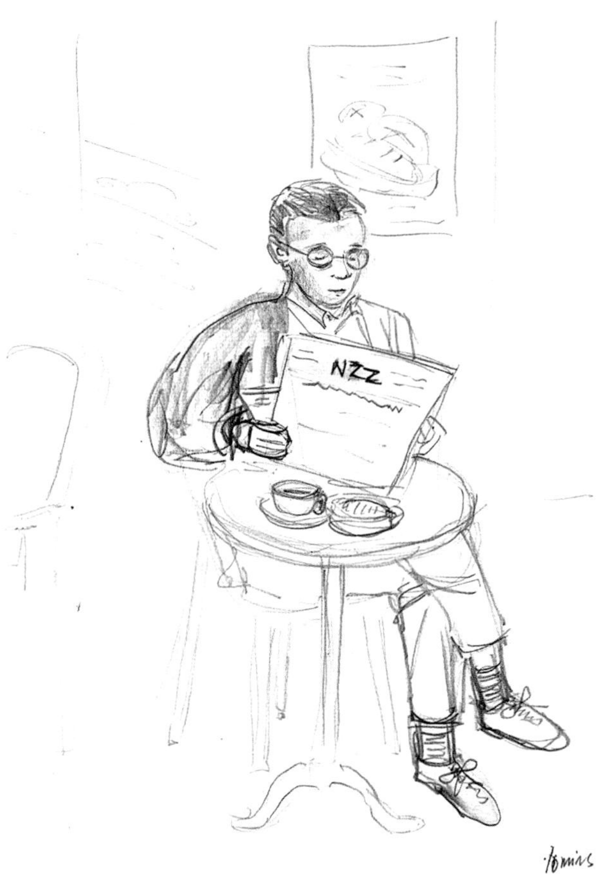

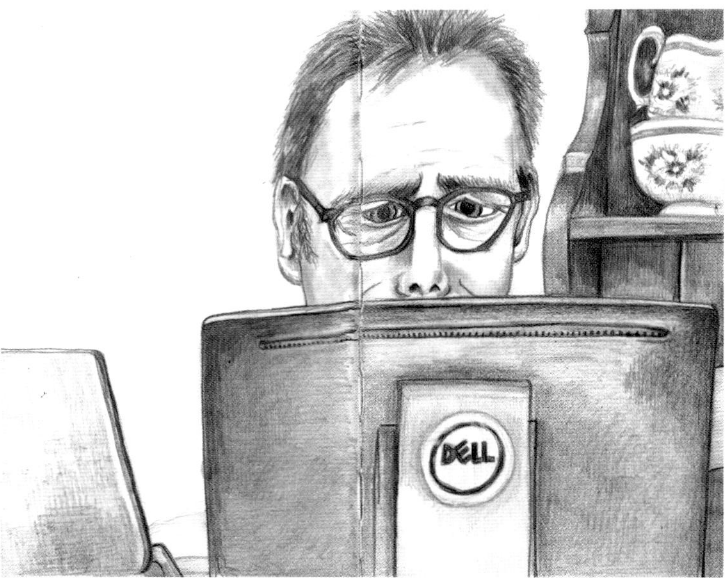

▲ *Lucy*

Lucy drew her husband while having breakfast in a café in Bern. It was early and the café was quiet, meaning she didn't feel too self-conscious. She specially chose to visit the café early in the morning for exactly this purpose – she had tried to draw later in the day, but she felt too uncomfortable getting out her sketchpad and pencil.

If, like Lucy, you are understandably feeling awkward about drawing in public, it's important to go slowly and make the adjustments you need.

▲ *Niki*

Niki chose to draw her husband Jon while he was working. She noted that Jon is the least vain person she knows, so he was very relaxed as to how the portrait would turn out. Drawing it made her feel a little sad, though, as he's a naturally upbeat and positive person, and drawing him made Niki realise just how much his job takes out of him and how demanding it is. When we look at the drawing, the computer takes up more space than Jon's head – we could read this as reflecting Niki's feelings.

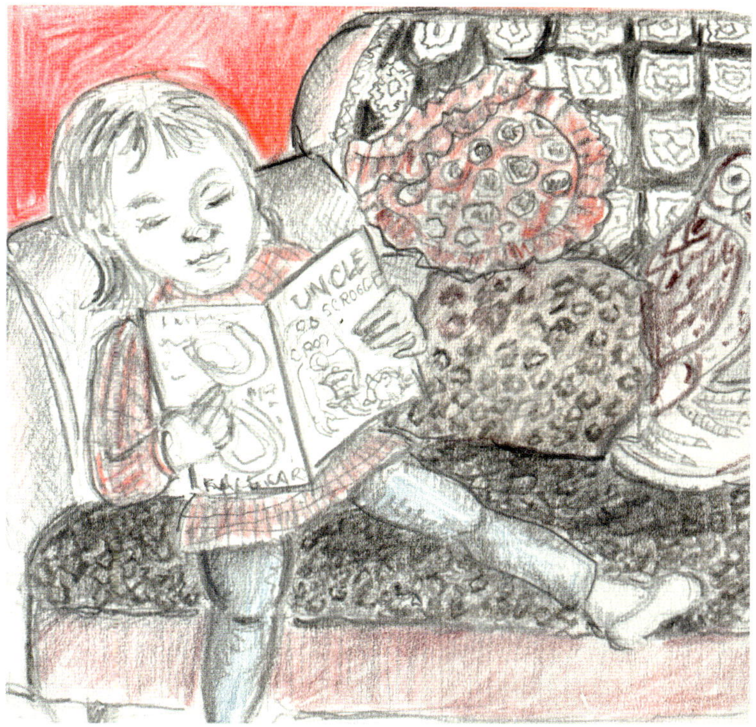

▲ *Phyllis*

This is a portrait of Sloane, Phyllis's granddaughter. Phyllis seized the opportunity to draw her while she was reading one of her favourite books, one that regularly holds and captures her attention. Even so, Phyllis knew she wouldn't have long, so she concentrated on drawing Sloane while she was sitting relatively still then finished the surroundings later in the day. This is a great idea if your sitter is short on time – prioritise drawing them first and you can always return to the background.

Final thoughts

This chapter proved to be the most challenging for the Sketch Squad so far. The self-portraits were especially difficult to navigate for some; the very act of spending time in front of a mirror, scrutinising your appearance, is bound to create feelings. However, if you can move past this and approach the drawing with curiosity and kindness, you will always have an available model to work with.

8
Imposter syndrome

When I first received an email from Bloomsbury Publishing asking me if I would be interested in writing a book about linocut, my first thought was, 'Have they got the right person? Surely they can't want me?' Even though, at that stage, I had been printmaking and teaching for years and had tons of experience, I still doubted myself and my abilities. If I'm honest, this feeling persisted while I was writing the book and is here now as I write this, my second book.

This is a common feeling called 'imposter syndrome'. I want to write about it, as I'm sure it's something that you have felt too. I hear about it regularly in my coaching sessions, especially when it comes to drawing in public with a sketchbook. One student said she feels that drawing out in public is almost like shouting, 'Look at me, I'm an artist!' This causes her to think, 'Who do I think I'm kidding?'

Imposter syndrome is where we doubt our genuine abilities and accomplishments to the point where we become convinced that we are frauds. It's a term used to describe a feeling of self-doubt, which is experienced by many of us, who – despite having evidence of our skill, abilities and accomplishments – still feel we are pretending to be successful.

Causes of imposter syndrome

Before I discuss ways to combat imposter syndrome, let's look at what the causes of this feeling may be:

- **Comparison to others:** We compare ourselves to others and feel we aren't as talented or successful.

- **The desire to be perfect:** As creative people, we have a strong pull towards perfectionism, which can make us feel like we aren't good enough.

- **Fear of failure:** We may be afraid of failing and being exposed as a fraud, which can lead to self-doubt.

- **Unclear goals:** We might not have a clear understanding of what we want to achieve, which can make it difficult to measure our success.

- **Lack of support:** We may not have a supportive network of friends, family or mentors, which can make us feel as if we are on our own and not good enough.

I found it easy to make this list as I have experienced all of these feelings at some time or another. They are common and natural, especially when it comes to artistic endeavours where success is subjective and difficult to measure.

Ways to combat imposter syndrome

Over the years, I've developed my own methods to help me deal with this uncomfortable feeling. Here's my list, which I hope you will find helpful:

- **Acknowledge your feelings:** The first step is to be aware of and accept your feelings – accept that you are feeling this self-doubt.

- **Focus on your own achievements:** Don't focus on other people's.

- **Reframe your thinking:** Instead of fixating on your weaknesses, focus on your strengths.

- **Set achievable goals:** Having clear goals can help you measure your success and give you a sense of direction. Start by setting small, achievable goals and gradually increase these as you become more confident.

- **Keep a book of praise:** Note down whenever you receive a compliment on your work.

- **You're worth it:** Tell yourself you deserve to be making art.

- **Embrace what makes your work special:** Remember there is no one right way to be an artist. Embrace your uniqueness and what makes your work different from everyone else's.

It's important to remember that everyone experiences self-doubt and imposter syndrome from time to time, and it doesn't mean that you're not good enough. By taking the steps to overcome this feeling, you'll be able to focus on your strengths, reach your full potential as an artist and become more confident in your abilities. With time and practice, you'll be able to look back on your journey and see how far you've come.

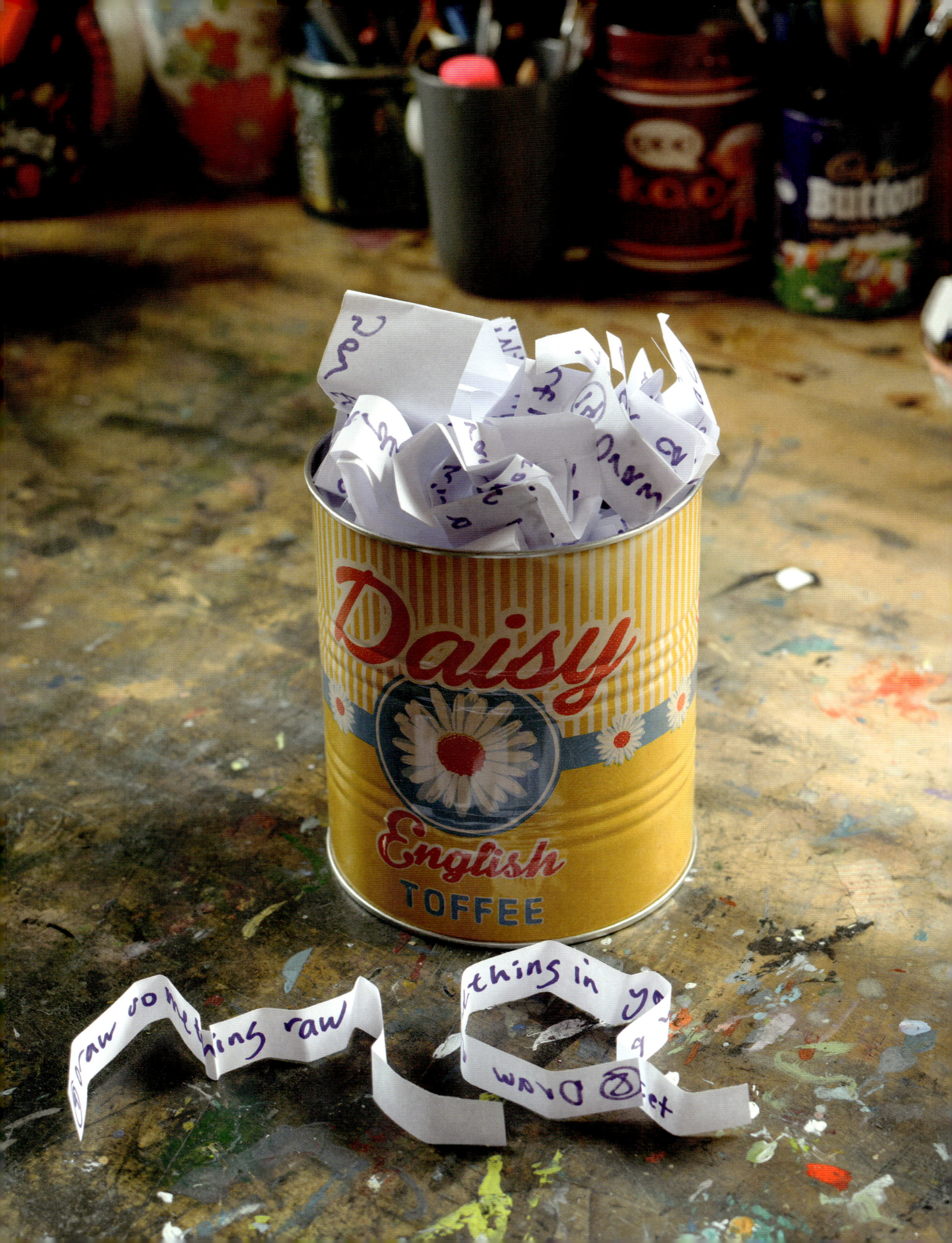

Daisy
English
TOFFEE
Draw something raw
thing in
Draw

9

A daily drawing challenge

Many of the Sketch Squad found drawing portraits challenging for a variety of reasons, so this chapter is a bit of fun – a sort of palette cleanser before we roll on to the rest of the exercises in the book.

As I write this, we are leading up to Christmas, almost halfway through the twenty-five days of Advent. Many of us have an Advent calendar, which we open every day to find a surprise waiting for us, be it in picture form or – if we are lucky – a piece of chocolate. I've designed this chapter with this in mind. For the next twenty-five days, you are going to draw something different – I've come up with twenty-five simple everyday items for you to sketch.

Making drawing a habit

So far, your drawing practice may have been a bit stop-start. The idea behind this chapter is to build up consistency in your drawing practice to get you making marks in your sketchbook every day or every other day. If you are able to do this, my hope is that drawing will become a habit – something that you look forward to every day and consider precious time for yourself.

Decide when to draw

It's important to consider carefully when you might slot in your daily drawing so that you build it into your routine. These drawings are meant to be quick – ideally not over thirty minutes – but this is entirely up to you and your schedule. Some days you might have more time than others. The important thing is to consider a time each day that works for you. Whatever you decide, commit to it and try to make it consistent.

Make it easy

If you want to build up a regular, consistent drawing practice, you must make it easy for yourself. I would suggest placing your sketchbook and drawing materials where you can't ignore them. For me, this is on the kitchen counter, near the kettle, as I spend a lot of time making cups of tea during the day.

If you are feeling confident, leave your sketchbook out so your friends and family can look through it. Tell them about the challenge. The more you share what you are doing, the more accountability you have.

Remind yourself why you are doing this

One of the goals of this challenge is for you to really begin to enjoy your daily drawing. When I open my sketchbook, I immediately feel excited and reassured – I'm returning to my peaceful place. I don't deny that sometimes it's challenging, but the overall feeling is positive. I would love you to feel this way.

To get better at anything you must keep practising, and when there is evidence in the form of your sketchbook – a record of your improvement – I hope this compels you to keep on going. As always, make notes of your thoughts and feelings as you work through the daily drawings. This will give you valuable insights into your creativity.

The twenty-five days of drawing

The best way to approach this challenge is to treat it like a lucky dip. I would suggest getting a piece of paper and writing out the list of drawing prompts. Then cut them up into individual strips, fold them and put them into a container. You can then pull one out daily, and that's the item you are drawing that day. This way, it means that you don't choose the ones you consider easiest first and leave the hardest ones until last. It's a bit like making sure you eat all the chocolates in the box and not leaving the ones you dislike until the end as you might not eat them!

Timings

Ideally, you want to be doing a drawing every day for twenty-five days. However, I'm aware that this might not be realistic or achievable for some of you. If you are unable to do a drawing a day, try to do at least one drawing every three days. This will keep you on track and motivated. Try and think of it as time for you to reflect and relax, not a chore. It's not supposed to be a burden on your life, but a way to relax and celebrate.

You are developing your own unique style. Let the pages of your sketchbook become a personal lens, a way to record your everyday life.

What you need

You can use any drawing materials you like – here are just some suggestions:

- Your small sketchbook – the size is less intimidating, encouraging quick drawings
- Pencils
- Coloured pencils
- Felt-tip pens
- Watercolour
- Charcoal
- Ink
- Wax crayons

The twenty-five daily drawing prompts

1. A souvenir from somewhere you have visited.
2. Something yellow.
3. Something smooth.
4. An ornament.
5. Something that grows.
6. Something related to one of your hobbies.
7. Something you can tie.
8. Something in your pocket.
9. Something raw.
10. Something to put on your head.
11. Any sort of toy.
12. Something you put on your face.
13. Something beginning with the first letter of your name or surname.
14. Something you can stroke.
15. Something that smells.
16. Something sweet.
17. Something from under your kitchen sink.
18. A tin of something.
19. Something spiky.
20. Something black and white.
21. Something you can put around your neck.
22. Something that jingles or makes a noise when moved.
23. A garden tool.
24. Something in your bedroom.
25. Something from the fridge.

My drawings: The twenty-five days of drawing

Even though drawing is my passion and something I love to do, I can't say that I do it every day. When I'm at home in the studio, my days are filled with admin and teaching, so drawing from observation often gets neglected. So, in a way, I planned this exercise for myself too – to see how it felt to draw something random every day.

I started with good intentions, wrote out all the prompts, cut them up and pulled one out of the tin every day. I noted some initial resistance as I started drawing, thinking there was something else I should be doing, but reminded myself that this was for my book and at present there wasn't anything more important. Once I settled down and started drawing, I enjoyed it. It was as simple as just sitting and starting. The problem then was when to stop as I was enjoying it so much – I ended up setting a timer to force the finish, and I found that I naturally drew to this pace.

Below is a selection of some of my daily drawings.

4. Draw an ornament

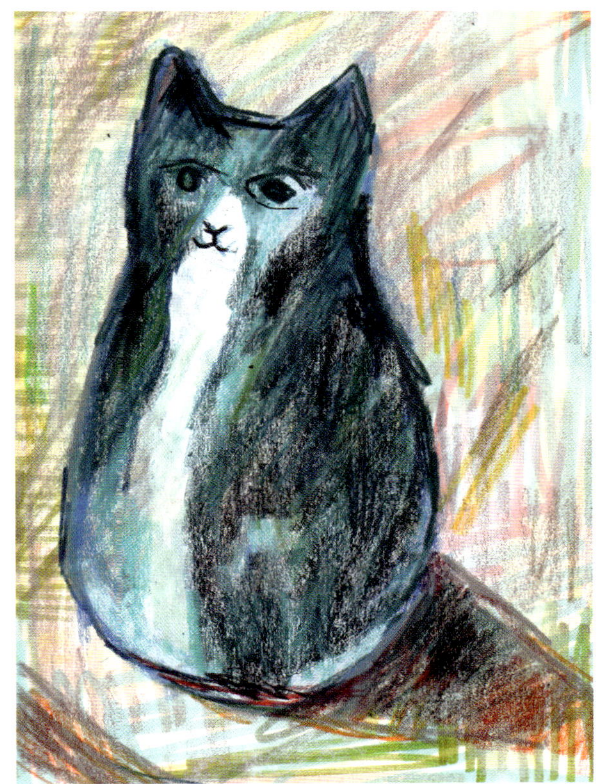

6. Draw something related to one of your hobbies

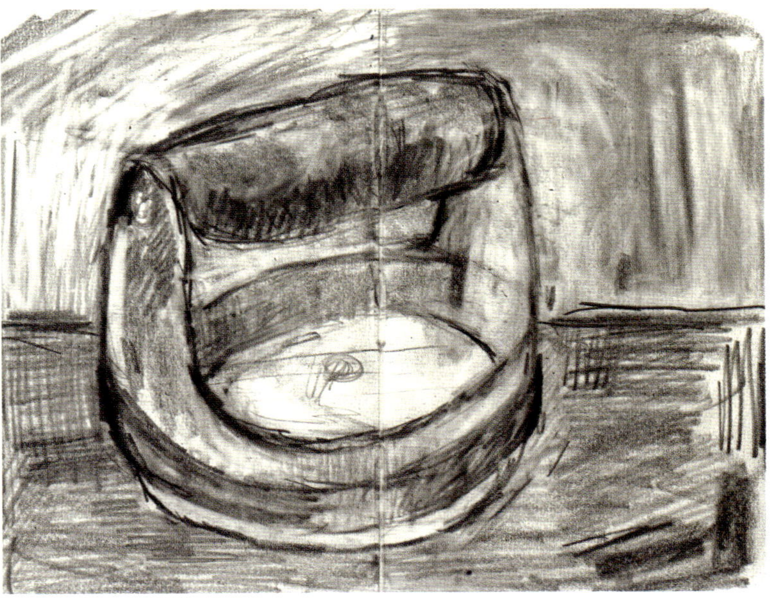

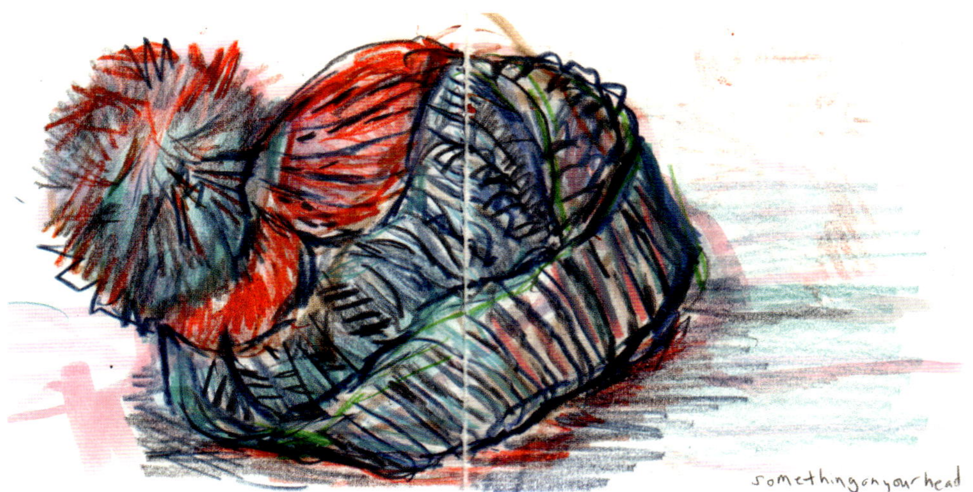

10. Draw something to put on your head

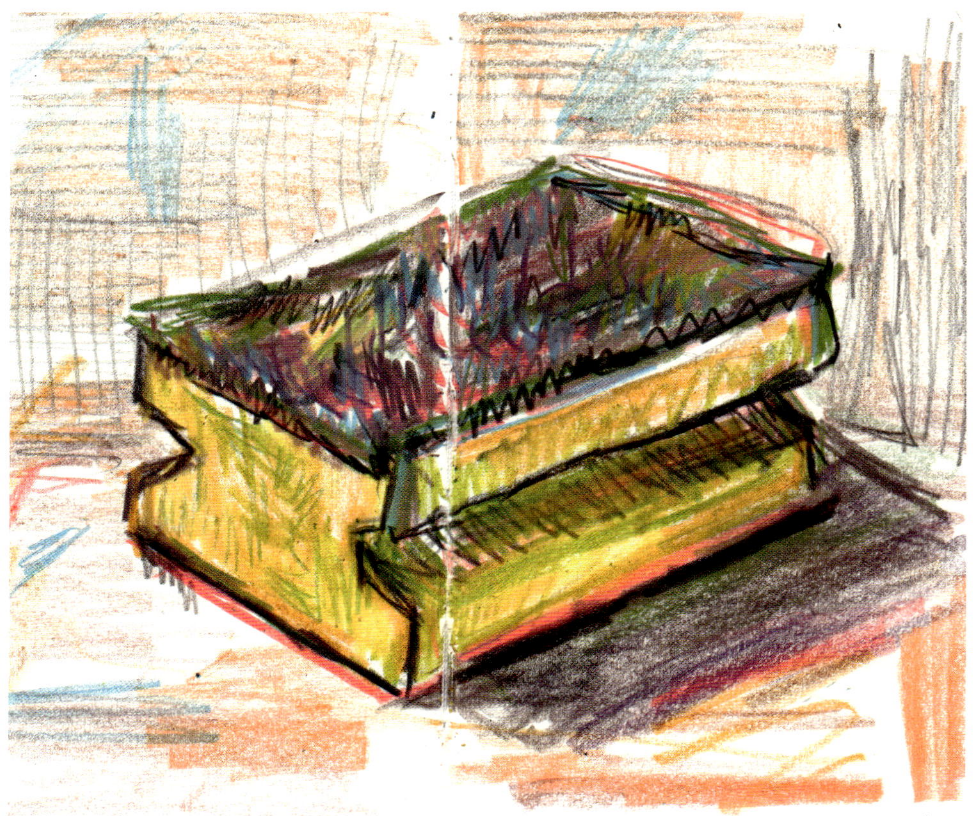

17. Draw something from under your kitchen sink

Sketch Squad: The twenty-five days of drawing

Now let's see how the Squad found the challenge. I asked them all to note down their thoughts on the experience individually, and what follows is a summarisation of their notes.

Initial reactions to the challenge

Everyone said that once they had read the brief, they felt excited about starting.

Anne said, 'I liked the idea of having a range of different prompts after the challenge of drawing portraits. I thought the range of seemingly innocuous items would be fun, particularly with the shorter, snappier sketching time suggested.'

Diane noted: 'Reading about the exercise made me excited about it. The Sketch Squad so far had me realise the importance of consistency for improving my drawings and enjoying the process.'

Jane was eager to get started. Having done nothing like this before, she said she felt a mix of nerves and excitement at the same time.

Finding and using the prompts

Many of the Squad commented that the objects themselves were things they wouldn't normally draw.

Niki said, 'It made me really look at the objects I was drawing, and I noticed things about them I hadn't previously.'

Kathi wrote that she found it practically hard as she didn't have many of the prompts. She lives in a small flat in the middle of Vienna, so a gardening tool wasn't something she had to hand. It's important to note that if this is the case for you, just choose an alternative. You don't have to stick religiously to each prompt. The important thing is that you are drawing every day, not what you are drawing.

Some of the Squad picked each day's prompt, while others, like me, popped them into a tin or container and pulled out a random one each day. Phyllis wrote the prompts on slips of paper and pulled them out of a hat. She said, 'It felt like opening the doors of an Advent calendar.'

Using different materials

The use of different materials was something that all the Squad enjoyed. Niki chose to use a different drawing material each day, Eva tried out ink that she had never used before, and Diane experimented with marker pens. Jane used it as an opportunity to try out the new coloured pencils that she got for Christmas.

Anne said she started to 'play' with the different drawing materials and that it really stretched her understanding of them and what they could do.

Making time for drawing every day

One of the main challenges the Squad encountered was how to fit the task into their schedules.

Paula was on holiday in Australia for the month and she found 'the most productive period of the day was first thing in the morning', so 'incorporating sketching into the daily routine worked well'.

Hannah is a busy mum of two young girls, and she found drawing at night helped her wind down and shift her mind away from the pressures of the day.

Claire was honest and said that even though she had every intention of drawing every day, 'in the end I ended up drawing in batches – sometimes life just gets in the way!'

Diane said the same: 'Initially I told myself I would try and do one drawing a day, but sure enough I ended up doing several a day to catch up.'

However, most of the Squad members found that once they got into the swing of the challenge, it became easier. Niki said that every day was a fresh opportunity and that it helped her become bolder and take more risks. Hannah observed that her drawings became freer and more expressive towards the end of the twenty-five day challenge. Lucy said, 'Drawing every day has made me less precious about my sketchbooks and more open to discussion and feedback.'

Example daily drawings from the Sketch Squad

1. Draw a souvenir from somewhere you have visited
▼ *Niki*

2. Draw something yellow
▼ *Safa*

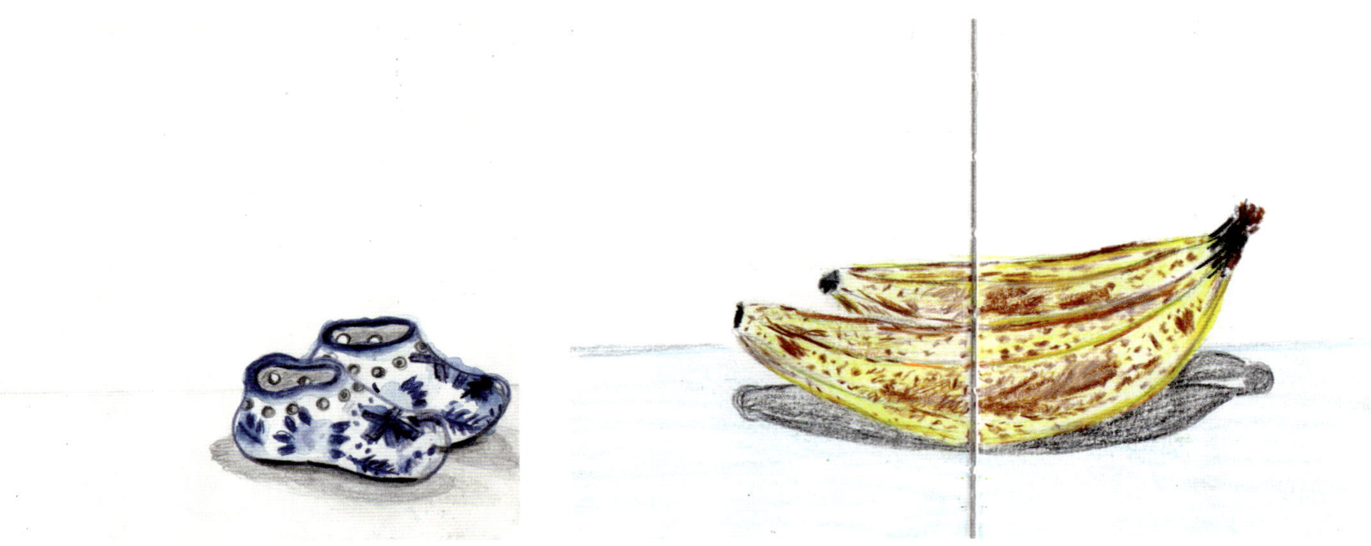

3. Draw something smooth
▼ *Hannah*

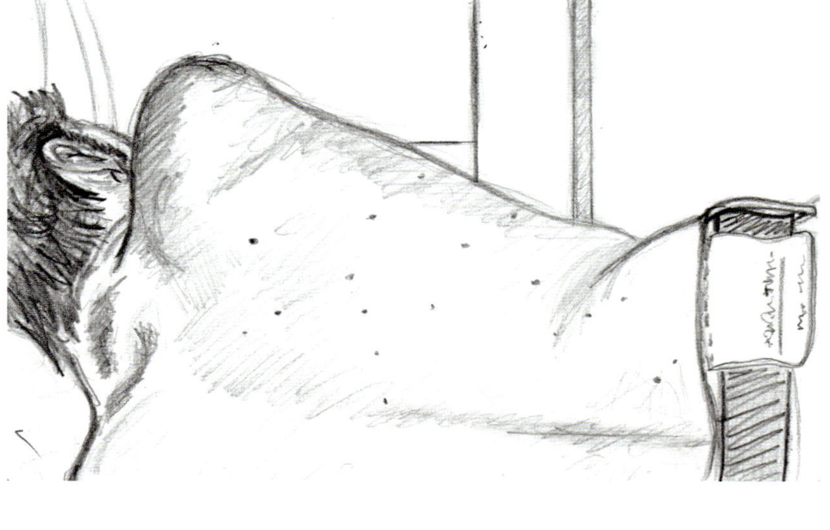

4. Draw an ornament
▼ *Jane*

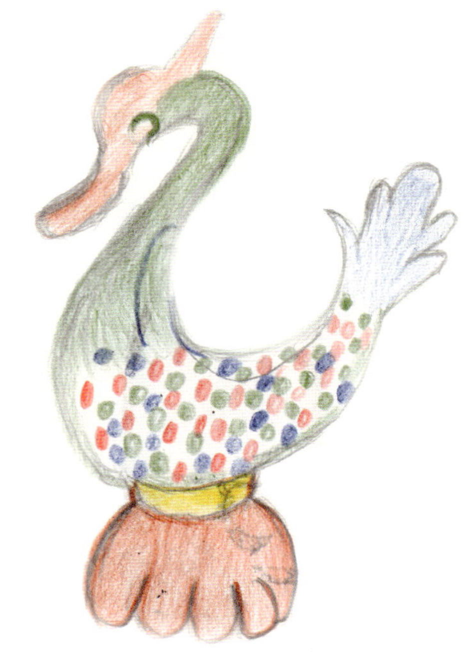

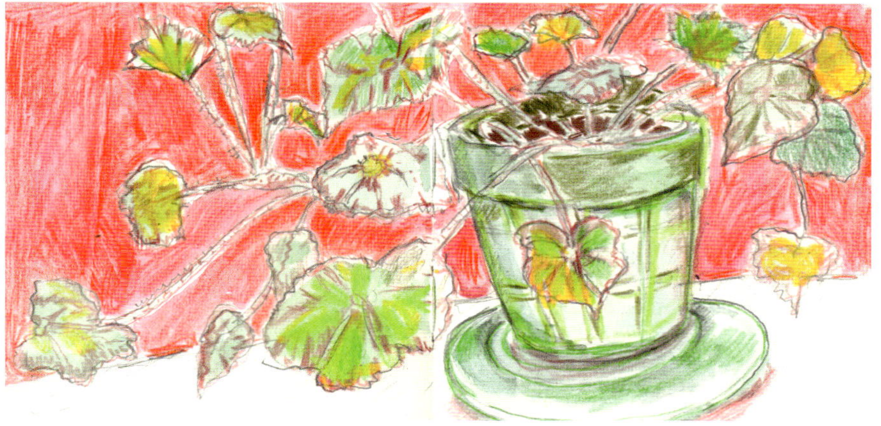

5. Draw something that grows
◀ *Phyllis*

6. Draw something related to one of your hobbies
▼ *Jane*

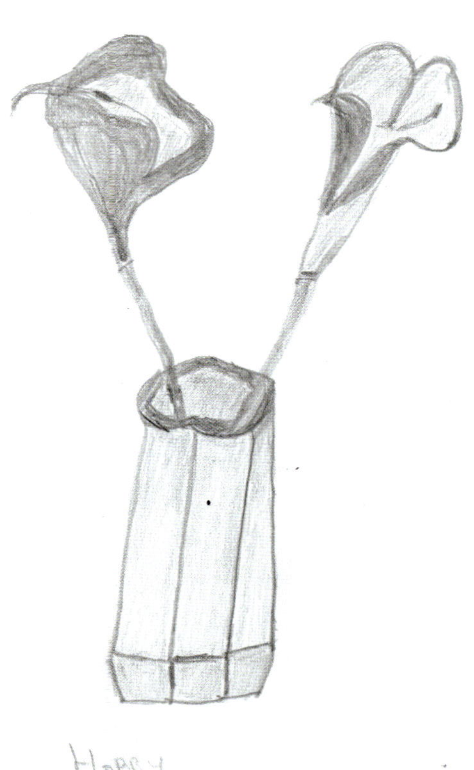

7. Draw something you can tie
▼ *Eva*

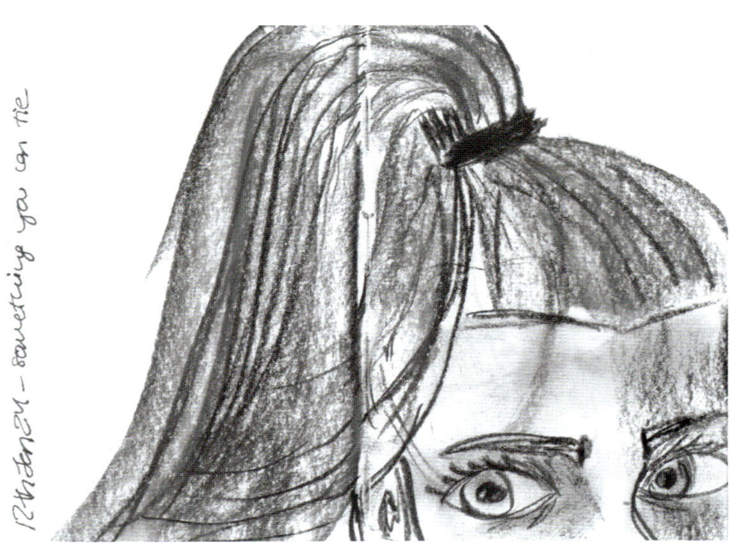

8. Draw something in your pocket
▶ *Niki*

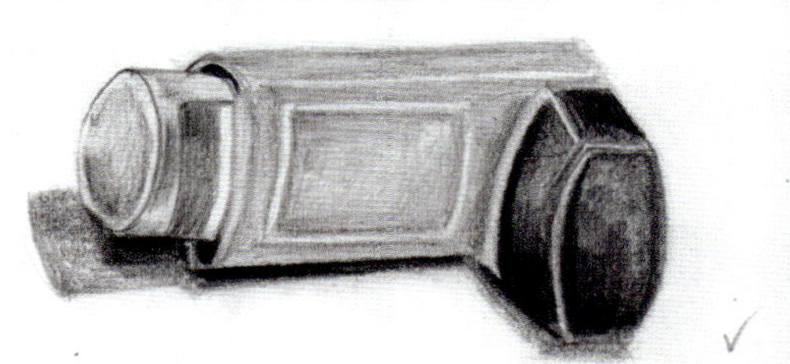

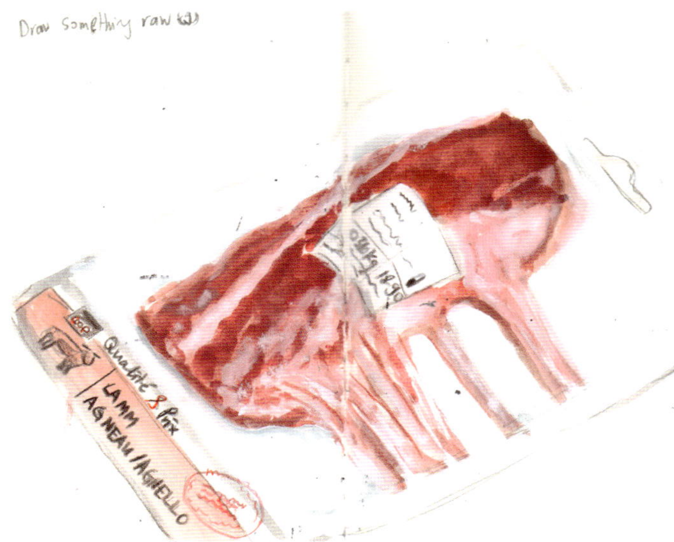

9. Draw something raw
▲ *Lucy*

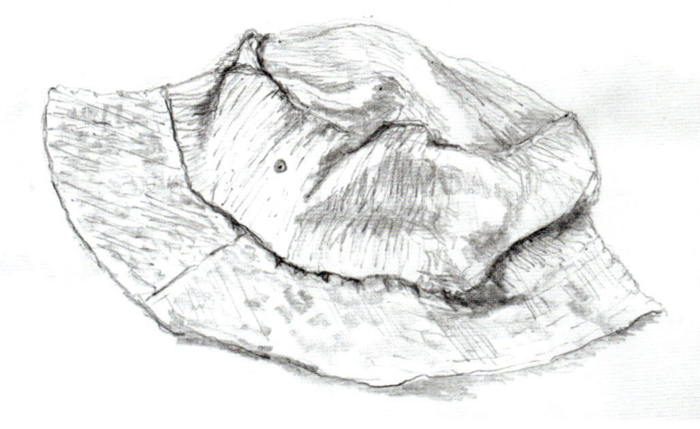

10. Draw something to put on your head
▲ *Paula*

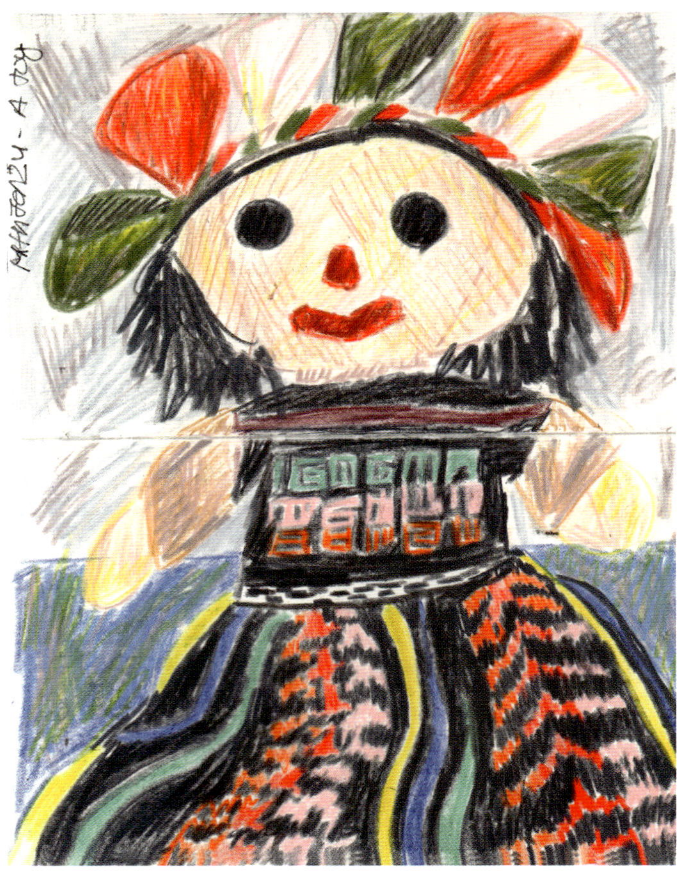

11. Draw any sort of toy
▲ *Eva*

12. Draw something you put on your face
▼ *Phyllis*

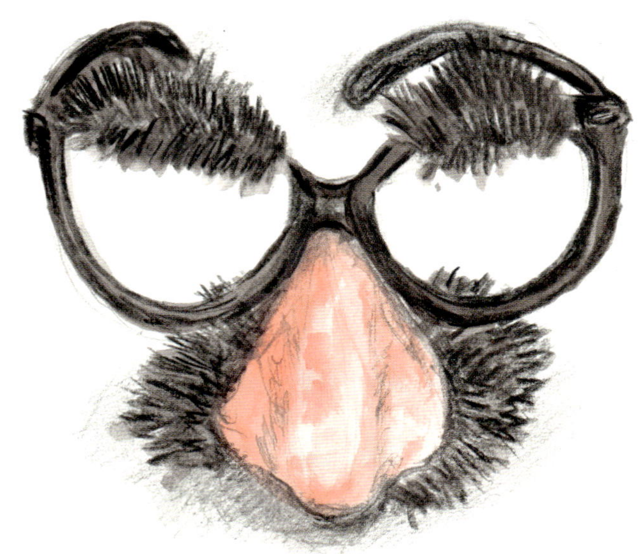

**13. Draw something beginning with the first
letter of your name or surname**
▼ *Claire*

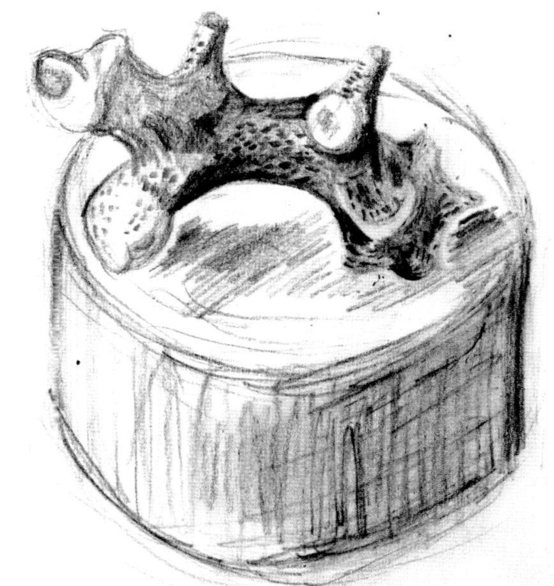

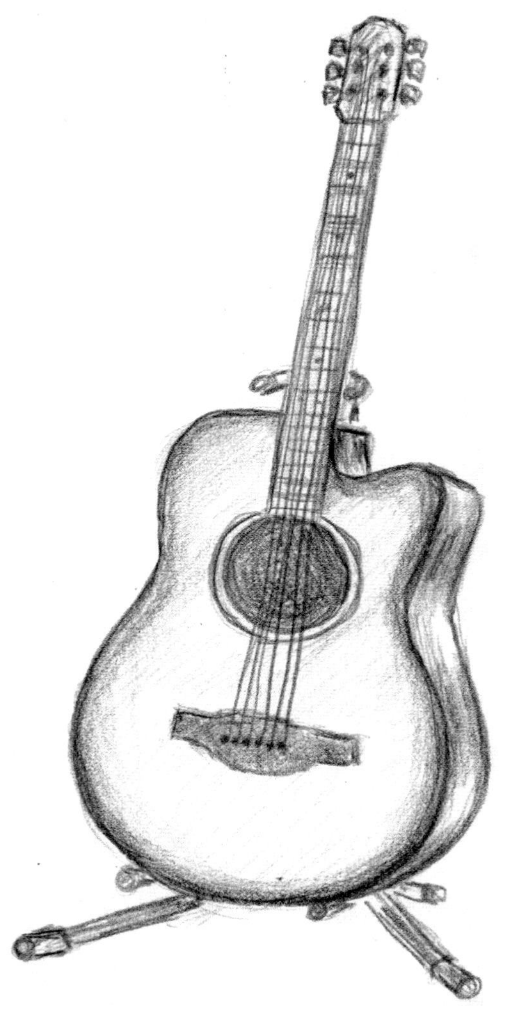

**15. Draw something
that smells**
◄ *Hannah*

**14. Draw something you
can stroke**
▲ *Kathi*

16. Draw something sweet
▼ *Safa*

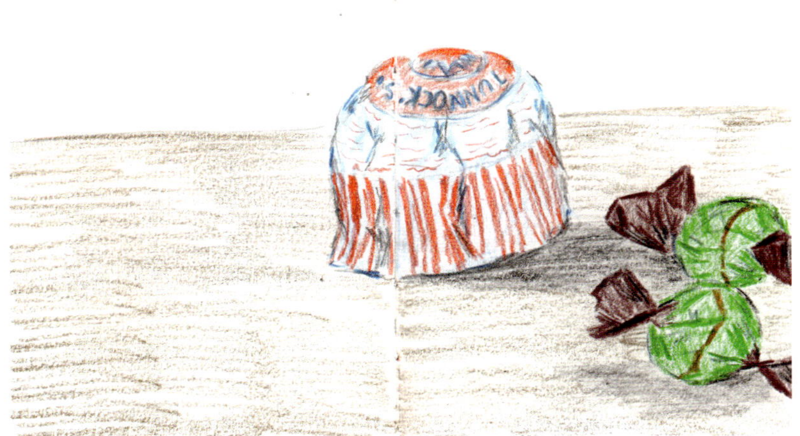

17. Draw something from under your kitchen sink
▼ *Claire*

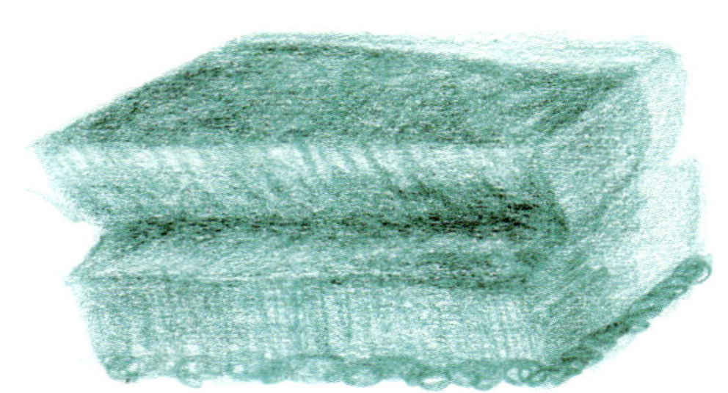

18. Draw a tin of something
▼ *Paula*

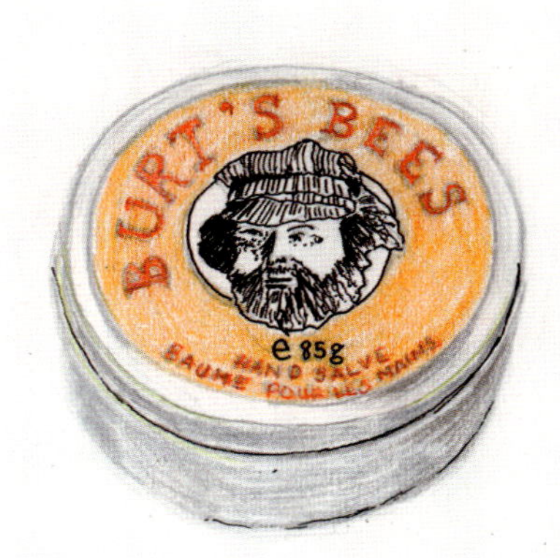

19. Draw something spiky
▼ *Anne*

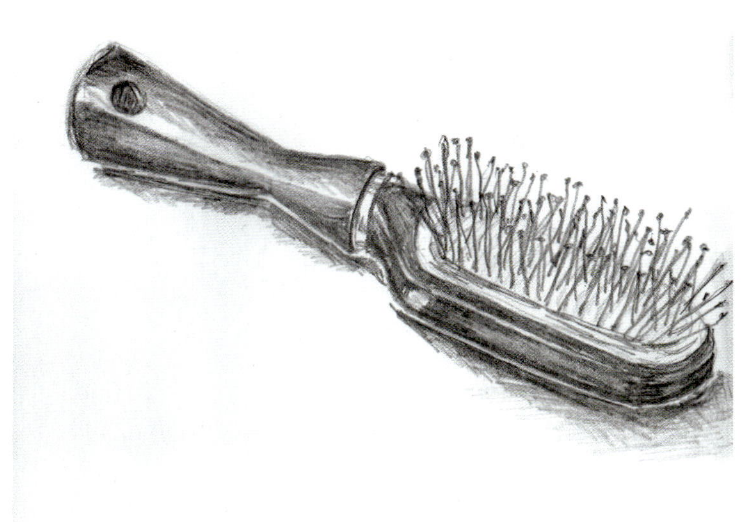

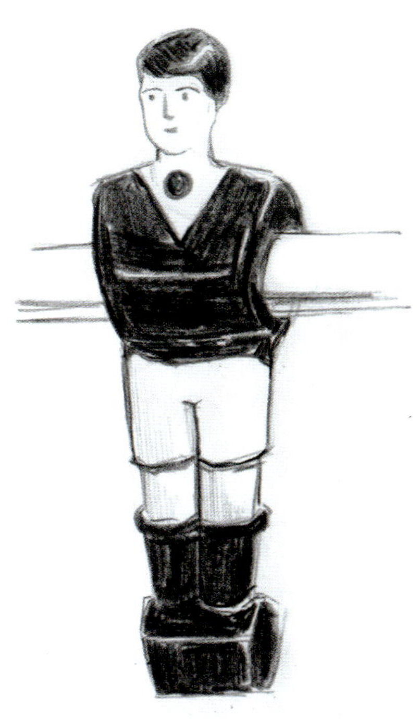

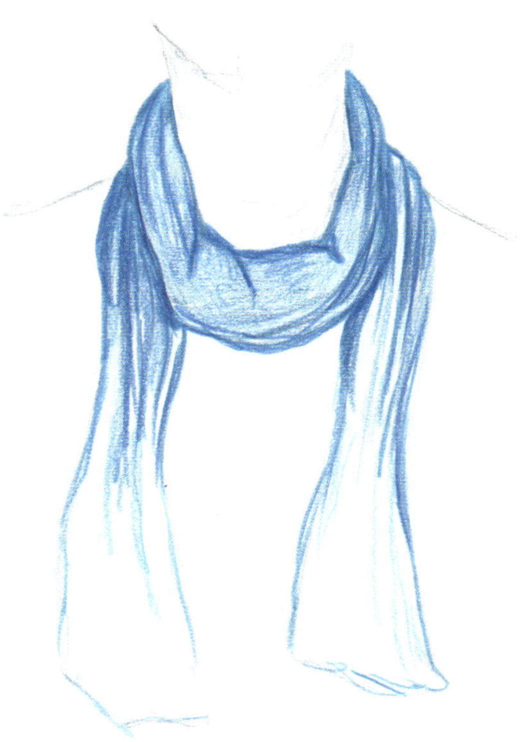

20. Draw something black and white
▲ *Diane*

21. Draw something you can put around your neck
▲ *Kathi*

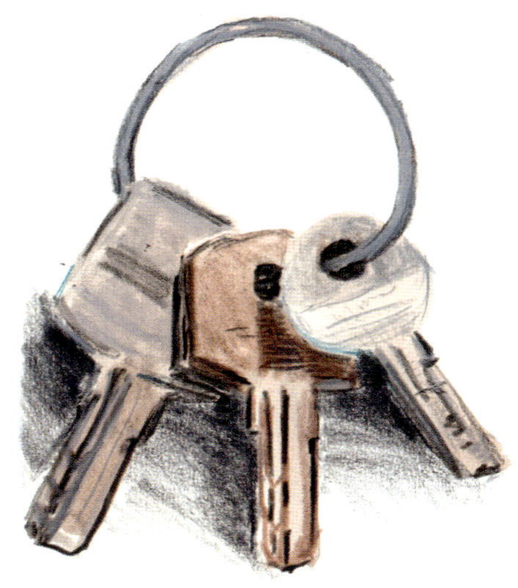

22. Draw something that jingles or makes a noise when moved
▲ *Lucy*

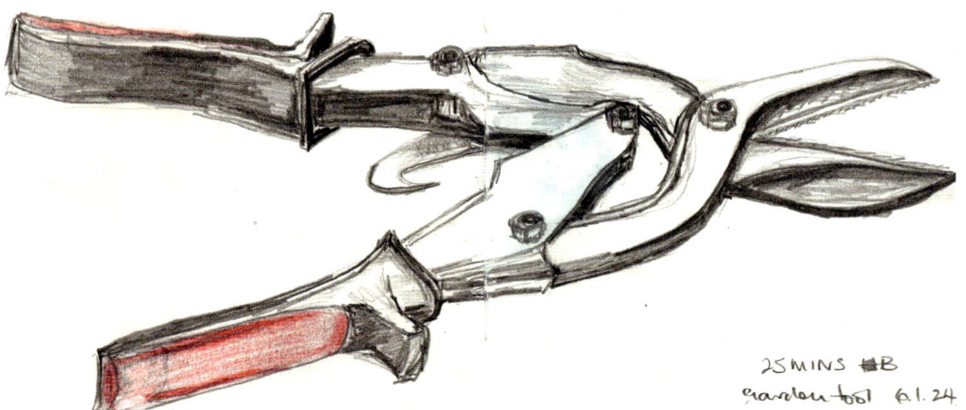

23. Draw a garden tool
▲ *Anne*

24. Draw something in your bedroom
◄ *Eva*

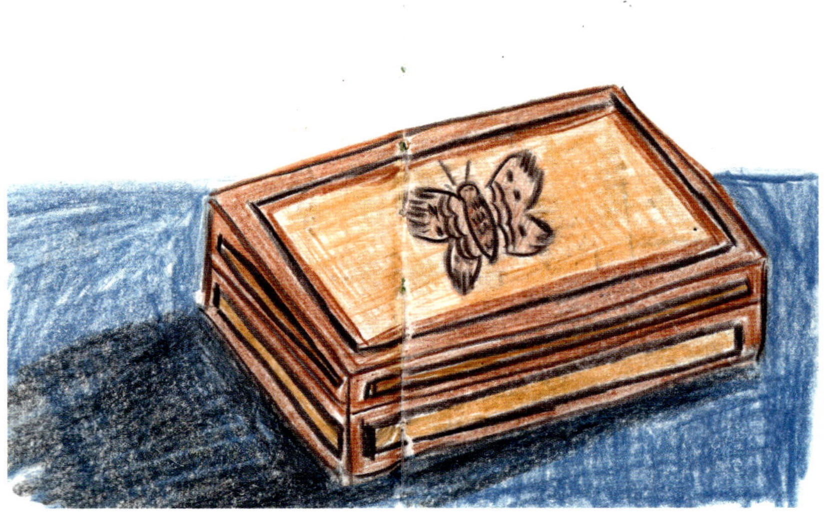

25. Draw something from the fridge
► *Diane*

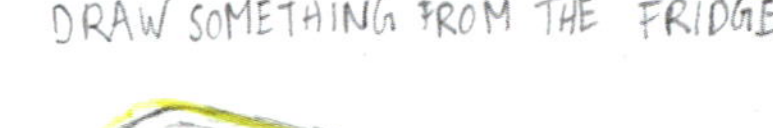

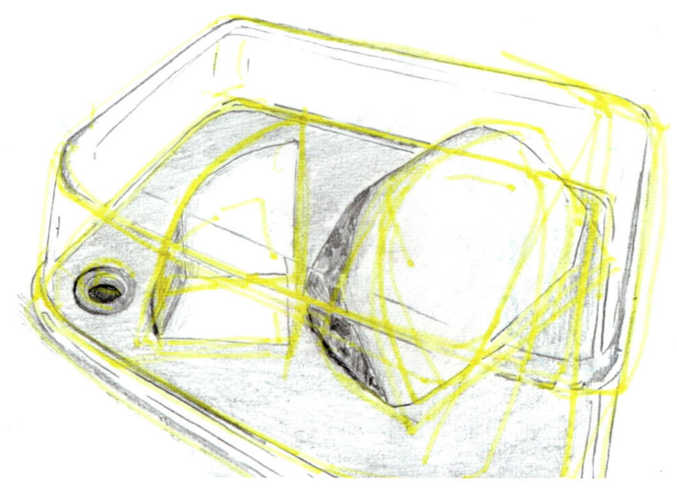

Sketch Squad: Reflections at the end of the challenge

On reflection, after the challenge had ended, Eva said that it made her realise that drawing every day isn't practical for her. 'Daily challenges are not for me as they add too much pressure to my already busy schedule. A more relaxed approach (one per week or every few days) would work much better for me.'

Hannah, however, noted that after the challenge was complete, she realised how much she missed drawing daily. She said, 'It was a brilliant insight into just how feasible it is to make drawing a part of daily life.'

Safa is a teacher, so she often did her drawings at school. She said it made her view her sketchbook as a 'travelling companion' and that the task meant she had it in her bag with her at all times.

At the end, Anne surprised herself (and me!) by stating that she thoroughly enjoyed drawing daily and setting time aside to concentrate. 'I felt refreshed, relaxed and self-satisfied, irrespective of the success of the sketch after each session.'

This feeling of accomplishment shone through all of the students' notes. Jane said that never before has she stuck to something so attentively. Kathi felt proud of herself for completing all twenty-five drawings, as some days it was a real struggle. Lucy said, 'I truly enjoyed every moment of these projects. They opened new doors for me, leading to a better understanding of my skills, my working methods and my passion for sketching every day.'

Final thoughts

Congratulations! Hopefully, you have now finished this challenge and have thoughts and feelings about it. I hope you enjoyed it. As we have seen, the Sketch Squad found daily drawing helpful in establishing a regular drawing practice. Hannah felt sad when it was over – it made her hungry to keep on drawing. I also hope it made you less precious about your sketchbooks and more familiar with your materials, and that you've grown in confidence with your drawing.

Even if you only managed to do some of the prompts, this is better than nothing. Every time you put pencil to paper it should be a chance to congratulate yourself. My hope is that drawing every day has made you feel inspired and ready for the next challenge.

10
Drawing in public

'A drawing is simply a line going for a walk'

Paul Klee

As we are now just over halfway through the book, your sketchbooks will be filling up – plump with memories and records of your daily life. Take some time here to look back through your drawings to reflect and congratulate yourself on how far you have come. Think about how differently you now feel about drawing as you did when you started. Consider the chapters you found difficult and how you found ways to navigate and complete the exercises, even though you perhaps weren't always happy with the result. I hope you are now able to enjoy the drawing process and feel how much it enhances your life. It's important to give yourself this pat on the back, as this chapter might prove to be challenging for some of you, and the more confident you feel, the easier it will be.

In this chapter, you are going to draw outside the home, in public, with your sketchbook. You are going to take your sketchbook out and about and draw in places like cafés, public gardens and on public transport. Throughout my years of drawing outside, some of the most common comments I've heard are: 'I would love to go out and draw in public but I'm just too scared' or 'I wish I had the confidence like you to sit outside and draw'. It's true, sketching in public can be a daunting prospect and one that might fill you with dread. If you place your trust in me and allow me to guide you with my helpful tips, I believe that you will build the confidence to do this with ease.

Worries about taking your sketchbook out in public

When I ask students what puts them off drawing in public, it mostly comes down to not feeling good enough or fear of being judged by other people. Some of the frequent things I hear are:

- 'I worry that someone is going to come up to me and say my drawing isn't any good.'
- 'I feel so self-conscious.'
- 'What if it rains/gets cold/there's a heatwave?'
- 'I feel vulnerable and exposed.'

Let's look at some of these fears more closely. Take the first one – someone comes up to you and says your drawing is no good. Ask yourself, why does it matter what a total stranger thinks of your drawing? After all, where's their sketchbook? Although this might happen, it is very unlikely – if someone does wander over to you and asks what you are doing, often they will say something along the lines of: 'Nice drawing. I wish I could do that.'

People are naturally curious. Art is a magnet, and they can't help but be drawn to it. People who approach you generally fall into two categories: people who want to sketch or people who already sketch. Most people who approach me don't hang around long enough for an extended conversation. If they do want to chat, then I am always polite but keep my answers short and keep drawing. This is normally enough to discourage more interaction.

If you are really concerned that someone might say something disparaging, it might be helpful for you to have some ideas about what you might do or say when someone comes up to you. You could just close your sketchbook and take a drink, pick up your phone or say something like, 'I'm having some time to myself, thank you.' It's good to remind yourself that people are always busy doing their own thing and you are just a momentary distraction. Think of that old saying, 'People aren't thinking of you as much as you think they are. They are too busy thinking about themselves.'

Let's look at the worry about the environment – that it might get too cold/hot/windy, etc. There are many things we can do to allay this fear. The first is prepare – make sure you have a raincoat/sunhat/sunblock with you. Second, accept that you are at the mercy of the weather – you can then adapt accordingly. I love the fact that the weather affects my drawing. I speed up if I see dark clouds looming; my marks become exciting when it's windy. Allow the weather to do its thing and see how you can use it to your advantage. Of course, if it gets too windy/wet/hot, the best thing to do is pack up and try again later!

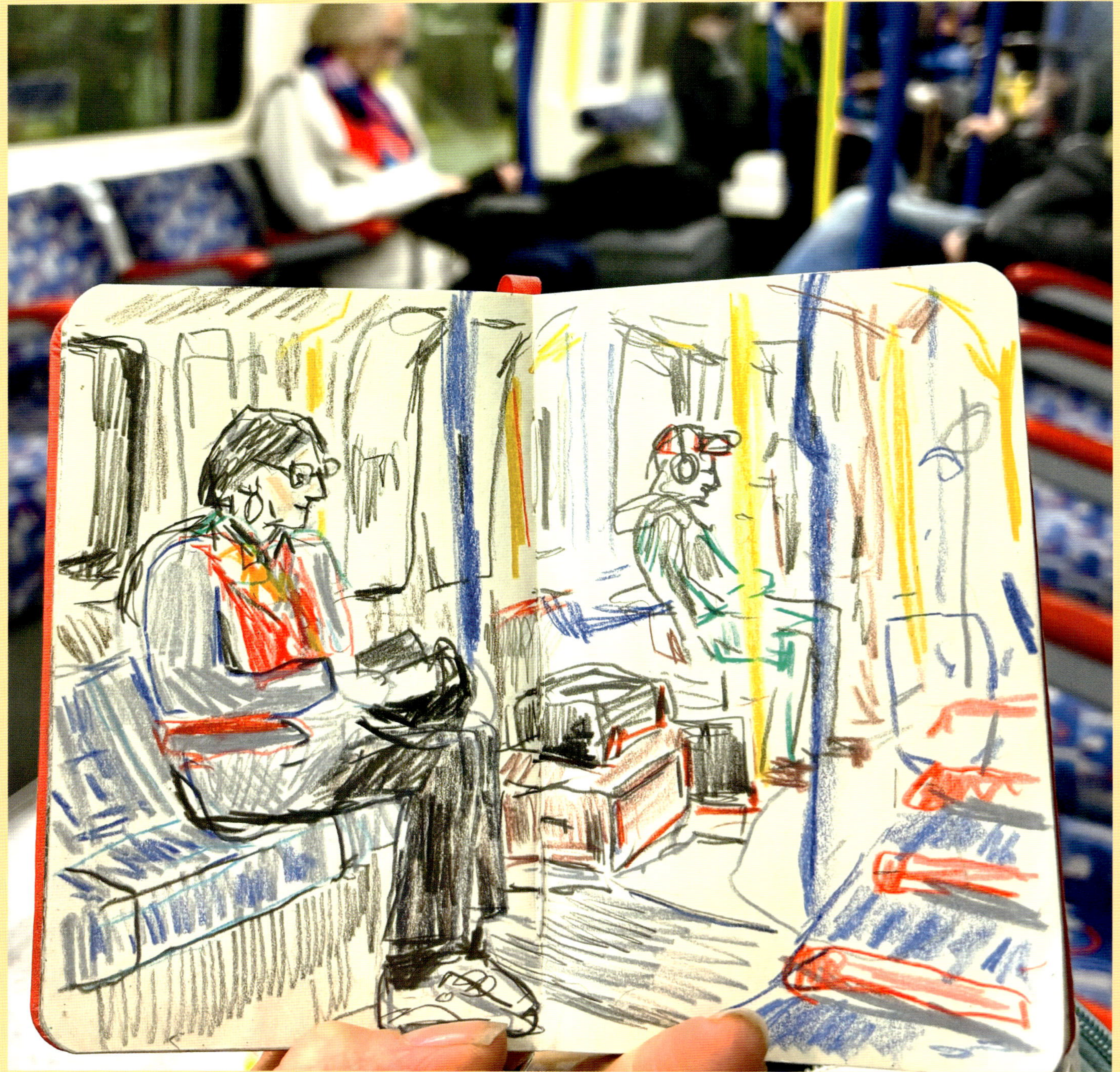

My tips for drawing in public

The following might help you to be mentally and physically prepared to draw in public:

- Wear headphones
- Wear sunglasses
- Sit in the car
- Wear a hat
- Dress simply

- Look busy
- Have all your materials to hand
- Get someone else to sit with you
- Start in a less crowded setting
- Sit against a wall or tuck yourself away
- Work small – it's unobtrusive and less likely to call attention to what you're doing

Drawing people in public

The exercises in this chapter involve you not only drawing out and about but also drawing people in places and spaces. Drawing people is tricky. Drawing people quickly while they are on the move is even more difficult. You will get the proportions wrong; people's legs, arms, heads etc. will look odd at the start but keep going. Just try and capture the essence. When you haven't got time, there's not much space for judgement. For me, capturing a fleeting moment forces me to a place where drawing becomes automatic. I just look and draw.

When you are starting out, keep it simple and choose a person that isn't moving much (someone reading or sleeping, for example). This ensures their movements are limited and you don't have to observe their pattern of movement. When you progress on to drawing people moving, start with sketching the big shapes very loosely. Allow your pencil to move quickly across the page.

Sketching people while out and about is different from drawing a portrait or trying to draw anatomically correct figures as you would in a life-drawing class. When I look back at my drawings of people, it's not the realistic ones that grab my attention. I'm not interested in realism. It's the sketches that capture the energy and spirit of the person that I enjoy the most.

Remind yourself that the way we are drawing is not about perfection or sheer technical ability but storytelling and experimentation. It's about recording part of your day – your emotions, memory and who you are as a person. We aren't perfect – neither is life – and it's unrealistic to expect our sketches to be.

Getting started

Practise at home

Before you start drawing in public – more specifically, drawing people in places and spaces – practise at home. While I'm not an advocate for drawing from photos exclusively, it can be helpful to get you used to drawing people. You might want to go out and take some photos in public places, of people just doing their everyday things, and then come home and draw them. Or you might find it useful to draw from footage on your phone. This way, you get used to trying to capture people quickly.

Dive straight in

Once you have spent some time practising at home, dive straight in. Follow the exercises below and see what happens. If your subject gets up and leaves, just move on to the next one and keep going until you have a page filled with small drawings. Don't worry about the results. As you practise, your drawings will improve and you'll learn which techniques work best for you.

Keep your materials in your bag

It's always helpful to have your sketchbook and a selection of pencils with you when you are out and about, as you never know when there might be an ideal opportunity to draw. In December last year, when I was driving back to my parents, I got a flat tyre and I had to wait for someone to help me out. I was so pleased I had my sketchbook with me as instead of scrolling on my phone, I could draw instead.

Keep it simple

Don't overcomplicate things. Just choose a spot and draw. If you are feeling overwhelmed, limit the area you are drawing in. Eyeball something to the left and to the right of your vision, then just draw what you see in between. Refer to one of the first exercises we did, when you were drawing a corner of your room (see pages 53–5) and remember how you selected what to draw in that space. Do the same when you have a scene in front of you. Remember, you don't have to include everything – just do what you can in the time you've allocated yourself.

Let go of perfection

Remind yourself you are learning and the process matters more than the result. You can't expect quick drawings to be flawless; they will be lively and have character.

Look back at your drawings a few days later. Drawings I was disappointed with when I made them often don't look half as bad after a couple of days. Step back and take time to see their qualities rather than their flaws.

Try new techniques

While I advise just using pencil when you are starting out, once you feel more comfortable drawing outside, experiment with your materials and try different techniques. You might want to try out pen and ink or maybe use watercolour, coloured pencils or felt-tip pens. The most important thing is to build up gradually as your confidence grows.

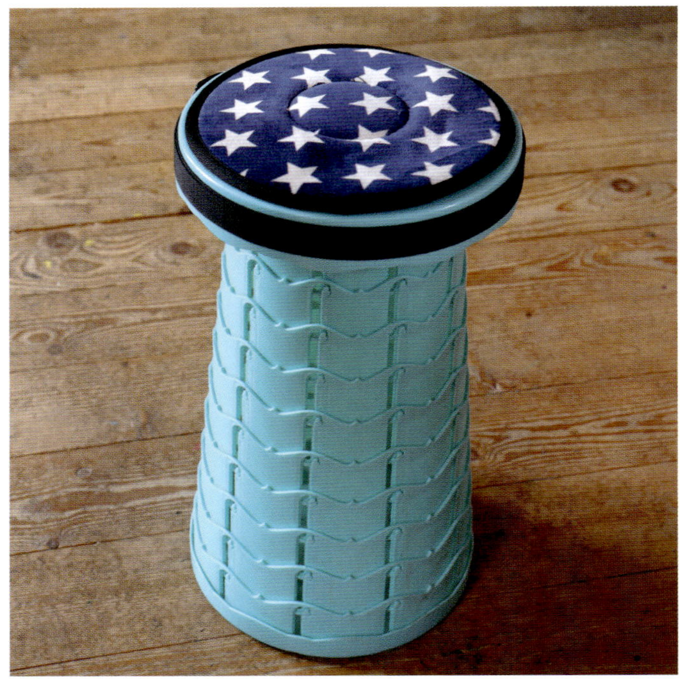

Practise and practise

There is no magic pill. It takes time to build a skill, and drawing out and about is no exception. Practise as much as you can, even if it's just a few minutes at a time. Cafés, bars, restaurants, parks and public spaces, trains, planes and waiting rooms are all great places to draw people.

What you need

- A bag to hold all your kit
- Sketchbook – it's up to you whether you choose your small or large sketchbook
- Selection of graphite pencils
- Selection of coloured pencils (optional)
- Marker pens (optional)
- Charcoal (optional) – if used, make sure you fix your drawings (I use hairspray) or put a sheet of copy paper in between
- Clips to hold sketchbook pages open
- Pencil sharpener
- Eraser
- Headphones
- Water and snacks
- Sun hat/warm clothes, depending on temperature
- Something to sit on – I use an expandable telescopic stool (pictured above and see page 33)

Exercise 1:
From a car (30 minutes–1 hour)

We're going to start off gently by drawing in a car. This is a useful stepping stone to sketching in public as the car provides a literal protective bubble around you. Sitting in the car also helps with staying warm. If you have your own car – great! If you don't, perhaps you can ask someone to drive you somewhere and you can sit in the car and draw while they go and do something.

When I draw from the car, I sometimes like to include parts from the inside of the car – the steering wheel or the rim of the window, for example – but this is entirely up to you. I take a piece of hardboard with me and rest it on the steering wheel as I can then use it to put my sketchbook on. Don't worry about choosing a particularly scenic spot, just go somewhere where it's easy to park and there is enough to keep you interested and engaged.

Exercise 2:
While waiting
(30 minutes–1 hour)

Rather than scrolling on your phone, drawing is a productive way to pass time while you are waiting for an appointment, for a friend to turn up, for a train, etc. Just pick up your sketchbook and start.

Try to include something in your drawing that identifies where you are. Let's say you are drawing while waiting at the dentist, consider what you could include to identify the setting. Have fun with it and keep your drawings light, quick and expressive.

Exercise 3:

On public transport (5–10 minutes)

One of my favourite ways to draw people in public is on train journeys, the reason being that they tend not to move much – they are either engrossed in their phone, reading a book or snoozing. It's an ideal opportunity to get out your sketchbook and begin to draw. Try to include their surroundings too – the seats often provide interesting shapes, and you can just capture parts of the body that you can see.

This is the exercise where you are most likely to have people notice that you are drawing them. Although it's perfectly legal to draw people in public, some might not like it, so try and avoid eye contact. I always hold my sketchbook close to my face and squint so it's not clear where I am looking.

Exercise 4:

In a café, pub or restaurant (1–1 ½ hours)

You will have more time in this exercise as people will be sitting down for a while, absorbed in conversation, their food and drink and their mobile phones. Include parts of the space that interest you and make sure you place the people in context; you want them to be sitting at the table, not floating in space.

In a park (1–1 ½ hours)

Here you have a lot of choices. You could just draw a part of the park that appeals to you – perhaps there is an interesting building, a statue or an area of water that you want to capture. You don't have to include people here, but it's often useful to feature a few figures as this gives a sense of space. People move around and play, but you can focus on those who are sitting on a bench or on the grass. You can also draw people from afar or focus on landscapes, if you need a break.

Exercise 6:

In an art gallery or museum (1–1 ½ hours)

Drawing in an art gallery or museum is wonderful as people are mostly preoccupied with looking at the works of art, and there are plenty of places to sit and draw. You may choose to sit in the foyer and just draw people in the entrance halls, or you might find a quiet spot – somewhere tucked away where you can get lost in drawing the details of the environment you are in. Try drawing people looking at the artworks; you could sketch them with their back to you and perhaps include part of the paintings.

My drawings: Drawing in public

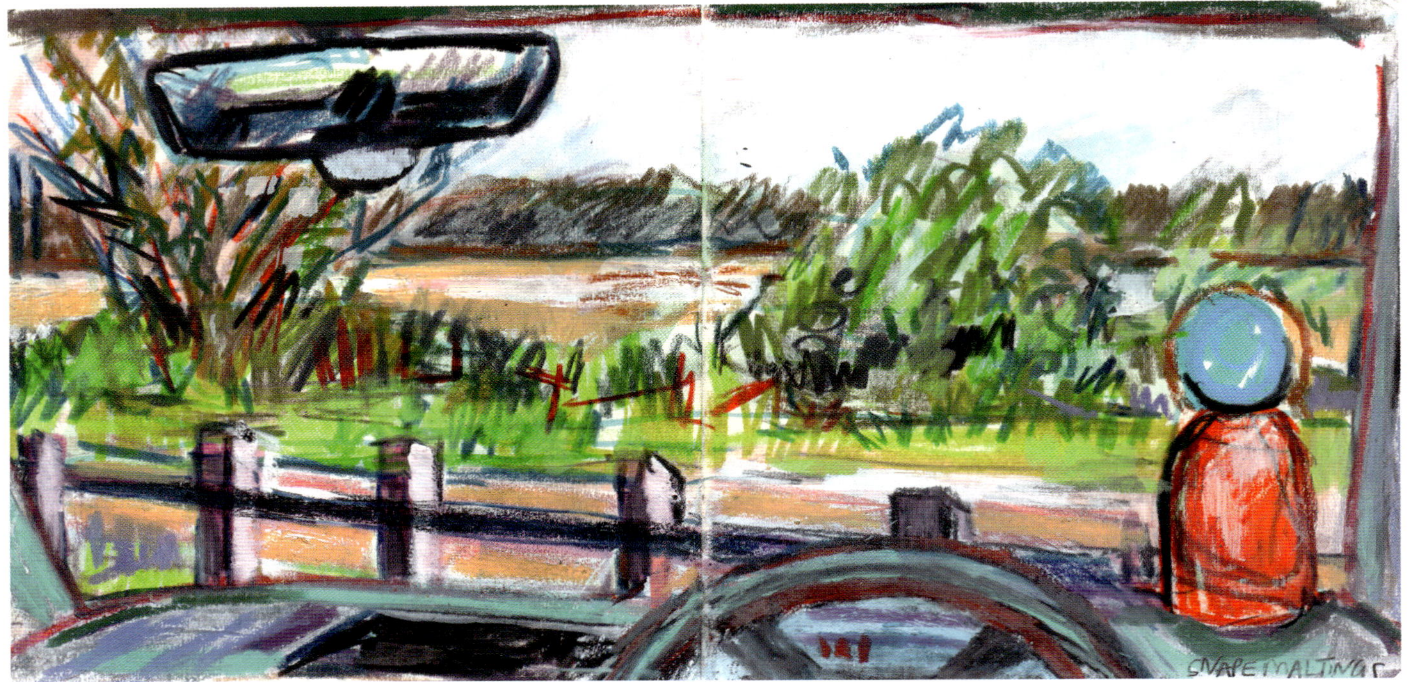

▲ Exercise 1: Drawing from a car

I drew this while on holiday in Suffolk in the camper van. It was a rainy day, and I decided to visit Snape Maltings; however, as soon as I parked the van, the weather took a turn for the worse, so I was proactive with my time and took my sketchbook out. It surprised me how quickly time passed, and, before I knew it, the weather had cleared and I could venture out. I used Caran d'Ache Luminance pencils for this, along with Caran d'Ache Neocolor® crayons.

▼ Exercise 2: Drawing while waiting

Airports are one of my favourite places to draw. There's always such an interesting energy in the atmosphere – excitement mixed with apprehension. There are also plenty of people sitting still, just whiling away the time chatting, eating or on their phones. I drew this while waiting for my flight to Japan. I loved the way the seat curved around and the composition of the chair and the suitcase. I used pencil and Caran d'Ache Luminance pencils for this drawing.

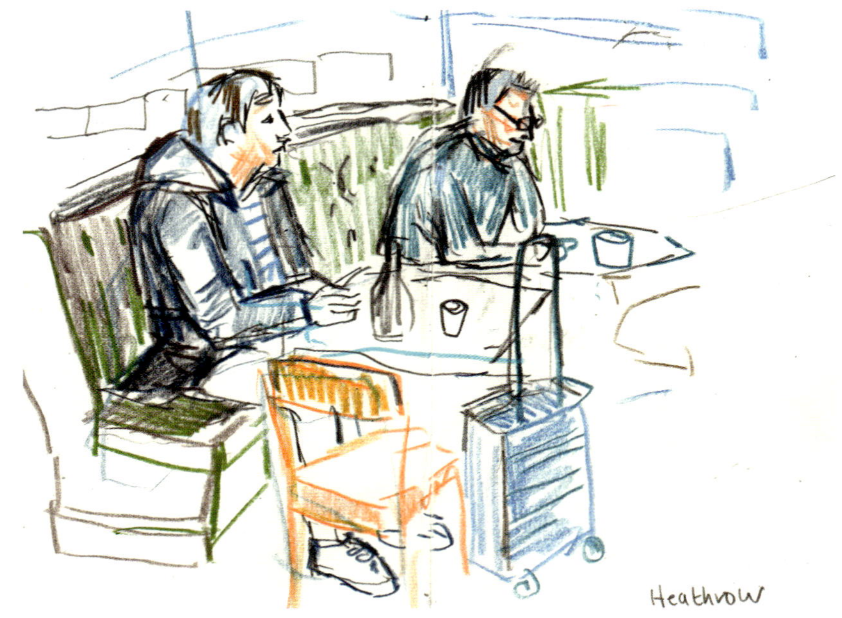

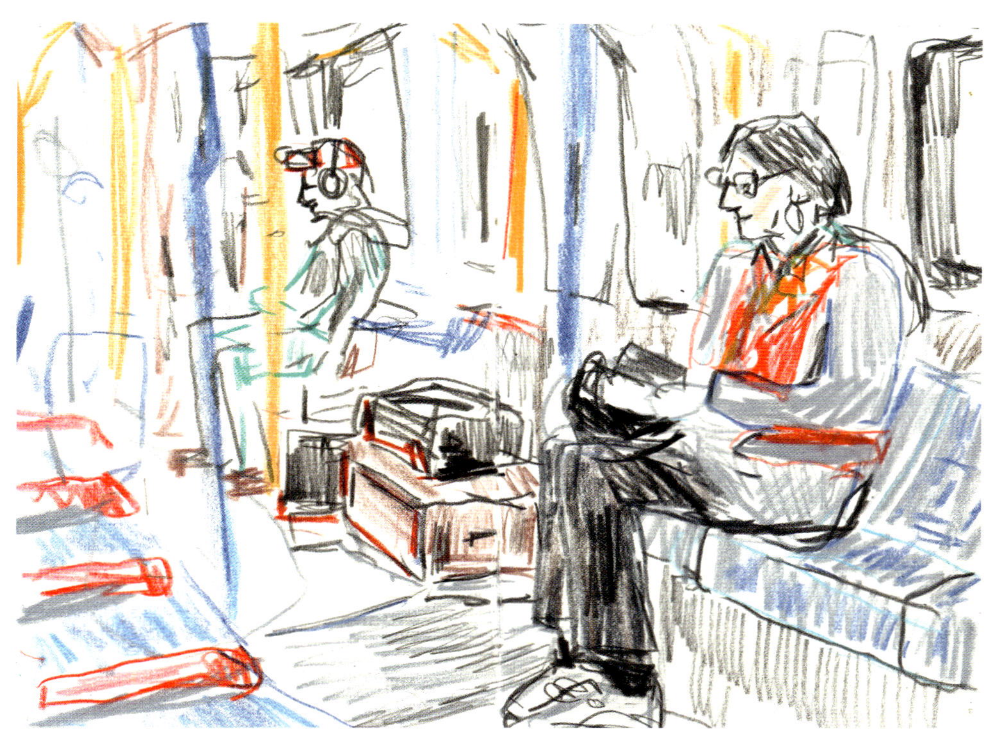

While on a relatively empty tube carriage en route to Heathrow, I seized the opportunity to do this quick sketch. I loved the colours the lady was wearing as they echoed the décor of the train. It took me about fifteen minutes; I moved very quickly across the page, concentrating on the lady first and then the other passenger to the left. I then filled in the details of the carriage interior as I knew they wouldn't move.

▶ Exercise 4: Drawing in a café, pub or restaurant

In March last year, I took a trip to Vienna for two reasons – to meet Kathi, one of the Sketch Squad members, and to draw in the wonderful cafés. Over the years, I had read so much about Vienna café culture and I was keen to experience it for myself. This is one of many drawings I did during my stay. I enjoyed an apple strudel and coffee at the famous Café Central and took my time to do this sketch. It took me just over half an hour.

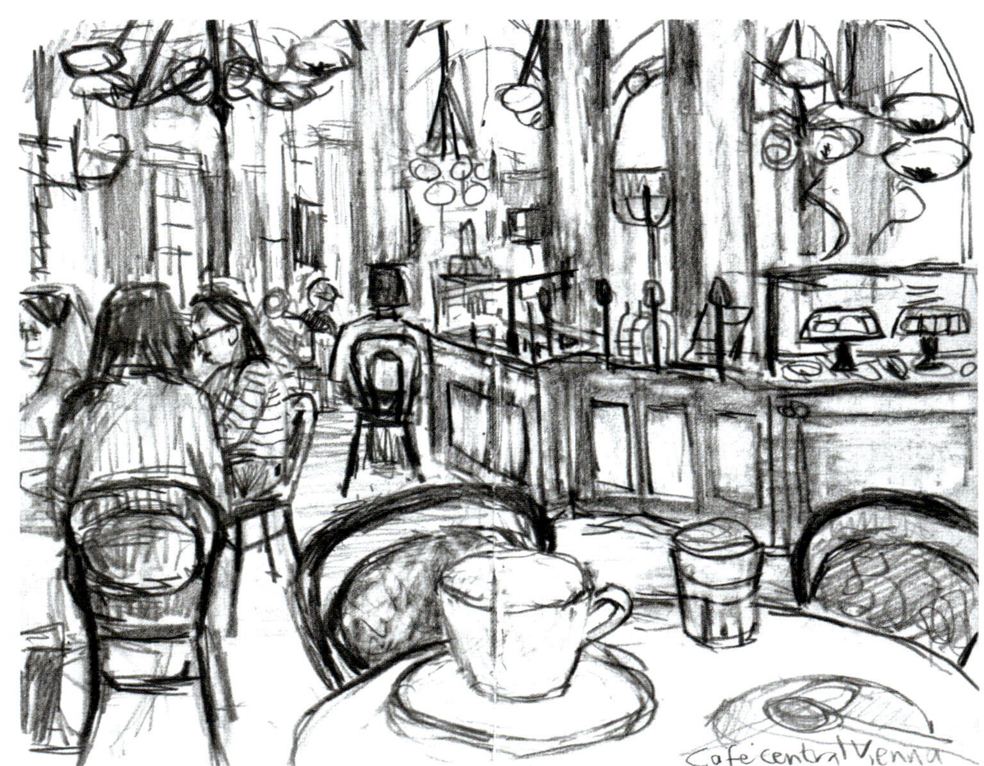

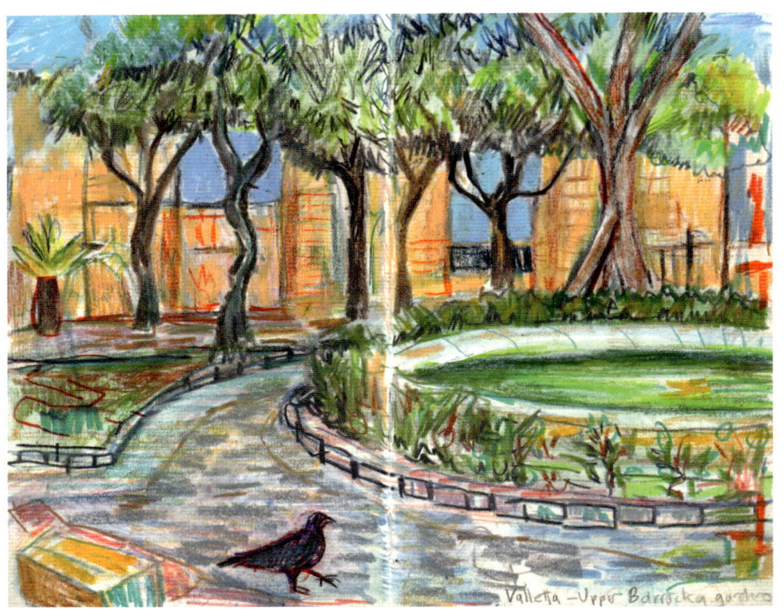

◄ Exercise 5: Drawing in a park

This drawing was done in Upper Barrakka Park in Valletta, Malta. I loved the way the park wall framed the intense blue sky and the succession of olive trees that lined the pond. It had been a busy day of drawing for me, and this was the last one I completed. I find the first and the last drawings of the day are often the most enjoyable for me. I felt relaxed and calm from my day of sketching and I feel this comes across in the sketch.

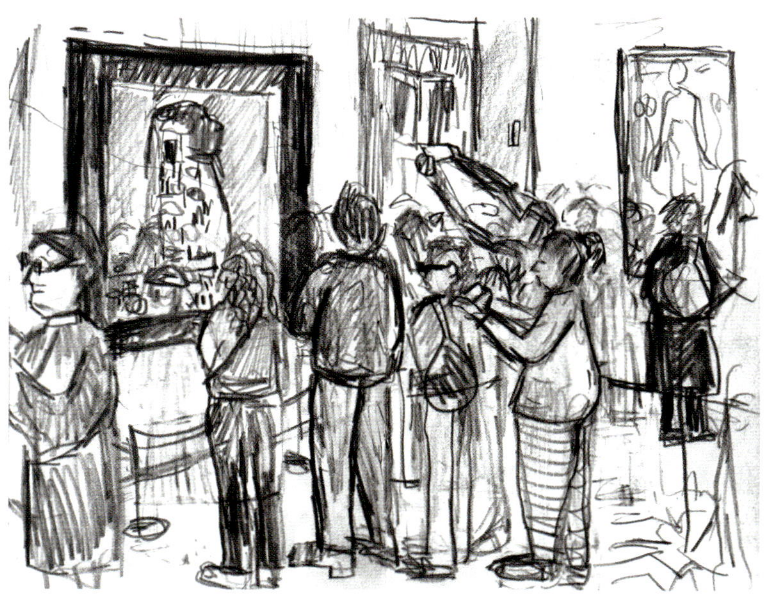

◄ Exercise 6: Drawing in an art gallery or museum

It always fascinates me when I'm in a gallery or a museum just how few people stop and look at the artwork but instead take photos. This was the case at Belvedere Museum in Vienna in the room that showcases Gustav Klimt's *The Kiss*. It was so busy in this room that it made for an exciting and dynamic place to draw. My pencil was flying across the page as I tried to capture the hungry hordes of people trying to take a photo or a selfie with the painting. This drawing took me forty-five minutes and I used a 4B pencil.

Sketch Squad: Drawing in public

Exercise 1: Drawing from a car

▶ *Kathi*

Kathi doesn't have a car so found this one difficult to complete. The logistics of having to get her mum to drive her somewhere made her feel anxious about starting the drawing and she began to overthink it. She had planned to draw with her coloured pencils, however, as she was feeling stressed out already, she made the decision to simplify her drawing and just use pencil. Do bear this in mind – you may set out with ambitious goals with your drawing, but sometimes it's better to scale things back and simplify your plans.

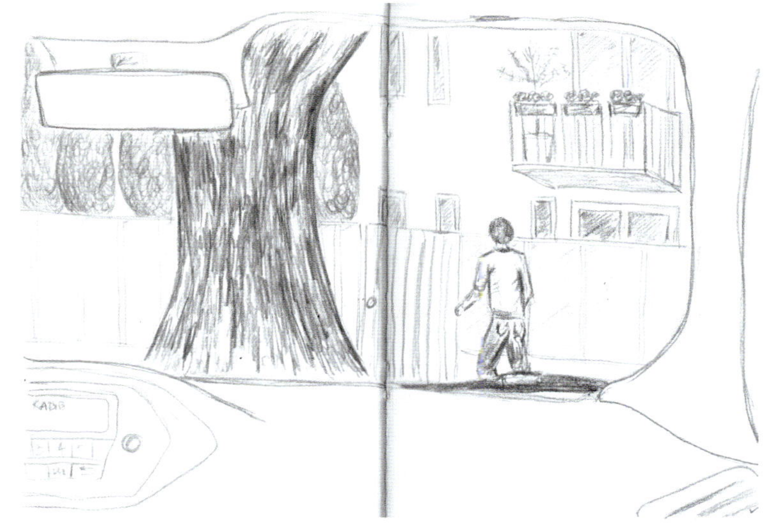

▼ *Eva*

Eva works from home in a remote part of Wales. She was having a busy and stressful day, so she decided to just drive outside her village, park in a layby and draw. She liked how the road disappeared around the turn and how the trees lined the side of the road. She wrote: 'Just taking some time to draw helped me stop and breathe for a little while. Drawing is really the best kind of mindfulness.'

▲ *Claire*

Claire uses her car a lot for work, so she was excited about doing this exercise, as it's something she hadn't thought about before. She chose to draw the inside as well as the outside as she liked the combination of non-organic material (the inside of the car) and organic material (the bush outside). Having completed the exercise, she wrote that she's keen to explore other scenes from her car: 'I live in a part of Scotland where my outside drawing plans are often hampered by the weather, so this is a brilliant option when I want to draw but don't want to get wet!'

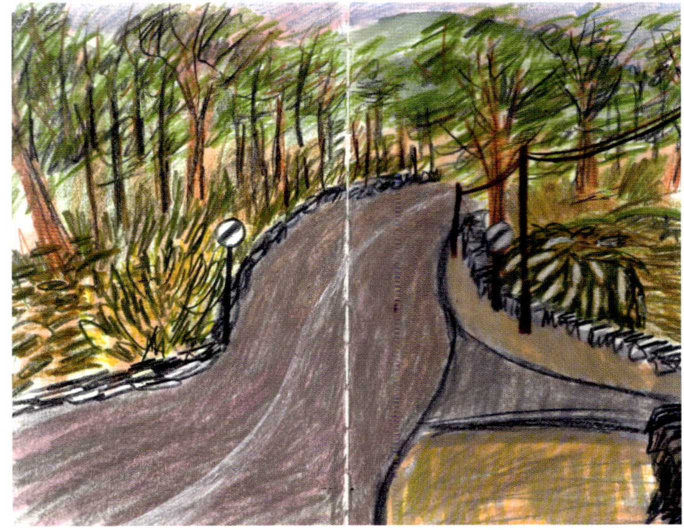

Exercise 2: Drawing while waiting

▶ *Eva*

Like me, Eva enjoys drawing at airports, so while waiting for her flight to Nepal, she did a series of drawings using her favourite coloured pencils, Derwent Chromaflow. Eva is conscious of not spending too much time scrolling on her phone and finds drawing a perfect way to fill that gap while waiting.

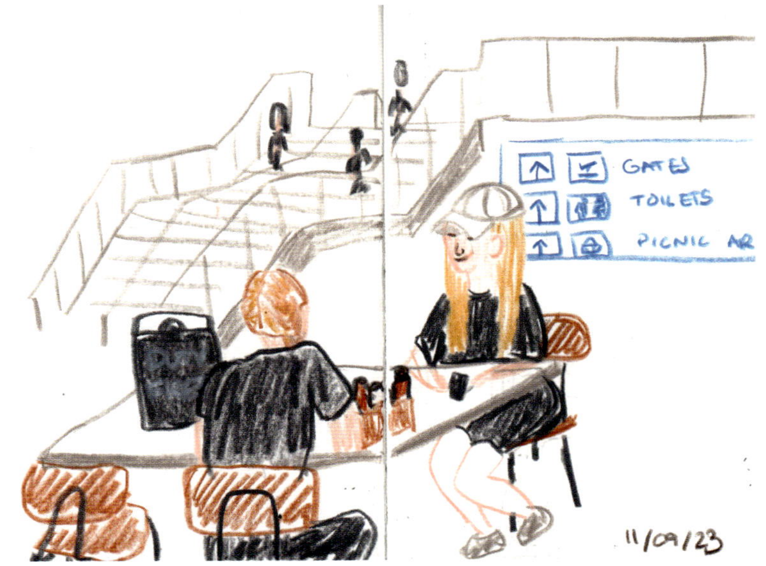

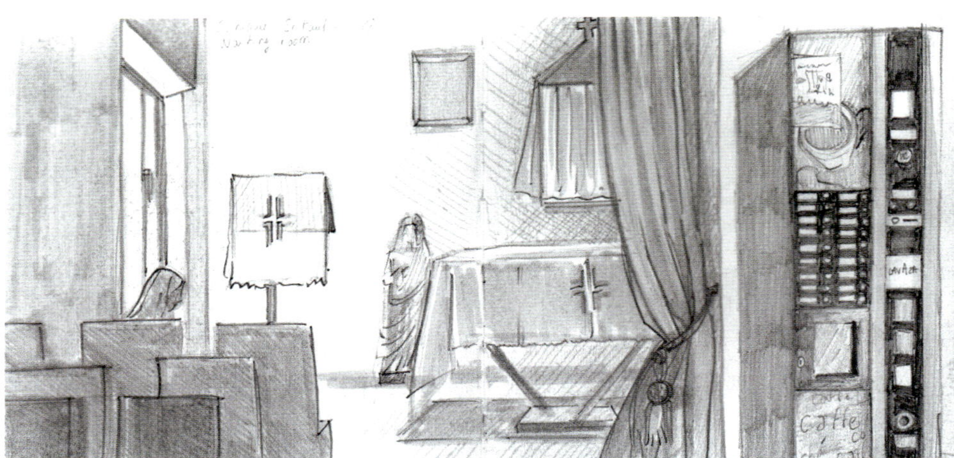

◀ *Diane*

Diane drew this while waiting for her grandfather, who lives in Martinique and was in hospital for some tests. There was a little chapel in the hospital, which she thought ironically looked like a funeral parlour. She chose to draw the scene as she liked the bizarre juxtaposition between the sombre chapel and the drinks vending machine. She also gets slightly anxious while waiting in hospitals, so this was a productive way to utilise the time while waiting for her grandfather.

▶ *Safa*

Safa was on her way to do Exercise 1, when she got a flat tyre. As she had all her kit with her, she took the opportunity to draw while waiting to get her tyre fixed. She had to make quick marks as the man fixing the tyres was moving at speed, so she just got down the key information. She surprised herself by how the drawing came together as she isn't used to working so fast. She realised that she was in a pattern of thinking: key information, mark making and dancing around the page.

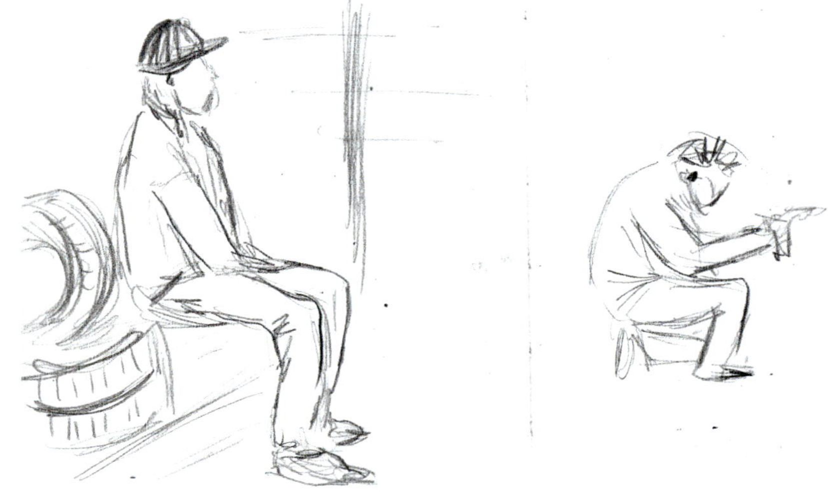

Exercise 3: Drawing on public transport

▶ *Anne*

This exercise was particularly tough for Anne, as she gets anxious on public transport and rarely uses it. However, she overrode her anxiety and gave it a go by drawing on a local tram. She chose to use fineliner pens as she finds their directness helps prevent her overthinking her lines. She then used a coloured brush pen to add detail of the interior of the tram. She admits that she didn't find the exercise enjoyable but the fact that she did it made her feel proud of herself, which is a good result.

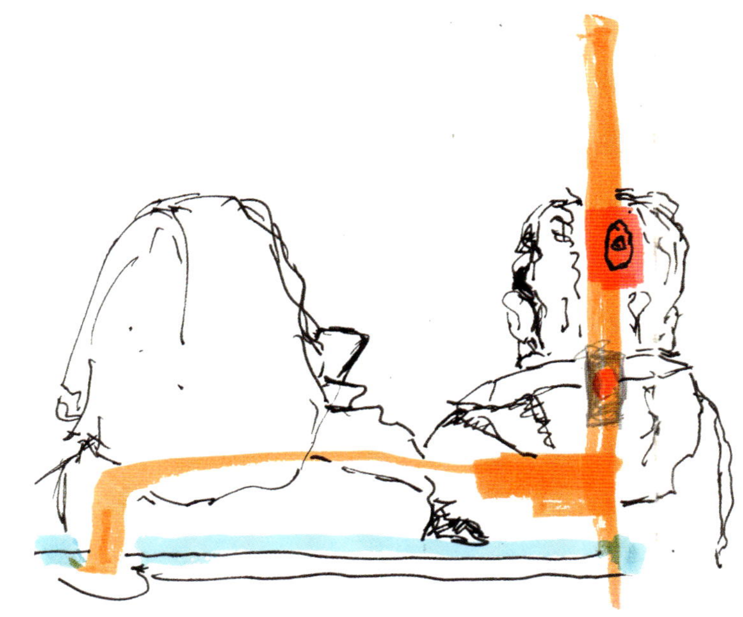

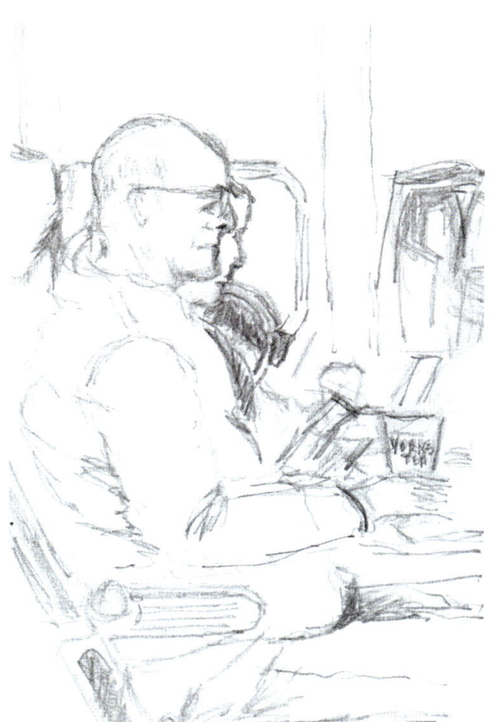

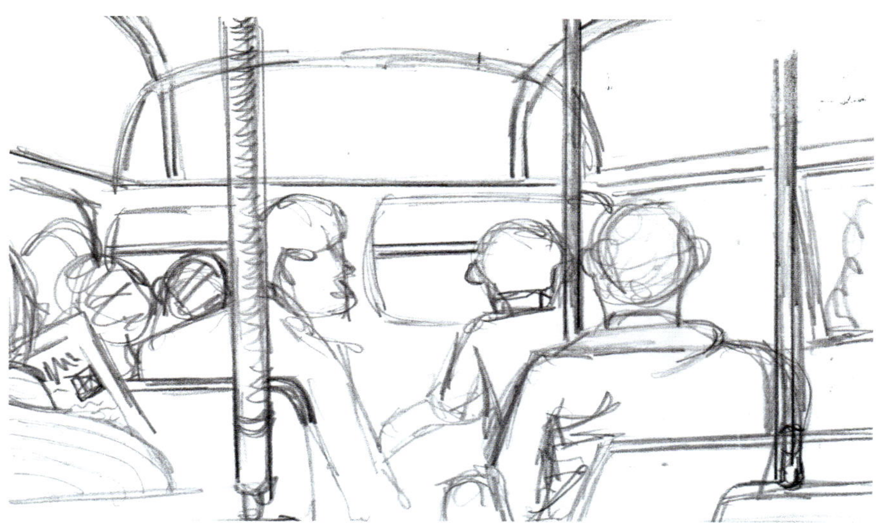

▲ *Hannah*

Hannah sketched this on a London bus. She found it exceptionally hard as the bus was busy and she was in such close proximity to the subject matter. She enjoyed the challenge but it's not something she would choose to do again.

As you progress through these exercises, there are inevitably going to be ones you enjoy more than others. This is part of discovering who you are as an artist – your likes and dislikes. The most important thing is that you give it a go, then you can make your mind up afterwards if it's something you want to revisit in the future.

▲ *Paula*

Paula drew this of her husband, Paul, while on a flight to Austria. Drawing on public transport was something she hadn't done before and she was curious to see how it would go. The flight was a little bumpy, but she enjoyed the way this affected her drawing as her lines became jagged and broken. How the environment we are in changes the way we sketch is one of the interesting things about drawing when out and about.

Exercise 4: Drawing in a café, pub or restaurant

▶ *Phyllis*

Phyllis drew this in her local café. The ladies sat there for over half an hour chatting away happily and enjoying their coffee. This meant that Phyllis had ample time to sketch them and their surroundings. She had to laugh at herself as she found she was getting irritated that the women were moving and changing position just when she was getting into the flow of the drawing.

As I mentioned before, this is one of the biggest challenges while drawing people out and about – the fact that they move. If you can accept this and approach it with excitement and anticipation as to what they do next, then you never know, you might just enjoy it!

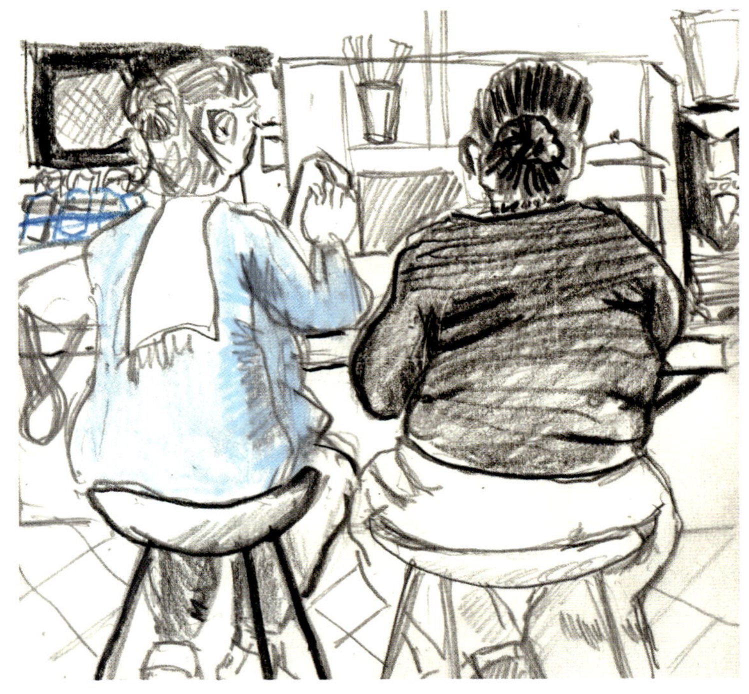

▶ *Jane*

Jane drew this while having lunch in a garden centre café. She carefully thought through her choice of venue, selecting a café that had a lot of space so she would feel more comfortable drawing in public. She deliberately chose a group who would be there for a while, as they were waiting for their lunch. She surprised herself by how much she enjoyed the drawing. Being inquisitive (I call it nosey) by nature, she found herself eavesdropping on the conversation and drawing for longer than she intended.

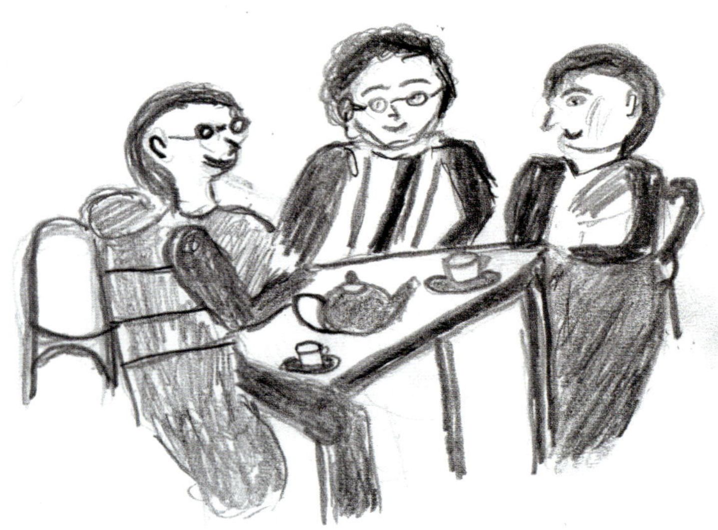

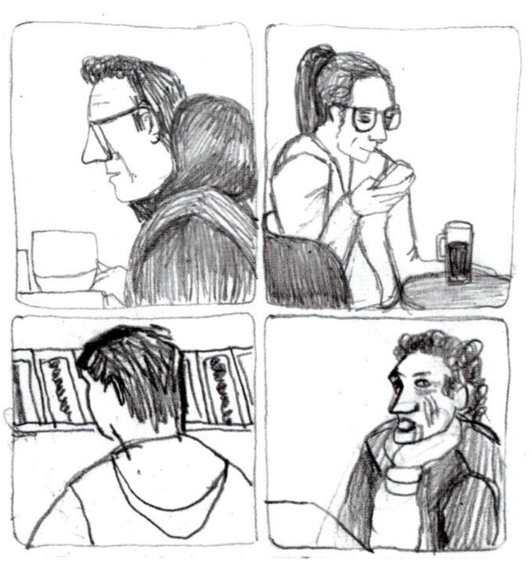

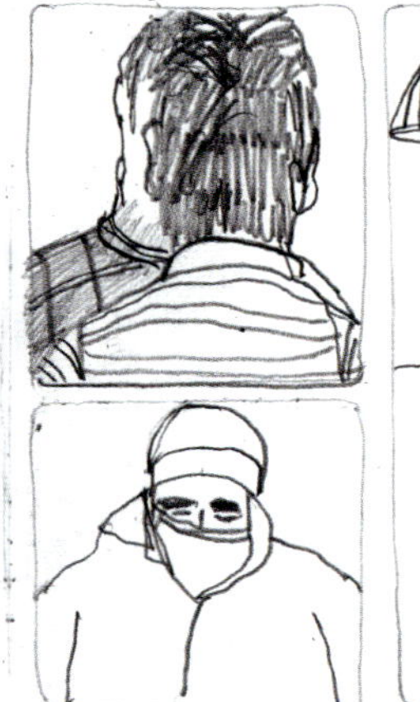

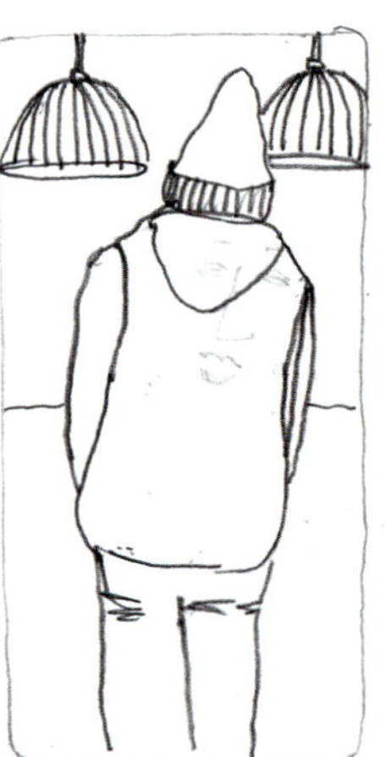

◀ *Niki*

Niki admits that she was nervous about the prospect of drawing in a café. However, to help her cope with this, she decided to use her smaller sketchbook and split her page into smaller, more manageable sections. This way she felt more capable of giving it a go. It is great if you find a way to make these exercises easier for yourself. I am only giving you guidelines; feel free to adapt them.

Exercise 5: Drawing in a park

▼ *Lucy*

Lucy and her family had a picnic in the park, and she told them beforehand that she would be sketching during their time there. She noted that while everybody was enjoying their sandwiches, she was enjoying doing her drawing. Drawing in a park is something she feels very comfortable with, and the confidence of the drawing shows this. She used watercolours, coloured pencils and a couple of Neocolor® crayons.

▶ *Diane*

Diane chose to draw in a park by the Seine, near where she lives in Paris. Initially, she intended to use multiple colours for the sketch, but after experimenting with a couple of warm-up drawings, she decided that a single colour was more effective in showing how the sun was shining through the trees. The red has a dynamic effect.

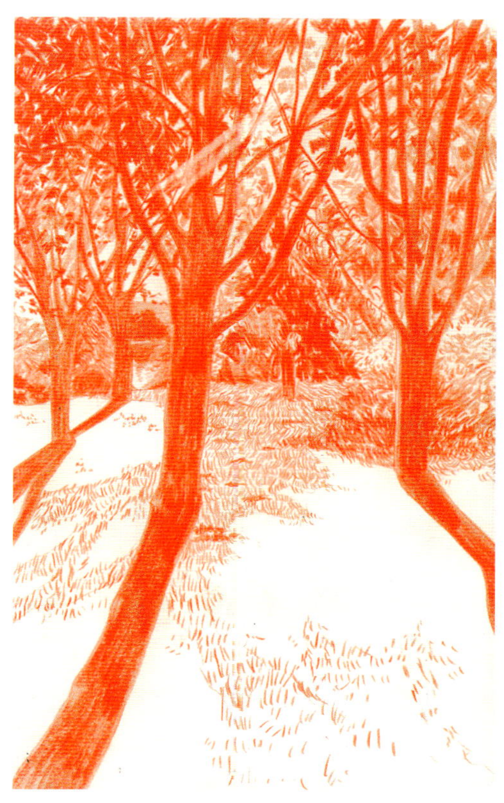

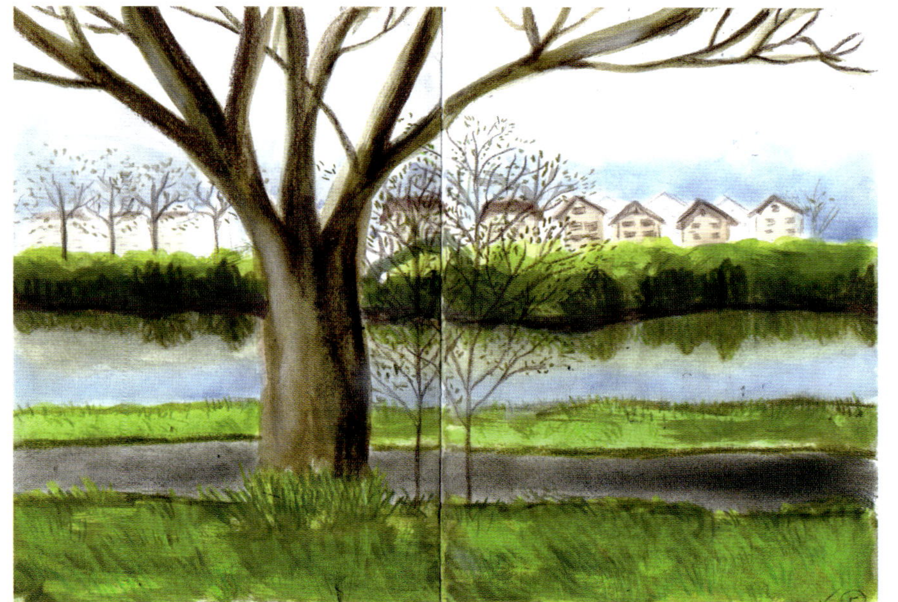

▼ *Phyllis*

This is a local park near where Phyllis lives in Santa Rosa. She takes her granddaughter there every week, so she decided to take her drawing materials and do this exercise there. She started drawing the pair on the table and thought she would stop there, but the park was teeming with activity and she didn't want to finish. The drawing took her around an hour using a mechanical pencil and a 3B graphite pencil.

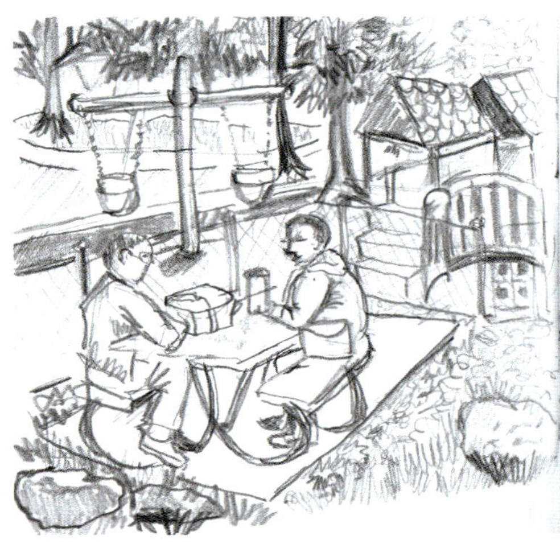

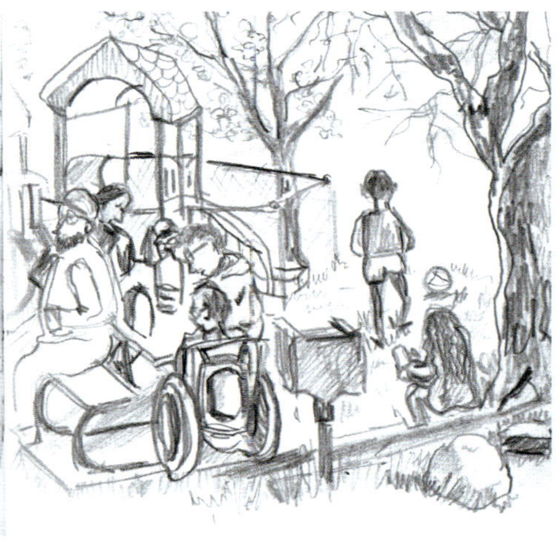

Exercise 6: Drawing in an art gallery or museum

▶ *Hannah*

Hannah found it really challenging to draw when visiting the Royal Academy of Arts in London. The main issue was that she felt the weight and gravitas of the artists on the wall around her – her imposter syndrome (see pages 96–7) was very loud at this point. To combat her nerves and ensure she completed the task, she aimed to get no more than a snapshot of the room itself and the people immediately in front of her. She also decided to spend no more than twenty minutes on the drawing. Having time limitations can really help to motivate you not to overthink and to get the drawing done.

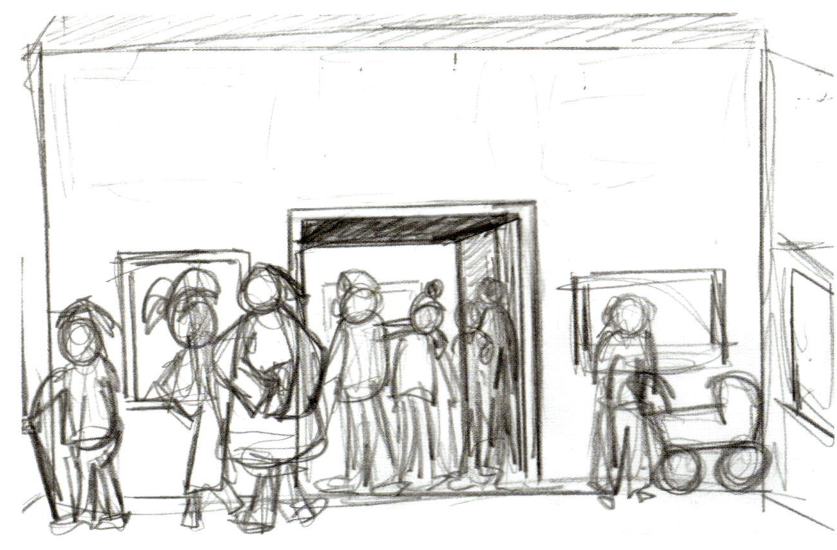

▼ *Anne*

Anne drew in a small museum in her home town of Sheffield. At first, she felt overwhelmed; however, she came up with the tactic of drawing the sculptures in the space and then populating the drawing with people in the museum. 'Taking time planning my approach really helped to not feel rushed when people were moving on.'

Anne found this a beneficial exercise to help build her confidence with drawing in public. This museum is a space where people are encouraged to draw and create, so the people who did come up and look at her work were supportive and interested in her drawing.

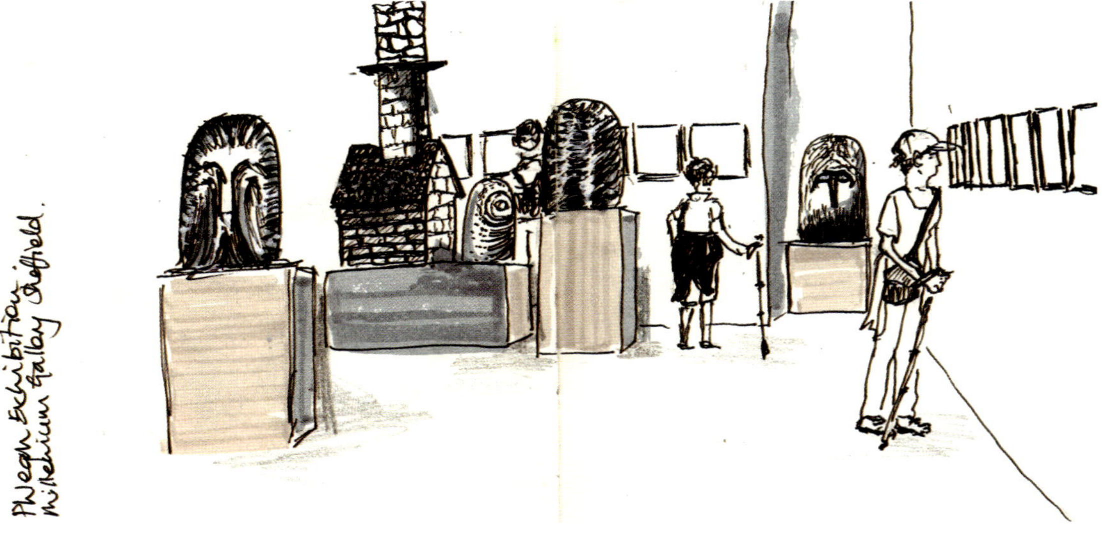

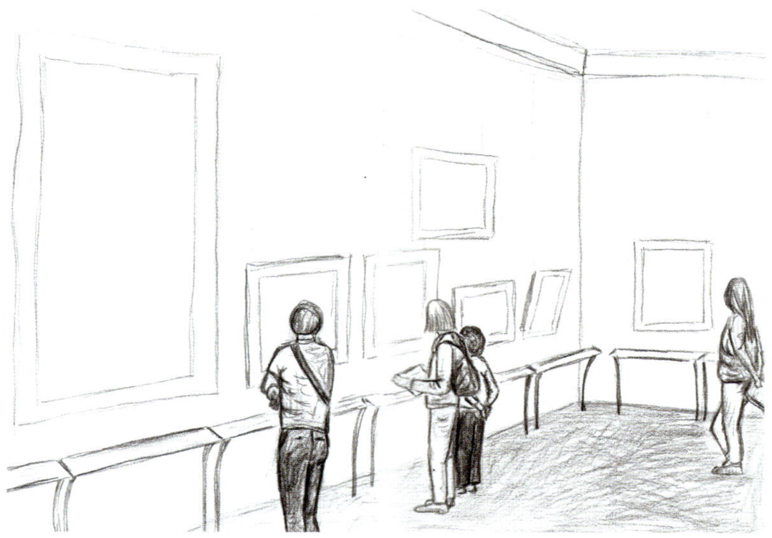

▲ *Kathi*

For Kathi, the most difficult part about drawing people in museums is that they move so quickly. She observed that people don't spend that much time looking at the paintings – they often just take a photo and move on. This drawing took her longer than anticipated, as she had to wait until people stood still enough for her to capture them.

What she found most interesting was that, as she was drawing, she became fascinated by what people were wearing – something she wouldn't have paid attention to normally. This is the joy of drawing the world around you; just taking the time to stop and sketch means that you observe things that might ordinarily pass you by.

Final thoughts

As we can see from the Squad's feedback, drawing in public to complete these exercises has been challenging for many different reasons. However, every member of the Squad completed all the exercises, and they all found them beneficial for building up their confidence with drawing in general, not just drawing out and about.

Safa wrote that, at the start, being outside with her sketchpad activated her imposter syndrome: 'Who do I think I am? An artist?' However, she gently reminded herself that she draws and prints regularly and that she is an artist, so there's no need to feel like an imposter at all.

This chapter will no doubt be challenging to you too, but I hope you enjoy it. Drawing in public can be great fun and very beneficial to your artistic journey. Once you have reached the end of this chapter, remember how you felt at the start. If this was something that you thought you couldn't do, and you did manage to do it then reflect on what other things in your life you might be putting off because you think you aren't capable. Drawing can be a gateway to achieving many other goals.

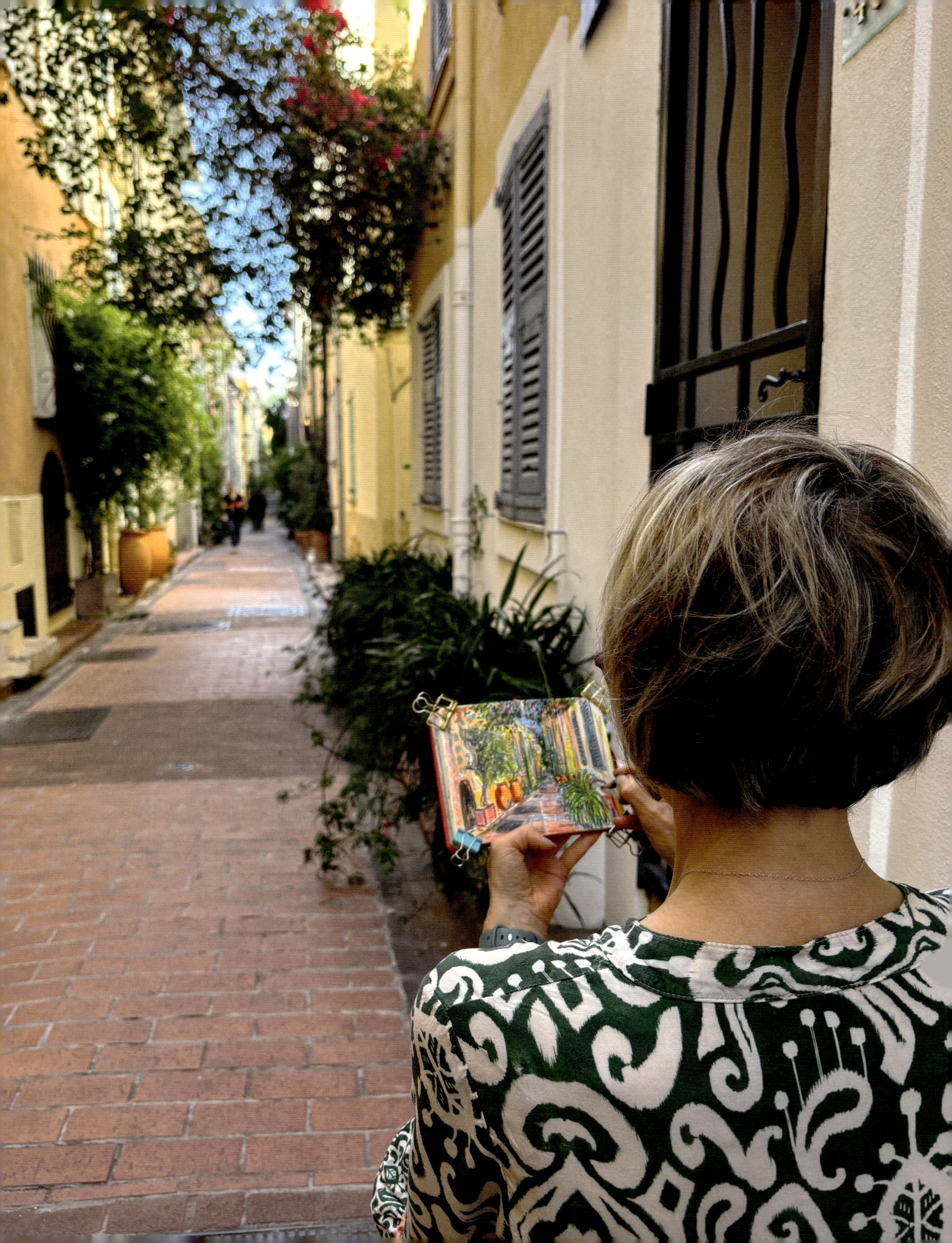

11
Dealing with comparison and envy

It would be remiss of me to not include a chapter on comparison and envy in this book. Alongside the inner critic, comparison and its partner envy are huge parts of our lives as creatives. Comparing ourselves to others is unavoidable, and if we compare ourselves negatively with others then we will inevitably become envious. Put simply, comparison is an action and envy is an emotion generated from that action – a potent emotion that can crush self-esteem, stifle creativity and inspire efforts to undermine others' successes.

The first thing we need to note is that comparison is totally normal. We all do it. There is no point beating yourself up for doing it. Comparing ourselves negatively is hard enough without adding a whole heap of shame on top. Throughout my years as an artist, comparison and envy have always been on my shoulder, sometimes weighing heavily and other times not so much.

From my experience as a teacher, I have seen many students suffer, often causing their work to come to a halt. Over the years, I've developed my own strategies to manage comparison and envy, turning it into more of a positive experience. By applying these strategies, I've become more confident, self-focused and balanced.

Tips to help you handle it

How does envy make you feel?

One of the first questions to ask yourself is: how does comparing yourself or envying others make you feel, both emotionally and physically?

Be brutally honest here, even if it makes you squirm to acknowledge you feel a certain way. Just write down all your thoughts and feelings – don't filter them.

How do you want to feel?

Now we have looked at how comparison and envy make you feel, consider how you want to feel instead. When I first asked myself this, I noted that I wanted to feel calm and centred, able to celebrate the success of others. I wanted to be clear about my own goals and confident of my path moving forward. So, over to you; how do you want to feel?

What can you do to combat these feelings?

Now that we have acknowledged how comparison and envy make us feel and how we want to feel, we can move on to dealing with it as it happens. You might want to use these suggestions when you are actively comparing yourself and feeling envious, or just reflect on a time when you were and try and put yourself back in that position.

Ask yourself if there's anything going on in your life at present as to why you might be feeling particularly susceptible to comparison and envy. I find if I'm feeling generally down on myself physically, I'm more likely to compare myself professionally.

The next thing I advise is to take a break. I find going for a walk helps me clear my head. There's something about the repetitive movement of putting one foot in front of another that quietens my mind and allows me to get my thoughts in order.

Exercises to combat it

Once you have returned from your break, it's time to ask yourselves some questions and dig a bit deeper. You might want to get a notebook and pen for this bit – or even better, do these exercises in your sketchbook.

What are you envious of?

Ask yourself what is it about someone else's work that you like and think is 'good' or better than yours? You might admire their use of line or colour or the way they draw trees. Be as specific as possible. Just keep reminding yourself you are gathering information to help yourself.

Celebrate their work

Now that you have this information, it's time to recognise the artist you are comparing yourself to and celebrate them. Acknowledge their hard work, the time they have invested in their creativity and the results they have achieved. Thank them for leading the way and providing you with a road map as to how you want to progress. Once you see them through the lens of kindness it's harder to see them as a trigger for your comparison and envy.

Let their work inspire yours

Once you have thanked them, use the information you gathered earlier to enhance your own work. Let's say you admire the looseness in their work – the way it appears full of life – and you would like your work to be freer and more organic, how could you achieve this? One thing you could do is set a time limit on your drawings so you don't overdo them. You could hold your pencil with a looser grip or draw with your non-dominant hand (see page 42). Make a list and work your way through it.

Be aware of time and experience

Acknowledge that we all have a different timescale. There's no point in comparing and envying someone who has been making art for years when you are just starting out. Remind yourself of the famous mantra, 'Run your own race'.

Don't be blinded by social media

Remember that social media is heavily curated. We all want to put our best work out there. Very few artists show what they think is a weak piece of work. We are often comparing our 'behind-the-scenes' work to their highlight reel.

Be your own cheerleader

One thing I'm sure of is that self-confidence helps to cure comparison and envy. It takes time, patience and practice to be comfortable with patting yourself on the back. It's always helpful to have a list of your artistic achievements to reflect on – something you can pull out and read in times like these.

Work on building an abundance mindset

Often comparison is linked to scarcity; we think if they've got that, we can't have it. This isn't the case. There's so much abundance in creativity, and there are plenty of people to share our creativity with. Just because someone likes someone else's work doesn't mean they don't like yours!

Let go of perfectionism

Remind yourself it doesn't have to be perfect; good enough will do just fine. Perfectionism often goes hand in hand with comparison – a lethal combination. I had to let go of perfectionism a long time ago as I just wasn't achieving anything. If I was still in a perfectionist mindset, I wouldn't have finished writing my first book!

See through others' eyes

It can be helpful to realise that someone else might be comparing themselves with and envying you. They might see your work as fabulous and think that you have your life sorted and you live in a constant bubble of happiness and creativity.

Look inward, not outward

If you must compare, try reflecting on your current work alongside your past creations. I can almost guarantee you will be surprised by how far you have come. You might also rediscover some of the qualities of your earlier work that you may want to revisit.

Trust the process

Turning comparison into a positive experience takes time and effort. I rarely experience a bad attack of comparison and envy now, but it's taken me years to get here. If you do the mental work, your physical work will benefit, I promise.

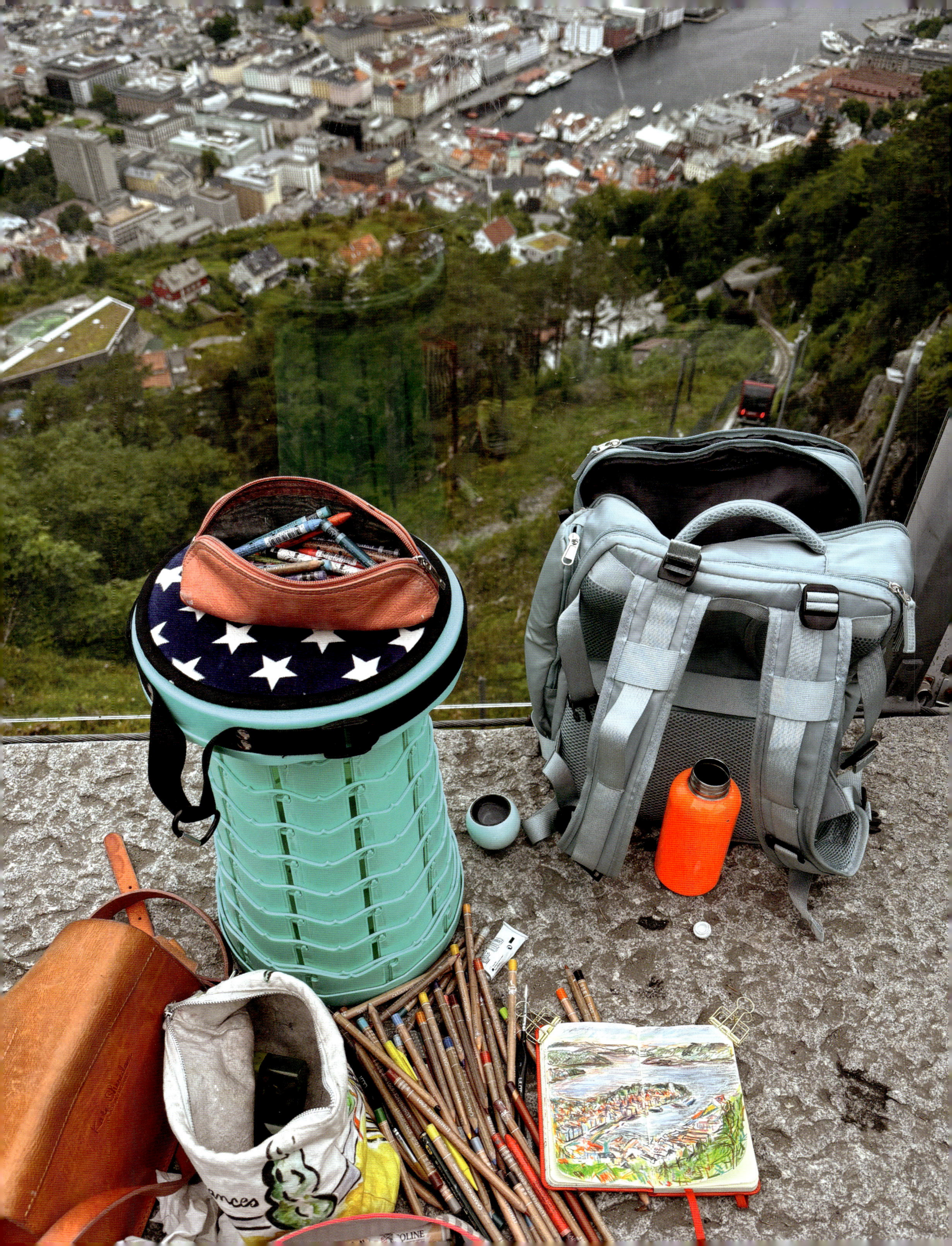

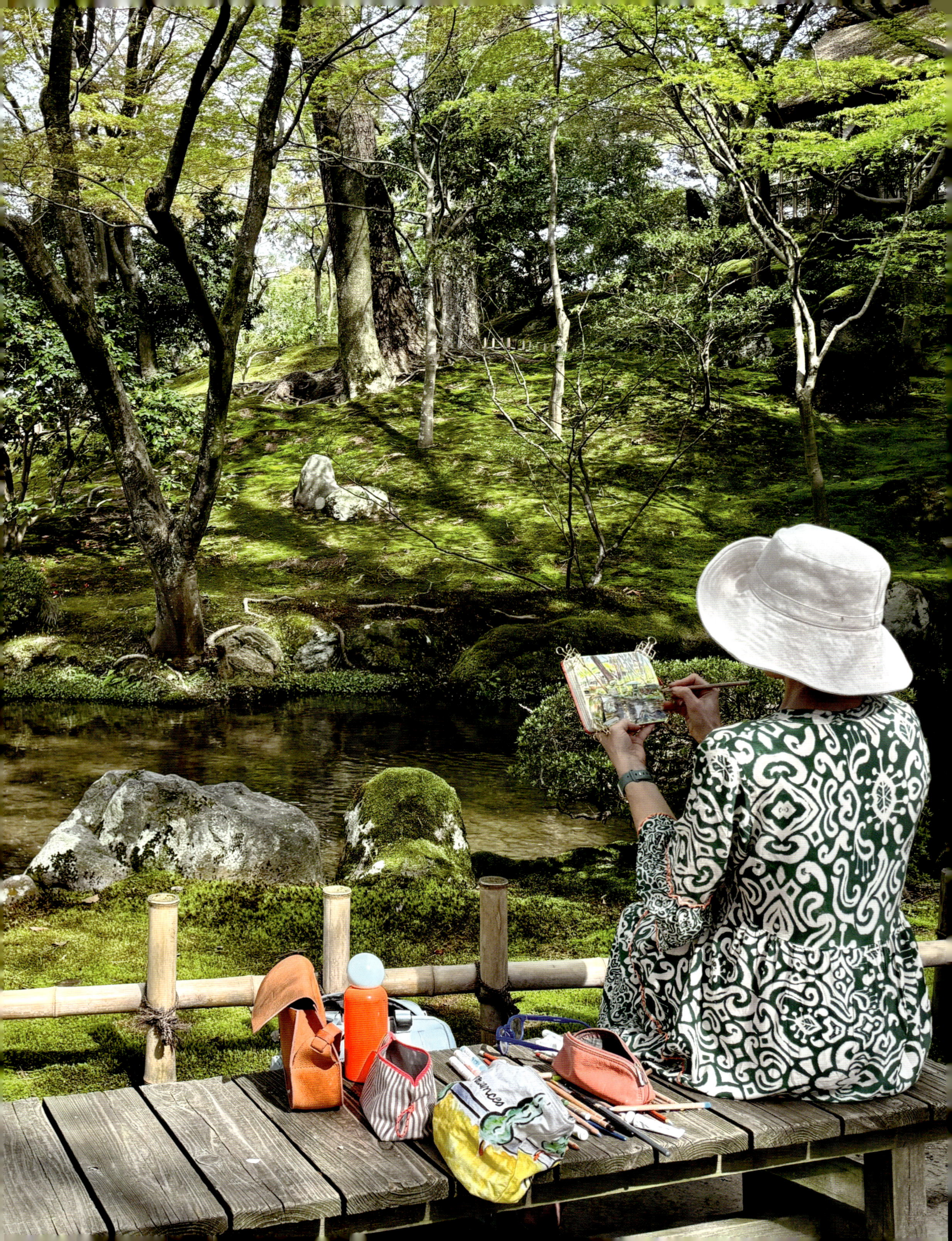

12
Drawing on holiday

Now you have plenty of experience in drawing outside in public, I hope you have gained enough confidence to take your sketchbook with you on holiday. I bet many of you have done this, with every intention of drawing while away, only to find that you bring them back untouched? I'll be honest and say that I have, many times. After too many trips like this, I took some time to reflect on what would make it easier for me to achieve my goal of drawing while away. I came up with a list of ideas and started to implement them on my travels.

Top tips to help you get drawing on holiday

Tell people your plans and compromise

Most of the time, I travel alone and I travel to draw. This means I only have myself to please, and if I want to spend the whole day drawing, that's just fine. However, most of you will be going away with friends and family with whom you want to spend time, and they'll want to spend time with you. Therefore, if you want to commit to drawing while away then I advise you to talk to them before you go. Make it clear that an important part of the holiday for you is to have some time drawing. This means that they will know what to expect and won't be surprised. You are also making yourself accountable and verbalising your intentions – they will be expecting you to draw now too.

Plan what to take with you

When you start travel sketching, it's important to keep your kit simple so you won't be overwhelmed with what to use. Look back at the kit list on page 66 and be selective with your choices – don't take everything, just the tools and materials you feel most comfortable with or those you are curious about experimenting with. Keep your bag portable and lightweight. You might want to think about tailoring your palette to the place you are visiting – for example, when I'm drawing in the UK in spring, I always make sure I have plenty of green pencils with me.

Draw on your first day away

I can almost guarantee if you don't draw the first day that you are on holiday then you won't draw at all. If you put it off, it will become something you start to fear. Your sketchbook will be glaring at you, making you feel guilty.

My advice is to jump straight in. As soon as you arrive, do a quick recce of your surroundings and just find something to draw. Don't overcomplicate it, just choose something that takes your eye and commit to drawing it as soon as you can. This way, you feel good that you have started and you are inspired to continue throughout your break.

Remind yourself to enjoy the moment

Don't worry about creating a masterpiece or a beautiful page in your sketchbook. Drawing on holiday is about the experience, not just the result. In other words, try to enjoy the moment and don't worry too much about the outcome.

Drawing while travelling is a great way to slow down and take in your surroundings. Keep reminding yourself of how much you enjoy drawing, how much better you feel after it and your 'why' (see Chapter 1).

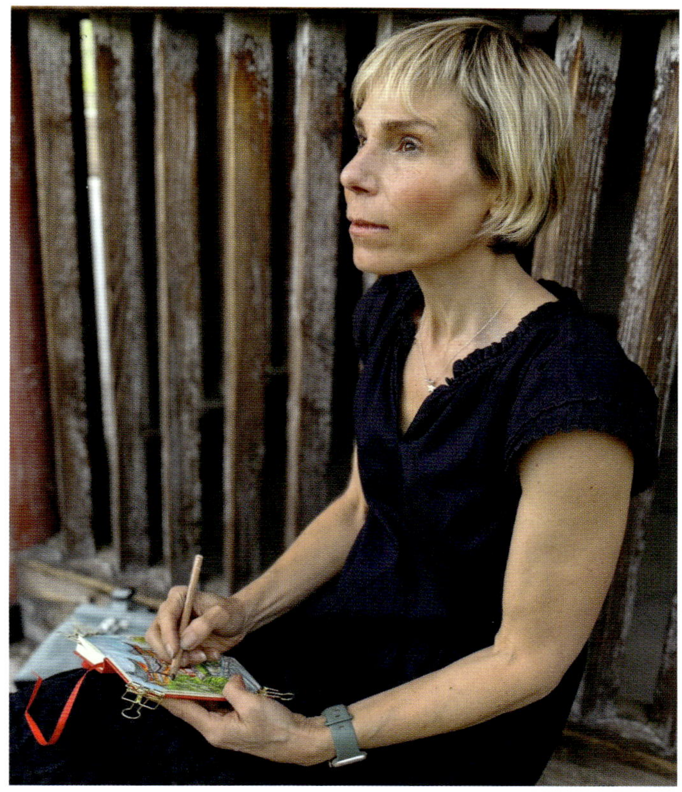

Focus on the future

Look ahead to when you are heading home and you have time to flick through your sketchpad. Imagine how good it will feel when you look at what you have achieved and think about how much you enjoyed your time just looking, slowing down and observing. I find forward-thinking like this really motivates me.

My travel sketchbooks are so important to me. I open a page and I'm instantly transported to the time and place – much more so than looking at a photograph. I remember where I was sitting, the people around me, the time of day, what the weather was like; some drawings can even evoke smells. It's a truly magical way of recording your trip.

With these tips in mind, here are the suggested exercises you might like to try when you are on holiday. I've designed them so that you can repeat them again and again for future holidays – they are easy to remember and can be done quickly.

Exercise 1:

First-day drawing (30 minutes–1 hour)

As I mentioned earlier, it's important to draw the first day so that you set the pace and feel excited about future drawings. It really doesn't matter what you choose; just put pencil to paper. Give yourself a timeframe, say half an hour, and really celebrate after you have done the drawing, no matter how you feel about it.

Why not show your work to whoever you are away with? This helps to build up confidence with sharing your work and getting feedback. Feel proud of yourself for honouring your commitment to doing something for you.

Exercise 2:

Draw your view (30 minutes–1 hour)

As we did in Chapter 5, Exercise 3 (see page 55) choose a view from where you are staying and draw from it. It doesn't have to be from a window; it could be from an open door or another viewing platform. The idea is to familiarise yourself with your new accommodation and surroundings and get to know them better.

This also serves as a good warm-up before you embark on drawing while out and about. I always try and do a drawing from my hotel window, even if the view isn't anything special. I normally find something of interest, and again, it's a lovely memory.

When the weather defeats you (1 hour minimum)

In an ideal world, the weather is beautiful when you go on holiday. You can sit in the sun (when it's not too hot) or the shade and draw to your heart's content. However, we all know this isn't always the case. This exercise, therefore, is for when you encounter days on your holiday that prevent you from drawing outside – when the weather is too hot, too rainy, too cold, etc.

Try drawing from your car or from any dry space that looks out to the weather. You might find a lovely little shelter from the sun while you are on a walk that provides the perfect location for a quick sketch.

Three drawings on location

I'm not going to be specific about the rest of the exercises as it's your holiday and you will all be going somewhere different. However, it would be great if you could do at least three different drawings. Here are some suggestions of places that you might like to draw:

A green space: I love to draw in parks and gardens when I'm away. It's a great way to see what's growing, how different cultures maintain their green spaces and how they use them. I was in Valencia last year and I loved how much outdoor exercise went on. I saw outdoor yoga, running clubs and numerous ball sports.

The beach: I could spend all my time on holiday drawing people on beaches. People act so differently on the beach; they move and sit in unusual ways. I love all the accoutrements that people bring along – it all makes such interesting subject matter.

A museum: If you are like me, one of the first things I do while away is visit the art galleries and museums. I often draw a couple of my favourite paintings or works of art. I also like to draw people when they are in the museum, looking at the art or meandering around the space. It's a great place for drawing people.

The markets: Another of my favourite things to do is draw the local markets. I love being among the stallholders, watching the hustle and bustle. I take my stool and perch in the corner or find a café in the market where I can place myself.

These are just some suggestions of what I love to draw. I look forward to seeing what you choose.

My drawings: On holiday

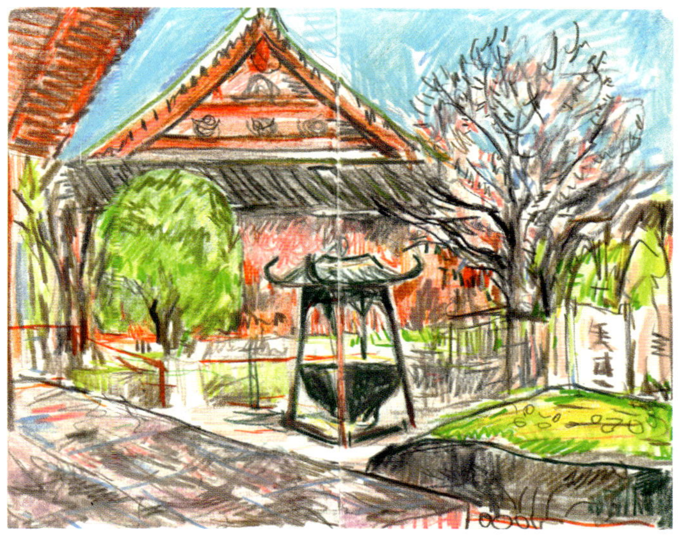

▲ Exercise 1: First-day drawing

Sensō-ji Temple, Tokyo
This drawing was done the first afternoon I arrived in Tokyo on my trip last year. After a fourteen-hour flight, I arrived at midday at my hotel in Asakusa. I couldn't check in until 3pm so I took my sketchpad out and headed to Sensō-ji Temple to draw. It was a beautiful day in April and the cherry blossom was out. I was terribly jet-lagged and felt all out of sorts, but I knew that drawing would help centre and ground me, and it worked its magic. This drawing took me around one hour.

▶ Exercise 3: When the weather defeats you

Charleston Farmhouse, Lewes, Sussex
Charleston Farmhouse in Sussex was the home of the artists Vanessa Bell and Duncan Grant, and it's one of my favourite places in the UK. Last August, during an exceptionally hot period, I spent three days drawing in the delightfully cool rooms. This drawing is of Vanessa and Duncan's studio. It took me around two hours to complete.

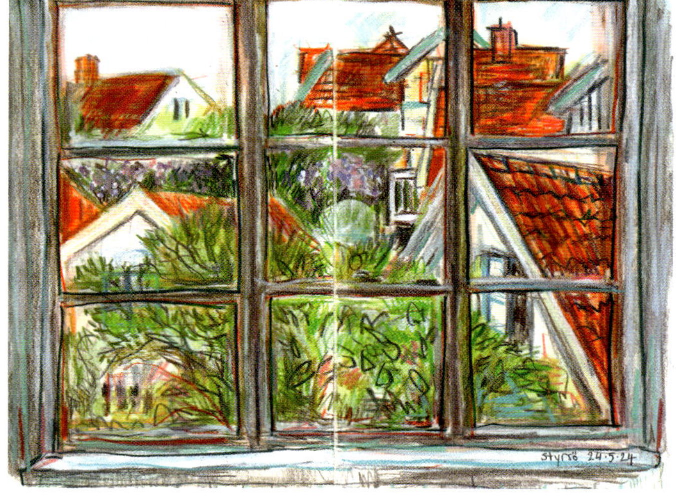

▲ Exercise 2: Draw your view

Styrso, Gothenburg
My Swedish friend, Susanne, is a photographer and took many of the photographs for this book. To take the photos, we stayed on Strysö island in the Gothenburg Archipelago for a few days this year, and this was the view from one of the windows in our accommodation. I used my Ecoline marker pens, Caran d'Ache pencils and Neocolor® crayons.

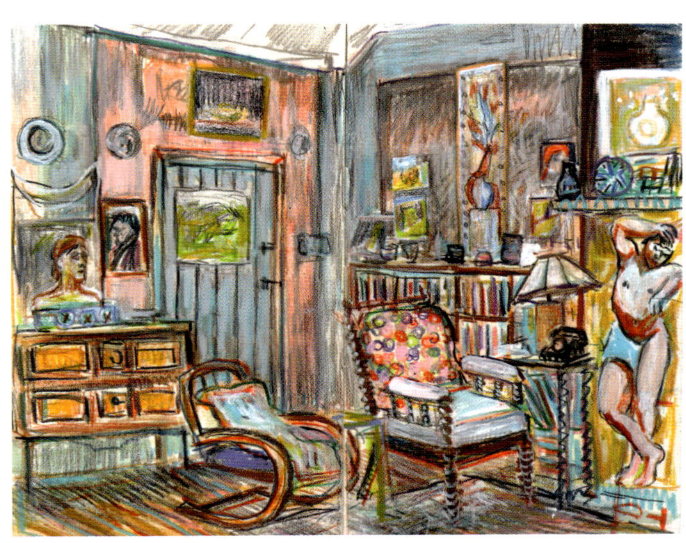

Exercise 4: Drawing on location

Here are a few of my drawings in different locations.

▶ *Nishiki Market, Kyoto, Japan*

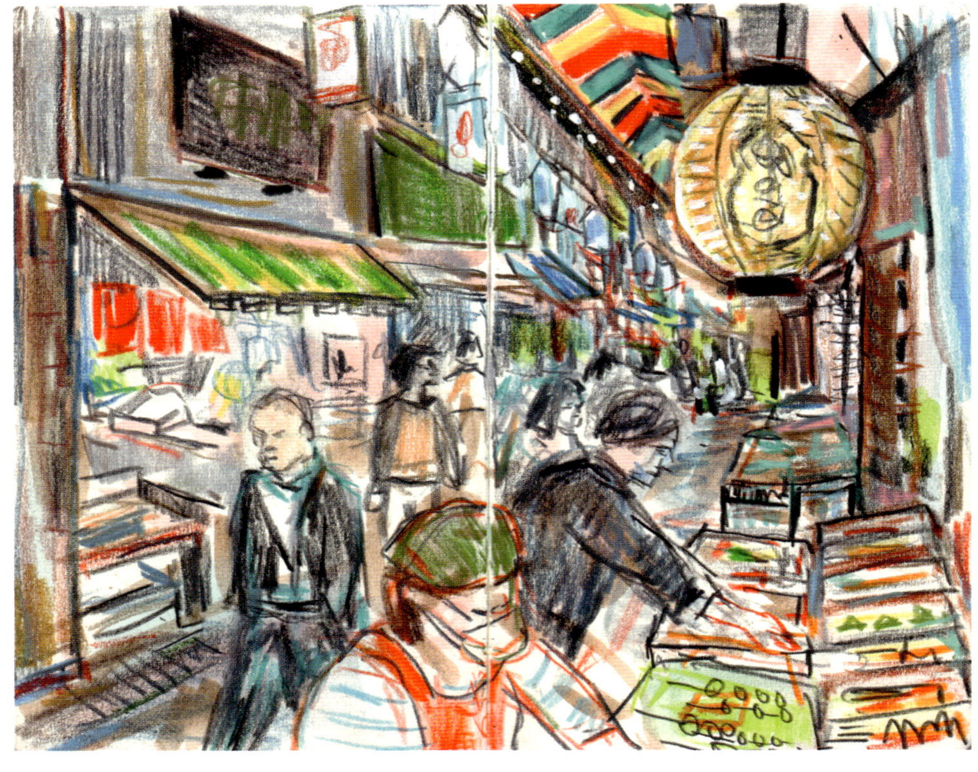

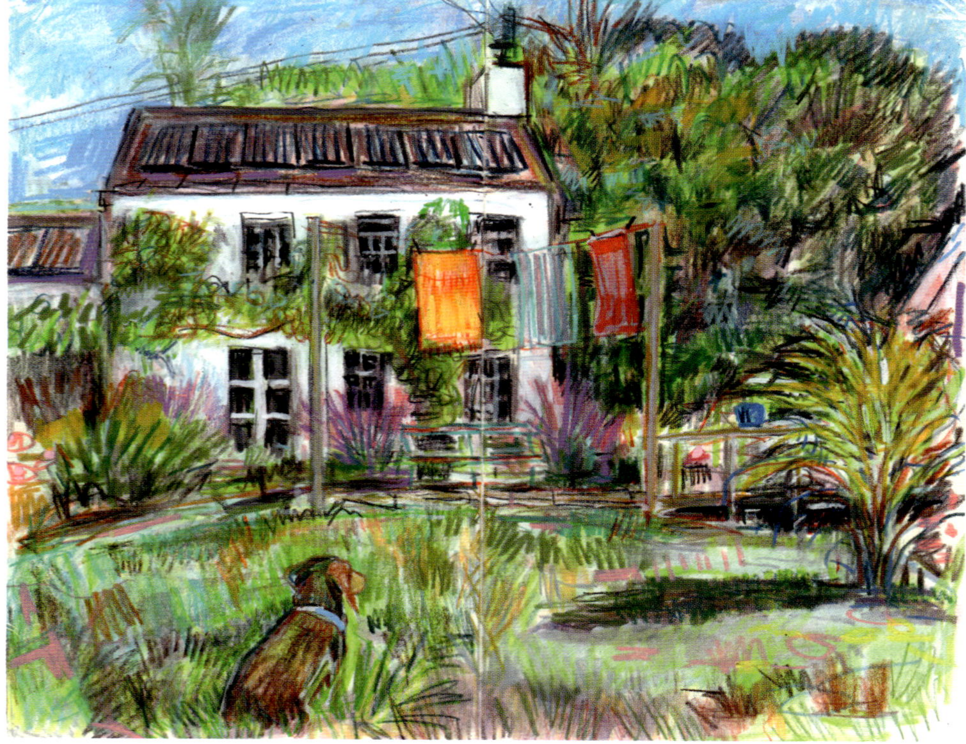

◀ *My friend Micki's garden in Wales*

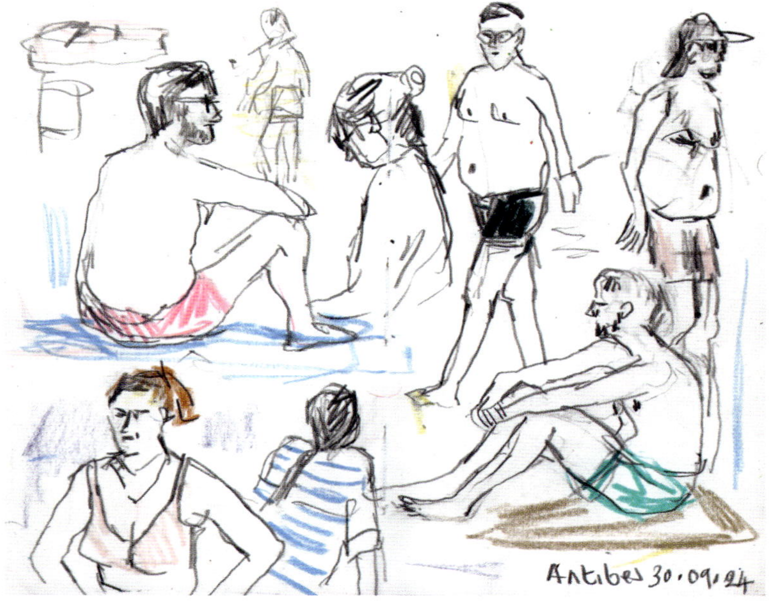

▶ *Antibes beach, south of France*

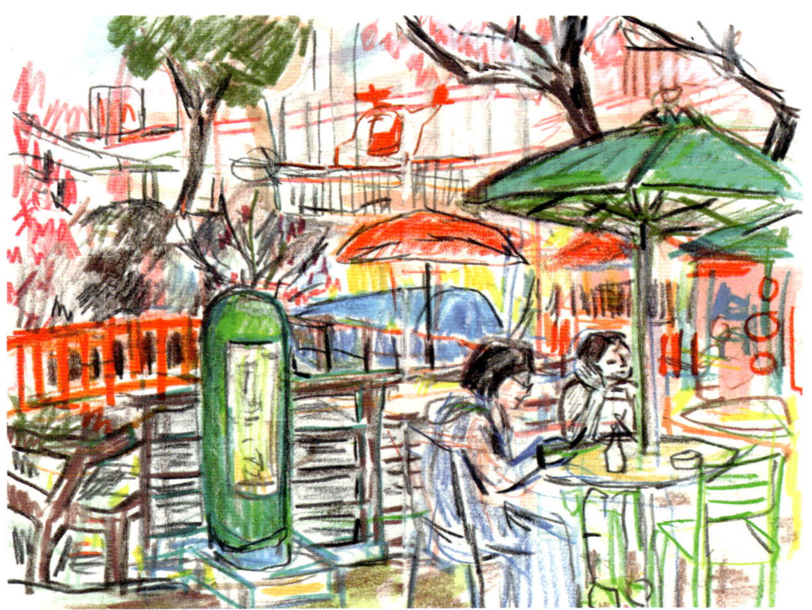

◀ *Asakusa Hanayashiki amusement park, Tokyo*

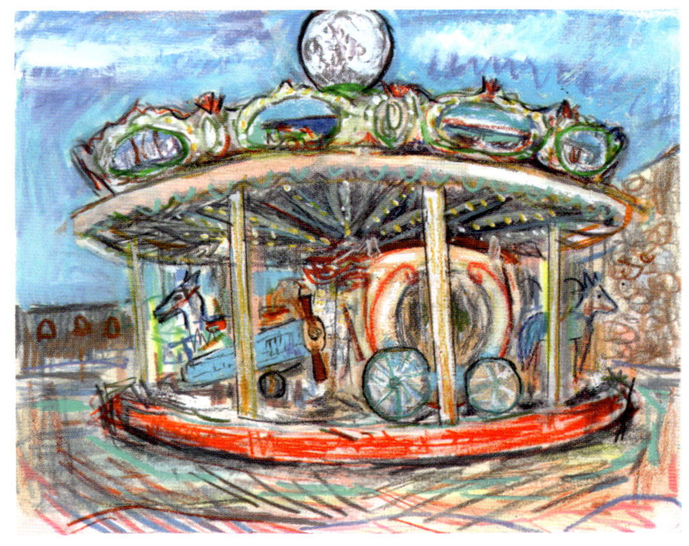

▶ *Carousel, Antibes, south of France*

Sketch Squad: On holiday

Now that we have looked at some of my drawings, let's see how the Sketch Squad got on with these exercises on holiday.

Exercise 1: First-day drawing

▶ *Niki*

Niki drew this on a plane to Barcelona. She admits that she is a very nervous flyer, so drawing proved to be a welcome distraction. She was tucked in a window seat, and this helped her feel more confident about getting her sketchpad out. 'I'm so pleased I did this drawing as it gave me the confidence to continue drawing once I got to Barcelona.'

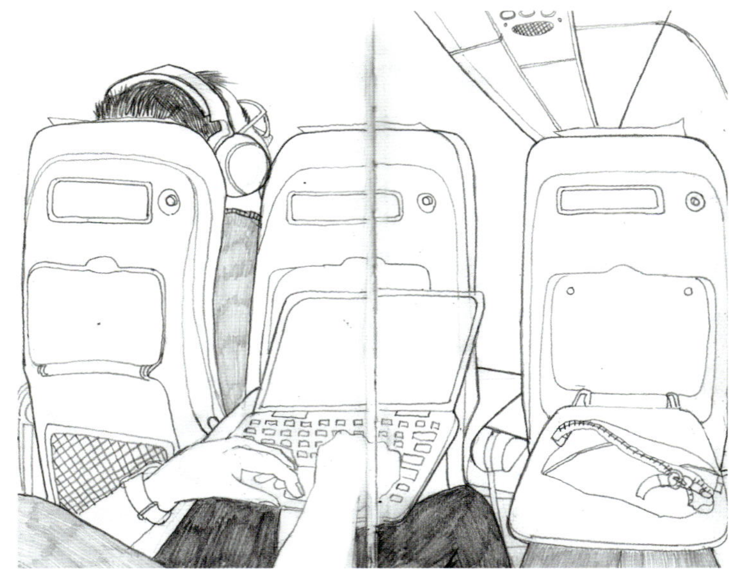

◀ *Lucy*

Lucy was travelling from Switzerland to visit her husband's family in the UK. She did this drawing while waiting to board the ferry. She writes: 'We were stuck in a long queue, and I knew I needed to seize the moment and draw, otherwise I would put it off. I'm pleased I did as it helped motivate me for the rest of our trip.'

◀ *Kathi*

Kathi spent the weekend in Prague with the intention of completing the exercises in this chapter. She writes that she felt a little overwhelmed at the start but decided to work in her small sketchbook and just get drawing straight away. She chose to draw the tea-making facilities in her room and says it helped to motivate her.

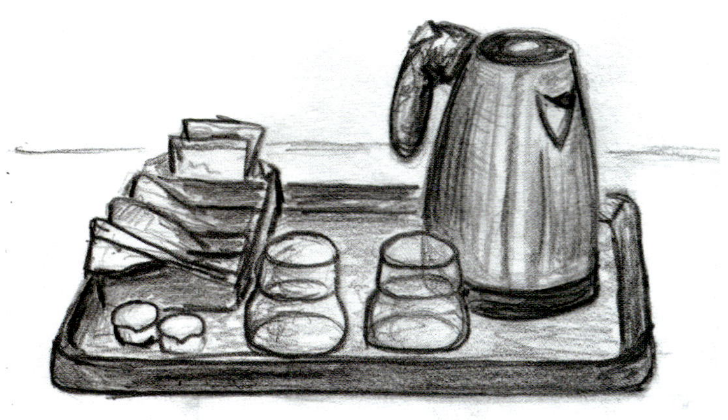

Exercise 2: Draw your view

▶ *Diane*

Diane drew this while visiting her granddad in Martinique. His house has huge windows to protect from the strong winds and the view from them is beautiful. She described how she got up early one day on a soft, misty morning. She chose to use a soft blue pencil to capture the delicate light and atmosphere.

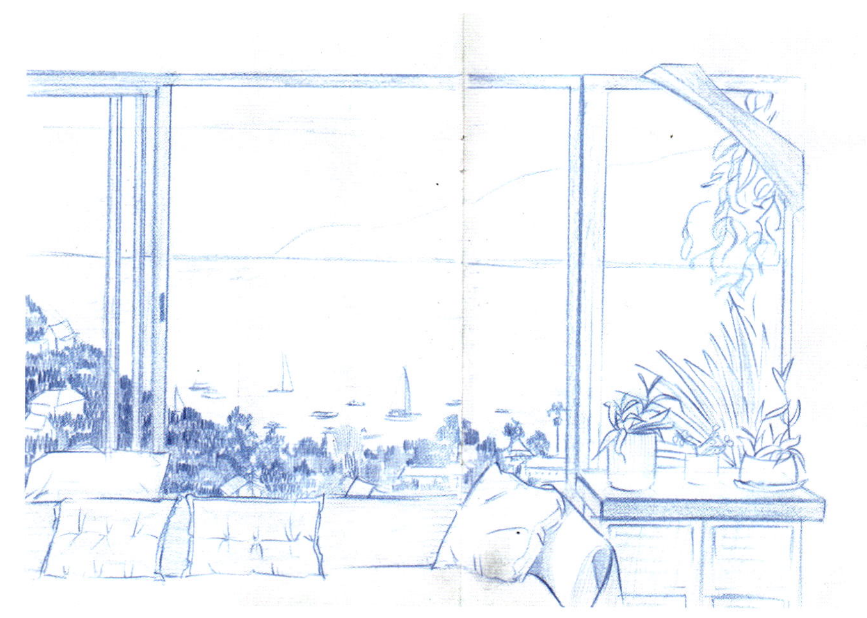

◀ *Hannah*

Hannah and her family holidayed with friends in Wales over New Year last year and she drew this from the room she was staying in. From her window she had the view of this magnificent gnarly tree. She wanted to capture the feel of it without it being too detailed so chose to use charcoal instead of pencil, which she felt she could be more expressive with. It was a busy holiday with lots of demands on her time, and the hour she spent by herself away from everyone else was very much enjoyed.

▶ *Safa*

This drawing of Safa's served as her first-day drawing and her view drawing. She arrived at her accommodation in Valletta, Malta, and opened her window to this lovely scene. Although she was tired from the travelling, she got her pencils out and started drawing, and found it gave her the motivation to draw for the rest of the afternoon.

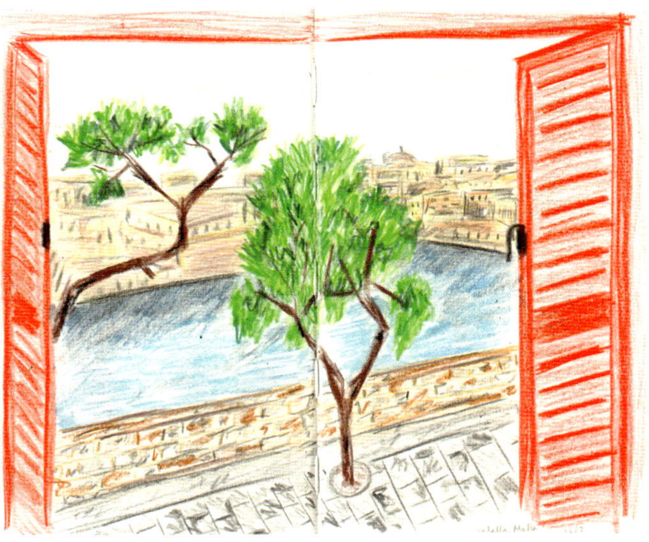

Exercise 3: When the weather defeats you

▶ *Claire*

Claire was on holiday in Nice. Although the weather was fine for most of her trip, one day it was so windy that she took refuge in the Villa Masséna museum. She liked the crisp shadows on the white marble and wanted to experiment with different marker pen colours to capture the tonal definition.

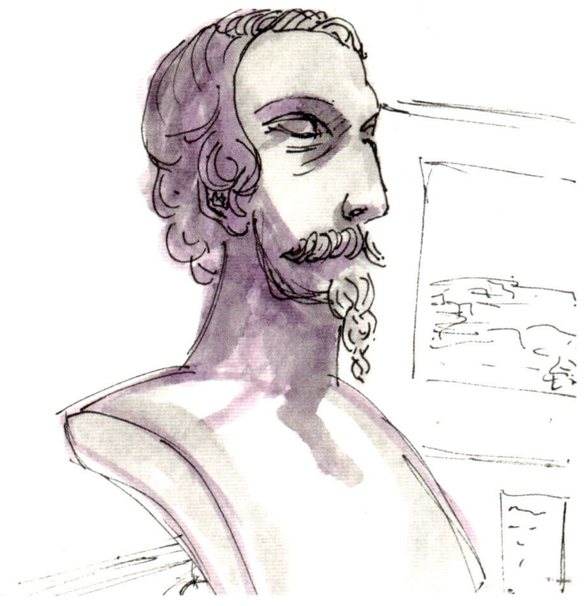

◀ *Phyllis*

Phyllis and her husband rented an apartment in Santa Barbara. One morning, she had the intention of going downtown to draw the old buildings; however, it started pouring with rain, so she had to rethink. As she had been admiring the French windows with their vibrant blue, she decided to spend an hour drawing the doors and the view outside instead.

She had only taken a few coloured pencils with her on this trip, so she was surprised how vibrant the final drawing was when using a limited palette. Sometimes having less choice can encourage us to be more experimental with the colours we have available.

▶ *Jane*

Jane drew this while on holiday in Tenerife. It was a hot day, so instead of venturing into the village, she chose to sit in the shade and draw the view from her balcony.

When I asked her how she approached this drawing, she said she just drew the things she could draw and left out the more challenging bits. 'Looking at it now, I can see it doesn't make sense but that's how I saw it at the time. I really enjoyed doing the drawing and I'm happy with it.' And, really, that's all that matters.

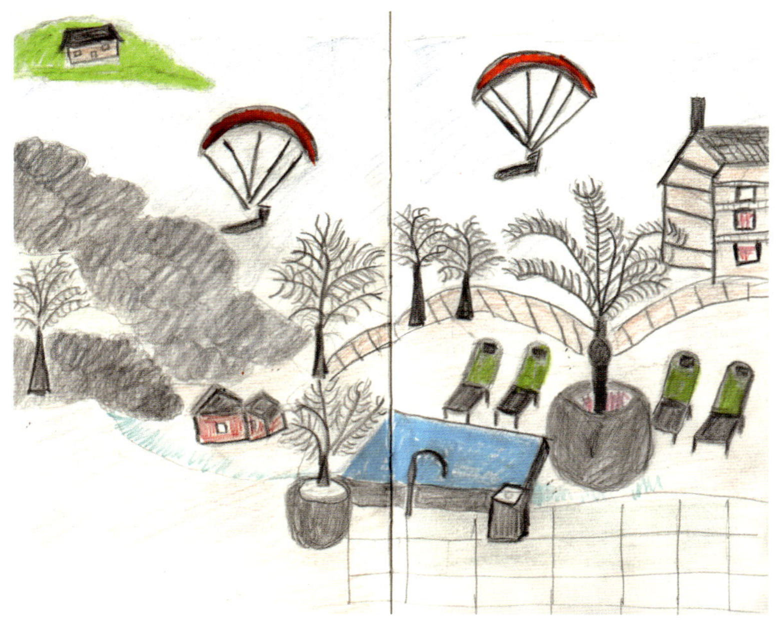

Exercise 4: Drawing on location

▶ Anne

Anne's husband is a musician, and she often travels with him to gigs in the UK and abroad. This drawing was done while she was at a folk festival in Ibiza. She was sat on the front row and decided to start sketching, even though she felt nervous. She got so absorbed in the drawing, and time just flew by.

She felt proud of herself for 'giving the drawing a bash'. It reminded her of how absorbing drawing from observation can be, along with providing a lovely memory of a wonderful, fun evening.

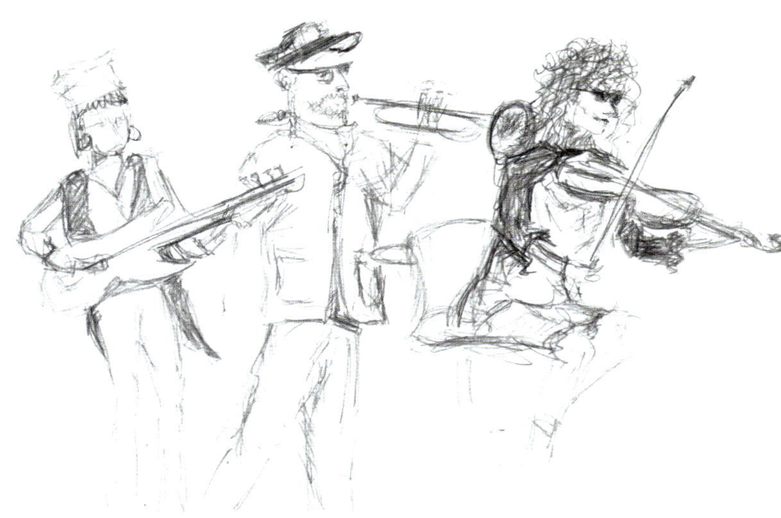

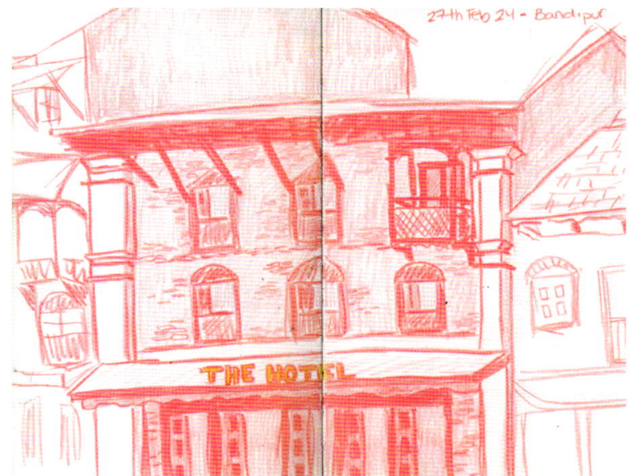

◀ Eva

Eva drew a hotel, ironically called 'The Hotel', near where she was staying in Bandipur, Nepal. The brickwork was a lovely warm red-brown colour, so she chose to use a dusky pink shade for the drawing and just highlight the name in yellow.

Although she admits she found it intimidating at first, as she isn't used to drawing buildings, she felt really focused throughout. This turned out to be one of her favourite drawings of her trip.

▲ Paula

Paula's daughter lives in Australia, so this drawing was done at a local pool near where she lives. She spent a relaxed afternoon there, reading, swimming and drawing. This drawing took Paula about an hour using Ecoline brush pens and coloured pencils.

Final thoughts

At the end of this chapter, my hope is that you return from your holiday with a selection of drawings from your trip that will provide wonderful memories in years to come.

We are now three-quarters of the way through this book, so take a moment to reflect on your work and congratulate yourself on your progress. I'm pretty sure that when you started the book, you didn't think you would be able to draw where people could see you – this is a huge achievement, so well done!

13
Drawing from paintings

Exercise 6 in Chapter 10 (see page 121) required you to visit a gallery or museum and draw inside the space. In this chapter, you are going to take this one step further to draw a painting from your chosen museum or gallery. The aim is for you to learn more about painting and your own preferences about which artwork you are drawn to. This also will help build on your confidence with drawing in public.

Choose a gallery you can get to easily, which has a good website showcasing the paintings they hold in their collection. You are going to draw from your chosen painting online, then to visit the painting at the gallery or museum and spend time drawing it in person.

Why draw from paintings?

I believe that drawing from paintings is one of the best ways to look at art. Taking time to draw a painting makes us look closer, allowing our minds to wander. We start to understand how the painting was created, allowing us to imagine the time when it was painted and think about the artist who created it.

One of my tutors said to me, 'When you spend time drawing a painting, for that time, that painting is yours.' This resonated with me. When you spend time looking so closely at a painting, you are committing that painting to memory. It will be etched in your mind. This also helps us develop as artists – it enhances our knowledge of art history, which benefits our own practice.

Choosing your painting

First, choose your gallery or museum and have a look online at the paintings in their collection. Choose a selection of paintings that interest you, then narrow it down to one after you have spent some time considering your choices. Make sure that the painting you choose is on show, as sometimes they are in storage. If you are feeling nervous about this, it might be wise to visit the gallery beforehand and choose a painting in a quiet room, so you don't feel too exposed.

Before drawing your chosen painting, I want you to look at it carefully and gather your thoughts. The first five exercises are written ones; use your sketchbook to make notes. It's up to you how much you write. The aim of the written exercises is to help you to get to know the artist and the painting. The questions are just prompts to help you dig a little deeper; don't worry if they aren't relevant to your chosen painting. You don't have to answer each question – just answer what you can.

Written exercises to get to know your painting

Exercise 1: Initial thoughts

You may feel a little daunted by the idea of looking at, responding to and analysing a painting, but I want to reassure you that there is no right or wrong answer. How you feel about and respond to an artwork is entirely unique to you. Treat these questions light-heartedly and with curiosity as to what you might uncover:

- Why did you choose this painting?
- What was your initial reaction to the work?
- As you continue to look at and experience the artwork, how does your mind and body respond?
- Does the artwork help you feel calm or does it anger, excite or irritate you?
- Does the artwork bring up any memories
- for you?

You have chosen your painting for a reason. Keep an open mind and let your eyes wander – you will naturally be drawn to certain elements in the artwork and your mind will try and make connections between these.

Exercise 2: Meet the painting

Do some research to find out as much about the artwork as you can to familiarise yourself with it and get into the mind of the artist. See if you can answer the following questions:

- What is the title of the artwork?
- Does the title have any significance?
- What is the medium?
- When and where was the artwork made?
- What are the dimensions?
- What is the artist's background?
- What else can you find out about the artist?
- Does it fit into a particular genre – religious, landscape, still life or fantasy, for example?

Exercise 3: Observe the visual elements

Visual elements are the components or building blocks the visual art is made up of and are any characteristic that we see, including line, shape, direction, texture and colour. Not all the visual elements may be present in the painting you are analysing. The absence of a visual element may be as important as the ones that are present in the artwork.

For this analysis, we are staying with four basic visual elements: colour, line, light and composition. Look carefully at the artwork and ask yourself the following:

Colour
- What are the main colours used?
- Is there a lack of colour?
- What moods do the colours – or lack of colours – evoke?
- If colours are used, what do they represent?

Line
- How would you describe the line?
- Are the lines definitive and hard, irregular, indistinct or broken?

Light
- What is the effect of light in the artwork?
- Does light illuminate the scene, objects or people in the painting? If so, how?

Composition
- How do images fit within the frame (cropped, truncated or shown in full)?
- Why is this format appropriate for the subject matter?
- Where does the composition lead the eye to?
- Do other elements, for example, shape and space, make up the artwork's composition?

Exercise 4: Try to make sense of the painting

By this stage, you will have a good analysis of your chosen artwork. Now it's time to find out what you think it might mean. Answer the following:

- Does the artwork communicate an action or narrative?
- Are there any recognisable objects, places or scenes? How are these presented (are they idealised, realistic, indistinct, hidden, distorted, exaggerated, stylised, reflected, reduced to simplified or minimalist form, primitive, abstracted, concealed, suggested, blurred or focused)?
- Have people been included? What can we tell about them (identity, age, profession, status, etc.)? What can we learn from their pose (i.e. frontal, profile, partly turned, body language)? Where are they looking (i.e. direct eye contact with viewer, downcast, interested in other subjects within the artwork)? Can we work out the relationships between figures from the way they are posed?
- Was the art part of a particular movement (Cubism, Impressionism, Pointillism, Futurism, American Abstract Expressionism or Surrealism)?

Exercise 5: Find the meaning

Ask yourself the following to gain a deeper understanding about the meaning of the piece:

- What do you think the artist was trying to convey?
- What do you think the meaning of the painting is?
- Has finding out about the context of the artwork changed your response to it in any way?

Practical exercises: Drawing from a painting

Now we move on to the practical part, where you pick up your sketchbook and drawing materials again. Keep your materials to a minimum if you find drawing in the museum or gallery challenging. Don't feel you need to use your coloured pencils – drawing in just pencil is OK. Most galleries are fine with you drawing with dry materials; however, most don't allow charcoal or paint – check before you visit.

What you need
- Sketchbook
- Pencils
- Coloured pencils (optional)
- Eraser
- Sharpener
- Drawing clips to hold your pages back
- Something to sit on (sometimes museums or galleries have their own stools)

Exercise 6: Draw from a painting on your computer (1 hour maximum)

Now you are acquainted with your painting and have analysed it, it's time to draw it. Before you draw from the painting in the museum or gallery, you are going to draw it from a reproduction on the computer or from a book. Treat this like a warm-up, a way to get to know the painting before you see it in real life and in the context of the gallery. Don't spend too long on this; a quick sketch is fine.

Exercise 7:

Draw from a painting in a museum or gallery

(as long as you need)

Now you have drawn the painting from the computer or a book, it's time to visit an art gallery or museum and draw it in real life. I don't get excited about seeing famous people, but I do get excited about seeing art I love. For me, there's nothing better than seeing a painting in real life that I have admired in a book or online. I hope you feel this excitement when you see your chosen painting for the first time (or even if you have seen it before, now you are seeing it with more educated eyes).

Sit in front of your chosen painting and make sure you feel comfortable. It's likely that you will get people looking at your drawing, but hopefully by now you feel confident enough not to let this derail you (revisit some of the suggestions for drawing in public in Chapter 10).

Pop a good audiobook on and wear your headphones. Start your drawing slowly, just sketching in loose areas. Take your time and have breaks if you need them. Try and enjoy the process. Keep drawing until you are satisfied and feel you have done enough. Reward yourself with a gift from the shop, tea and cake, or any other appropriate treat.

My drawing from a painting

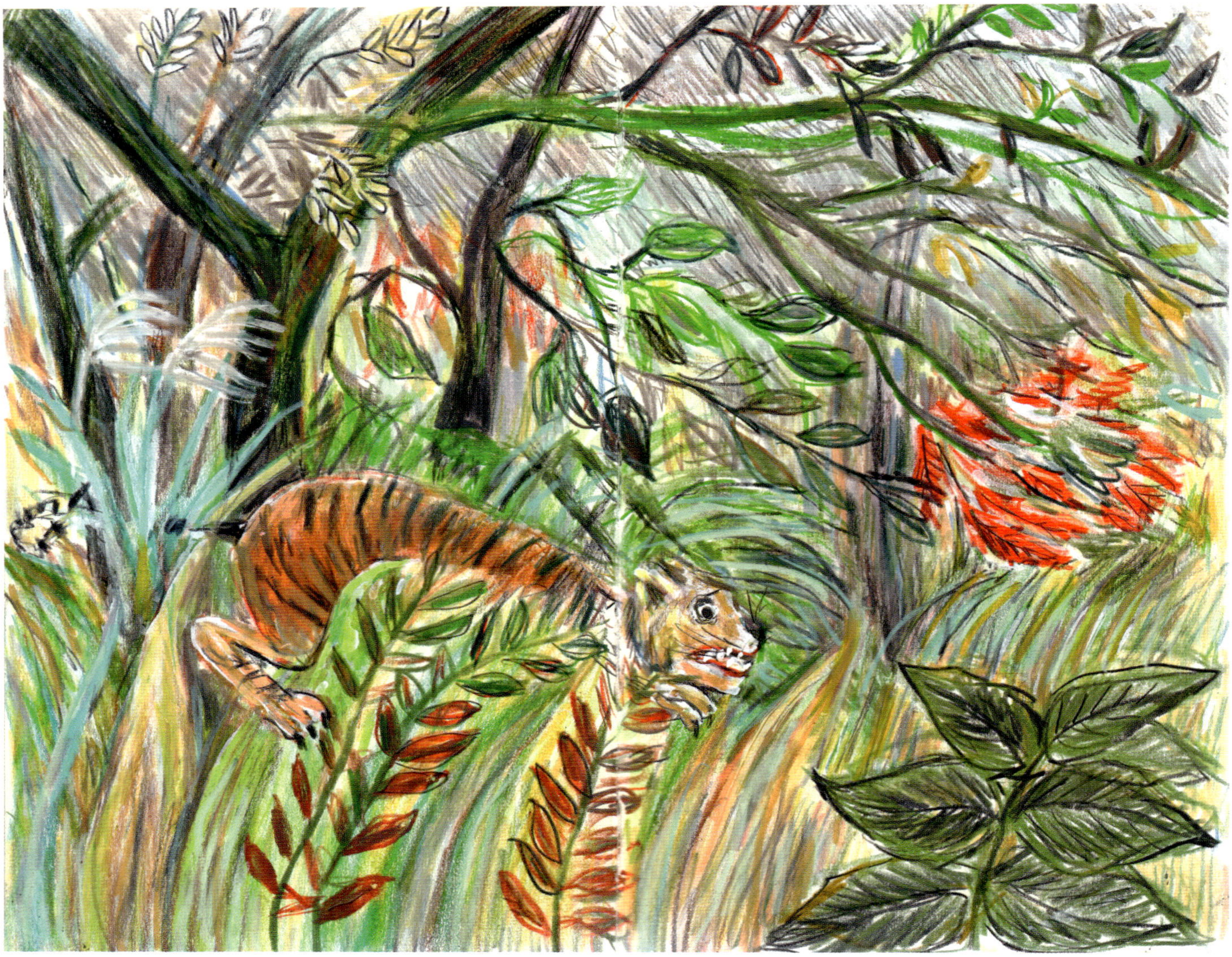

▲ *Surprised!* **by Henri Rousseau (1891), The National Gallery, London**

This is one of my favourite paintings in the National Gallery, so this exercise was a perfect opportunity for me to spend time drawing and studying it. The National Gallery is always busy, and this room is especially packed. I have been drawing in galleries and museums for years, so this wasn't too nerve-racking for me. I always feel a little daunted at the start, but once I've started, I can fully immerse myself in the painting and time just floats away.

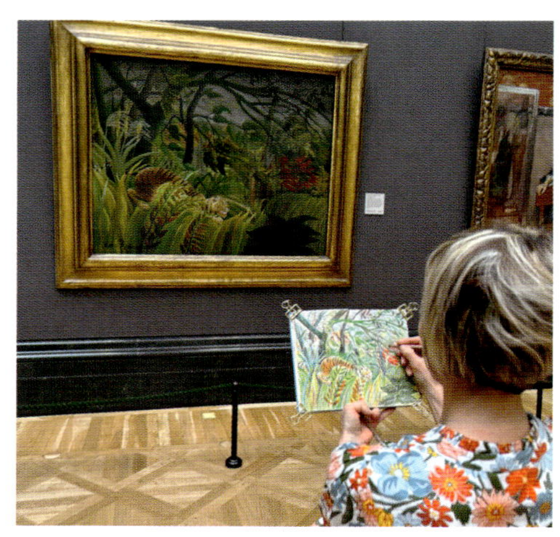

Sketch Squad: Drawing from a painting

All of the Squad completed this exercise but not everyone took photos of themselves with the paintings, and therefore they aren't shown here.

▶ *Holidays* **by Henry Watson (1920), Bristol Museum & Art Gallery, Bristol**
Safa

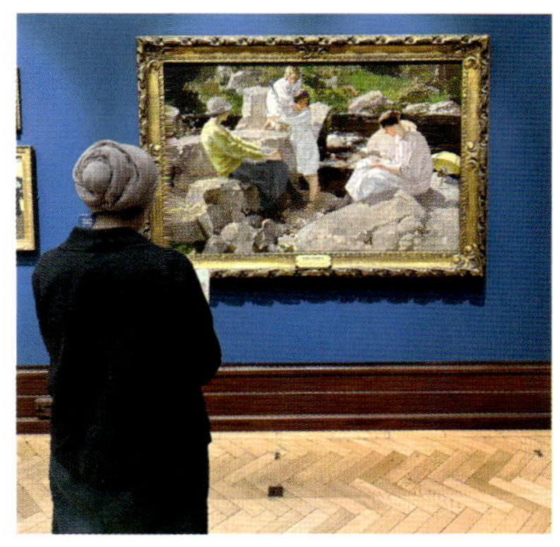

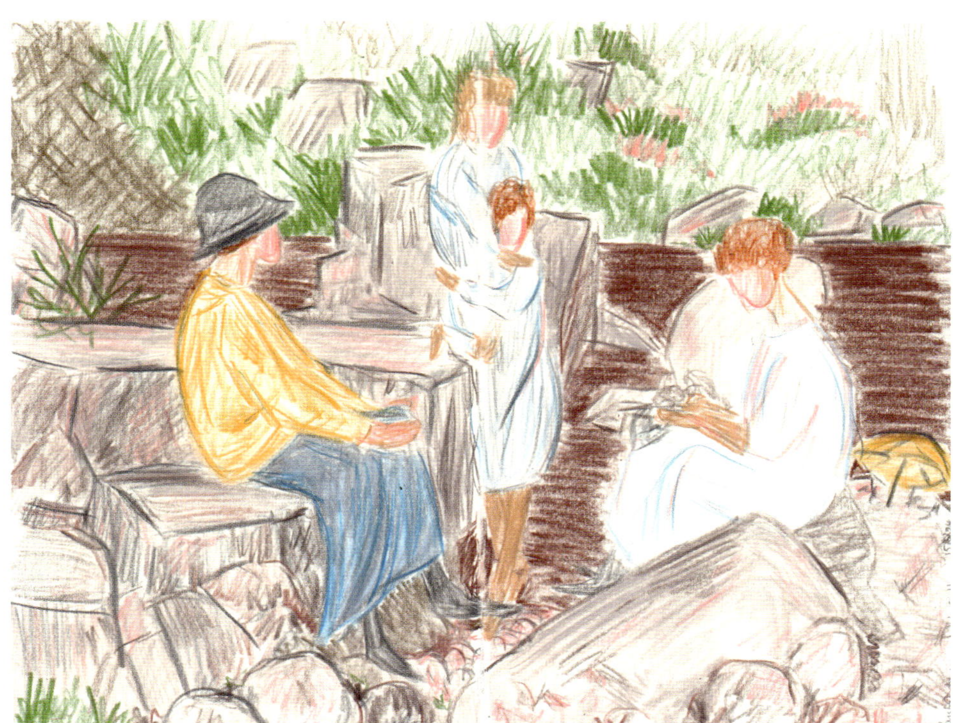

▶ *Figure on a Bed* **by Anne Rothenstein (1996), Graves Gallery, Sheffield**
Anne

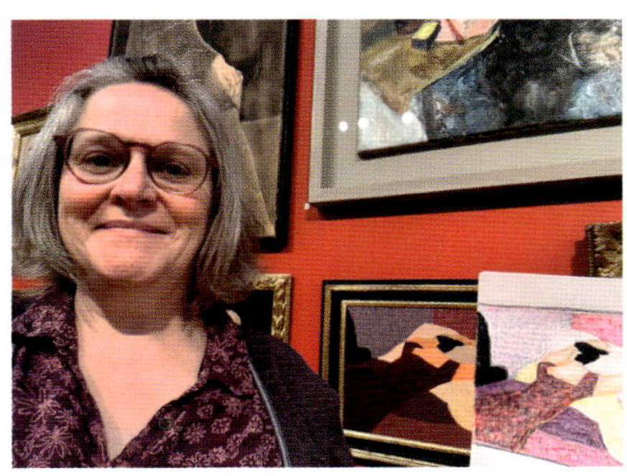

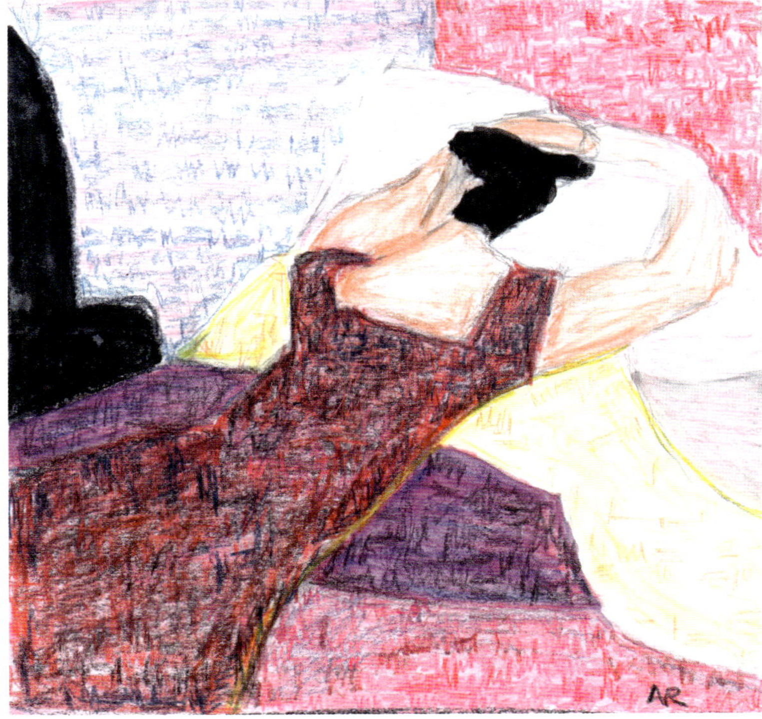

▶ *Red Tulips* by
**Christian Rohlfs (1920),
Leicester Museum and
Art Gallery, Leicester**
Paula

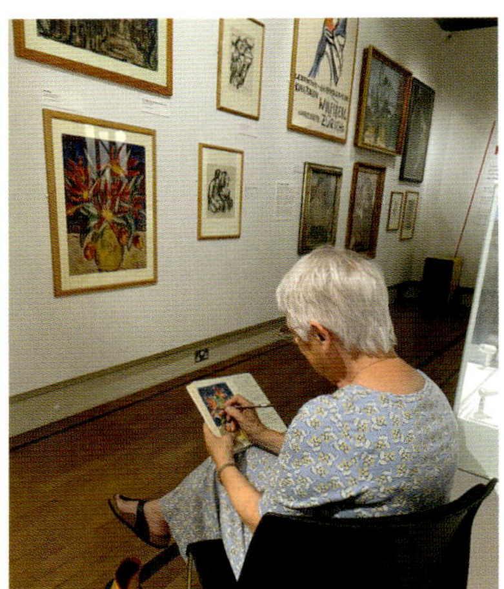

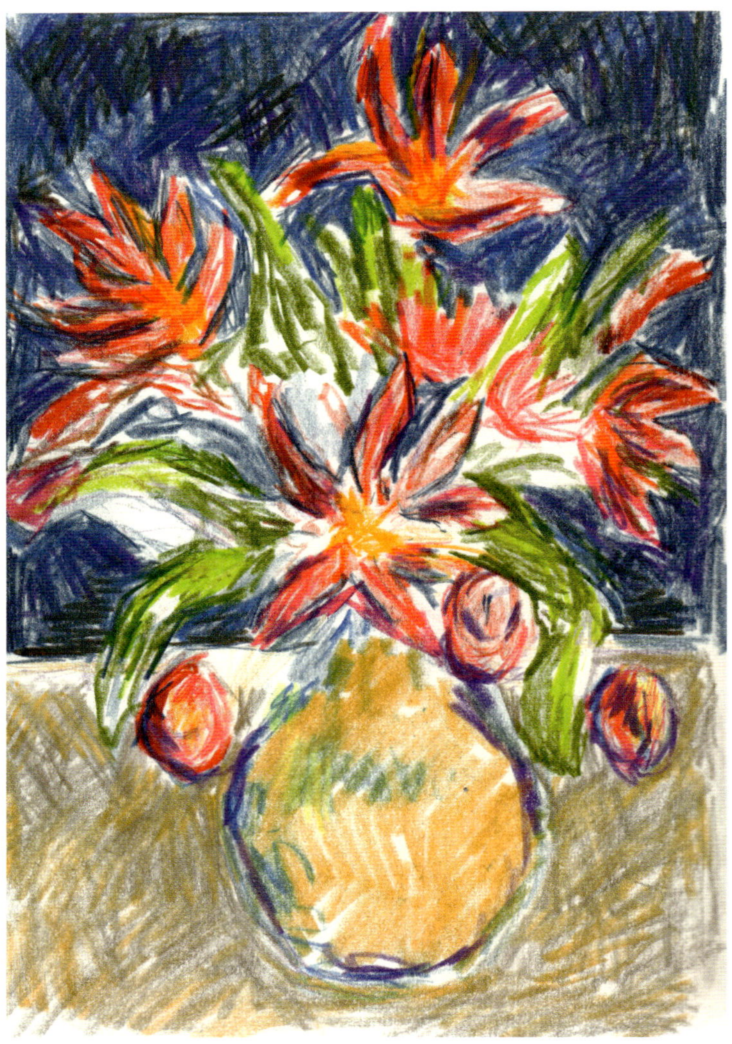

◀ *From my room in
Madrid – Santa Teresa
Street* by **Carlos
Quizpez Asín (1924),
MALI, Lima, Peru**
Claire

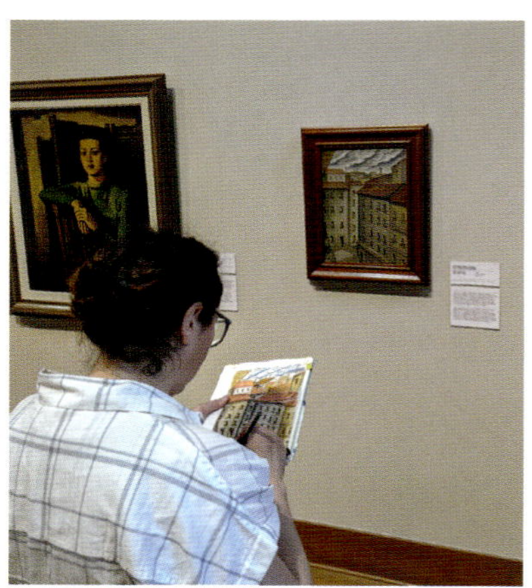

► *Laura Knight with model, Ella Louise Naper ('Self Portrait')* **by Laura Knight (1913), National Portrait Gallery, London**
Eva

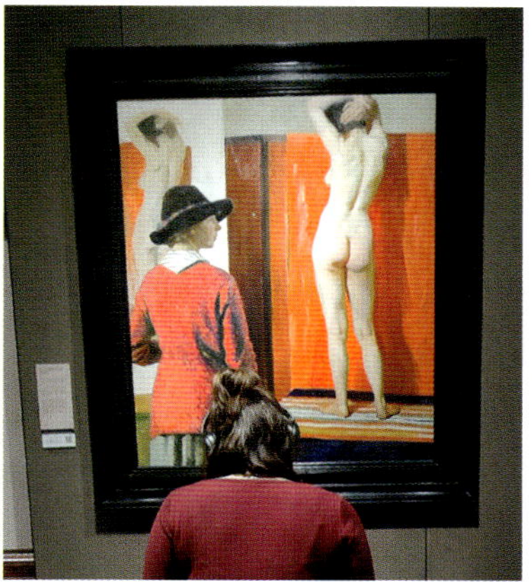

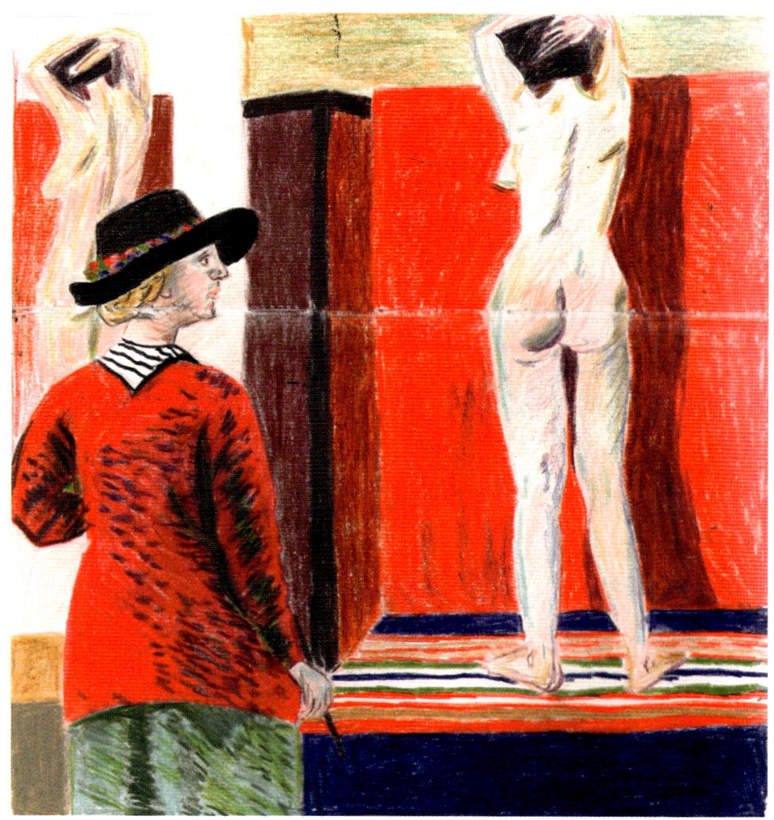

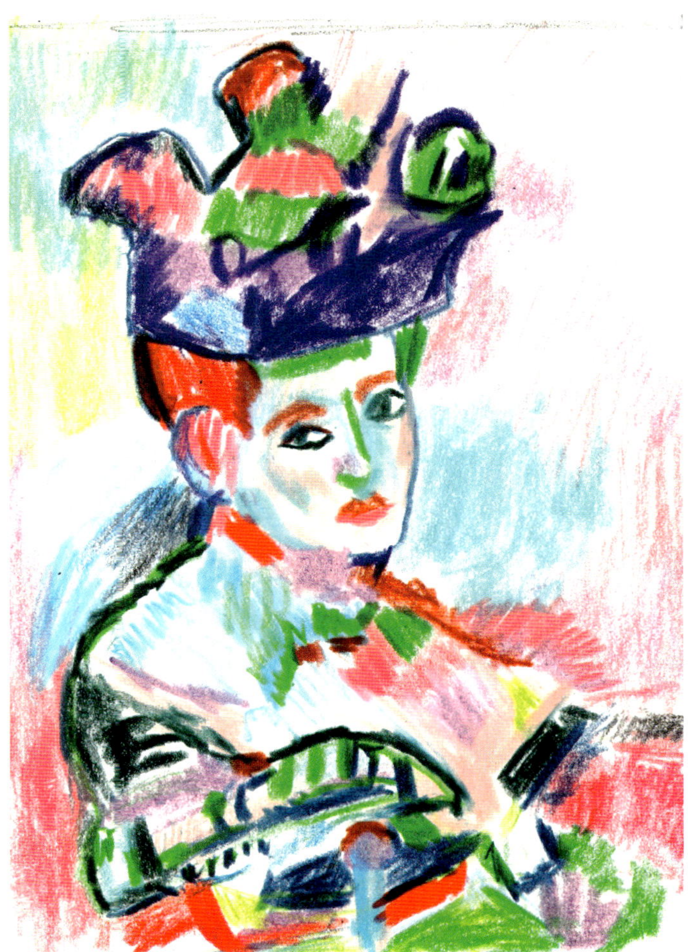

◄ *Femme au chapeau* **(*Woman with a Hat*) by Henri Matisse (1905), SFMOMA, San Francisco, USA**
Phyllis

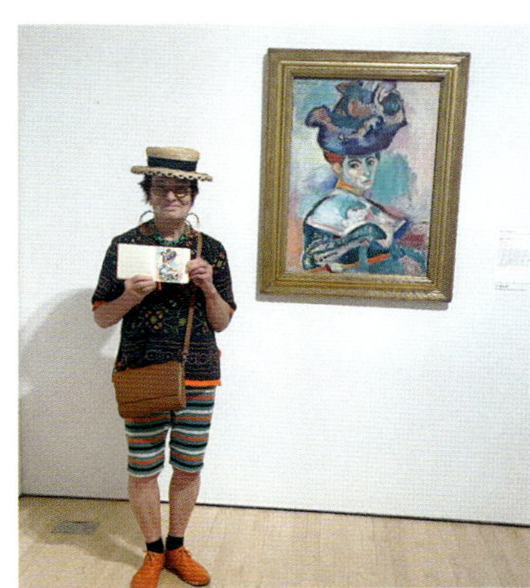

► *Bathers at Asnières* by
Georges Seurat (1884),
The National Gallery,
London
Jane

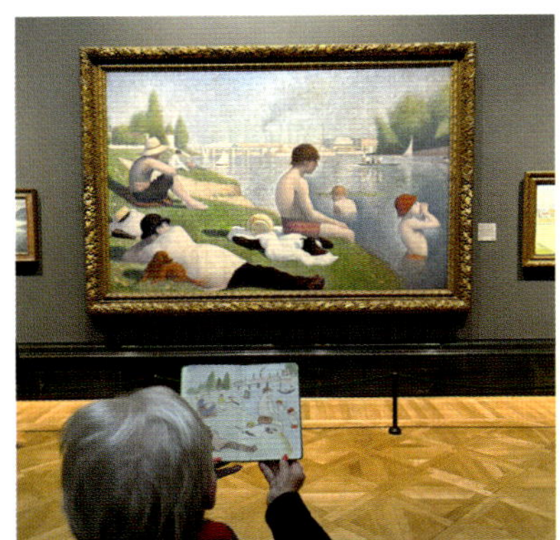

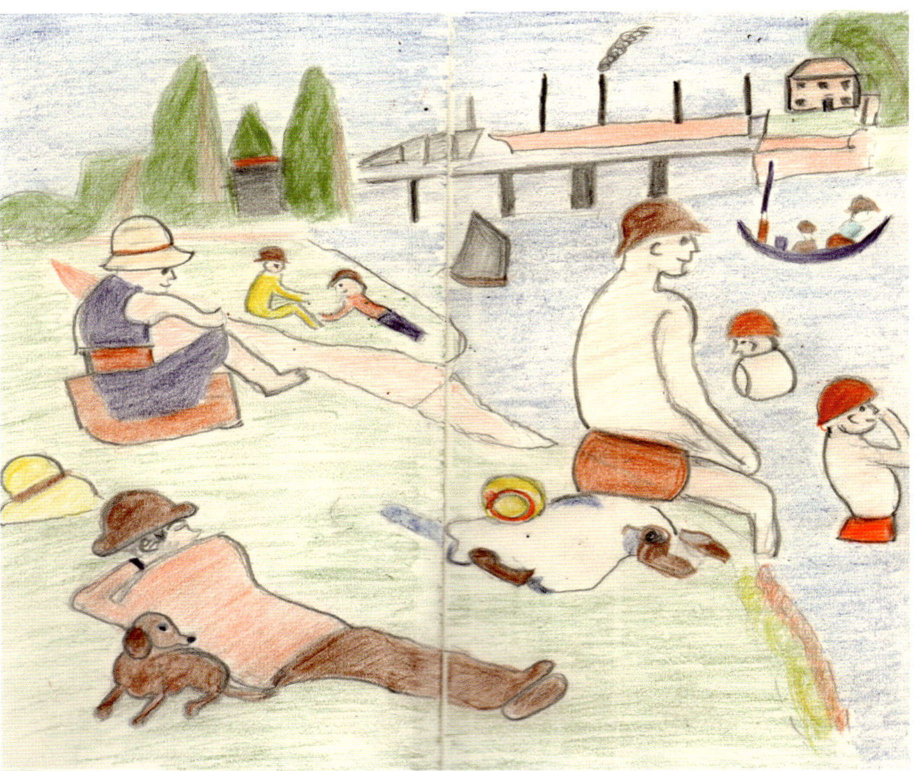

◄ *Girl with Bread* by
Albert Anker (1887),
Museum of Fine Arts,
Bern, Switzerland
Lucy

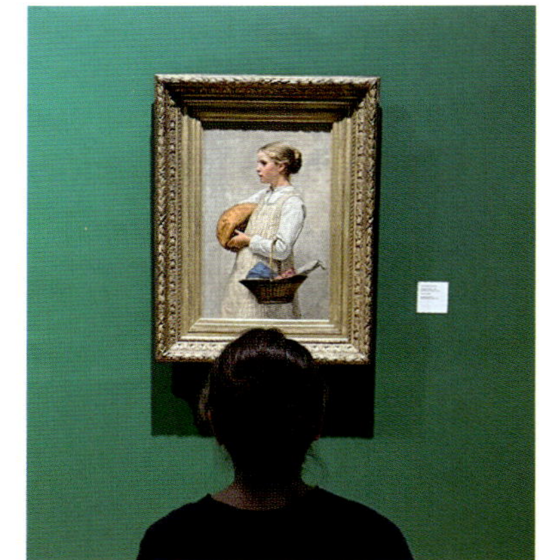

Sketch Squad: Reflections on drawing from a painting

The Squad all followed the written exercises in this chapter and wrote fulsome accounts of their thoughts and feelings. Here's a summary of their notes and my observations.

Choosing the paintings

It was interesting for me to read why the members of the Squad chose the paintings they did as they were all so varied.

Paula chose her painting based on practical reasons; the gallery is near to where she lives so it was easy to access. She looked at the paintings online and chose which painting appealed to her.

Since completing Chapter 7, Eva has a newfound interest in drawing portraits, so she chose to combine a trip to London with a visit to the National Portrait Gallery to draw from her painting.

Claire chose her painting carefully. She was on holiday in Peru, so researched the online gallery and selected her painting as she was intrigued by the scene. She notes that it had 'a strange quality' and she was curious to know more.

Phyllis is a milliner who loves colour. She chose to draw from a Matisse in her gallery in San Francisco. She discovered that the colours that Matisse used in his portrait of his wife were meant to convey her emotional state – the green could represent envy and the orange passion or energy.

The research stage

Once the Sketch Squad had chosen their paintings, they followed the exercises and started their research into the paintings.

Anne noted she really enjoyed having time to draw the painting in detail after she took her time to fully acquaint herself with it.

Jane notes that, after drawing her painting from the computer screen, she was eager to see it in the flesh.

Phyllis echoes this. After spending so long with the painting online, she was curious and excited to see what it looked like in the gallery.

Painting in the gallery or museum

The final exercise was, of course, to draw the painting in the gallery or museum. Overall, it was a positive experience for the Squad. Everyone confessed to being a little apprehensive before embarking on their drawing; however, they all had various strategies to help combat their nerves. Phyllis took her husband along and Paula had her friend accompany her. Lucy promised herself a nice lunch in the museum café, and Anne focused on how good it would feel once she had done it, as she knew it was way out of her comfort zone.

The practical aspects of drawing in a gallery were a challenge to some. Lucy had to hunt out a seat (galleries and museums often have fold-up chairs to use). Sometimes the lighting in the rooms was an issue, as were the way the actual paintings were lit.

Lucy had to contend with a large group of schoolchildren who were being taught about the painting and who crowded around her, trying to see her drawing. She reminded herself to stay calm and relaxed: 'By blocking out the distractions and focusing solely on the painting and the sketch, I felt more at ease.'

Final thoughts

All the Squad members found this exercise beneficial for a range of reasons. Anne found it rewarding as it built her confidence with drawing in public and showing her work. Eva enjoyed it as it enriched her art history knowledge: 'It was a great experience; I loved learning more about the paintings and the artist I chose.' For Paula, it was a fantastic opportunity to visit a local art gallery, which she hadn't visited before and to have a lovely day out.

14

Self-sabotage

Self-sabotage is when we do things that undermine our goals and stop us from reaching our full potential. I wanted to include a chapter on self-sabotage towards the end of the book as it's when you are most likely to be running out of steam. The novelty of drawing regularly is wearing off, your inner critic has become louder, and you may have hit a block with your practice. I too am suffering from this right now as I reach the end of writing this book; the closer it comes to my deadline, the more real it becomes and my fears around its publication grow bigger. I want to do anything but crack on and finish it, so instead I'm filling out my taxes and decluttering my cottage. I've seen this in my many years of teaching. Students set off on their projects with enthusiasm and energy, but, towards the end of these projects, many of them sabotage their efforts for a variety of reasons.

Self-sabotage can take different forms, including procrastination, perfectionism and negative self-talk. When we engage in self-sabotage, we reinforce the belief that we're not good enough or capable of success. We so often get in our own way, avoiding getting on with our work and putting out obstacles to prevent ourselves from achieving our dreams. Behind most forms of self-sabotage – particularly with creatives – is the fear of failure and, surprisingly, sometimes the fear of success.

Types of self-sabotage

Here are some forms of self-sabotage that I've seen in my students and myself:

- Not setting aside time or filling your time with other things

- Leaving things to the last minute

- Exhausting yourself with other things so you are too tired to be creative

- Putting others' needs, wants and schedules ahead of your own

- Making excuses as to why you aren't getting on with your artwork

- Always starting new projects but not finishing them, or having trouble considering finishing any piece of work

- Telling yourself that creating is selfish

- Stopping when things get hard ... or boring

- Filling in an application or submission then not submitting it

- Holding on to unrealistic expectations for yourself or your work

- Waiting for everything to be perfect before starting something

- Trying to make your work 'perfect'

- Overwhelming yourself with ideas so you do nothing

- Comparing yourself, or your efforts, to others

- Not acknowledging your past achievements

- Working hard on a piece of work and then being careless in the final stages

- Setting prices way too low or high

Why do we engage in these behaviours?

I'm so excited to get this book finished and for it to be published. It's always been a dream of mine, so why am I madly decluttering my cottage instead? For me, it's the fear of failure. What if no one likes the book? What if people think it's a 'how to draw' book and leave negative reviews? By procrastinating and not finishing it, it remains a dream where I can imagine the golden, glittering future outcome.

Fear is likely the case for most of us, but it could also be that you don't believe you deserve good things, so you unconsciously push them away. You could be afraid of success and your brain is telling you that you're not good enough, or you could have had a bad experience in the past, like a poor art teacher or art workshop, which is impacting your current decisions.

Questions to ask ourselves

Take a moment to reflect here and then ask yourself these questions:

- What am I afraid of? Is it a fear of failure, a fear of success or maybe a fear of change?

- How real is that fear? Once you have established what you are afraid of, ask yourself how likely it is. For example, how likely is it that everyone will laugh at your drawings and tell you you're wasting your time?

- Do you do this in other areas of your life? Think carefully about the rest of your life. In what other ways do you self-sabotage? Can you see any links or any similar causes as to why you do this?

Ways to help you stop self-sabotaging

The following thoughts and actions can help you to avoid self-sabotage:

- **Develop awareness:** Get to understand how and why you do it. Just by asking yourself the questions above, you will have a greater sense of why you get in your own way.

- **Write it down:** Writing it down can be a great way to notice patterns in your thoughts or actions that are related to self-sabotage.

- **Consider the reward:** Reflect on how good it will feel if you don't get in your own way and you finish all the drawing exercises in the book. For me, a big motivation to stop self-sabotaging is the reward of accomplishment.

I hope you have found this chapter helpful. I feel better by writing it – it's helped me understand the barriers I put in my path. In fact, it's inspired me to finish the book (thank goodness)!

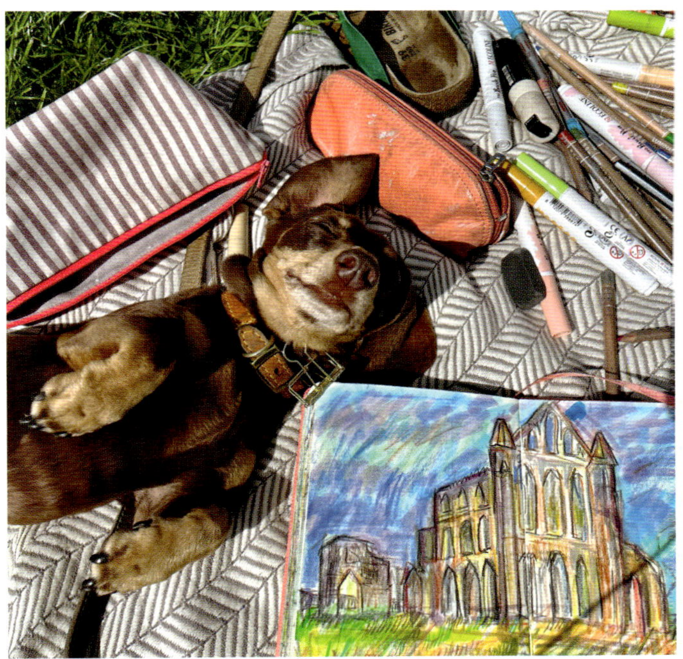

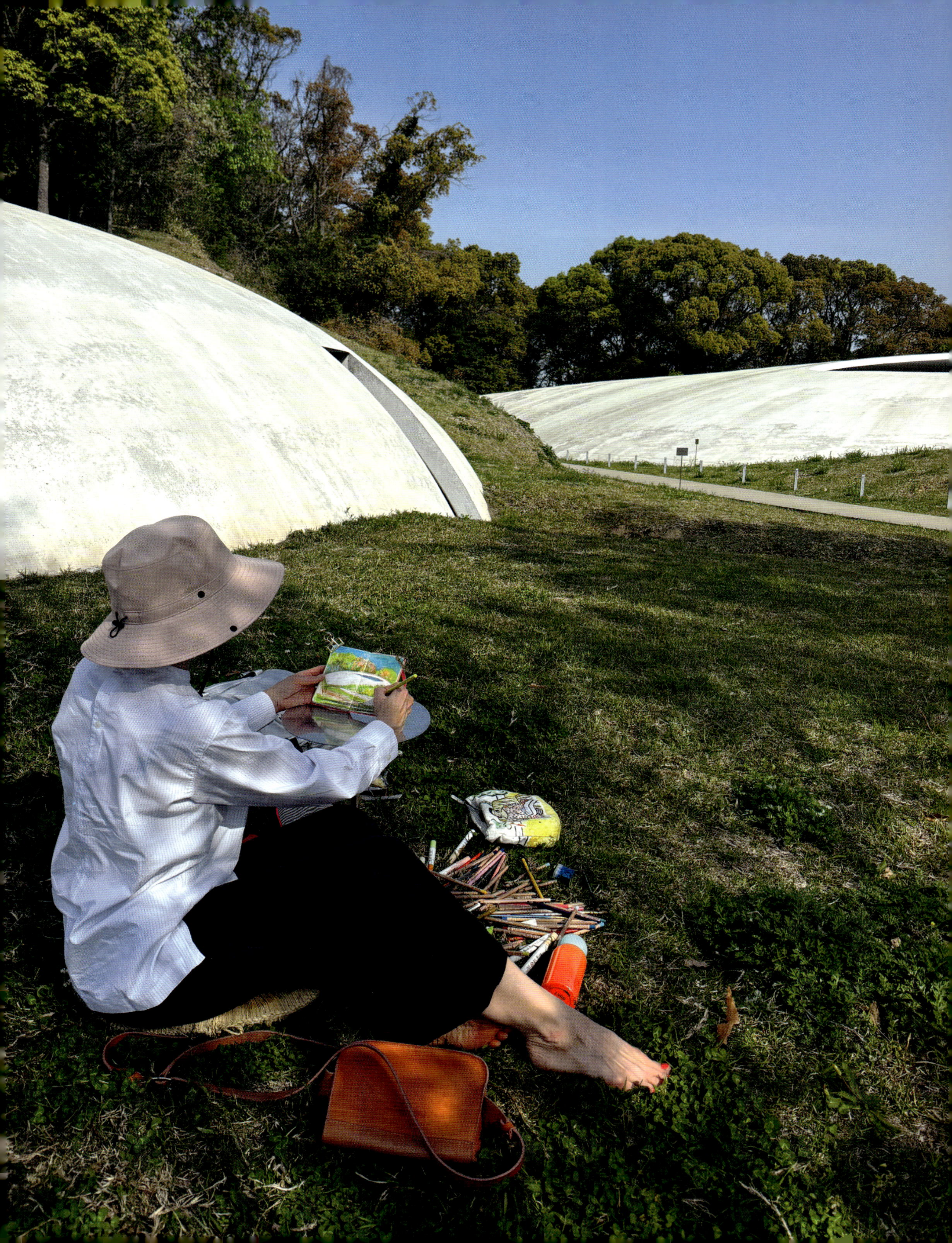

15
Experimental drawing

As you should now be feeling more confident in your drawing abilities, this chapter contains a set of exercises that encourage you to ask questions about what drawing is. The exercises are designed to investigate the conventions of drawing and inspire you to experiment with unfamiliar or unexpected ways of approaching drawing. My hope is that the exercises will reveal something about your practice that you haven't considered before and will unlock a way of drawing that you can use moving forward with your work.

With all these exercises, there is no right or wrong result – your interpretation will be entirely your own. Let go of any expectations of how you think the drawing should look. Instead, concentrate on exploring new ways of drawing and approach the exercises with curiosity and a sense of anticipation about what may be revealed.

In all these exercises, I haven't specified which drawing materials to use. This is entirely up to you. I encourage you to use materials you don't ordinarily use as this can help to free you up. For example, if you haven't used oil pastels before and you have some to hand, now might be the time to have a go. I also haven't specified how long to take on these exercises (apart from Exercise 2, where I've provided a guideline). I trust by now you have a sense of how long you want to spend on a drawing and when you feel it's time to stop.

Drawing from music

Instead of using our eyes to draw, we are now going to rely on our ears to inform what and how we draw. This exercise is designed to encourage you to interpret what you hear into marks on your sketchbook page. Listening to a variety of music tracks can evoke different emotions and ideas and hopefully encourage you to experiment with mark making, colours, shapes and subjects in your drawing.

What you need
- Three pieces of music from varied genres and styles, preferably instrumental
- Something to play your music on
- Sketchbook
- Selection of drawing materials

Start by listening to the first music track, all the way through, with your eyes closed. You could use an electronic track, a classical piece, a heavy metal song, a hip-hop beat or a folk song, for example. Try thinking about it in relation to marks, lines and physical movements.

After you have listened to it once, play it again. This time, try and translate the sounds you hear and how the music makes you feel into marks on paper. It's important to remember that there is no right or wrong here; this is entirely your own interpretation. Don't overthink the marks you are making; allow yourself to intuitively respond to what you are hearing without getting in your own way. You might want to draw things, objects or places or you may just want to draw lines, follow rhythms or express your emotions with marks.

Play the track as many times as you want until you feel the drawing is complete, then repeat the exercise for the other two tracks.

Drawing from film

Drawing from film is a wonderful way to expand your skills. It is a unique way to experience cinema as if you are editing the rushes frame by frame. By stopping the film where you choose and drawing for a specified time, you become aware of the construction of each frame – you look closely at the content, spatial effects, composition, lighting, narrative and emotion. You also gain insight into your own preferences, to what draws your eye and creates a good picture. It also helps your understanding of sequence and narrative, as by studying the film in terms of its visuals, you get an insight into how the director created the story and constructed the film.

In this exercise, you are going to choose a film to draw from, pause the film eight times and draw for six minutes from each paused film still. Make sure that you can regularly pause the film, so you are able to draw from the paused film still.

Make a note of why you have chosen the film you are drawing from. Be specific here: is it because the narrative interests you or maybe it's the costume design or the lighting? If you have chosen a film you haven't seen before then why have you chosen it? What has made you want to draw from it?

Press play and watch the film. When an interesting, exciting or dynamic image appears, press pause.

Set your timer to six minutes. Draw quickly from the film still using your drawing materials. If you are watching the film on your computer, be careful to keep any inks etc. at a safe distance to avoid spills. Go for the big shapes first before attempting any detail.

When the six minutes is up, turn the page, start the film and repeat the process seven more times.

What you need
- A film
- Something to play your film on
- Your larger sketchbook
- Selection of drawing materials
- Timer

Drawing from collage

A collage is a work of art in which pieces of paper, photographs, fabric and other ephemera are arranged and stuck down onto a supporting surface. In this exercise, you are going to create a collage that reflects your interests, tastes and desires – a kind of self-portrait from scraps of paper. You will be cutting and tearing fragments out of magazines, newspapers or anything that interests you and takes your eye. You will then experiment with different ways of organising these fragments before sticking them down. Once you have done this, you are then going to use the collage as inspiration for a drawing.

Collage is a freeing and liberating way of working. It enables you to experiment with composition, colour, space and shape in an intuitive way. You will tend to choose imagery, colours and words that reflect your unconscious thoughts and emotions. This will make for a very interesting and personal piece of work.

Artists have often used collage as the work itself or as inspiration for another piece of work – this is what we are doing here. To inspire you, here are some artists who use collage: Hannah Hoch, Richard Hamilton, John Stezaker, Henri Matisse, Eileen Agar, Robert Rauschenberg and Mark Hearld.

Just as a reminder, there is no right or wrong way of doing this. How you interpret the exercise is entirely up to you. This reflects you and no one else.

What you need
- Magazines, newspapers, pages from old books, photos, fabric, coloured papers etc.
- Glue
- Scissors
- A piece of paper that is larger than your sketchbook
- Your larger sketchbook
- Selection of drawing materials

Place your sketchbook on the piece of paper and draw around it. The space inside the outline is where you will create your collage.

Using your first magazine, flick through and tear or cut out anything that interests or reflects you – colours you like, text, interiors, clothes, things that give an insight into you. Give yourself a time limit when going through the magazines.

Once you have created a collection of collage papers, you are now ready to start experimenting with different combinations. Place a selection of your pieces onto your paper with the outline of the sketchbook.

When you move the collage pieces around on the paper, you learn a lot about composition. You can feel in your body when it 'clicks' and the collage is coming together. Experiment with at least five different versions before you stick anything down. Take photos on your phone as this can often help you to see the images more clearly.

Once you have decided on your chosen setup, it's time to stick down the collage. As soon as the collage has dried to the paper and is secure, you are now going to draw from it. The idea is that you use it as inspiration for a new drawing in your sketchbook. You might choose to draw the whole collage, exploring what it's like to draw the rips and tears of the corners of the pieces of paper or how you draw written text. Or you might draw just a segment of it, a small area of the collage that interests you. You can use whatever drawing materials you like – you may choose to draw it in pencil or go full out with colour. Again, it's your choice. Do what you feel is best. Try and fill the whole page of your sketchbook.

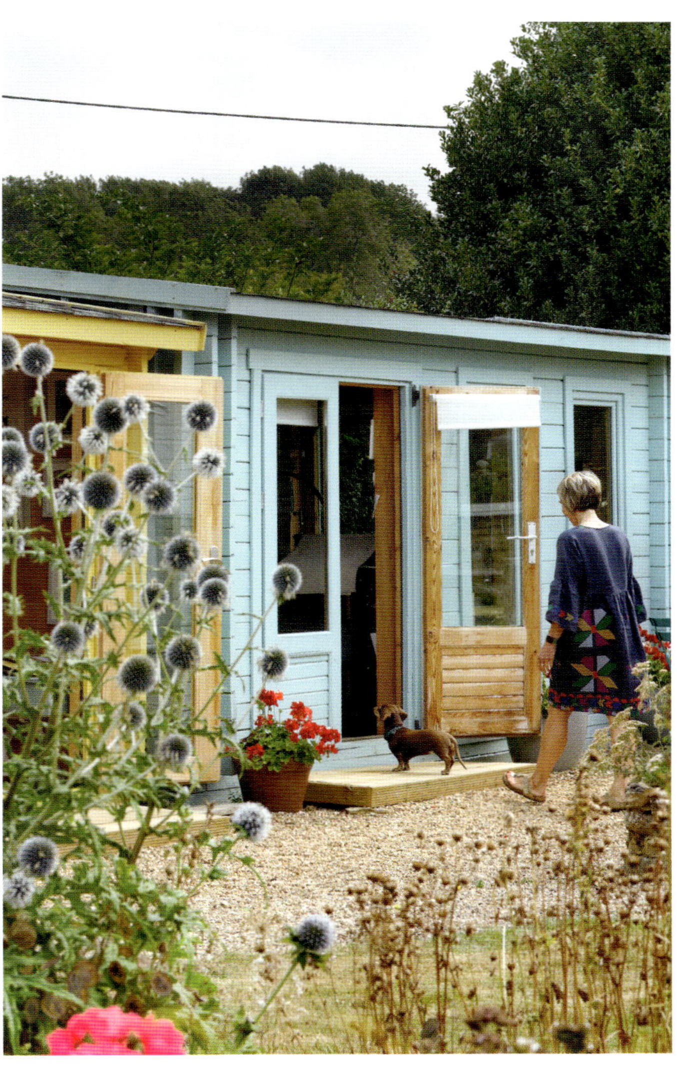

Drawing your dream

This exercise is designed to help you draw from memory, to draw without any reference or props and use your imagination to create a drawing from out of your head. Drawing without any reference is always going to be difficult and your drawings won't look 'accurate' but this isn't the point. Dreams by their nature are unusual and don't make sense, so don't expect your drawing to make sense either. The more you do it, and the more you approach it with the spirit of enquiry, the more you will enjoy it.

Many artists use their dreams as source material, and it might inspire you to look at the work of artists such as Max Ernst, Leonora Carrington, René Magritte, Giorgio de Chirico, Marc Chagall and Paula Rego.

Over a period of a week, keep a notepad or sketchbook by your bed. When you wake, note down or draw anything you remember from your dreams. After you have collected a week's worth of dream imagery, you will then make a drawing based on the things you dreamt about.

Use one double page in your large sketchbook, or just a loose sheet of paper if you prefer, and let your imagination guide you with making marks on the page. Just enjoy the process of working freely without any constraints, being curious about your nocturnal wanderings and seeing how they translate on to paper.

What you need
- Notepad
- Large sketchbook or loose paper
- Drawing materials

My drawings: Experimental drawing

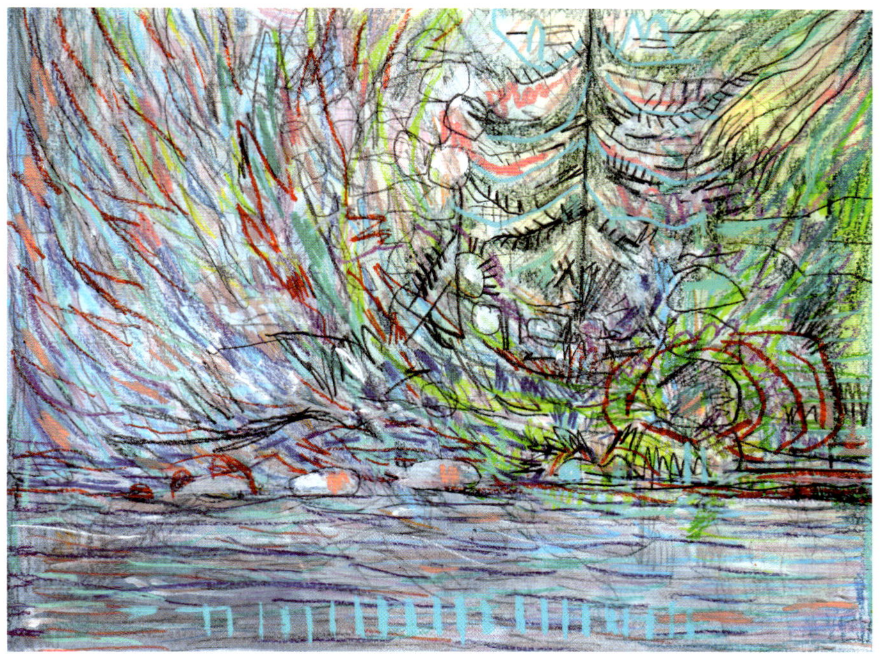

◀ Exercise 1:
Drawing from music

This drawing was done while listening to an instrumental music track, 'Tristana', which is from *Wintermusik*, a thirty-minute album from the German musician and composer Nils Frahm. It is a meandering, rich and contemplative piece of music featuring piano, celeste and reed organ.

At the start, I built up the layers using short marks with cooler colours, allowing myself to respond to the sounds I was hearing. As the track progressed, and the music intensified, I picked up greens and reds. I then finished off with pencil, roaming around the paper, making marks where I saw fit. As the music is so soothing and melancholic, I almost felt I had entered a meditative state where the marks were just forming themselves. I emerged from the drawing feeling much calmer and more focused.

▼ Exercise 2:
Drawing from film

I chose to draw from one of my favourite films, *Our Little Sister* (2016) – a Japanese film directed by Hirokazu Kore-eda. It tells the story of three sisters who live in their grandmother's home and the arrival of their thirteen-year-old half-sister. It's a beautiful poetic film that moves at a gentle pace, which made it a delight to draw from. This was my third viewing of the film, and drawing it enhanced my appreciation of the cinematography. The problem for me was selecting the frames to draw from as each was worthy of more attention. This drawing took me just over six minutes.

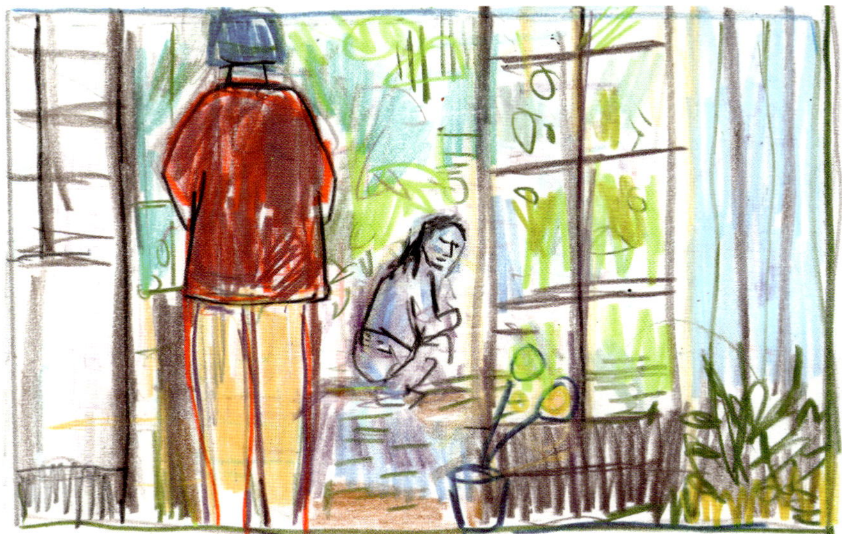

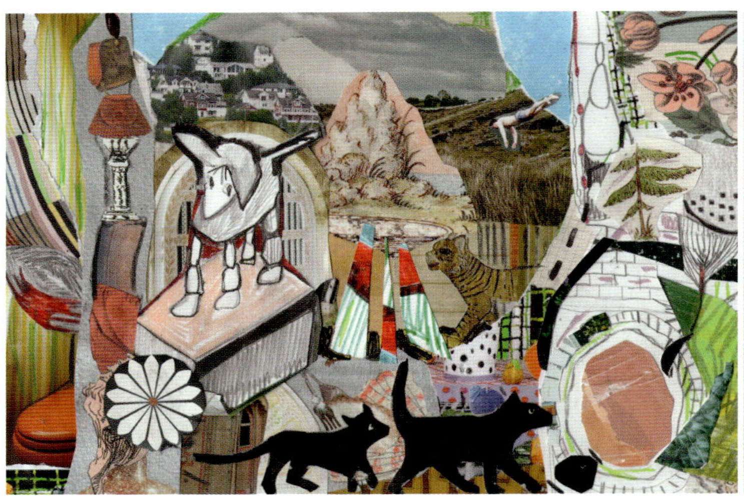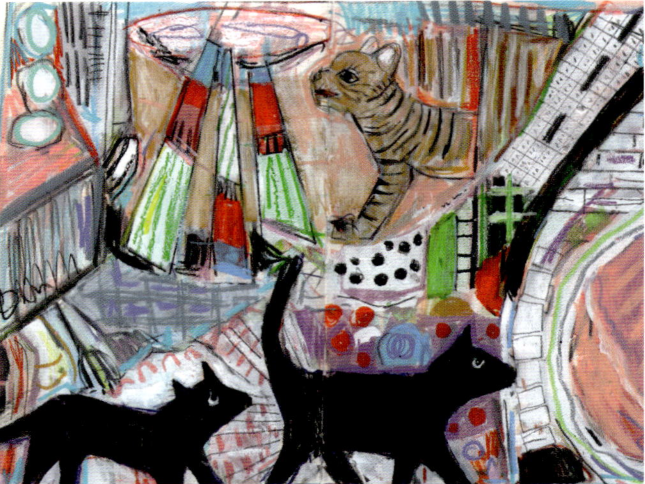

▲ Exercise 3: Drawing from collage

For my collage (above left), I used a selection of magazines and a couple of old drawings. I gave myself a time limit of thirty minutes to go through the magazines and tear out things that immediately appealed to me. I didn't overthink it; I trusted my intuition, aware that anything I was attracted to would reflect my taste and aesthetic.

At the end of the thirty minutes, I had a heap of material to work with – and then the fun started. I played around with various compositions and then started to stick the papers down. I got the collage to a place where I couldn't 'see' it anymore, so I left it for a couple of days. When I came back to it, I knew it needed something more at the bottom to pull the image together. On my studio wall, I had an image of two walking black cats from a medieval bestiary. I photocopied the image, cut the cats out and stuck them at the bottom. The collage then 'locked' into place.

▼ Exercise 4: Drawing your dream

My dreams almost always feature animals, but not usually as many as featured in this particular dream, hence why I chose to draw it. Looking at my notes the morning after the dream, I had hastily scribbled down 'a menagerie of animals surrounding me, like on a merry-go-round in a landscape'. And so, from this slightly bizarre sentence, and my hazy memory of this dream, this drawing emerged. I have a collection of toy animals, which I used to draw from initially, and the rest came from my imagination.

This exercise reminded me of how much I enjoy combining drawing from imagination and observation and blending the two. As I spent most of the past two years drawing directly from observation, it's made me eager to pick up this way of working again.

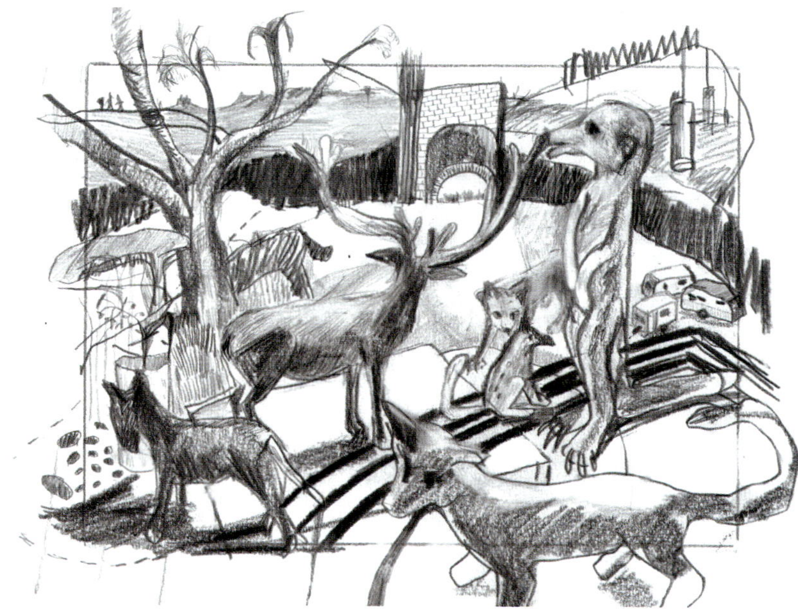

Sketch Squad: Experimental drawing

I've shown you my interpretations of the exercises, so now let's look at some of the Sketch Squad's drawings.

Exercise 1: Drawing from music

▶ *Safa: 'The Returning Light/ Late Frost', Tamsin Elliot and Tarek Elazhary (2023)*

Safa chose this track as the folk musician Tamsin Elliot originates from her home city of Bristol and she was intrigued by her collaboration with the Egyptian composer, Tarek Elazhary. Tarek plays the Arabic oud, and Tamsin plays the lever harp, accordion and flute.

Safa had only heard this track once before, so had no expectations going into the drawing. She allowed herself to listen while directly responding with the materials she had to hand. Once she had finished the drawing, she was able to review it more objectively. She observed that the colourful vertical lines used were a response to the harp and accordion with their jaunty melodies, while the black lines that cut over the top are reminiscent of the sound of the oud.

It's interesting to note that Safa finished the drawing feeling 'lighter and inspired'. She said that in future she will use music drawing as a warm-up to other work in the studio.

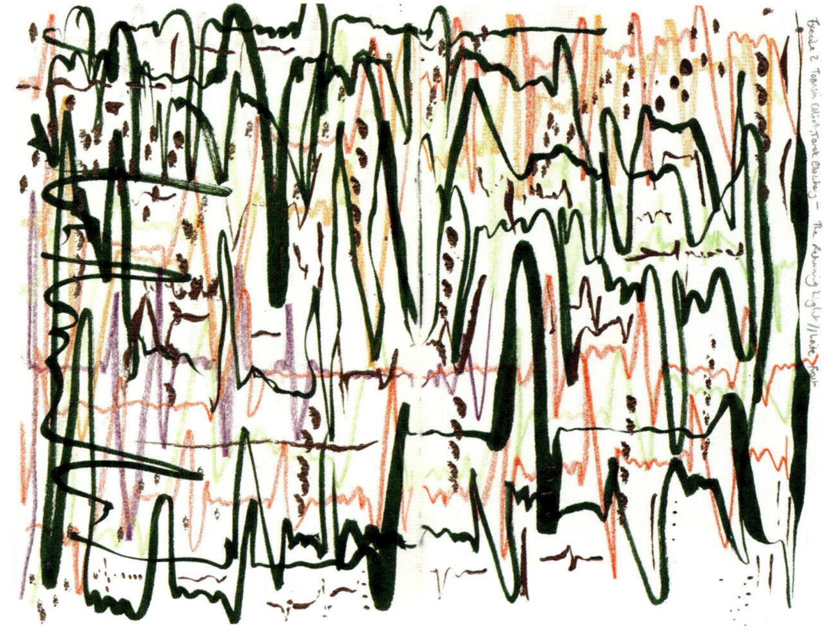

▼ *Anne: 'Piano Concerto No. 1 in F# minor', Sergei Rachmaninov (1891)*

Anne chose this classical music track as it's one she knows well and she was curious to see how she would translate it into a drawing.

After listening to it a couple of times, she attempted to document the two emotional states as she sees it – depression/anguish and calm/tranquillity. When the music was darker, she drew the stronger lines and the colours became more intense; when the music transitioned to something calmer, her mark making changed.

As she continued, she found herself drawing a 'scene', which wasn't intentional. 'I felt it was becoming autobiographical, indicating the struggles and triumphs of my own life.' At the end of the drawing, she felt emotionally exhausted.

This drawing was enlightening for Anne. She said it was almost like a therapy session, where she uncovered things about herself she hadn't observed previously. 'Maybe I will use this exercise again when I feel I need to unblock some emotions!'

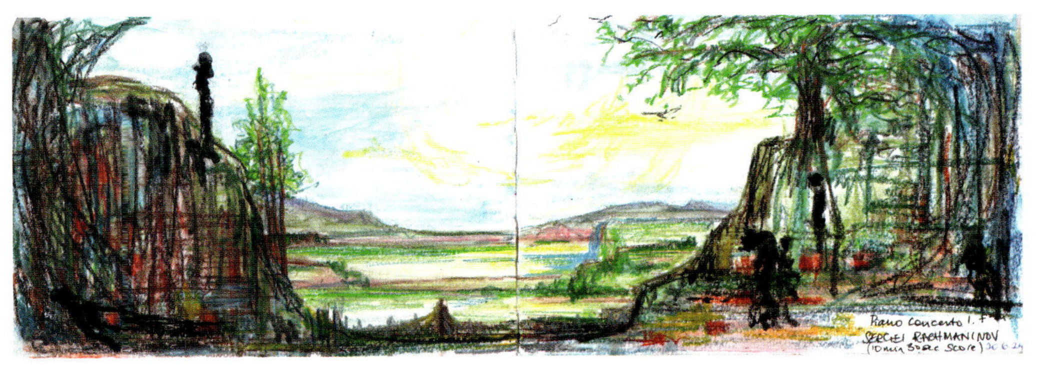

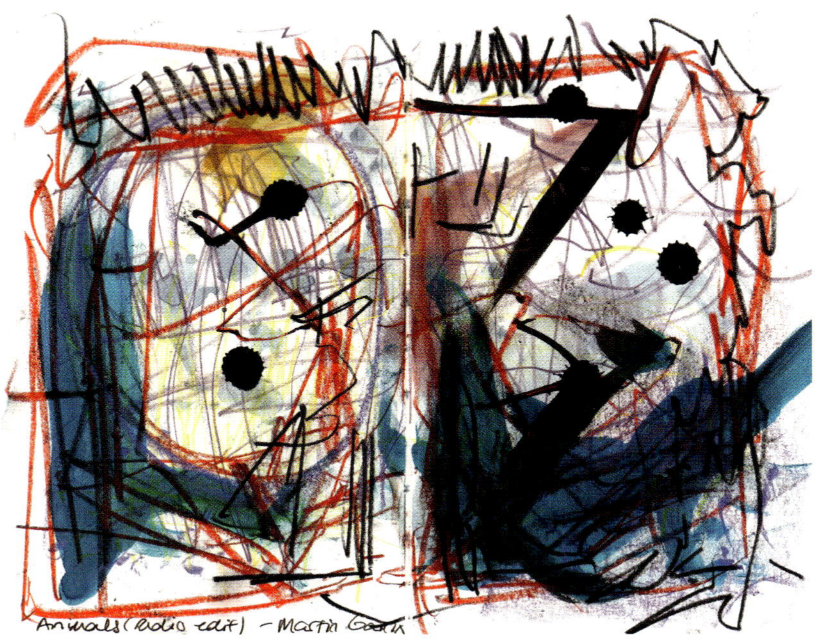

◀ *Eva: 'Animals (Radio Edit)', Martin Garrix (2013)*

Eva used music she hadn't heard before as she wanted her response to be fresh and original. She browsed online, approaching the exercise with openness and curiosity. She ended up choosing this house music track. She was drawn to it as it made her want to dance; it reminded her of her party days. She wrote: 'I started the drawing sitting down, but I ended up dancing while drawing.'

There is such an immediacy to Eva's drawing that it comes as no surprise that she completed it in one listen. There was no need to listen to the track again as the drawing was done. 'It was such a good exercise for me to do, as I didn't overthink it.'

Eva makes a great point here. So often we overthink or overdo our work, thinking that, for it to be complete, it needs to be worked on for a long period of time. As Eva has proven, shorter is often better.

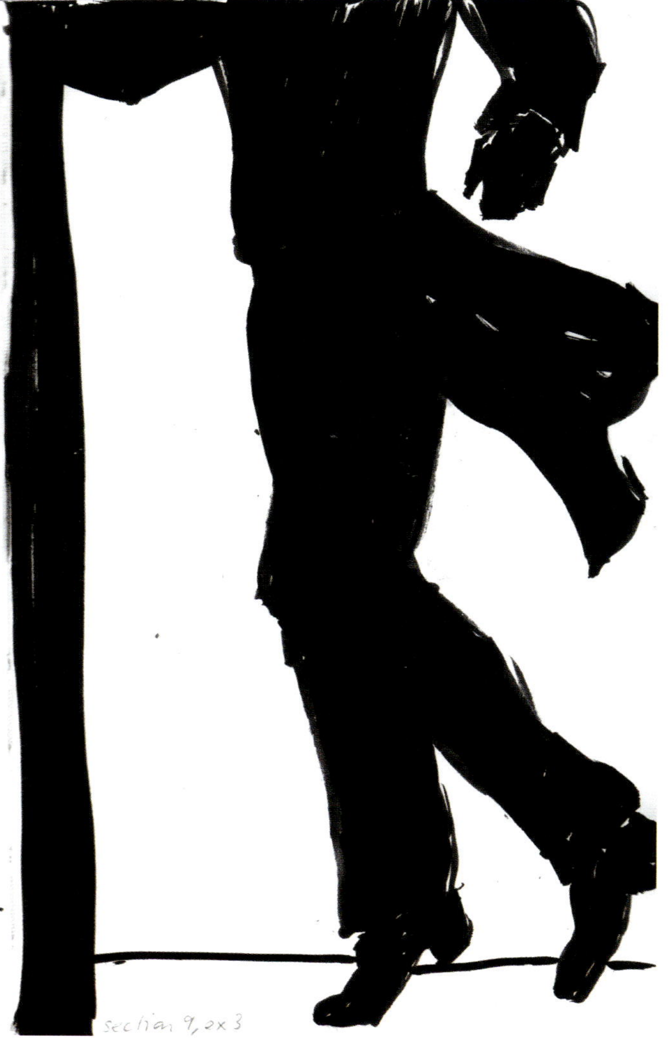

Exercise 2: Drawing from film

◀ *Claire:* Strictly Ballroom *(1992)*

Claire chose to draw from *Strictly Ballroom* as it was the first film she thought of. 'The costumes and the whole movement of the film had a real impact on me'. Clare decided to just use pen and ink for her film drawings, so she could respond quickly without overthinking. I chose to include this drawing of Claire's as I feel it sums up the essence of the film so simply and successfully.

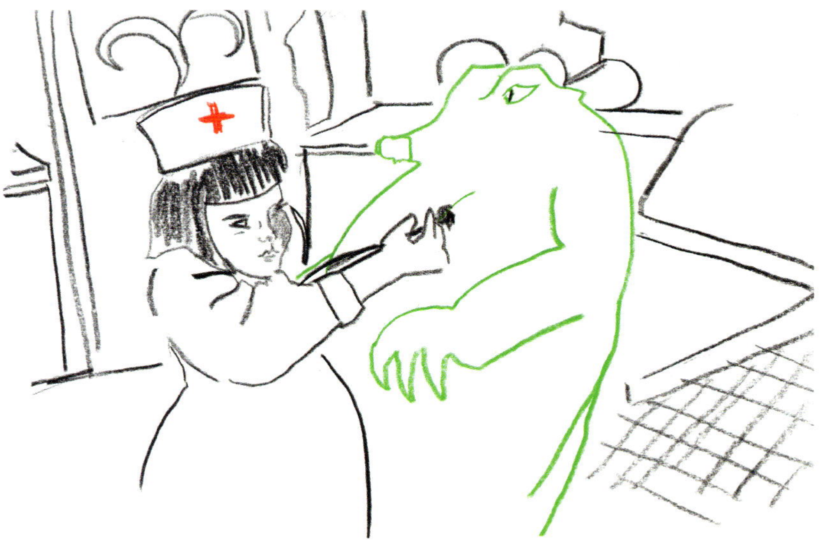

▼ *Jane:* Chitty Chitty Bang Bang *(1968)*

Jane chose to draw from her favourite film, *Chitty Chitty Bang Bang*, as it's one she knows well. 'It's such a magical, colourful film that is so visual, I knew I wanted to draw it'.

Jane confesses that, at first, she was a little unsure of the exercise, but, once she sat in front of the screen with her sketchbook, she started to enjoy the film. She realised that she wouldn't be able to draw the whole scene within the time limits so she simplified it by just drawing one element in the frame, and here we see her drawing of the magical car from the film. Jane noted that drawing from the film made her enjoy it even more as she was paying greater attention to the details.

◀ *Phyllis:* Amélie *(2001)*

Phyllis knew straight away that she wanted to draw from *Amélie* – one of her favourite films. 'It has humour, mischief, whimsy and romance, all which appeal to me.'

At first, she struggled with the time constraint, anxious that she wasn't 'going to get all the details in'. But after doing the first drawing, she realised that wasn't the point of the exercise. She started to enjoy just drawing the essentials – the essence of the scene.

In her summary, she notes that the exercise 'made me think carefully about composition. I realised that all the scenes I chose had a strong composition, which made it easier for me to draw.' Phyllis also notes that drawing from the film made her appreciate it even more. 'When you are looking that closely at the scenes it makes you realise just how much work has gone into creating every frame.'

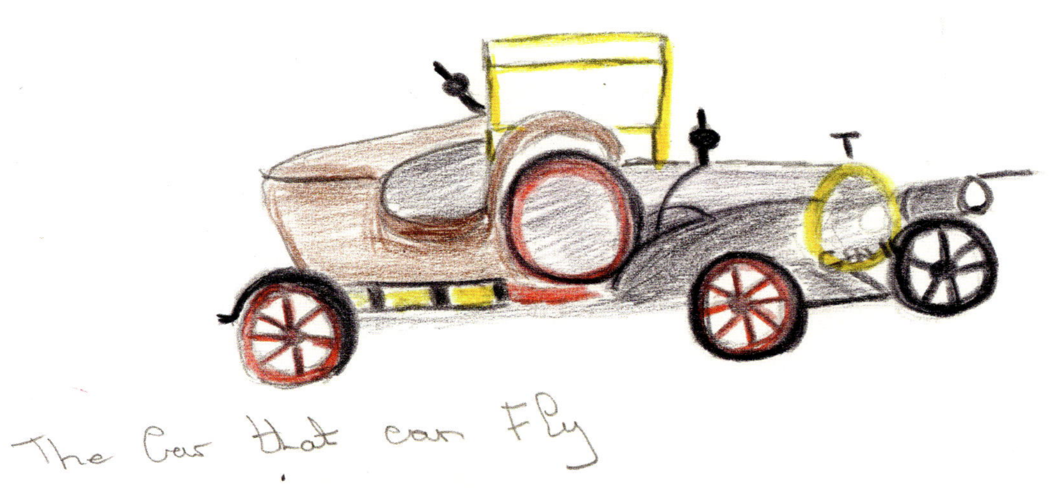

Exercise 3:
Drawing from collage

▼ *Niki*

Niki used textured papers and images from old books for her collage. She chose to interpret the brief literally, creating a self-portrait of her face based on one of the drawings she did for Chapter 7. The other elements in the collage reflect her interests and part of her personality.

She was surprised by how much she enjoyed creating the collage. As an artist whose work is always quite controlled, she found a sense of play and freedom involved with creating it. Niki then chose to draw the collage directly, as she was curious to see how it would translate into a drawing with the texture and colour removed. She found that this helped her mark-making skills and made her think carefully about tone.

As Niki gained so much from this exercise – it helped to loosen her up and have some fun – she is keen to use collage in her work in future. 'There is something about selecting, cutting and sticking that I found really liberating.'

▶ *Hannah*

Hannah has a great passion for collage and enjoys the whole process of selecting images that reflect her interests, tastes, personality and palette. 'I gave myself half an hour to select the images, but I was enjoying it so much that I allowed myself another half hour.'

She experimented with many different compositions for the collage. While she was making it, she was focused just on the task and wasn't considering the drawing of it. 'I wanted to approach the drawing with fresh eyes, in a different mindset.'

She felt her first attempt at drawing the collage was too literal. It had too many clashing colours and felt cluttered. She was happier with the next attempt, 'It felt more instinctive, cleaner, crisper and pared down.' This is evident when we look at Hannah's drawing. It isn't a direct response; instead, she has used elements of her collage to form her drawing – simple line work to highlight the structure of the composition.

This was a reminder for Hannah not to overdo her work, as sometimes she feels she can spend too much time on a piece and it loses something in the process. She acknowledges that she works best with a time limit.

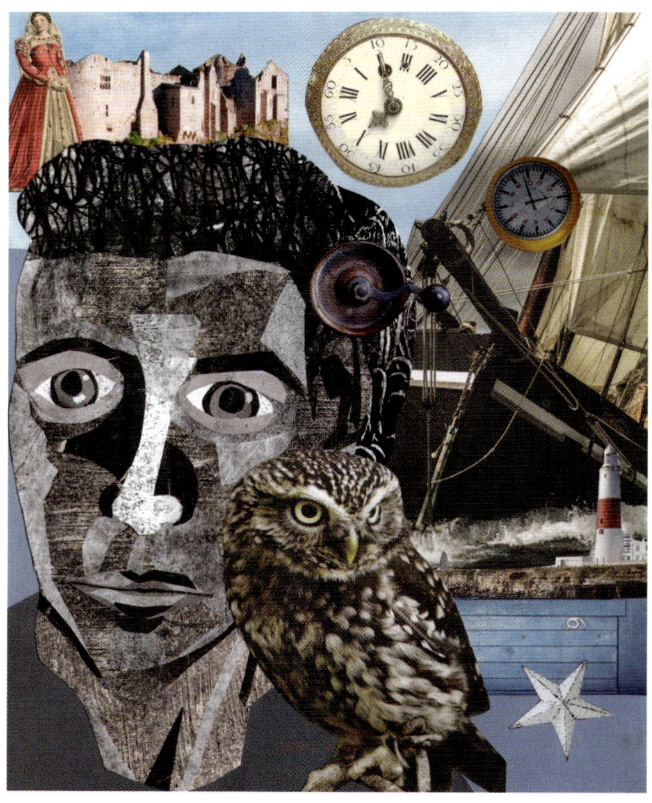

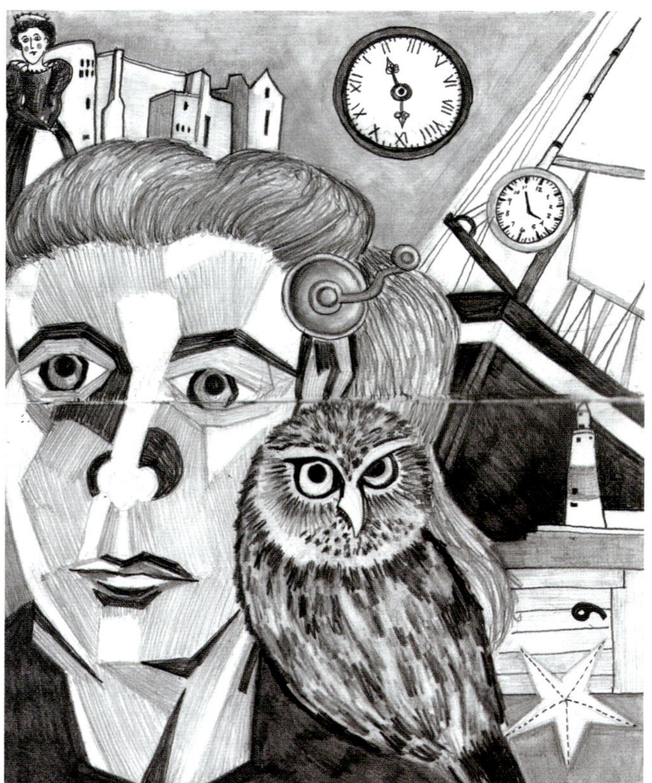

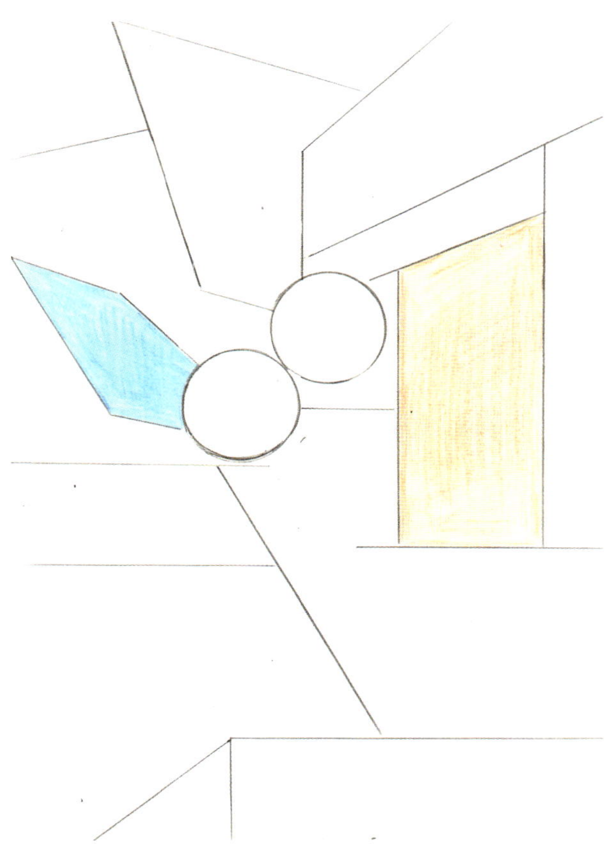

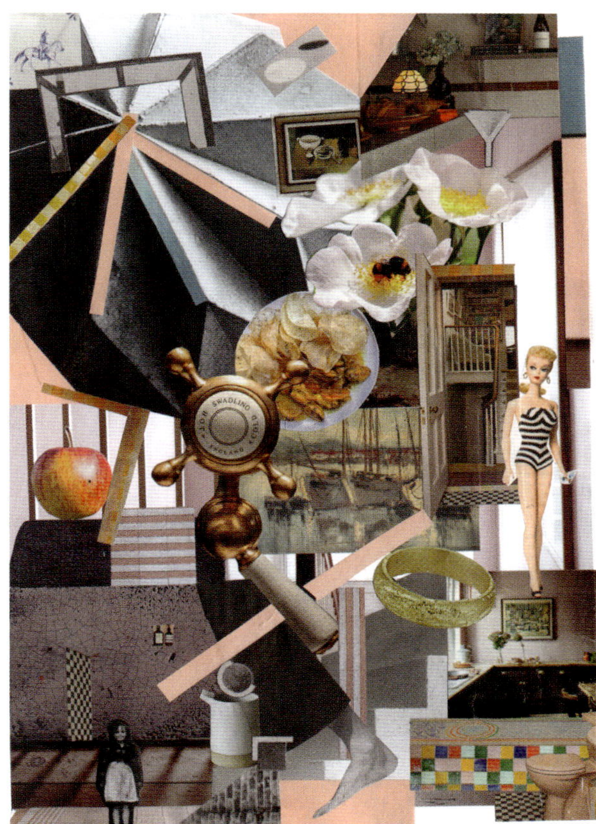

Exercise 4: Drawing your dream
▶ *Lucy*

Lucy rarely dreams anymore, but, when she does, it's always the same dream. 'It features a large house, with white curtains. It is situated in the middle of nowhere, in a deep forest. The setting is dark, but not in a frightening way; it's a peaceful and safe darkness. I am being chased by an animal in the wood and end up running into the house, into the dining room, and hiding under the table, so the animal can't see me. The animal always walks through the curtains but never sees me.'

Lucy wanted to work on black paper with white chalk, as she felt that they suited the atmosphere of the dream. Once she started the drawing, it came together quickly, 'Because it's a recurring dream, it's lodged in my memory'.

Lucy found this exercise helpful as it made her reflect about why she is having this recurring dream. Lucy is an artist who connects deeply to her emotions to help her create her work, so the more understanding she has of herself the better. 'This exercise was a real turning point for me. It made me realise that images from my memory and imagination are valid as starting points for my work and also can be works in themselves.'

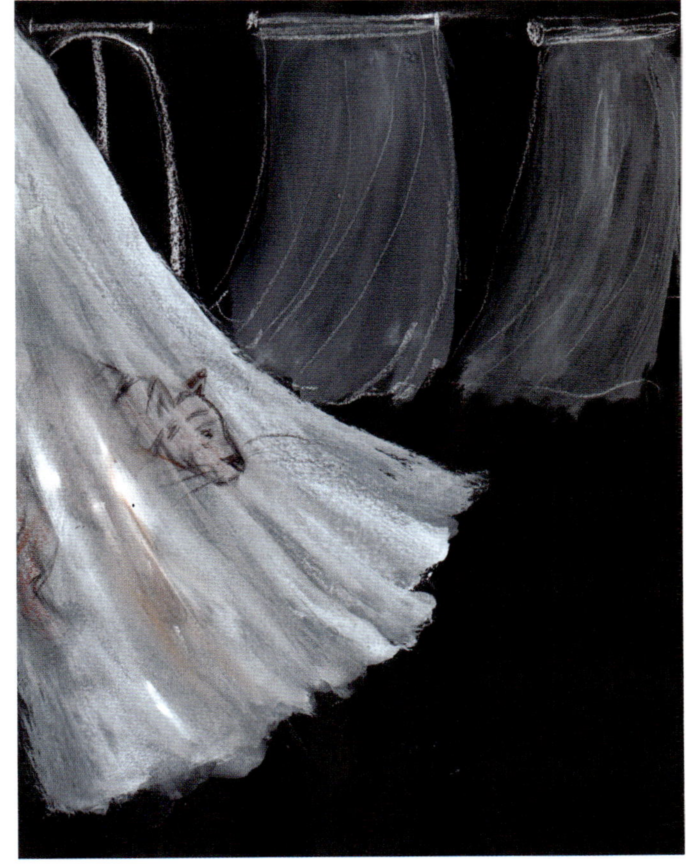

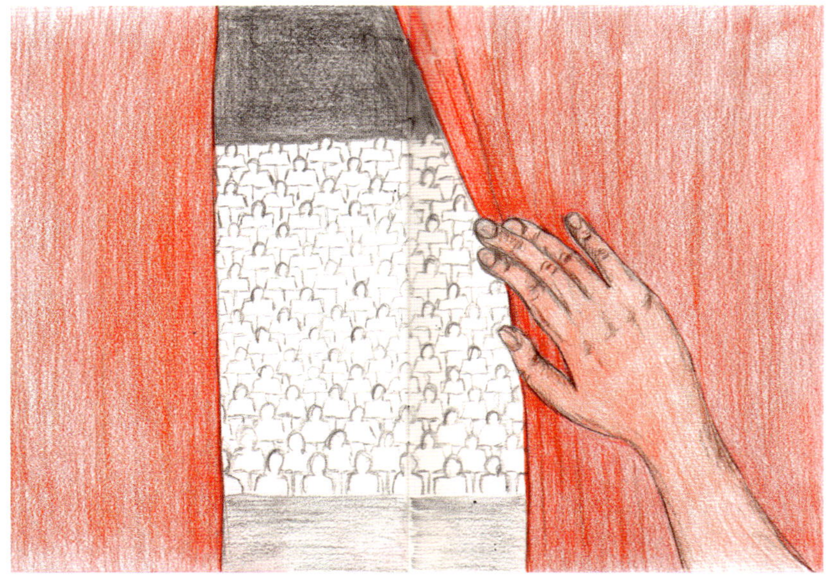

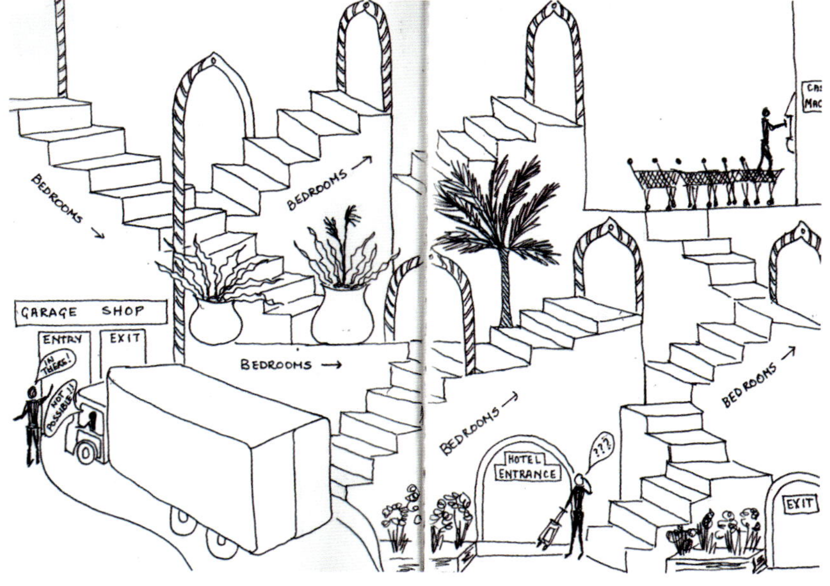

◄ *Kathi*

Kathi is an aspiring actor. This past year, she has taken part in a couple of shows, both of which caused her understandable anxiety and disrupted her sleep. 'When I did get to sleep, I found myself having the same dream, where I was opening the heavy red velvet theatre curtain and staring out into an audience of blank faces.'

For Kathi, the image was an easy one to recollect, so vivid in its simplicity. By drawing her dream, she realised that she had drawn her arm in the same red of the curtain, and that the audience were all left in pencil. 'It allowed me to discover that I see myself as the actor as very separate from the audience and that maybe, to build more of a unified performance, I could perhaps view us all as one.' For Kathi, drawing her dream has enabled her to make connections between her artwork and theatre work.

◄ *Paula*

Paula took note of her dreams over a period of a week and decided to combine elements of them into one drawing.

On the bottom left, we can see Paula driving a huge articulated lorry. Her husband then directed her the wrong way and she drove the lorry into a shop. At the top right, she was trying to get cash out but the only way she could get to the cash machine was by climbing over lots of trolleys.

The simplicity of the drawing itself was a revelation for her. 'I hadn't realised that I could draw in such a bold, direct and diagrammatic way. I've previously doubted my abilities to draw from my imagination, but this exercise made me realise that it is possible. I'm curious to see how I can include this more in my other work.'

▼ *Diane*

Like Paula, Diane decided to merge different dreams
into one drawing but in a more naturalistic way. In the
drawing, we see Diane's mum and brother having lunch
while Diane's arm, which is covered in maggots, holds out
a plate of food.

Diane admits she normally struggles to draw without
reference, so was hesitant about this exercise. However,
she surprised herself by just how much she gained from
it. 'Using some elements of my dreams as a starting
point could be a great way to come up with an original
composition and push myself out of my comfort zone.'

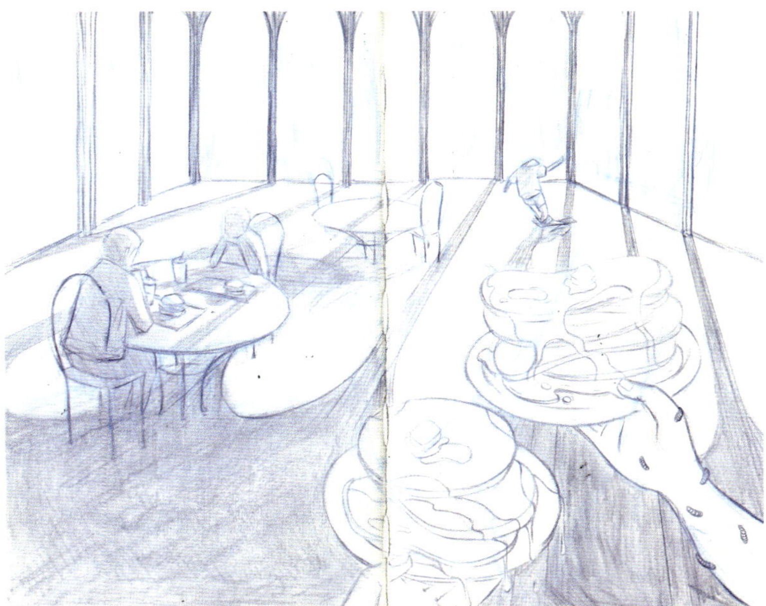

Final thoughts

I hope you have enjoyed these four exercises
and that they have opened you up to new
ways of drawing. Take a moment to reflect
on these exercises and answer these following
questions in your sketchbook:

- Which exercise did you find the
  most challenging? Why?
- Which exercise did you find the
  most enjoyable? Why?
- What have these exercises allowed
  you to discover about yourself?
- Have these exercises changed the
  way you feel about drawing?
  If so, why?
- Why do you think these ways
  of drawing could be beneficial to
  your practice?

As you can see from all these exercises, and
the rich and varied responses to them, the
Squad and I all discovered something about
our work that we would like to explore
further. I hope that by doing these exercises,
there has been an 'aha' moment for you too.
And, if that isn't the case, don't lose hope.
You might find, by leaving the drawings for
a while and coming back to them later, you
will see something in them you didn't see
earlier that you would like to develop further.

16
Personal project

'To create one's own world takes courage'

Georgia O'Keeffe

As the book is now coming to an end, I want to celebrate all the hard work you have done by using your drawings as inspiration for a more sustained and consolidated piece of work. This will take the form of a personal project. It is your chance to really have some fun, to use your drawings as inspiration for a bigger, more ambitious artwork.

I don't want you to feel intimidated by this. I'm not suggesting that the final piece of your project must be gallery-worthy or highly polished – it's more an opportunity to move drawings out of your sketchbook and utilise them in your own way. Think of it as a pause rather than a conclusion; time for you to experiment with what you have learnt and to consider things you might want to explore after the book finishes. My hope is that, by working on this project, you will discover strands in your artwork that you want to take further and that will fuel you on your artistic journey.

What might your project look like?

It's entirely up to you how you interpret this chapter and what work you make. I'm not giving you any limitations or restrictions. You have complete freedom to make whatever you want. The only thing I ask is that you use your sketches as inspiration for your artwork and that you set yourself a deadline, but beyond that it's up to you. For example, you may want to turn a small sketch into a larger drawing or painting. Or you might want to experiment with printmaking, a linocut or a monoprint. Or maybe you want to try your hand at creating a sculpture or a textile piece, an illustration or collage. The list is endless, and it doesn't have to be just one piece; it could be several works that take the form of a series.

Materials

Obviously, the materials you choose are up to you, and it all depends on the artwork you are making. However, it might be helpful to use your sketchbook for all your artist research and preparatory sketches.

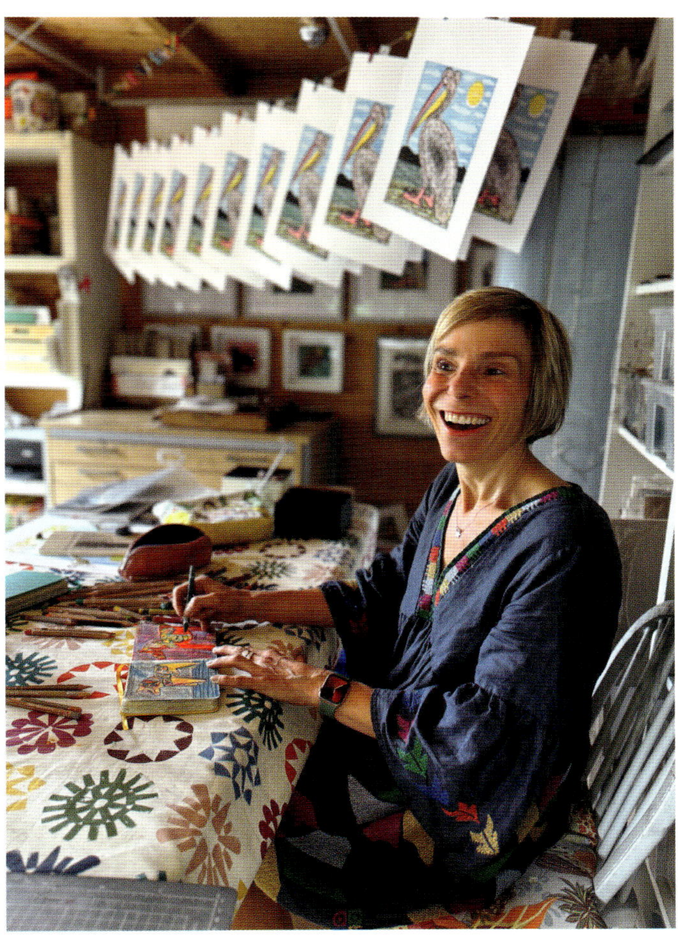

Project checklist

I've compiled this list to help guide you with your project and to give you some structure.

Set a deadline

It always helps to have a deadline. Setting a date to complete the project will help to ensure you finish the work, and it will motivate you to achieve your goals. It's also good practice as you embark on your life as an artist, as setting your own deadlines forms part of your practice.

Choose your drawings

Go through all your sketchbooks with an open, curious mind and see which drawings resonate with you. Try not to overthink this – just trust your intuition and create a collection.

Decide why

Now it's time to dig a bit deeper and question why you have chosen the drawings you have. What is it that attracts you to this sketch? Maybe it's the mark making that you have used or the colours you have chosen. Perhaps it reminds you of a special place you visited – if so, why was it special? Keep asking why until you have a clearer idea as to why you have chosen the drawings you have – this will help you decide how to progress with your project.

Gather your ideas

Once you have your drawings and a clearer sense as to why you have chosen them, take some time to put some ideas down on paper:

- What might your piece look like?
- On what kind of scale should it be?
- What materials might you want to use?
- What techniques do you want to try?

Draw or write any ideas that come to mind – be adventurous and ambitious. Think of it like a big shopping basket that you are filling with wholesome food – you aren't putting together the final dish yet, you're just gathering the ingredients.

Just a warning, your inner critic will be busy here, telling you, 'You can't do this. Who do you think you are?' Hopefully by now you can just let it sit in the corner while you crack on with your plans.

Create a timeframe

With any of my projects, I find it helpful to give myself a timeframe. For example, if I'm working on a project whereby I must deliver the final piece in a month, I would give myself a week for gathering my ideas and research, a week for the prep work and two weeks to create the actual artwork. If this sounds helpful to you, I would suggest you create a rough schedule too.

Research

What artist or maker comes to mind when you think of your project? Who would you like sitting on your shoulder to guide you? Cast your net wide and see what comes up. Once you have found an artist or maker whose work inspires you, see who they are or were inspired by. Keep adding to your list. You will also need to research materials at this point.

Preparatory studies

Now you have done your research, it's time to start experimenting, to try out ideas, mediums and techniques. Again, keep things loose and free at this point.

Work on the final piece

Once you have reached a place where you are happy with your idea, and you've had some time to experiment, you can pull together your consolidated piece of work, whatever form that might take. I always take process photos of my work as it's coming together, and I encourage you all to do this too. Note down any thoughts and feelings you have along the way as these will be helpful for the evaluation.

Decide when it's time to stop

One of the most difficult decisions we must make as artists is when to stop working on our piece of art. You can ask for advice from others, but ultimately, it's up to you to decide when it's done. I tend to overdo a print or a drawing; however, some of you might finish too early for fear of 'ruining' your work.

The more work you make, the easier this will be. You will become aware of your tendencies and make allowances accordingly. Remember, this isn't a full stop – you can always go back, edit, add, remove – it's just important that you reach a place where you think you are done, even if it's just for the time being.

Evaluation

Now you have reached that point of 'doneness', I want you to reflect on and evaluate your work. You might want to answer these questions in your sketchbook:

- What is it?
- Why did you make it?
- How did you make it?
- How do you feel about it?
- What do you think works?
- What do you think doesn't work so well?
- What did you learn?
- If you had to start this project again, what would you do differently?
- What further work could you do that is inspired by this project?

My personal project

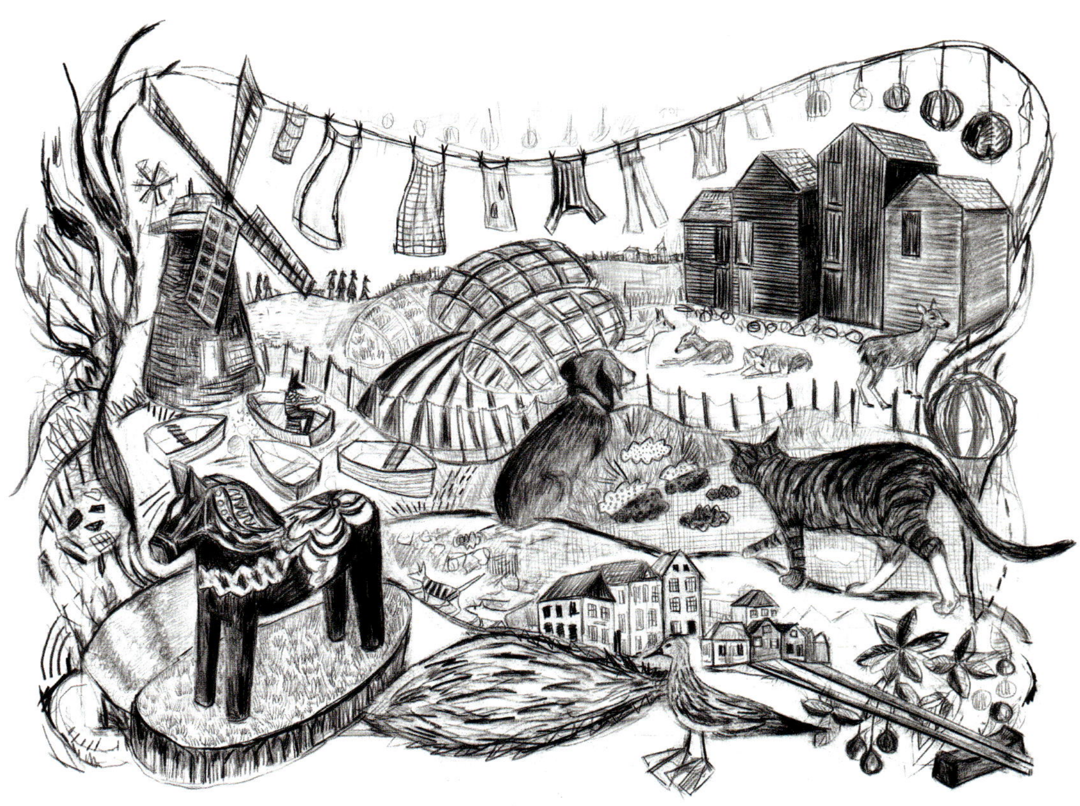

Title: *Playtime*
Medium: Graphite pencil on heritage drawing paper
Size: 56 x 76cm (22 x 30in)

For my personal project, I wanted to bring elements from my sketchbook drawings, drawings from my imagination and drawings from memory and combine them into one large piece. The 'Drawing your dream' exercise (see page 176) reminded me of how much I enjoy working this way, so I was keen to push it further.

I started by carefully selecting the sketchbook drawings I wanted to use and then redrew them onto a large sheet of paper. As with all my drawings, I loosely sketch in the main elements and keep it free flowing; I shift and move things around, constantly erasing and adding. The drawing then starts to suggest things to me, to have a pace of its own – spaces emerge that need filling, and the forms almost draw themselves.

I worked on this drawing over two weeks, and I looked at the work of Paul Noble, William Kentridge and Ilse Weber. It's a work in itself and one that has future potential. I would like to make a linocut inspired by it and I'm excited to create even larger drawings that fill whole walls. Let's see what happens....

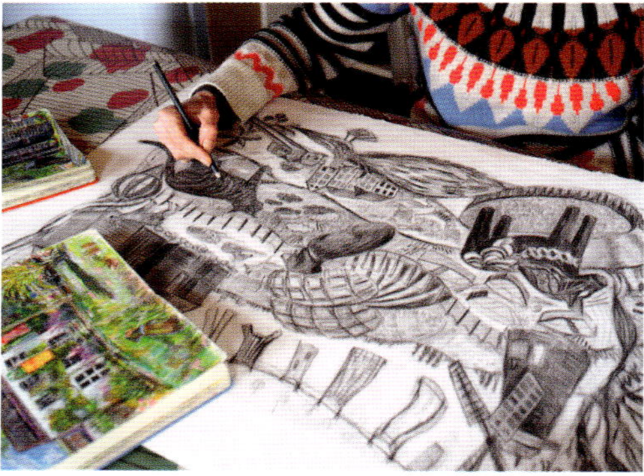

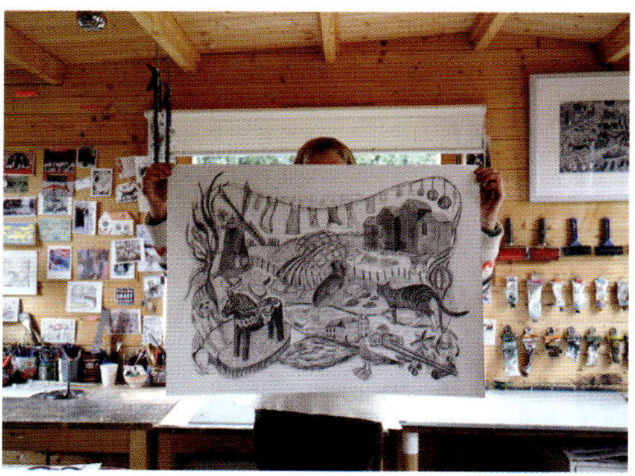

Sketch Squad: Personal projects

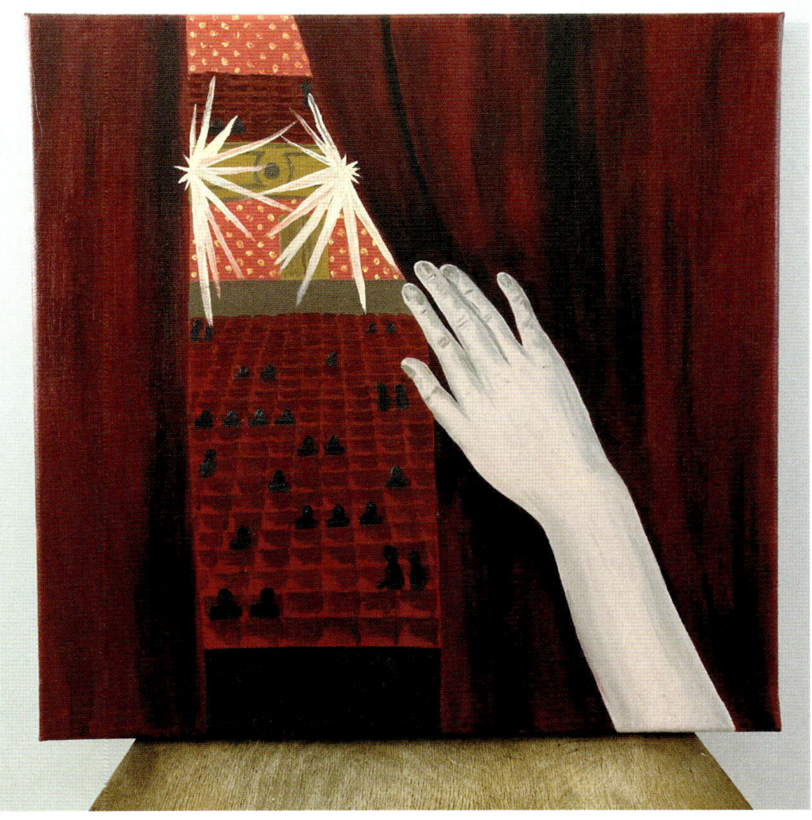

▲ *Kathi*
Title: *Before the Show*
Medium: Oil painting on canvas
Size: 50 × 50cm (20 × 20in)

The inspiration for Kathi's personal project was also the 'Drawing your dream' exercise on page 182. Kathi is part of a theatre group in Vienna – acting and performing are a big part of her life. After carefully reflecting on her sketchbook work, she felt the most connection with this drawing as it features the theatre. She wanted to develop it further.

Kathi has painted in the past and it's something she enjoys, so she decided that her personal project would take the form of a painting. She started her project with research into artists who used the interiors of theatres in their work, looking at the paintings of Walter Sickert, Gustav Klimt and Eugene Spiro. These gave her a good base of inspiration to build upon.

Initially, she procrastinated with the project as she felt it was too overwhelming. However, she utilised some of the tactics that have helped her with exercises in the book – one of which was breaking the task down into smaller, more achievable chunks. She committed to adding a small part or a layer to the painting every day, using water-based oil paints, which have the same qualities as oil paints but dry faster.

While working on this project, Kathi realised that her procrastination is due to the fear of failure, and she recognises that this holds her back from doing what she wants in many aspects of her life. Having had this realisation while successfully completing this project has made her determined to face her procrastination problem head on.

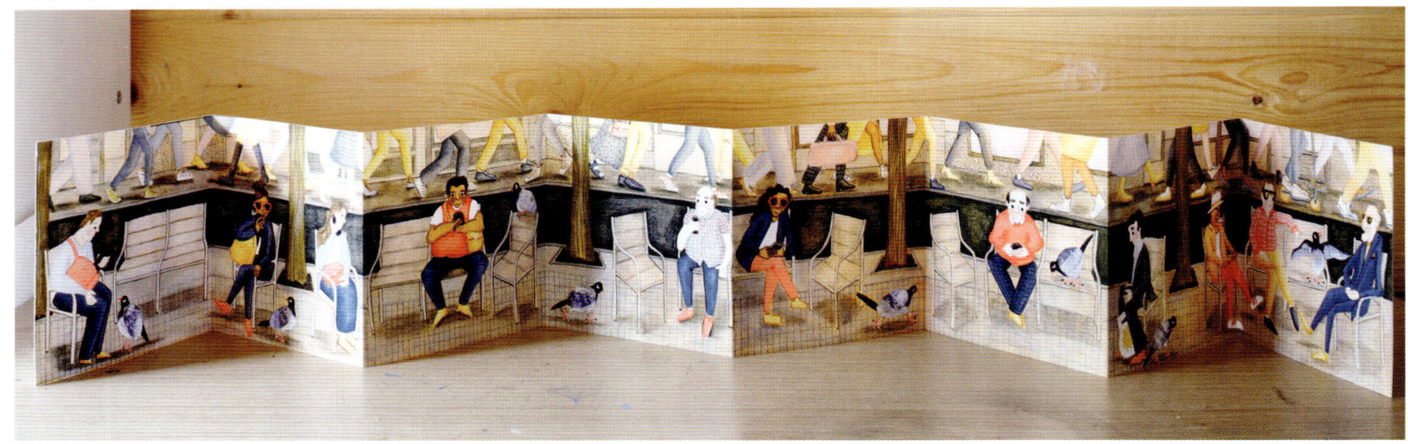

Title: *La Rambla*
Materials: Ink, gouache, coloured pencil
Size: 168 x 21cm (66 x 8in)

Niki's starting point for her personal project were the holiday drawings she did in Barcelona. One of the highlights of the trip was drawing people on La Rambla. She was fascinated by the contrast between the generations. She noted that everyone her age or below was sitting on their own, glued to their phones, whereas the older generation sat next to one another, chatting and enjoying each other's company. This formed the idea of creating a long sequential drawing, reflecting these observations, and perhaps turning it into a concertina book.

She created the long drawing strip by joining three sheets of A3 paper. Starting with an underpainting of ink, she then drew on top using gouache and coloured pencils. She used her drawings as reference and added in observations she'd had at the time – the warmth of the sun, how busy the street was, how many pigeons there were, etc. She also looked at the illustrators Louise Lockhart and Sarah van Dongen for inspiration.

Niki is currently working on a BA in illustration, and, as a result, is completing lots of briefs with a tight turnaround. For her, this project was a respite away from all of that – she was able to enjoy it purely for herself. She says, 'I loved how meditative and unpressured it felt. I was able to let the ideas flow without forcing them.'

For further work, Niki is keen to develop and expand this project by turning it into a short illustrated story with the pigeon as the main character. She found the project helpful in generating ideas for work in the future.

▶ *Phyllis*
Title: *Amélie's Hat*
Material: Corriedale fleece, soap paste
Size: 27 x 30cm (10½ x 12in)

Phyllis's inspiration for her personal project was the drawing she did for Chapter 13, 'Drawing from paintings', where she drew from the Matisse painting *Femme au chapeau* (*Woman with a Hat*).

While she was drawing the painting in SFMOMA, she had an 'aha' moment and knew that she wanted to recreate the hat – this project provided the perfect opportunity to do so. Phyllis chose to hand felt as it's a technique she enjoys and so often she finds herself surprised by the result. She used Corriedale fleece, which she laid out in many layers for each section. Then she applied a thick soap paste and water to the fleece, with friction, and the fibres came together to felt. This was all then manipulated into the shape of the hat. She looked at the work of Alice Neel, Paula Rego and Picasso for inspiration.

In her evaluation, Phyllis admits that she is not normally immediately pleased with her work, but she felt an immediate sense of achievement on completion of this hat. 'I feel that I captured the colours, the textures and the character of her hat. It was an experiment that worked.'

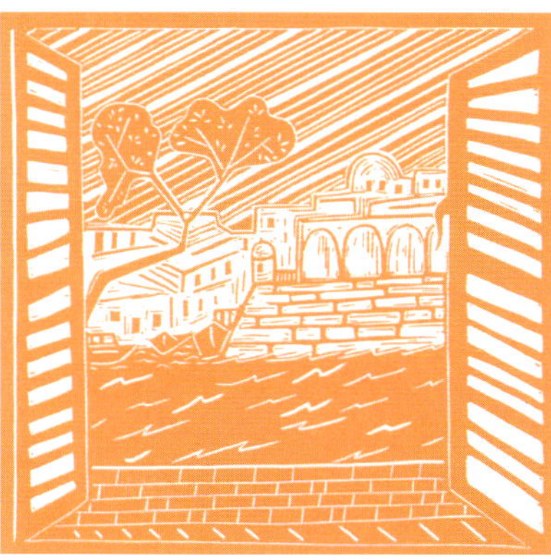
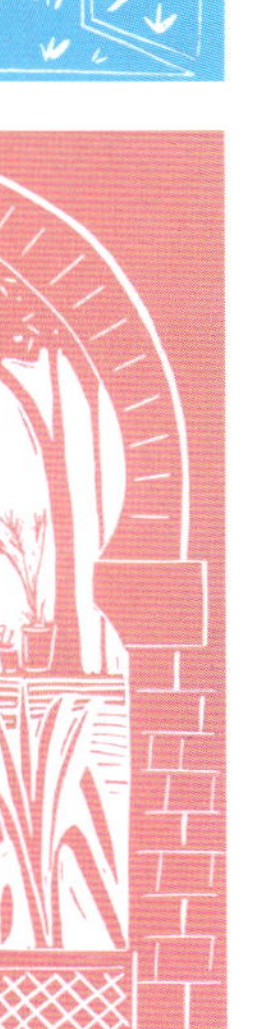
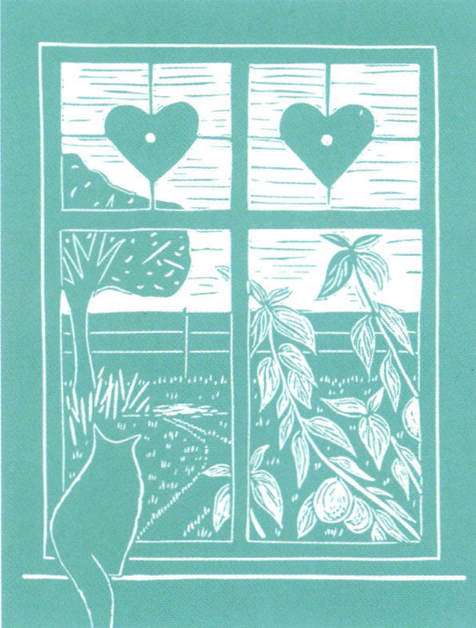

Title: *A Room with a View*
Materials: Four lino blocks, various sizes, printing ink
Window 1: Faro, Portugal – 12 x 18cm (4¾ x 7in)
Window 2: Valetta, Malta – 15 x 15cm (6 x 6in)
Window 3: My Home – 15 x 20cm (6 x 8in)
Window 4: Granada, Spain – 15 x 20cm (6 x 8in)

Safa is an avid traveller and has been keeping sketchbooks of her travels for a couple of years. One of her favourite things to draw is views from windows, so she particularly enjoyed the 'Draw your view' exercise (see page 149). As she has accumulated many of these window drawings, she selected her favourite four and decided that these would be the inspiration for her project.

First, she experimented with different print techniques and decided that linocut would work best. She researched artists who include windows in their work, such as Henri Matisse, Alice Neel and Lois Dodd. She then redrew her original drawings in preparation for her linocuts to help figure out what areas she needed to carve away and what she should leave. Once she was happy with the drawings, she began carving her linocuts. After she had completed all four, she carefully chose her colours, ensuring they complemented the individual linocuts so they all worked together as a whole.

My main observation after reading through Safa's notes is how important preparation was for her project. She normally starts a linocut with just a loose sketch and frequently finds she loses her way. However, this time, she was rigorous with her drawing and had a clear idea of the plan before she started. She says that in future she 'will always start a linocut with a solid drawing as its basis. Drawing is the stimulus and generator of the next process. My drawings are now essentially windows to the next body of work I create.'

Safa is keen to expand this project by further exploration of inside and outside views. She plans to include more details inside which will create a narrative for the observer.

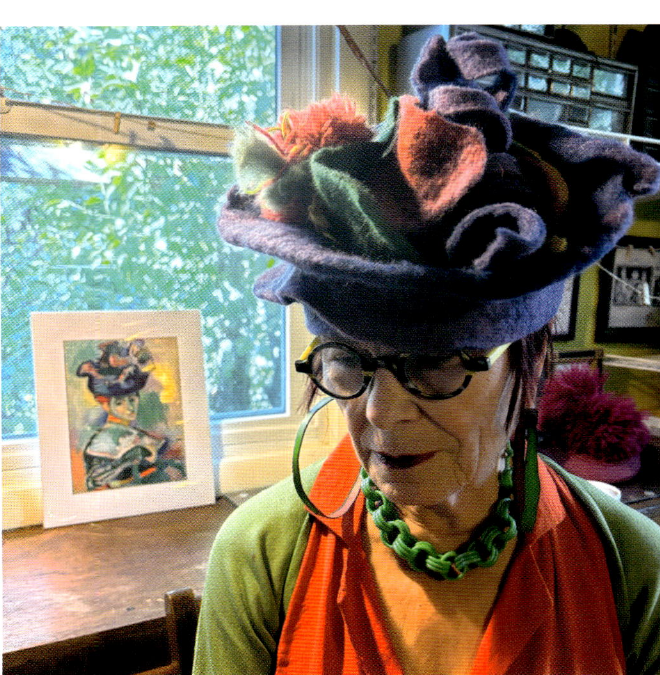

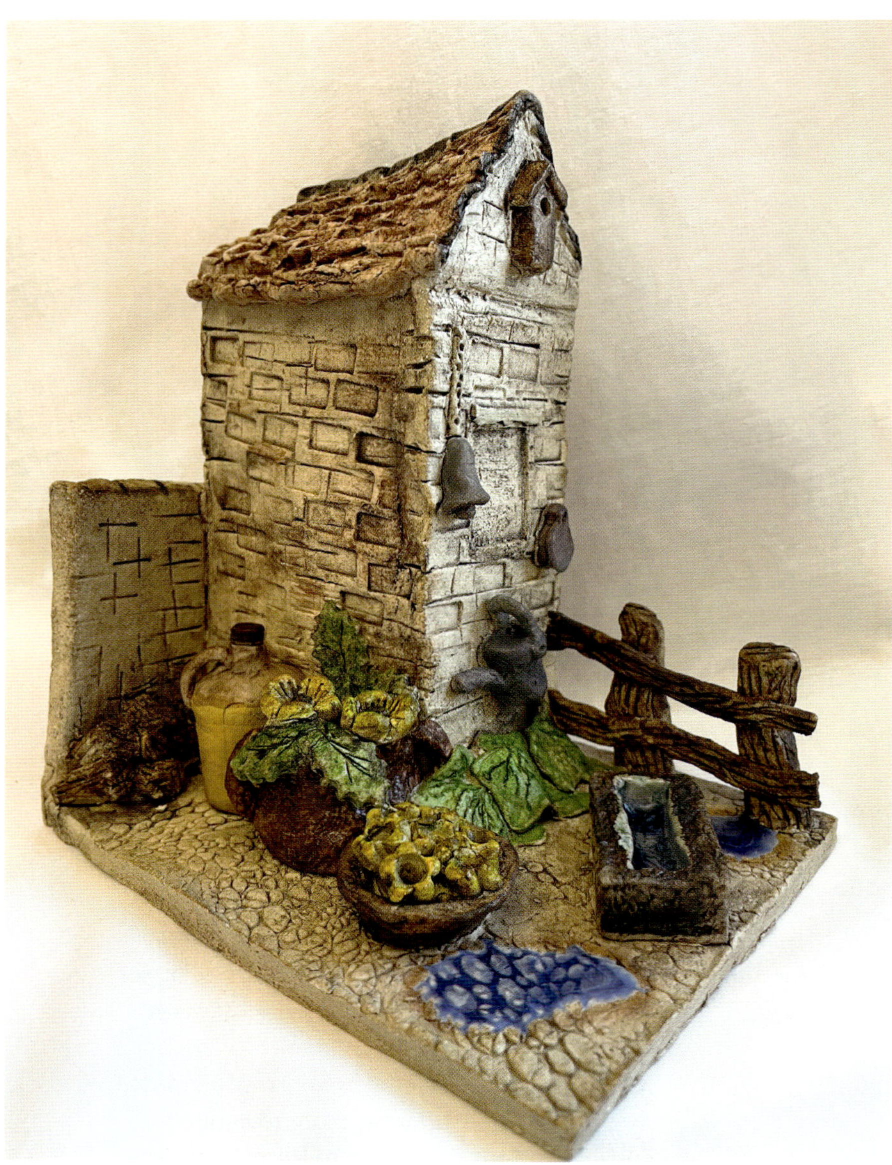

◀ *Paula*
Title: *Lynda's Netty*
Material: Clay with glazing
Size: 18 x 13 x 18cm
(7 x 5¼ x 7in)

Paula lives in a very sociable village – she knows many of her neighbours and has spent a lot of time drawing in their gardens. One of her favourite drawings for the book was of her friend Lynda's garden with its old outside loo, known as a 'netty'. She decided to use this drawing as the focus for her project.

She started out with a linocut inspired by the drawing and was keen to push the idea further. As she had recently started a pottery class and had previously experimented with relief ceramics, the idea began to form of creating a 3D piece of Lynda's garden. She looked at artists who used ceramics in their work for inspiration, including Pablo Picasso, Edmund de Waal and Betty Woodman, and began experimenting. You can see the result here. As it was only her second time working with clay, Paula is keen to point out the things she feels don't work but also notes how much she enjoyed the process.

One of my main observations while looking at Paula's personal project is just how far you can push an idea. It can start with a small sketch that only takes a few minutes but this can form the basis of a whole set of explorations that lead in all sorts of directions.

Paula realised while creating this ceramic piece that she knew very little about glazing pottery, so extending her knowledge of glazing and firing options is something she is keen to explore in her further work.

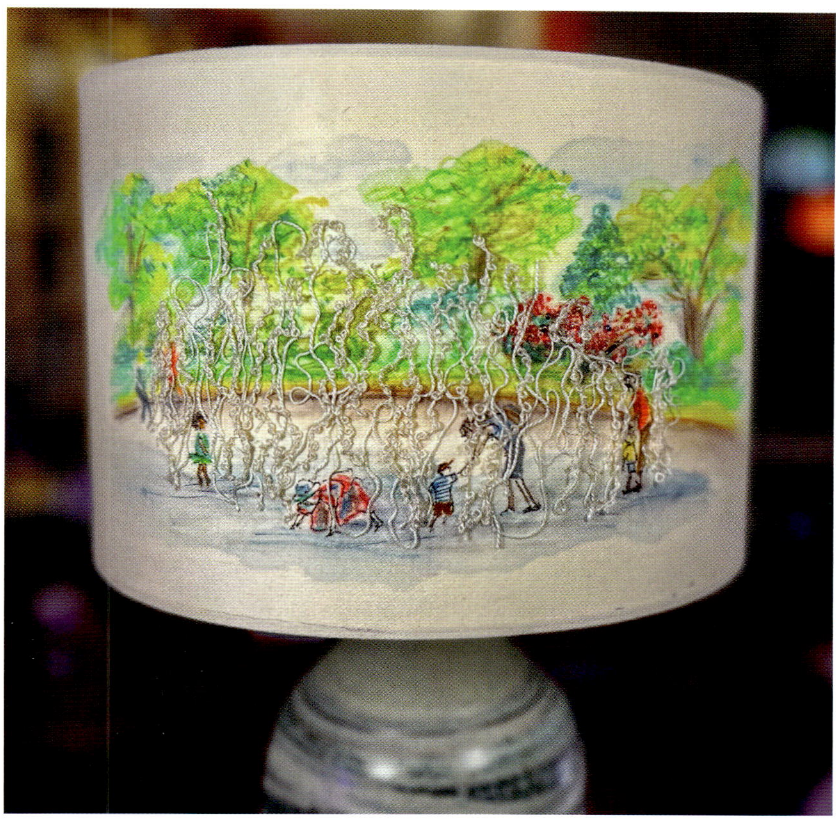

Anne is someone who uses an abundance of materials in her work and she was keen to explore a range of resources in this project. After careful consideration, she decided to use a selection of her sketchbook drawings, transfer them onto fabric and then make a 3D piece out of this fabric. She chose the drawings she's made in public as 'these were the ones she felt most connected to' and then researched artists such as Eric Carle, Cas Holmes and Sue Lancaster.

After a couple of weeks of playful experimentation with different printing methods and drawing onto various materials, she landed on the idea of using the structure of a lampshade to showcase her drawings. Using heavyweight cotton and fabric inks, Anne redrew her selected sketches directly onto the fabric and added more details by stitching onto the fabric using couched threads and bead embellishments.

For Anne, the whole process was a sharp learning curve, from researching the inks, paints and pens to learning about lampshade options. She feels proud of this piece and finished her evaluation by saying, 'I have learnt to not underestimate or undervalue my own design and artistic expression because I recognise that the lampshade, if I saw it on display, would impress, intrigue and inspire me.' This is a massive achievement for Anne, who is keen to keep pursuing this idea of translating her sketches into textile form.

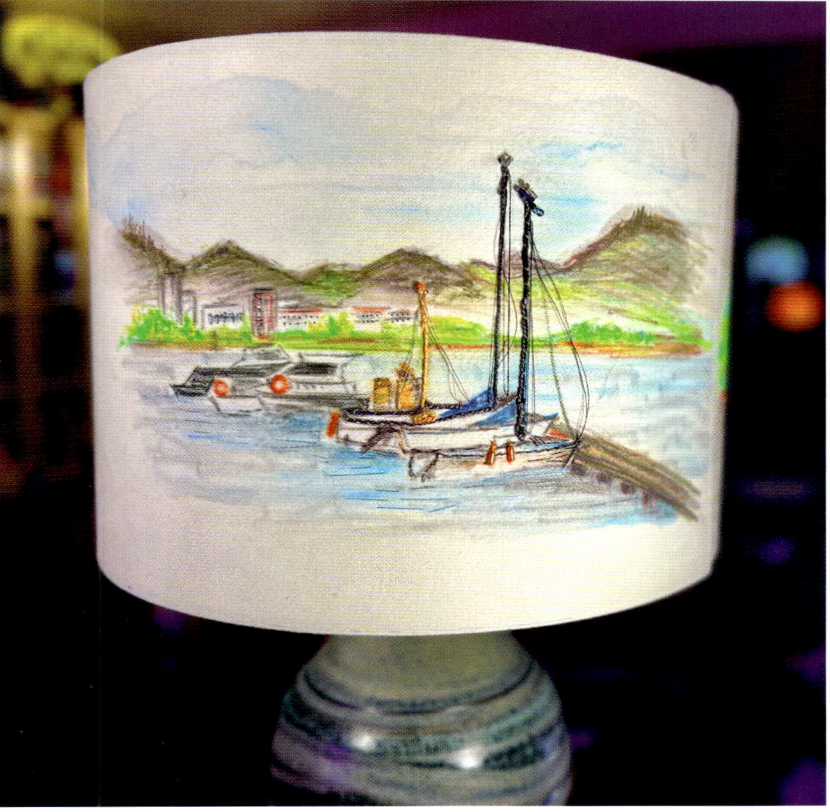

Title: *Las isleñas del Perú*
Material: Drypoint plastic, printing ink, etching tools
Size: 21 x 30cm (4¼ x 12in)

Claire travelled to Peru during her year in the Sketch Squad, and, when looking through her sketchbooks, she decided to focus on her drawings of the local people while she was there. She particularly enjoyed drawing people at work on their textiles, in their traditional workwear. Claire admits she has always struggled with drawing people, and these Peru drawings were a breakthrough for her, so this project was a perfect opportunity to push the drawings further.

She started by experimenting with different forms of printmaking and researching artists such as Vincent van Gogh and Pieter Bruegel. Initially, she tried out monoprint, but she didn't feel it was the right technique for the images, so she attempted drypoint printmaking – a simple form of intaglio printmaking that involves scratching an image onto a metal or plastic plate with a sharp tool to create an impression. Claire scratched the drawings onto a plastic plate then inked it up, as you would do for an etched plate, and hand printed it. Normally, to get a successful drypoint print, you would use an etching press; however, Claire managed to print successfully using wooden spoons and printmaking barens.

Reading through Claire's evaluation of her project, three things stood out:
1. It was a real confidence boost for Claire to realise that she could enjoy drawing figures and not be so critical of her abilities.
2. The prints provide her with a unique souvenir of her time in Peru.
3. It reiterated the value of sketching while travelling to her and reaffirmed that drawings can be used in many different ways in the future.

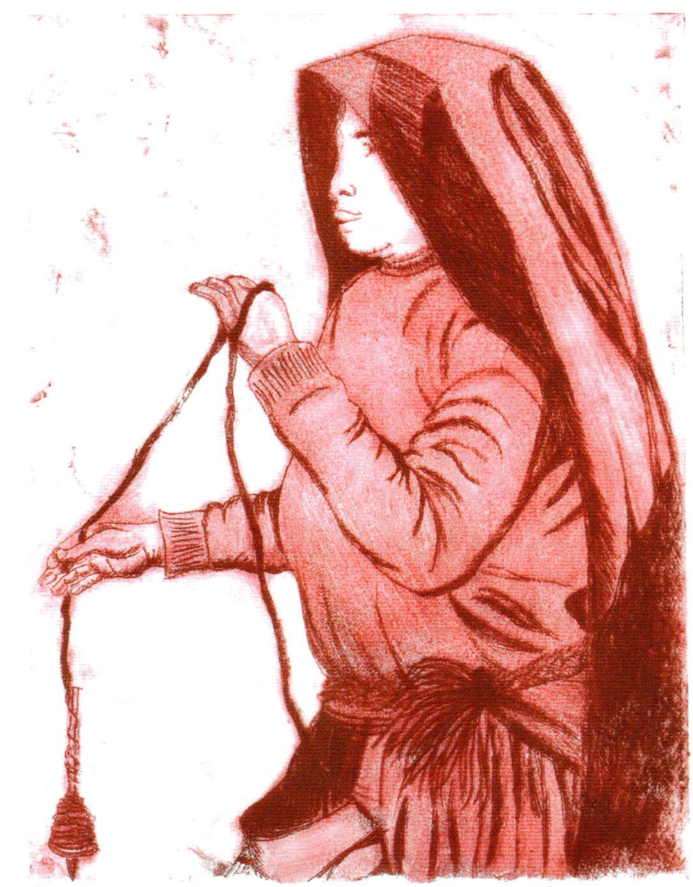

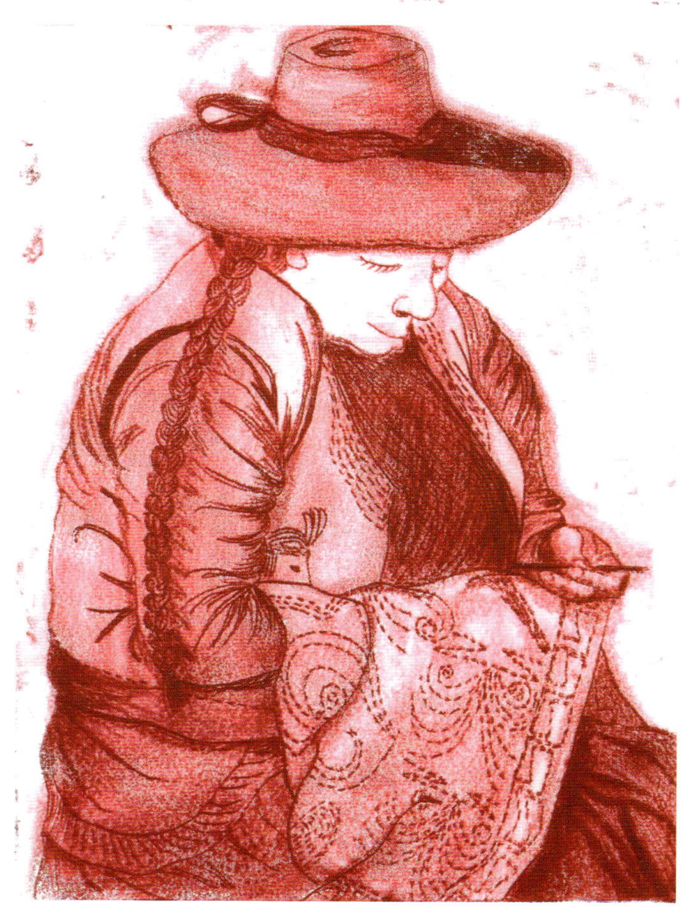

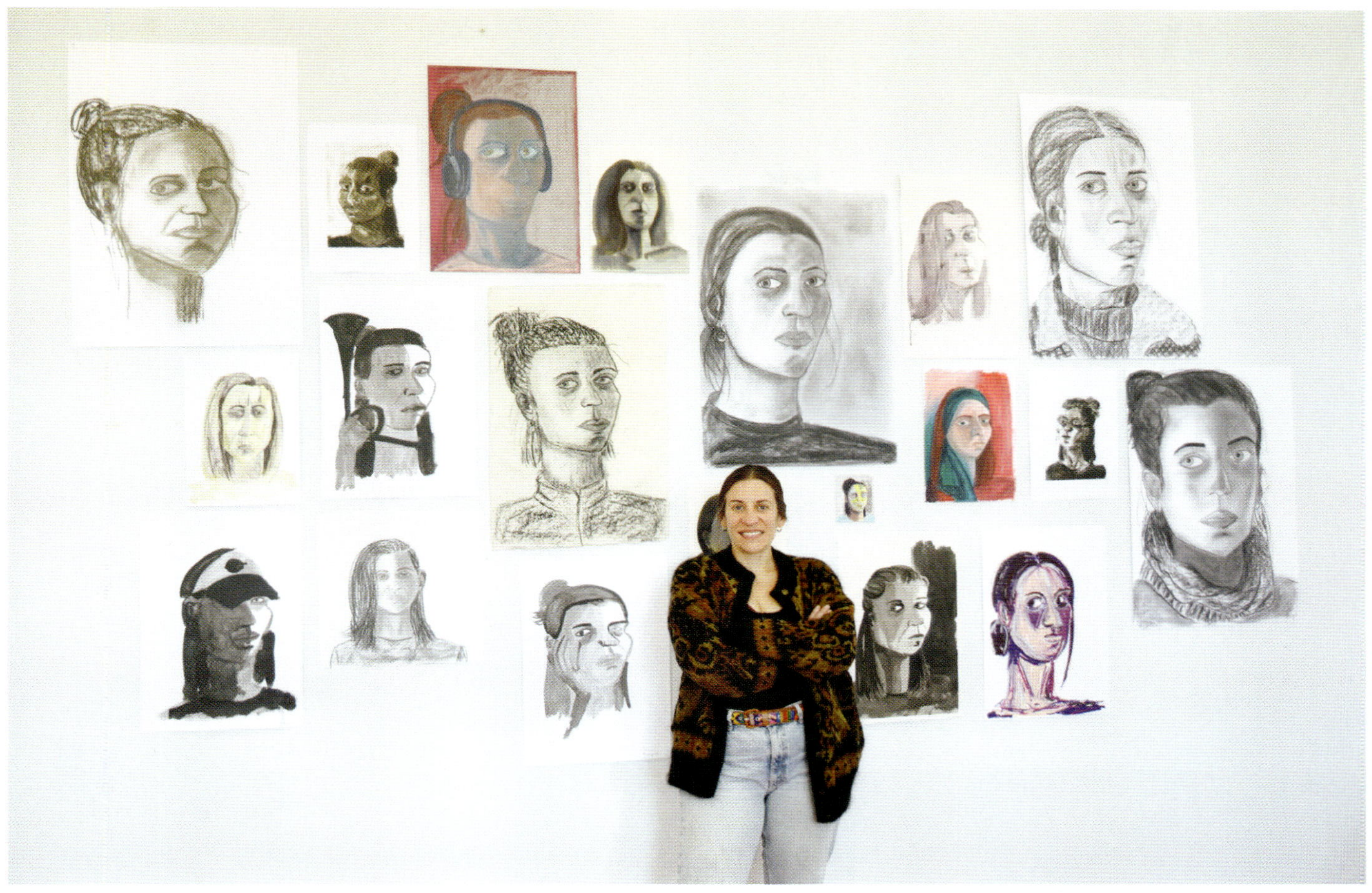

Title: *Self-portrait Wall*
Materials: Paper, ink, charcoal, gouache, graphite pencil, coloured pencils
Size: Twenty-one drawings in various sizes, from 25 x 30cm (10 x 12in) to 60 x 84cm (24 x 33in)

For Eva, it was Chapter 7, 'Drawing portraits', that had the most impact on her during her year in the Sketch Squad. Eva normally gets her inspiration from the landscape and, having never drawn portraits or self-portraits before, she surprised herself by how much she enjoyed drawing these. Therefore, choosing portraits for her project seemed the obvious choice.

Initially, Eva considered creating portraits of her friends and family; however, with time constraints and work commitments, it made more sense to use herself as the model and the idea for this project began to take shape. Eva has a busy job, so part of her preparation for the project was looking carefully at her schedule and seeing when she could fit drawing in. She came up with the idea of creating one self-portrait drawing per week until the project deadline. She decided to keep the drawing time fluid, depending on what time she had, and the project began to take shape organically. She found that some weeks she had one hour or more, and other weeks she had only ten minutes.

The paper size and materials differed every time to allow for experimentation with composition and techniques. 'I approached it as an exploration and playtime, rather than anything else, with no expectations – wanting to enjoy the process and learn more than thinking about the result'. Eva also looked at the artists Marlene Dumas, Frida Kahlo and Laura Knight.

She finished the project with twenty-one portraits in total and was then faced with the question of how best to display them. She ended up using the local village hall, which had a large wall space. Having the opportunity to view her work all together in a new environment made her see it differently; it was almost as if she was viewing it in a gallery space.

Next, Eva would like to work on a series of drawings that combine both portrait and landscape.

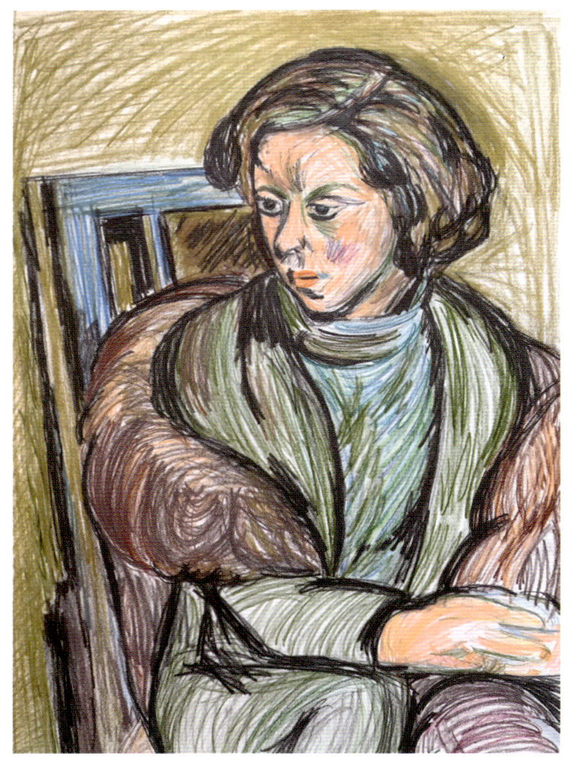

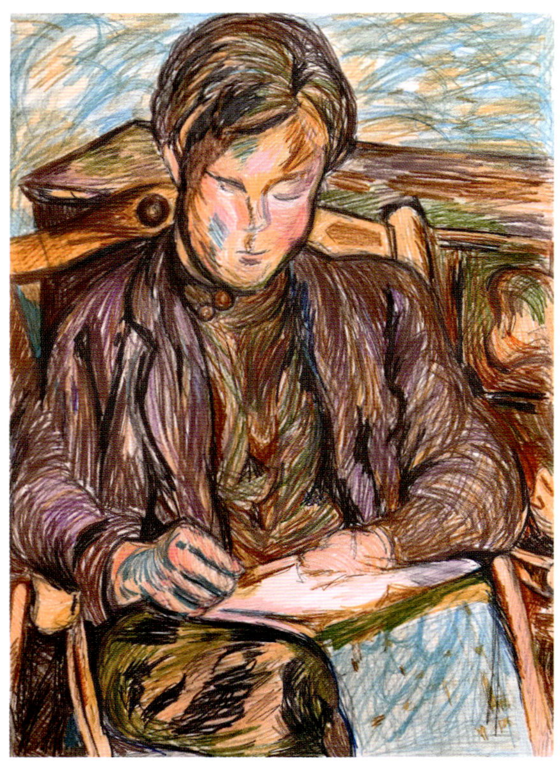

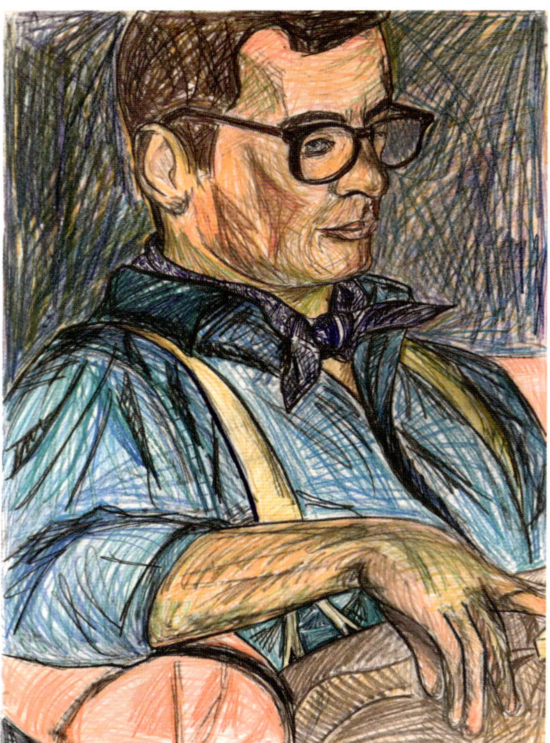

▲ *Hannah*
Title: *Three Colour Studies*
Material: A2 paper, coloured pencils
Size: 60 x 85cm (24 x 33½in)

One of the most enjoyable chapters for Hannah, and the one she felt she learnt a lot from, was Chapter 13, 'Drawing from paintings'. It helped her loosen up her way of drawing and become freer with her mark making. Therefore, after sifting through her sketchbooks, she decided to use this as a starting point for her project.

As she has always felt an affinity to the Bloomsbury group of artists, with their use of colour and subject matter, she decided to use a selection of their paintings to draw from – particularly the work of Duncan Grant, Vanessa Bell and Roger Fry. She noted: 'I had no preconceived idea of where the drawings were going to take me, just that I wanted to try to draw like someone else to break old habits.'

Hannah then went about deciding what materials to use. She knew she wanted to work larger, so she chose A2 paper, and she was curious to see how she could use coloured pencils to emulate the artists' paint strokes.

On reflection, Hannah felt surprised and pleased with the results. Working on a larger scale meant that she was freer with her arm and hand movements, and subsequently the drawings had a sense of spontaneity. She is keen to work on larger drawings in the future.

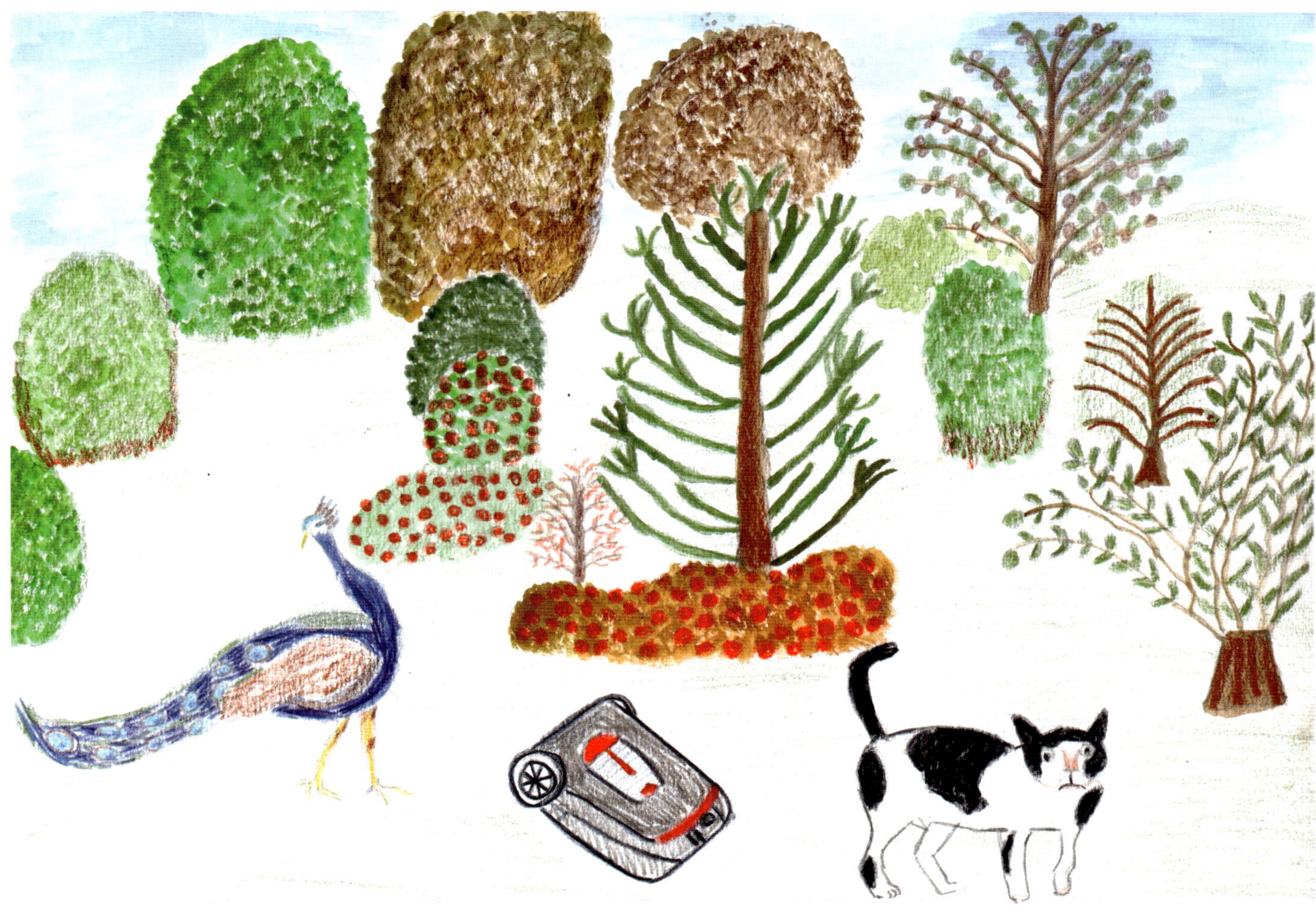

▲ *Jane*
Title: *Our Garden*
Materials: A3 paper, watercolour, coloured pencils, graphite pencils
Size: 29.7 x 42cm (11¾ x 16½in)

Jane knew her focus for her personal project was going to be her garden and its inhabitants – a resident peacock called Percy, a stray cat called Puss Puss and a robot lawnmower called Ernie.

She chose to work larger and experiment with using watercolour, graphite pencils and coloured pencils all in one piece. She started by using her sketchbook garden drawings from Chapter 6 (see page 74) as inspiration – redrawing onto a large piece of A3 paper. She then added Percy, Ernie and Puss Puss.

She attempted the painting a couple of times until she felt that she had got the scale and composition just as she wanted it. She looked at the work of L. S. Lowry, Helen Bradley and Grandma Moses for inspiration. For Jane, there was no internal angst about completing the work: 'I don't overthink my artwork, I just sit down and get on with it. If I enjoy it, then I'm happy!' In future, Jane is keen to continue to work larger and to experiment with mixing different techniques and materials.

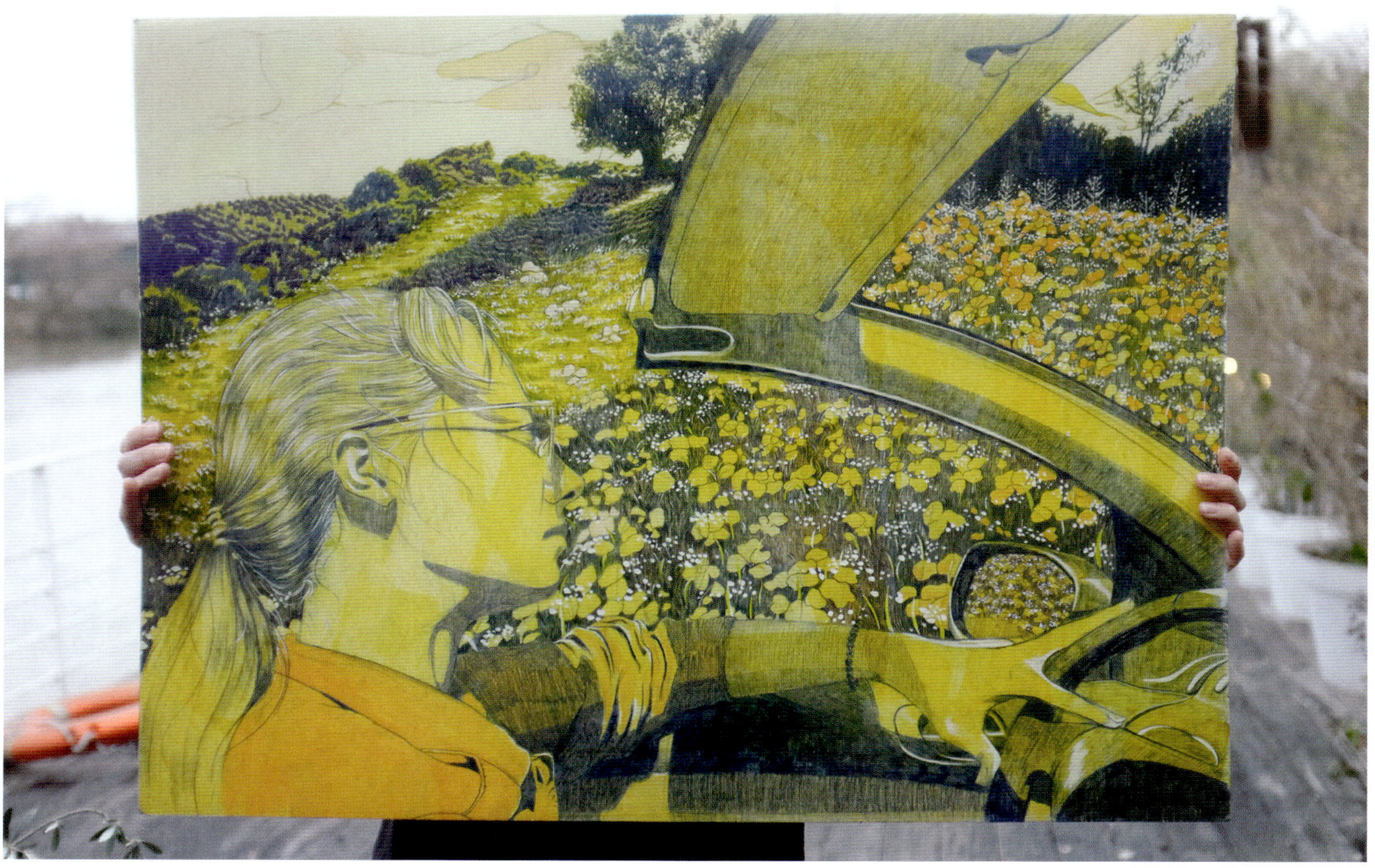

▲ *Diane*
Title: *Driving Up the Hill*
Materials: Hardboard, paper, coloured pencils, gouache, acrylic

Diane's inspiration for her personal project came from sketches done while visiting her friend in the south of France in the spring of 2024. When revisiting these sketchbooks as research for the projects, she struck upon the idea of combining both the drawing she did of her friend driving and one of her landscape drawings. She looked at the artists David Hockney, Alex Katz and Peter Doig for inspiration.

Having painted in the past, she decided to attempt a large drawing/painting on board. She started with a light yellow wash onto the board as a base and then redrew the drawing of her friend driving. Using coloured pencils, gouache and acrylic, she started to build the drawing up using multiple layers. As inspiration for the background, she printed out some of her landscape photographs, collaged them together and then used these as reference for the background painting.

She worked on the piece for over a month, adding layers, redrawing, painting and just letting the work evolve. This was a new and welcome approach for Diane as she normally works quickly: 'I found that this slower pace really suited the complexity of the work. I was able to reflect and assess and to let the work guide me, rather than me pushing it'. Diane is hoping to experiment with combining screen print, painting and drawing in future works.

▶ *Lucy*
Title: *The Forest's Quiet Stream*
Materials: Paper, printing ink, gouache, watercolour, coloured pencils, wax crayons, gel plate
Size: 27 x 35cm (10½ x 13¾in)

When reflecting on the drawings she had done over the year for the Sketch Squad, it was clear to Lucy that the ones she enjoyed the most were those she did in nature, in green spaces. Many of her drawings were completed in her local forest, a place that she feels a strong connection to. So, it was an easy decision for her to base her personal project around the forest, exploring her feelings towards it through her artwork.

Lucy started the project by spending more time drawing in the forest, really immersing herself in the space. She notes: 'Sitting quietly in the forest, with a calm mind, helped me see more clearly. I noticed the small details that bring the forest to life, like the way the leaves move in the breeze or the textures of the tree bark.' After completing a series of observational studies, Lucy returned to her studio and considered her next steps.

She was keen to experiment with combining printmaking, drawing and painting for this project, as this is something she had recently been playing with in her practice. Using her sketches as reference, she used a gel plate to create a monoprint with gouache paint; this then provided a base upon which she used her coloured pencils and wax crayons to bring the image to life.

Reflecting on the work, Lucy was happy with the overall result but is aware of her limited understanding of the monoprint technique and is keen to learn more to add to her evolving skill base.

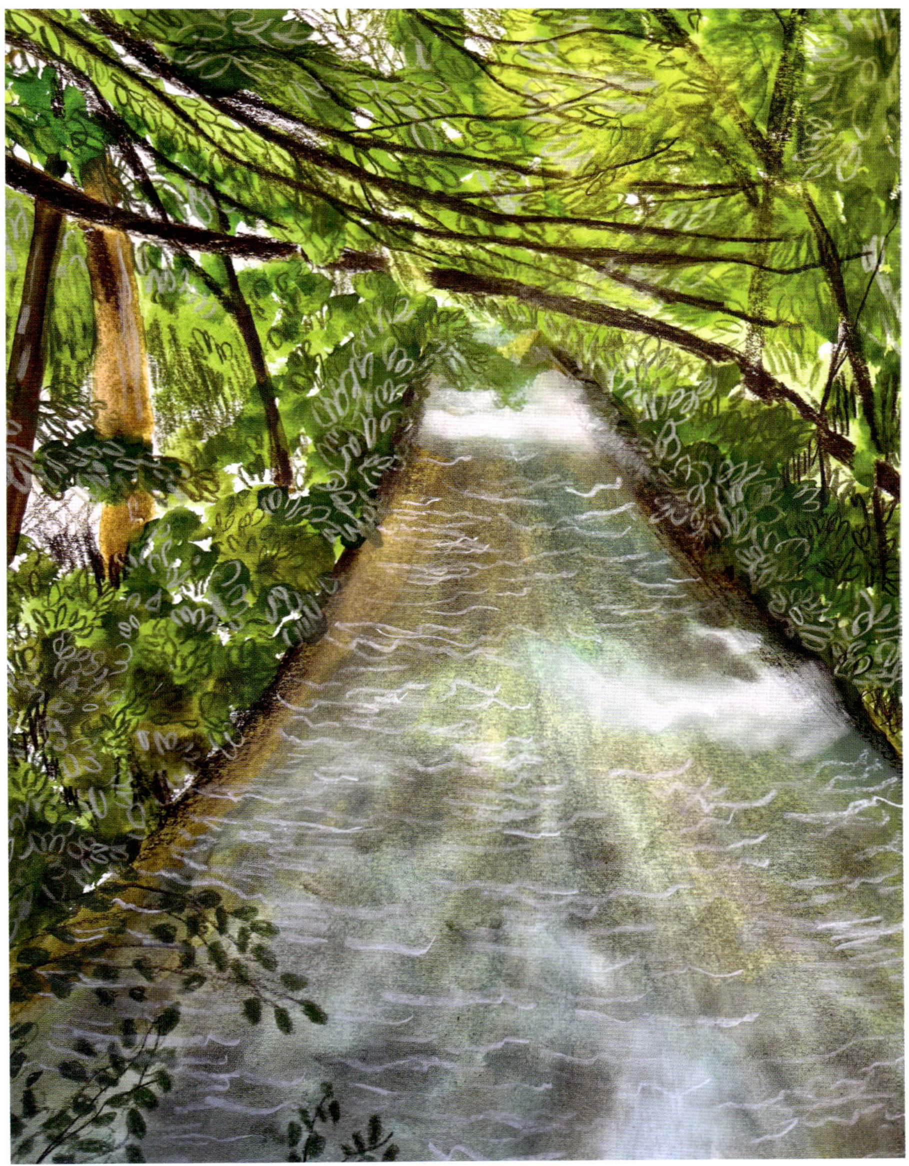

17
Final words from the Sketch Squad

Once the Squad had completed the exercises, we organised to meet up in real life and spend an afternoon together in London. Apart from Phyllis and Niki, who sadly couldn't make it, everyone else came – Kathi from Vienna, Lucy from Bern, Diane from Paris and the rest of us from the UK.

During this meet-up and over email, I asked them five questions about their experience of their year of drawing and of being part of the Squad. What follows below is the questions and a summary of their answers.

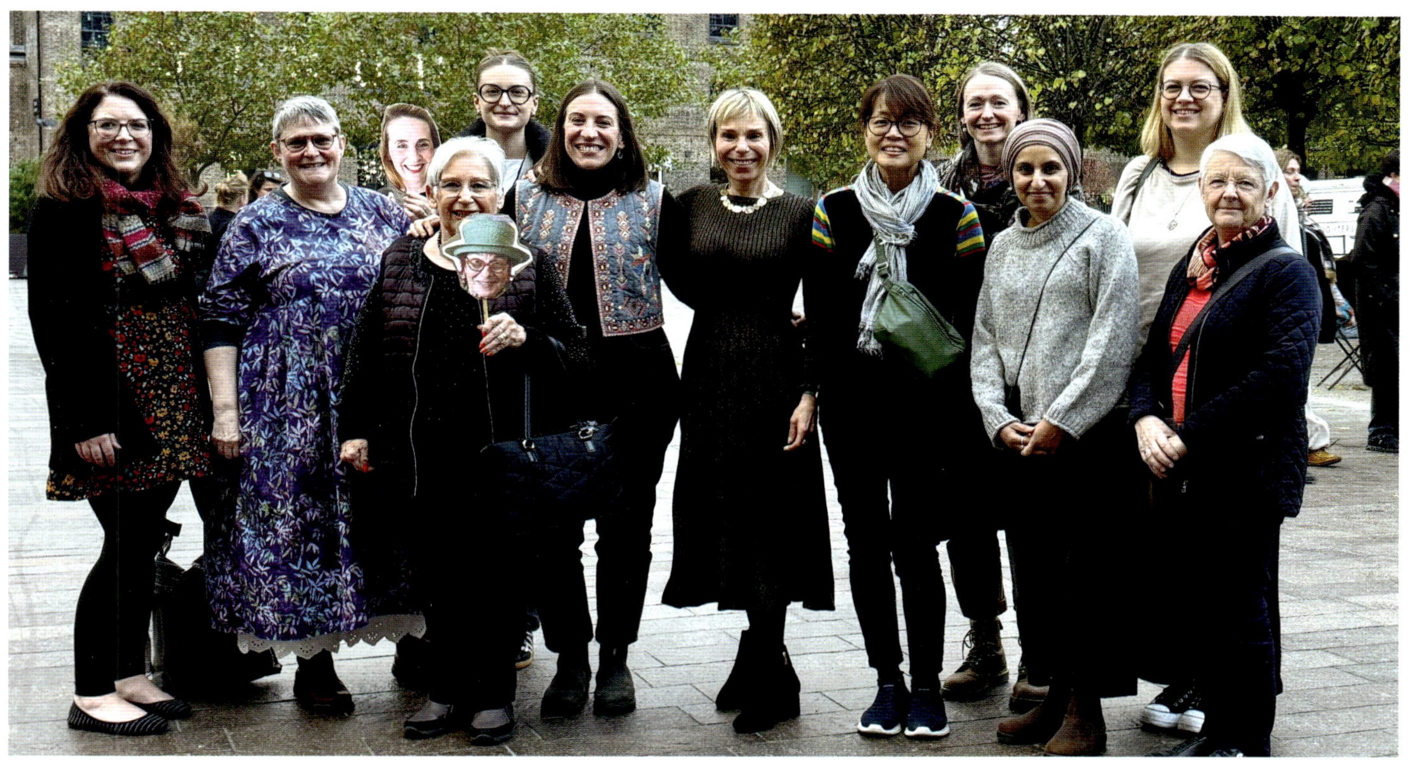

Questions for the Sketch Squad

What did you enjoy most about being part of the Sketch Squad?

Without a doubt, the most common answer to this question was that being part of the Squad itself was the most enjoyable part of the experience. They all said that working together, being part of a team and having the same goal was rewarding. Hannah said, 'Knowing we were all in it together, meeting the same deadlines, feeling the same panic, gave me the impetus to keep going.'

Reading through their answers, it's clear that seeing how differently they all interpreted the same exercises and how unique everyone's drawings were made them realise how each of them has their own style and their own way of drawing.

Claire enjoyed not having to think about what to draw as that was something she had struggled with in the past. Diane and Paula both enjoyed having deadlines as it made them commit to drawing. For Jane, it was finding enjoyment in creating again, and having a goal made her feel more motivated.

What did you find the most difficult?

There were a variety of responses to this question. Paula said that sometimes the most difficult thing was starting, but that, once she had got going, she was fine. Anne found that overcoming her lack of self-belief was the most challenging part. For Niki, the most difficult part was sharing drawings she wasn't happy with. 'It's the drawing equivalent of standing in your bra and knickers with all your lumps and bumps on view.'

For Hannah and Lucy, the trickiest part was overcoming their imposter syndrome. Lucy experienced this when drawing in public, and Hannah's emerged when looking at the work of other artists.

Phyllis struggled with trying to live up to her own expectations and was overly critical of herself – something that Claire also battled with when comparing her work to that of the other members of the Squad.

Paula and Eva both said that drawing in public spaces was initially tricky for them. For Eva, her resistance to some of the chapters was the most difficult part; however, on reflection, these chapters were the ones she learnt from and enjoyed the most. Jane said that sticking to the suggested timeframe was difficult; she would just get carried away as she was enjoying it so much!

What are you most proud of during your time in the Sketch Squad?

Safa and Anne both said they were most proud of finding ways to deal with the critical voices in their heads. For Kathi, Niki and Eva, it was the fact that they made it to the end and finished all the exercises.

Paula found that doing the exercises increased her confidence, and this inspired others in her local village to start sketching, which then resulted in getting funding to build a village 'Art Hub'. Diane also found that being consistent with her drawing practice improved her confidence, and she's most proud of this.

Hannah realised that tackling subjects she had never considered exploring before, such as portraiture, ended up being the thing she was most proud of. 'It informed my personal project in a way I would never have imagined possible at the start.'

Phyllis is most proud of her enthusiasm and dedication, something I know the group were all grateful for. Claire is proud that she drew in public and that she now shares her drawings with other people. And, for Lucy, she is proud that she pushed through the exercises she found challenging, as it gave her a deeper understanding of her drawing style.

How will what you have learnt over this past year help you in the future with your work or life in general?

There was such a rich set of responses to this question, highlighting what a unique and personal journey it has been for the Squad. Kathi and Eva said they learnt that having a structure helps them achieve their goals, and that having something to work towards is a big motivating factor. Niki has learnt that everyone struggles and that by being part of a group that have shared with such honesty and openness, it's made her realise that everyone has moments of frustration, where they think nothing is working out like it should.

For Safa, it's simple; she's realised that drawing is now at the heart of her printmaking practice. Where, before, her drawings were just a means for her to plan her linocut, now, they are the backbone to her work.

For Paula and Anne, it's been the realisation of how important their creativity is to their well-being and sense of purpose. Claire said she has learnt to place value on her work, to see herself as an artist, not just someone who 'doodles'.

Both Hannah and Diane have learnt how important consistency is – just by getting their sketchbooks out once or twice a week, they have surprised themselves with how much they have achieved. Lucy has learnt not to give up or devalue her work – reminding herself that it doesn't have to be perfect has been a big learning curve. And Jane learnt that it's never too late to start something new.

Anything else you would like to add or further thoughts that might inspire readers?

Kathi encourages you all to not give up, to find new ways of thinking and creating and to be proud of what you have accomplished, even if it's just a two-minute drawing of your kettle!

Eva and Hannah both advise you to do all the exercises, even the ones you feel daunted by, as Hannah says, 'You just don't know what you will discover, and the results might be formative.' This is backed up by Anne who encourages you to just have a go, as, like her, you might exceed your expectations.

Claire points out that, despite what you have been told in the past at school or college or by friends and family, there is no right or wrong way to draw. Niki suggests finding a friend who draws or creating your own drawing group – her time in the Squad has made her realise that everyone tackles the same sketching exercise differently. Safa backs this up by saying that, if we are all drawing an orange, we all draw the orange differently; it's about taking the time to discover your own individual way of mark making.

Lucy advises not to be too hard on yourself, as trying new things and being open to different perspectives will help you grow, not only in your life but as a person. She says, 'Embracing this mindset will make you more flexible, creative and open to learning in every area of life.'

As you can see from all the responses from the Squad, the year of drawing meant different things to each of them, enriching their lives in different ways. For me, it was about sharing my passion for drawing, being able to be a leader of sorts, and creating a space where everyone could have ideas and feel valued.

Finding your own squad

It's clear that for the Squad, drawing together as part of a group was essential for their motivation, commitment and enjoyment of the exercises. If you feel that drawing with other people would help spur you on, then think about ways you could make this happen. Search out local drawing classes, look for drawing workshops, draw with a like-minded friend or share this book with others and form your own drawing group. And, of course, you are more than welcome to join me in my online monthly sketch club.

18
Concluding with confidence

'I believe that confidence in our work comes through doing. It comes through turning up, making art, seeing improvement and continuing to grow'

This morning, I met with Safa for our regular coaching session. She was beaming as she told me that the other day she was drawing from a painting in Bristol Art Gallery. A lady who was observing the same painting started chatting and admiring her drawing. She asked Safa, 'Are you an artist? Do you paint?' Safa replied, 'Yes, I am an artist, and I draw'. A year ago, Safa wouldn't have had the confidence to say this out loud, and she credits this year of drawing for giving her the confidence to say 'I am an artist' with pride and conviction.

I believe that confidence in our work comes through doing. It comes through turning up, making art, seeing improvement and continuing to grow. As we practise drawing and making art in whichever way we want, there comes a time when we suddenly realise 'this is who I am as an artist'. It happens gradually. We begin to recognise our own unique way of making marks, of capturing a scene. We see ourselves in the soft, delicate line, or the bold, heavy dark lines. The pressure of creating a 'good' drawing diminishes as we play with our pencils and make new discoveries. We lose our inhibitions and our desire to 'get it right'.

By the simple process of turning up and drawing, we get a sense of what our interests are. You might have started this book with no idea of what you wanted to draw, but I hope, by following the exercises, you have discovered areas you want to explore more, which speak to you and ask to be investigated further.

I have held your hand and guided you through this first stage, but now it's over to you to commit to your practice, to keep getting out your pencils, to continue to draw and develop. If you show up day after day, it will become second nature. It will become your thing – the thing that you protect and value. It will become your place of comfort, and a place you can access any time.

One drawing won't change much, but consistently drawing will change the way you see the world. When we draw, we aren't on our phones; we open our eyes and observe. The more we sketch, the more we see and appreciate the world around us, and the more we feel connected.

I will be honest with you; there will be days when it's hard. Sometimes you will feel like giving up, that you aren't getting anywhere, but this isn't true. Keeping going during these tough bits is where the magic starts to happen. Acknowledge the feelings of despondency and see it for what it is – a moment of confusion and uncertainty. Remember the good times, remind yourself of how far you have come, then let it go and move on. If we are kind and supportive to ourselves, marvellous things can happen.

I'm convinced that drawing can be a balm to all our souls. When we take the time to look and sketch, we can change the way we feel. So, let's keep getting out our sketchbooks and making marks on paper, as good things will happen, I promise.

Love,
Sam
X

Acknowledgements

The focus for this book came to me while I was on a train in Switzerland. I had been thinking about writing a drawing book for a while, and instead of forcing the idea, I decided to mull it over. And so, that day in mid-April 2023, on a train to Lucerne, the idea to create 'a drawing class' within a book where the reader would feel part of an inclusive workshop alongside other students came to me.

I immediately emailed Niki to see if she would be interested in taking part. Her enthusiasm spurred me on, and then I was off and the Squad took shape. It goes without saying that I'm hugely grateful to all the Sketch Squad members for all their hard work, commitment, honesty and support. It's amazing how much more enjoyable writing a book is when there are others on board too!

Thank you to my wonderful friends Carly, Frances, Perienne and Suse. I can't tell you how much your words of encouragement have meant to me.

To my photographers and friends, Rachael and Susanne.

To Clare and Natasha from Bloomsbury, who have held my hand throughout.

To all my fantastic followers on social media. I have talked non-stop about this book for a couple of years and they have cheered me on and believed in me all the way.

A special thank you to my mum, who joined the Sketch Squad with such enthusiasm, and to my dad, who cheered us on from the sidelines.

And, of course, to the small brown dog who is on my lap as I type.

Further reading

Bayles, David and Ted Orland, *Art & Fear: Observations on the Perils (and Rewards) of Artmaking* (London: Souvenir Press, 2023)

Bennett, Cat, *The Conscious Creative* (Vermont: Findhorn Press, 2010)

Congdon, Lisa, *Finding Your Artistic Voice: The Essential Guide to Working Your Creative Magic* (San Francisco: Chronicle Books, 2019)

Durant, Will, *The Story of Philosophy* (New York: Simon & Schuster, 2012)

Foxton, Dr Ali, *The Green Sketching Handbook: Relax, Unwind and Reconnect with Nature* (Basingstoke: Pan Macmillan, 2022)

Gilbert, Elizabeth, *Big Magic: Creative Living Beyond Fear* (London: Bloomsbury, 2016)

Rubin, Rick, *The Creative Act: A Way of Being* (Edinburgh: Canongate Books, 2023)

Stanton, Philippa, *Conscious Creativity: Look, Connect, Create* (Brighton: Leaping Hare Press, 2018)

Wiest, Brianna, *The Mountain is You: Transforming Self-sabotage Into Self-mastery* (New York: Thought Catalog Books, 2020)

Resources

Caran d'Ache
www.carandache.com
Grafwood graphite pencils
Luminance coloured pencils
Neocolor® II watercolour pastels

Copic
www.copic-shop.co.uk
Copic multi-liner pens

Derwent
www.derwentart.com
Derwent Chromaflow coloured pencils

Faber-Castell
www.faber-castell.co.uk
Castell graphite pencils
Latex-free erasers
Polychromos coloured pencils

Royal Talens
www.royaltalens.com
Ecoline brush pens
Talens Art Creation sketchbooks

Sakura
Widely available
Sakura Pigma Micron pens

Suppliers

Australia

Eckersleys
www.eckersleys.com.au

Canada

Opus Art Supplies
opusartsupplies.com

France

Rougier and Plé
www.rougier-ple.fr

Germany/ Austria

Gerstaecker
www.gerstaecker.de

Italy

Poggi Art
www.poggi1825.it

Netherlands

Van Beek Art Supplies
www.vanbeekart.nl

UK

Cass Art
www.cassart.co.uk

Edinburgh Art Shop
edinburghartshop.co.uk

Evans Art Supplies
store.evansartsupplies.ie

Jacksons Art
www.jacksonsart.com

USA

Blick Art Materials
www.dickblick.com

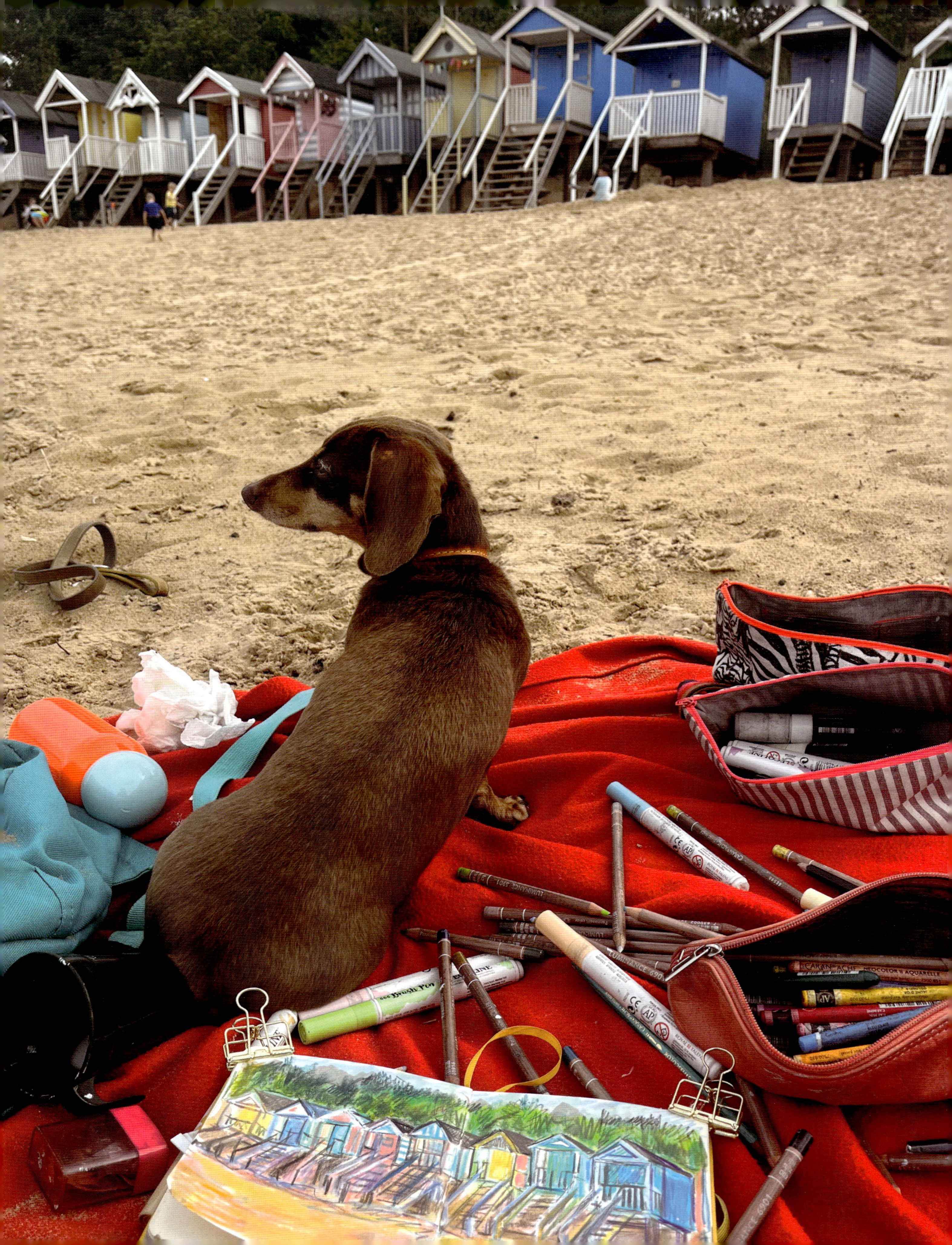